Foundations of
Criminal Science

FOUNDATIONS OF CRIMINAL SCIENCE

VOLUME 2:
The Use of Knowledge

GLENN D. WALTERS

New York
Westport, Connecticut
London

Library of Congress Cataloging-in-Publication Data

Walters, Glenn D.
   Foundations of criminal science.

   Includes bibliographical references and indexes.
   Contents: v. 1. The development of knowledge—
v. 2. The use of knowledge.
      1. Criminology.   2. Crime—United States.
I. Title.
HV6025.W37   1992   364   91–4202
ISBN 0–275–94128–0 (set)
ISBN 0–275–93953–7 (v. 1 : alk. paper)
ISBN 0–275–93954–5 (v. 2 : alk. paper)

British Library Cataloguing in Publication Data is available.

Library of Congress Catalog Card Number: 91–4202
ISBN: 0–275–94128–0 (set)
      0–275–93954–5 (vol. 2)

First published in 1992

Praeger Publishers, One Madison Avenue, New York, NY 10010
An imprint of Greenwood Publishing Group, Inc.

Printed in the United States of America

The paper used in this book complies with the
Permanent Paper Standard issued by the National
Information Standards Organization (Z39.48–1984).

10 9 8 7 6 5 4 3 2 1

Contents

PART IV   CONCLUSION

Tables and Figures

FIGURES

Preface

In this second volume of a text on the interdisciplinary study of crime and criminals we find ourselves shifting gears as application begins to supplant development in importance. We must remain mindful, nevertheless, that acquisition and application are interrelated to the extent that knowledge accumulation is at least partly motivated by the prospect of knowledge utilization. A review of historical trends in crime reveals that criminals, lifestyle or otherwise, have been with us since the dawn of civilization. Cross-national comparisons, on the other hand, inform us that while some countries may experience lower rates of criminality than others, the prospect of a veritably crime-free society is a fantasy. Likewise, research investigations demonstrate that choice is an essential component in the events that define a particular criminal act. As such, it would be inane for us to set as our goal the development of a crime-free society, although as this volume demonstrates, neither do we need to view ourselves as hapless victims who have no choice but to accept crime, violent or otherwise.

One vehicle by which we might understand criminality as a means to achieving a reduced level of crime is what was referred to in Volume 1 as the five foundations of criminal science. This, in fact, is a theme that finds itself a home in the pages and chapters of this volume as well. The reader may recall from our discussions in Volume 1 that context exists as the first foundation or pillar of criminal science endeavor. Consequently, crime does not occur in a vacuum but must be considered within its proper historical and cultural context. As part of our journey through the first foundation we considered crime within the context of several centuries of American history and entertained cross-national comparisons of crime-related issues, the results of which subsequently established that crime is influenced by both time and place.

Wide-range data collection, discussed in Volume 1 under the heading of research, is the second foundation of criminal science inquiry. Characteristics of the individual, features of the environment, aspects of the person × situation interaction, and the choices one makes relative to various life conditions were all surveyed in an effort to develop an effective system of causes and correlates by which criminal action might be explained. So that we might form a more complete understanding of crime we must consider the person, the situation, the interaction of the two, and the choices the individual makes relative to this interaction. In addition to the three primary interactive domains of attachment-social bonding, stimulus modulation-orientation and self-image–role identity, person variables like heredity, intelligence, and temperament; situation variables like alcohol and/or drugs, family atmosphere, and the physical environment; and choice variables like opportunity, cognitive processing, and fallibility were all found to be potentially important concomitants of crime.

The third pillar upon which the criminal science effort is built is that of theory. Put another way, research data are meaningless unless accompanied by a logical and coherent system of theoretical thought. Six major theories of criminal conduct, partitioned into person- (Hare), situation- (labeling, subcultural), interactive- (social control, Mednick), and choice- (rational choice) oriented models, were explored in the final section of Volume 1. A multi-pattern theory of criminal involvement, in which the six patterns are defined according to the person × situation interaction existing in three domains—the physical (stimulus modulation), the social (attachment), and the psychological (self-image)—rounded out our discussion of theory as a fundamental aspect of the criminal science effort.

The fourth foundation of the criminal science model is assessment and prediction. This foundation is grounded in the assumption that knowledge accrued through research and observation can be used to effectively evaluate, classify, and predict criminal behavior. Issues of assessment and prediction are therefore addressed in the second section of Volume 2, which is dedicated to the systematic examination of evaluation and classification procedures. In addition to investigating specific assessment techniques and reviewing major systems of inmate-criminal classification, this section explores such tenacious prediction problems as institutional adjustment, recidivism, and dangerousness.

Intervention is the final column in the edifice that is criminal science. Like assessment and prediction, intervention is a focal point of discussion in this second volume. Our review is organized around selected person, situation, and interactive issues. Therapeutic, medical, and choice procedures are treated as person-oriented strategies, while situation-oriented concerns like prevention and social policy decisions are probed in a second chapter. Interaction-based strategies consider ways in which the individual offender interfaces with the criminal justice system through trends in retribution, deterrence, incapacitation, rehabilitation, and restitution. It is hoped the reader will become increasingly more cognizant of the interlinked nature of intervention strategies, not to mention the inseparability of knowledge development and utilization, as we proceed through this second volume of a text on the science of criminal investigation.

The author would like to thank Dr. Donald Denney for his assistance with several of the figures contained in this volume. Gratitude is also extended to my wife, Patti, and our two children, Christopher and Tara, whose patience and understanding permitted me the time and opportunity to write this two-volume text.

The assertions contained herein are the private views of the author and should in no way be construed as official or as necessarily reflecting the views of the Department of Justice or Federal Bureau of Prisons.

PART I

INTRODUCTION

1

More Questions About Crime

As we discovered in Chapter 1 of Volume 1, there are many questions and concerns that arise when the subject of crime and criminals is broached. We subsequently organized these questions into five domains and labeled them the five foundations of criminal science: context, research, theory, assessment/prediction, and intervention. In this second volume on the scientific study of criminal behavior we consider the fourth and fifth foundations, assessment/prediction and intervention, and in this inaugural chapter we entertain four questions that correspond with issues central to each of these foundations. Since application has seemingly been ignored by many of the scholars who have entered into the scientific study of crime and criminals, it seems appropriate that we commence our discussion with a question probably on the minds of many academic criminologists: "Why be concerned with application?"

WHY BE CONCERNED WITH APPLICATION?

There are, in reality, at least three subquestions contained in the framework of the larger question concerning application of criminal science information. Whereas these subquestions are probably best conceptualized as rhetorical in nature, they do bring to light certain issues requiring a great deal more attention than they have thus far received. The first subquestion ponders the relative significance of application versus understanding as the true goal of science. The second subquestion queries whether the data on research and theory reviewed in Volume 1 stand on their own merit. The final subquestion doubts whether we need to devote an entire book to application-type issues. Let me address each of these inquiries as to the feasibility of criminal science application in turn.

First, I respond to the interrogatory concerning the "true" goal of science by reminding the reader that application is viewed as important by many fields of scientific endeavor, whether biochemistry, entomology, or nuclear science. Despite the fact that understanding and discovery are predominant goals of science, these goals will rarely come to fruition if the issue of application is ignored. Ever since humankind's invention of the wheel and the discovery of fire, efforts in the scientific arena have been guided by practical necessity: a desire for increased mobility in the first case and warmth in the second. The criminal science movement is no different in that the quest for understanding is piloted by the practical necessity of doing something about a problem that has existed for centuries—the problem of crime. Therefore, while science is principally geared toward understanding, this knowledge must be tempered with the prospect of and potential for application.

My initial response to the subquestion that ponders the independent value of Volume 1 is also a qualified yes. Volume 1 is most certainly significant in its own right or I would never have conceived of it as a separate work. However, it is equally critical that we appreciate the interdependence of these two volumes on criminal science. Therefore, while both volumes bring important issues into focus, their true value, like that of the classical and positivist schools of criminology, is found in their combination rather than in their juxtaposition. Issues presented in Volume 1 become clearer when integrated with information in Volume 2. Consequently, while Volumes 1 and 2 are independently meaningful, their pairing leads to a substantial increase in the value of each.

The final subquestion ponders whether we, in truth, need to devote an entire book to the topic of application. In point of fact, very few authors of criminology or criminal justice texts have invested much time, space, or effort in addressing the issue of application. However, the majority of students attending classes where these texts are in use will probably never become academic criminologists. Most will likely find employment in applied settings, be it corrections, probation, or law enforcement. It is essential, then, that such individuals be exposed to the concept of practical application as it relates to crime, criminals, and their future occupations. Though the study of applications issues is fraught with difficulty, ignoring these issues is clearly no solution. For this reason application is the axis around which our discussion of topics in Volume 2 revolves.

IS ASSESSMENT REALLY NECESSARY?

Psychological assessment contributed immeasurably to the rise of clinical psychology as a profession. It is therefore ironic that as this field has evolved it has not more clearly valued its assessment roots. Treatment and consultation have grown in popularity while assessment has often been relegated to a course or two in graduate school and an occasional Rorschach or MMPI in one's routine clinical work. Concern has also been expressed about such issues as deception, invasion of privacy, test bias, and pigeonholing as each pertains to the application of psychological assessment procedures in clinical practice (Cronbach, 1970). The aforementioned concerns, notwithstanding, I prefer to think that assessment is not only an integral part of the criminal science enterprise but is, in fact, indispensable to the effective implementation and orderly management of any science of human behavior.

Before proceeding, it is crucial that we distinguish between psychological testing and assessment. Psychometric testing, with its roots in the psychology of individual differences, concerns itself with the systematic observation and comparison of two or more persons through use of a standardized numerical scale or category-classification system (Cronbach, 1970). Psychological assessment, on the other hand, is a more general term used to describe ways in which one might organize available information on an individual offender. Maloney and Ward (1976) consider testing a mechanical procedure, while they conceive of assessment as a matter of problem solving. The process of problem identification and the generation of various alternative solutions to such problems are viewed as critical steps in the sequence of events that define criminal science.

Assessment and the psychology of individual differences have been treated with suspicion by many in the sociological community in the mistaken belief that *different* conveys a value judgment of *better* or *worse*. As Hirschi and Hindelang (1977) point out, however, *different* in a psychological sense does not necessarily connote good or bad, better or worse. The psychology of individual differences makes note of variations in temperament, mood, and personality but typically avoids affixing moral judgments to these divergencies. Instead of being concerned with what is proper or correct, the psychology of individual differences catalogs that which is statistically frequent and infrequent. In this way, psychological differences have no affective or subjective value other than that which is assigned by the investigator or reader.

The Declaration of Independence holds that "all men are created equal. . . . " While this was originally intended as a statement of equality under the law, there are some who would argue that this reflects a basic parity of temperament, personality, or ability. There is amble research evidence (much of which was reviewed in Volume 1), however, to suggest that the assumption is false. Wanting to believe that all differences are a function of learning or environment does not make it so, nor does it do anything to repudiate a growing body of research knowledge that shows that genetic and other nonenvironmental factors can impact on everyday human behavior. A psychology of individual plurality is not only fundamental to our understanding of criminal behavior but also is central to the problem-solving approach that upholds the fourth and fifth foundations of criminal science.

CAN PREDICTION BE MADE MORE ACCURATE?

There are many questions about prediction that remain unanswered. Those that are particularly puzzling to criminal scientists include forecasting recidivism, prognosticating institutional adjustment, and predicting dangerousness. We need only turn to a local television news program to find evidence of how troublesome prediction can be. It is difficult to fathom the countless number of picnics and ski vacations ruined because someone trusted a weather report that eventually turned out to be incorrect. Prediction can be just as problematic when applied to criminal science data, although the consequences are often more serious. Instead of a wet picnicker or a disappointed skier, we may have before us a rape, assault, or murder victim, or we might decide to retain an individual in custody who is no longer a threat to society.

In predicting future weather conditions, meteorologists enjoying the greatest measure of success (and probably receiving the fewest irate calls from viewers) rely on probabilistic, rather than absolute, predictions of future events. Instead of offering a blanket forecast of rain or snow, they report a 40, 60, or 80 percent chance of showers based on how often it rained in the past when weather conditions were the same. This way the viewer understands that there is also the possibility of no showers and is informed of the relative probability of each occurrence. One way to improve the utility of our prognostications of criminal science events might therefore be to offer probabilistic statements rather than absolute ones.

A great deal has been written about our inability to forecast violence. What is less apparent is that the issues involved in the prediction of dangerous behavior are more complex than they would appear. What was once thought to be a simple matter of selecting one of two future occurrences has evolved into a variegated system of divergent possibilities that vary on the basis of certain person and situation characteristics. We must therefore couch our questions about danger-ousness and recidivism in terms that more adequately address the relevant issues and maximize the prognostic capabilities of existing measures, procedures, and techniques. As many meteorologists have come to realize, we are in a position to better auger future events if we specify the contextual and probabilistic pa-rameters of our predictions.

IS THERE ANY TRUTH TO THE "NOTHING WORKS" VERDICT ON REHABILITATION?

First, I believe it is important that I acknowledge my dissatisfaction with the term *rehabilitation* as it is applied to changing the behavior of criminal offenders. In many cases the habitual criminal has never been habilitated, let alone reha-bilitated. Though I am disenchanted with the term, it finds its way into our discussion by virtue of its communicative value and continued popularity. We should keep in mind, however, that the defining theme of rehabilitation is change, and change is something only the individual offender can effect. The possibility of change is therefore an assumption that guides our search for efficacious pathways of intervention. Even though change is a personal issue that can be realized only by the individual, it is a fundamental tenet of criminal scientific intervention that there are ways in which society and certain of its agencies can facilitate the process of change, which of course takes place in the individual offender.

Martinson, Lipton, and Wilks reviewed the research on the effectiveness of educational, vocational, supervisory, and treatment programs in preventing future episodes of criminal outcome in adult and juvenile offenders. On the basis of this review, Martinson (1974) concluded that there was no good evidence that such programs had any effect on the relatively high rate of recidivism experienced by most criminal populations; thus, he offered the conclusion that "nothing works." A closer reading of Martinson's original paper, however, reveals that there was no good evidence that these programs were ineffective, either. Rather than being an indictment of rehabilitation programs, therefore, Martinson's review more clearly points out the deficiencies of research studies conducted on the rehabilitation issue prior to 1974. More recent investigations (Gendreau & Ross, 1979, 1987), as well as meta-analyses of the rehabilitation literature (Davidson et al., 1984; Garrett, 1985), provide preliminary support for the utility of selected vocational, supervisory, and treatment programs with specific groups of adult and juvenile offenders.

I would submit that the "nothing works" verdict is one of the greatest fallacies of our time. It is actually nothing more than a convenient excuse employed by correctional administrators who want to cut programs, clinical practitioners who want to avoid their treatment responsibilities, and offenders who want to continue engaging in self- and other destructive patterns of behavior. If spending the last nine years in the correctional field has taught me anything, it is that the "nothing works" verdict is little more than a ruse, whether the culprit is a prison official, criminal offender, or society at large. Even Martinson renounced his conclusion that "nothing works" in an article published just prior to his death (Martinson, 1979). In sum, there are programs that do, in fact, work; it is just a matter of discerning which programs work best with which offenders under which specific circumstances—always mindful, of course, that in the long run change is primarily the responsibility of the individual.

COMMENT

As the reader can probably gather, the emphasis in this volume is on the application of relationships outlined in Volume 1. Application of basic research findings and theoretical conceptualizations augments the growing body of knowledge that is criminal science and adds a new wrinkle to our investigation of crime and criminals. As we prepare to traverse a maze of studies on assessment, prediction, prevention, and intervention we must remain cognizant of the interrelated nature of Volumes 1 and 2. Findings that were two-dimensional in Volume 1 become three-dimensional in light of information in Volume 2. Thus, while a microbiologist may comprehend the physical features of an amoeba, this knowledge is of little value unless accompanied by information on how the amoeba moves, eats, reproduces, and interacts with its environment. Such a caveat applies whether we are investigating a microorganism, a nuclear generator, or a habitual criminal.

PART II

ASSESSMENT AND PREDICTION

2

Assessment Techniques

Cronbach (1970, p. 26) defines psychological testing as "a systematic procedure for observing a person's behavior and describing it with the aid of a numerical scale or a category system." In defining psychological assessment, Goldstein and Hersen (1984) assert that assessment involves the study of individual differences, testing being just one of several evaluation techniques available to clinicians and researchers. I argue that psychological assessment is an area in which science and art interface, and while this chapter centers on the methodological merit of individual assessment techniques, we should remain open to the possibility that clinical application of these procedures is as much an art form as it is a science. Hence, though I believe we must continue refining the science of psychological assessment, the evaluator brings to the assessment situation certain behaviors and characteristics that either augment or weaken the final outcome.

A prime consideration for scholars interested in criminal science assessment is the reliability and validity of one's procedures. Reliability is an estimate of the precision, stability, and consistency of a specific set of data. Thus, we might explore the inter-rater reliability of a specific procedure to determine its precision across observers, test-retest reliability to gauge its stability over time, and split-half reliability to assess the degree to which the instrument is internally consistent.

The question of validity, on the other hand, asks whether a test or procedure measures that for which it was originally designed. Like reliability, validity is measured in several different forms. Content validity surveys whether the procedure or test adequately samples the domain of behaviors purportedly being measured. Concurrent and predictive validity are empirical forms of validity that consider whether a test or procedure correlates with contemporaneously (concurrent) or subsequently (predictive) measured criteria. Construct validity ponders the theoretical meaningfulness of a specific assessment procedure, with particular emphasis placed on how this measure fits into a wider nomothetic net or multitrait-multimethod matrix.

Whereas reliability and validity are essential to the effective implementation of assessment techniques, we need to take other factors into account as well. For one, we must be clear as to the context of the evaluation and the questions proposed. No procedure, regardless of how reliable or valid, is capable of adequately addressing all of the questions of interest to criminal scientists. To a large extent, the more pertinent a technique is to one question, the less relevant it is for answering other questions—an artifact of the bandwidth-fidelity dilemma discussed with greater specificity in the concluding section of this chapter. We must therefore determine which procedures are maximally effective under which circumstances, with which types of clients, exhibiting which kinds of problems.

It would seem that the universe of assessment procedures of interest to criminal scientists is greatly reduced by the fact only a handful of assessment techniques have been used with any degree of regularity in criminal populations, although many different techniques might be called upon to answer a specific diagnostic question. These special-circumstance evaluations might include an intelligence test in one situation, an interest inventory in another, and an institutional climate survey in yet a third. This chapter covers three major categories of criminal science assessment: person-oriented assessment, environmental or situation-oriented assessment, and interaction-oriented assessment.

PERSON-ORIENTED ASSESSMENT

Interviewing

In this age of computer-assisted assessment, the clinical interview is still an invaluable source of individual-level data. A well-conducted interview not only provides a wealth of information but also helps facilitate a helping relationship between the interviewer and interviewee. With its roots in medical history taking, the clinical interview has grown beyond its humble beginnings to the objective, scientific analysis of interviewer-client transactions. Accordingly, it is essential that we not overlook the clinical interview as a source of criminal science knowledge. As experience has shown, an interview is capable of providing valuable information to scientists (Shover, 1983) and clinicians alike. It is vital, therefore, that we strive to maximize the potential of this particular form of clinical and research data collection.

In optimizing the potential of interviewing as an assessment technique, the type of interview employed—structured versus unstructured—is of paramount significance. The initial model upon which the mental health interview was based was the semistructured medical history–taking procedure. From the question-and-answer format of medical history taking evolved a more indirect, free-flowing approach commonly referred to as the unstructured interview. It was soon realized, however, that unstructured interviews were too widely influenced by the experience and personal characteristics of the interviewer to provide reliable research results (Hakel, 1982). This led to the structured interview, several of the more popular versions being the Diagnostic Interview Schedule (DIS: Helzer et al., 1977), Psychiatric Diagnostic Interview (PDI: Othmer, Penick, & Powell, 1981), and Schedule for Affective Disorders and Schizophrenia (SADS: Endicott & Spitzer, 1978).

Techniques such as the PDI and SADS have led to increased specificity, consistency, and stability of diagnostic and clinical impressions. In one study, for instance, it was determined that a moderately strong level of inter-rater agreement and temporal stability could be attained with the PDI when it was used to appraise the diagnostic status of 14 state prison inmates (Walters, Chlumsky, & Hemphill, 1988). However, such findings do not necessarily portend the demise of unstructured interviewing, since it allows for the formation of a therapeutic alliance between the interviewer and client. Siassi (1984) has considered this dilemma and recommends that evaluators employ a combined approach in which the interviewer elicits an unstructured dialogue initially and then gradually moves to a more structured format. The following six-step interview sequence is offered as a model of information exchange designed to produce results that are thorough, yet cost-efficient.

Collateral Background Information. Although one may not always have access to background information, when available such data can help frame the interview contextually. Medical and mental health interviewing have rested on the assumption that a client is invested in providing the truth about his or her problem. However, this is an assumption that may not always be true with criminals, many of whom have forged dishonesty into a way of life. We are therefore in a better position to evaluate a case if we have access to any background or historical information contained in a file or source independent of the offender him or herself.

Purpose of the Interview. It is essential that before conducting an interview we are clear as to the purpose of this face-to-face encounter with the offender. Such knowledge will not only help determine the type of questions to be asked but also the length of the interview. If there is an identified problem, the interviewer will probably want to explore with the offender the behavior's frequency, duration, and intensity. The interviewer should also seek to identify the circumstances under which the behavior occurs and any exacerbating or mitigating factors that may be contributing to the current problem. Once the purpose of the evaluation has been established and the presenting complaints (if, indeed, there are any) determined, the interviewer can move on to the personal history section of the interview.

Personal History. The interviewee's personal background and history should be explored in some depth, the amount of detail depending, of course, on the purpose of the evaluation. Areas that should be assessed routinely include family history, marital and/or sexual relationships, educational attainment, employment record, mental health (to include substance abuse) context, and criminal background. Although available data are oftentimes more negative than positive, efforts should be made to identify personal strengths as well as personal liabilities. Hence, the fact that an individual has experienced a stable marital relationship for 15 years or graduated from high school can be as important in formulating a program of change as understanding that he or she began engaging in criminal activity at age 14 or never held a job any longer than six months.

Modified Mental Status Examination. Unlike a psychiatric interview, which is normally dedicated to acquiring a detailed understanding of a client's mental status, the criminal science interview is designed to assist in forming an appreciation of the client's past criminal behavior and current criminal thinking. Of course, this focus will shift in situations where an individual is being evaluated for the express purpose of determining his or her suitability for transfer to a mental health facility or ability to stand trial and assist in his or her own defense. Under most circumstances, however, the mental status examination should be geared toward attaining a rudimentary appreciation of the individual through an examination of physical appearance, mood and affect (emotional state and reactivity), speech (designed to determine whether the individual exhibits any abnormalities of perception or thought), intellectual awareness, insight, and judgment.

Cognitive Review. Throughout Volume 1, much was made of the condition-choice-cognition sequence. Efforts should be directed at gathering information pertinent to each of these dimensions of human experience. A reasonably accurate assessment of the conditions of one's life can be derived through the personal history section of the interview. The choices a person has made relative to these conditions may also be inferred from statements made by the individual during this portion of the interview. However, the personal history section of the interview normally reveals very little about a person's style of thinking. A preliminary understanding of such thinking can be obtained by listening for evidence of cognitive errors as discussed by Walters (1990) and Yochelson and Samenow (1976). Asking the offender to describe his or her involvement in the instant offense (or some earlier offense) can be particularly illuminating in this regard.

The criminal science interview usually takes no more than 30 minutes to conduct, although there are exceptions to this general rule. Whether the interview requires 20 minutes or two hours, the interviewer should follow the fundamental rules of good communication. In his book *The Helping Interview*, Benjamin (1981) describes several general maxims he has found helpful in improving his own interactions with clients. These include lowering one's defenses and preconceptions, suspending judgment until the client has had the opportunity to tell his or her "side of the story," listening to the client rather than to one's own internal self-talk, and avoiding common roadblocks to good communication (for example, interrupting the client, talking too much). It has been my experience that following guidelines such as these will result in a more productive interview, whether the interview is conducted for research purposes or as part of one's general clinical practice.

As I have tried to show here, the length of the interview, as well as the amount of time one spends on each of the individual steps, can be modified as a function of the interview's purpose. A screening interview conducted routinely with all inmates who enter a particular correctional facility should not be approached in the same manner as an interview designed to provide information to a subject's initial parole board, and both will differ from the procedure of a research analyst investigating the community adjustment of newly released felons. All, however, can follow the general outline presented in this section. In sum, flexibility is quintessential to the interview procedure, although a common structure or methodology must be retained in order to facilitate communication among professionals studying the same general questions.

Objective Personality Assessment

With an emphasis on structured and standardized routes of administration, scoring, and interpretation, objective measures of personality are typically self-report inventories that ask the individual to describe him or herself through use of a specific set of close-ended questions (for example, true-false, agree-disagree). Though popular with practicing clinicians, objective personality inventories are not without certain limitations. Two of the more common criticisms leveled against personality assessment procedures are their vulnerability to response sets, like acquiescence (Edwards & Diers, 1962), and their reliance on the often maligned concept of personality traits (Mischel, 1968). With these issues in mind, we commence with a review of several of the more popular methods of objective personality appraisal.

Minnesota Multiphasic Personality Inventory. The Minnesota Multiphasic Personality Inventory (MMPI) is the most widely utilized objective measure of personality (Lubin et al., 1985). With its roots in early to mid-twentieth-century empiricism, the MMPI provides for a structured response format that facilitates scoring and encourages research. Though the MMPI is not flawless (Shweder, 1977), it is buttressed by an impressive amount of empirical support. Several hundred studies and research investigations are published on this instrument each year (Graham, 1987; Greene, 1980) and over a thousand students have earned advanced degrees on the basis of having completed a doctoral dissertation or master's thesis on the MMPI (Dahlstrom, Welsh, & Dahlstrom, 1975). Moreover, Carlson (1990) determined that 85 percent of a group of 200 state and federal correctional psychologists reported using the MMPI in one capacity or another. It would seem advisable, then, that we spend some time inspecting this instrument, starting with how it was conceived, derived, and normed.

From a pool of over 1,000 true-false items, Hathaway and McKinley (1940) selected questions that successfully discriminated between groups of psychiatric patients and a sample of 724 friends and relatives of patients at the University Hospitals in Minneapolis. Clinically depressed inpatients were contrasted with the 724 control subjects in assembling the Depression (*D*) scale, while a sample of juvenile offenders served as the index group in developing the Psychopathic Deviate (*Pd*) scale. This culminated in an inventory composed of four validity scales—*?* (Cannot Say), *L* (Lie), *F* (False) and *K* (Defensiveness)—and nine clinical scales—1 (Hypochondriasis: *Hs*), 2 (Depression: *D*), 3 (Hysteria: *Hy*), 4 (Psychopathic Deviate: *Pd*), 5 (Masculinity:Femininity: *Mf*), 6 (Paranoia: *Pa*), 7 (Psychasthenia: *Pt*), 8 (Schizophrenia: *Sc*), and 9 (Hypomania: *Ma*). Several years later, Scale 0 (Social Introversion: *Si*; Evans & McConnell, 1941) was incorporated into the standard MMPI profile as a tenth clinical scale.

Originally published in the early 1940s, the MMPI has passed the test of time, in part because of the plethora of empirical studies conducted on this measure each year. Nonetheless, an updated version of the MMPI was introduced in 1989. Though the architects of this revision, referred to as the MMPI-2 (Butcher et al., 1989), insist that the basic integrity of the original MMPI has been preserved, this conclusion has not yet been substantiated by wide-spectrum empirical support. What is known is that the MMPI and MMPI-2 do not produce identical profiles, a fact borne out by subjects who have completed both versions of the MMPI in a single sitting. Thus, while there is evidence to suggest that the original MMPI is an effective discriminator in correctional and forensic settings, it is uncertain whether the MMPI-2 is capable of generating the level of robust empirical support enjoyed by its predecessor.

The literature available for review at the present time is almost exclusive to Hathaway and McKinley's original version of the MMPI. Before reviewing the MMPI literature on offenders, however, it seems advisable that we consider several more general issues involved with the administration, scoring, and interpretation of this objective measure of personality. First and foremost is the issue of subject testability. The testee should possess the intellectual and reading acumen to comprehend the nature of the MMPI task and items. It is unlikely that an individual with an IQ under 80 or reading ability below the fourth- or fifth-grade level will be able to produce an interpretable MMPI record. Consequently, alternative methods of assessment should be entertained under such circumstances.

A second but equally important issue concerns the notion of profile validity. Traditionally, scores exceeding a *T*-score of 70 on any of the four MMPI validity scales were taken as evidence of an invalid test protocol. However, such a standard is overly liberal in some instances (for example, *?*) and unduly harsh in others (for example, *F*). Thus, deleting as few as 55 items on the MMPI (a *T*-score on Scale *?* of only 57) will result in an average drop of five to six *T*-score points on each of the clinical scales (Clopton & Neuringer, 1977), while eliminating profiles with Scale *F* scores in the 70 to 110 *T*-score range can lead to a loss of important diagnostic information (Apfeldorf & Hunley, 1975). Greene (1980) proposes that a score of 5 or greater on the TR Index (repeated items), the presence of 30 or more unanswered items, and a *T*-score $\geq$ 120 on Scale *F* be viewed as evidence of an inconsistent or inaccurate MMPI response set.

Walters, White, and Greene (1988) ascertained that several special MMPI validity scales, most notably the Gough (1954) Dissimulation Scale and Weiner (1948) Obvious-Subtle Subscales, outperformed the standard MMPI validity scales (that is, L, F, and K) in discriminating between malingering and genuinely disturbed male prisoners. This study further revealed that clinical judges failed to improve upon the results obtained with single-scale actuarials, and in many cases failed to achieve the level attained by the actuarials. These findings are limited, however, by the fact that the judgments of clinicians familiar with the everyday behavior of subjects served as the malingering-disturbed criterion measure. With this in mind, Walters (1988) compared the MMPIs of inmates requesting single cells (high motivation to exaggerate psychopathology) with inmates completing the MMPI as part of a preparole evaluation (low motivation to exaggerate psychopathology). The outcome was largely supportive of Walters, White, and Greene's earlier findings and demonstrated that the Dissimulation Scale and Obvious-Subtle measures were more effective than the standard validity scales in identifying certain categories of subject test-taking attitude.

Additional studies have been conducted in an effort to discover the MMPI's ability to identify malingering in general forensic and state prison populations. Hawk and Cornell (1989) denote that approximately half the defendants in their study produced "invalid" profiles, though of the "interpretable" profiles they did receive, defendants judged to be malingering scored significantly higher on Scale F and several of the MMPI clinical scales relative to defendants diagnosed as psychotic. Roman and associates (1990) witnessed a similar outcome wherein malingering forensic patients scored significantly higher than a group of genuinely disturbed patients on several "fake bad" indices ($F–K$, Obvious–Subtle) and all of the clinical scales except 5 and 9. Schretlen and Arkowitz (1990) compared several groups of state prison inmates with mentally retarded and psychiatrically disturbed males, and determined that a battery of psychological tests (which included the MMPI) was more effective in discriminating between prisoners instructed to fake pathology and truly disturbed inmates than any solitary measure.

A third issue that needs to be considered within the context of MMPI research on high-rate offenders concerns the potential influence of moderator variables like age, gender, race, and education on the MMPI profile. There is evidence, for instance, that black offenders score higher than white offenders on a number of MMPI scales (Panton, 1959), although not all of the research on this topic shows a consistent racial effect (compare Costello, Fine, & Blau, 1973). The intricacy of this issue is illustrated by the results of a study directed by Rosenblatt and Pritchard (1978) in which 104 black and 191 white male inmates, organized according to IQ, were compared. Although there were no black-white differences in the high IQ (≥ 93) group, lower IQ blacks achieved significantly higher scores on MMPI Scales 1 (Hs), 8 (Sc), and 9 (Ma) and significantly lower scores on Scale 3 (Hy) in comparison to lower IQ whites. This interaction between two moderator variables demonstrates the complexity of MMPI research on criminal offenders and moves us into a discussion of the literature proper.

Single-Scale Elevations: Scale 4 (*Pd*) is frequently elevated in samples of adult and juvenile offenders. Hathaway and Monachesi (1963) carried out a three-year follow-up of persons administered the MMPI in the ninth grade and discovered that boys with subsequent records of criminal involvement scored significantly higher on Scales 4 (*Pd*), 8 (*Sc*), and 9 (*Ma*) and significantly lower on Scales 2 (*D*), 5 (*Mf*), and 0 (*Si*) than did noncriminal boys. Panton (1958a) reviewed over 1,300 MMPI profiles of persons incarcerated in the North Carolina penal system and determined that the mean profile and many of the individual profiles displayed elevations on Scale 4 that exceeded a *T*-score of 70. However, there were no MMPI differences noted between different crime categories (white-collar, aggravated assault, robbery or burglary, property theft, sexual perversion, sexual assault). Quinsey, Arnold, and Pruesse (1980) witnessed much the same outcome in a group of offenders referred for pretrial psychiatric evaluations.

Though Scale 4 does not appear to differentiate between crime groups, it may still prove useful to researchers and clinicians exploring various criminal science issues. Walters (1985), for example, discerned that young male military prisoners satisfying diagnostic criteria for Antisocial Personality Disorder on the Psychiatric Diagnostic Interview (PDI; Othmer et al., 1981) obtained substantially higher scores on Scale 4 than prisoners not fulfilling these criteria, the only moderating effect being that property offenders achieved higher scores on Scale 4 than inmates serving sentences for more violent transgressions. Similarly, Hare (1985) observed a moderately strong correlation between Scale 4 and a DSM-III diagnosis of Antisocial Personality Disorder and checklist rating of psychopathy. Holland, Beckett, and Levi (1981) witnessed the presence of a modest but statistically significant elevation on Scale 4 in a group of violent offenders, while Erikson and Roberts (1966) noted that more poorly adapted inmates achieved significantly higher Scale 4 scores than inmates with records of better institutional adjustment. The cross-national validity of the Scale 4–criminality connection was demonstrated in a study by Ono (1980) in which Japanese delinquents achieved elevated scores on Scale 4.

Researchers have also addressed the possible influence of selected moderator variables on the relationship between Scale 4 and assorted indices of criminality. Elion (1974), for instance, compared the MMPI profiles generated by youthful black offenders and a group of black college students, and found Scale 4 to be as effective in identifying black criminals as has been repeatedly demonstrated with white offenders (Greene, 1980). Elion also observed a direct association between Scale 4 scores and the level of antisocial behavior displayed by the subjects in his sample, although Scale 4 elevations do not always correspond reliably with the severity of crimes committed (Holland et al., 1981). It is worth noting that this inconsistency might reflect the presence of another moderator variable effect. In this regard, Heilbrun (1979) carried out an investigation of adult white male offenders and observed a correlation between elevations on Scale 4 and the frequency of violent criminality, but only in inmates with IQs below 95. Since that time, Heilbrun (1990) has provided data showing that his criminal dangerousness index (high scale 4, low IQ) increases monotonically with the severity of the confining offense.

Scale 4 is often conspicuously elevated in groups of psychopaths, delinquents, and criminals, but it is important to recognize that there are noncriminals who also obtain high scores on this scale. King and Kelley (1977) discovered that Scale 4 elevations were routinely observed in college students, although many of the students with T-scores on this scale in excess of 70 had a history of academic and/or legal difficulty and the majority received a variety of personality disorder diagnoses. Peak scores on Scale 4 have also been observed in nursing trainees (Hovey, 1953), public clinic patients being treated for impotence (Munjack et al., 1981), and the mothers of emotionally disturbed adolescents (Smith et al., 1984). Therefore, while many offenders elevate Scale 4 of the MMPI, high scores on this scale are in no way pathognomonic of criminality, although they probably suggest a certain degree of unconventionality.

High-Point Pairs: A common practice in MMPI interpretation is to consider the two or three most highly elevated clinical scales on a protocol (high-point pairs and triad, respectively) in combination. As one might expect, Scale 4 is prominent in the high-point combinations produced by criminal offenders. A spike 4 profile occurs as a solitary elevation on Scale 4, with all other clinical scales falling below a T-score of 70. Greene (1980) describes persons attaining the spike 4 profile as being impulsive, rebellious, egocentric, and lacking in insight. Gilberstadt and Duker (1965) ascertained that one-half of the spike 4 subjects in a sample of VA inpatients exhibited seriously assaultive behavior and a full 65 percent were heavy consumers of alcohol. In a study cited earlier, King and Kelley (1977) noticed a rising rate of legal involvement in college students achieving the spike 4 profile—arrests for shoplifting, possession of a controlled substance, grand larceny, assault, and murder all being mentioned.

MMPI profiles sporting prominent peaks on Scales 4 (*Pd*) and 3 (*Hy*), particularly in cases where Scale 4 > Scale 3, suggest that the respondent is hostile, rigid, and overcontrolled (Walters, Greene, & Solomon, 1982). Davis and Sines (1971) observed an increased incidence of violent, acting-out behavior in state hospital, university-based medical center, and state prison inmates registering the 4–3 profile pattern. Persons and Marks (1971) witnessed hostility and violence in the actions of inmates achieving this high-point constellation, though Buck and Graham (1978) were unable to replicate these findings in an independent sample of subjects. It has been suggested that the 4–3 high-point pair and Megargee, Cook, and Mendelsohn's (1967) Overcontrolled-Hostility (*O-H*) scale measure many of the same behaviors (Greene, 1980), a supposition which has received some empirical support in the present author's own work (Walters, Greene, & Solomon, 1982).

A third high-point combination regularly encountered in persons owning records of serious criminality concerns the dual elevation of MMPI Scales 4 (*Pd*) and 8 (*Sc*). Since one of the correlates of Scale 8 is cognitive confusion, it makes sense that the crimes committed by individuals achieving the 4–8/8–4 pattern are often poorly planned, bizarre, and violent in nature (Greene, 1980). Sexual acting-out behaviors have also been observed in offenders achieving this particular MMPI high-point combination (Dahlstrom, Welsh, & Dahlstrom, 1972; Erickson et al., 1987). As such, this high-point pair has been observed in child molesters (Hall et al., 1986), rapists (Rader, 1977), and exhibitionists (Moncrieff & Pearson, 1979). Forgac and Michaels (1982) compared exhibitionists who had committed a variety of different offenses (criminal group) with exhibitionists who had never been arrested for anything other than exposure (pure group). While univariate analyses revealed significant variations on Scales F, 4, and 8 in favor of the criminal group, multivariate analyses failed to identify a significant overall difference between the two groups.

A fourth MMPI high-point pair commonly observed in offender populations betrays peaks on Scales 4 (*Pd*) and 9 (*Ma*). Persons attaining this high-point profile often act out in ways that bring them into conflict with their environment (Carson, 1969). Marks, Seeman, and Haller (1974) discerned a history of juvenile delinquency, substance abuse, and sexual promiscuity, with current indications of immaturity, hostility, and manipulativeness, in psychiatric patients displaying the 4–9/9–4 composite. Marks et al. (1974) and Gilberstadt and Duker (1965) both deduced a modal diagnosis of Antisocial Personality and/or Sociopathy in psychiatric patients achieving this particular high-point configural pattern. The 4–9/9–4 high-point coalition has been observed in persons displaying marital discord and child abuse difficulties (Paulson et al., 1974), chronic levels of drug and alcohol abuse (Loper, Kammeier, & Hoffmann, 1973), and delinquent patterns of personal adjustment (McCreary, 1975).

Profile Configuration: The configural pattern of MMPI scale relationships has also been of interest to researchers probing the personality correlates of criminal behavior. In contrasting violent and nonviolent criminal offenders, Jones, Beidleman, and Fowler (1981) determined that a multivariate composite incorporating 22 MMPI scales and four demographic measures successfully discriminated between subjects in these two groups. Violent offenders were found to achieve more highly elevated MMPI profiles, with Scales F, 6 (*Pa*), 7 (*Pt*), and 8 (*Sc*) carrying the brunt of the multivariate weight. Twomey and Hendry (1969) also witnessed a higher mean profile elevation in difficult-to-manage federal prisoners confined in a maximum security federal penitentiary, although use of general population state prisoners as a control group vitiates the meaningfulness of Twomey and Hendry's conclusions.

Besides serving as a dependent or outcome measure, the MMPI has also been used to assign subjects to conditions. In one study, Anderson and Holcomb (1983) cluster-analyzed the MMPIs of a sample of males charged with first-degree murder. The group achieving within-normal-limits profiles (*T*-scores on all clinical scales < 70) tended to possess higher IQs, were more likely to have been employed at the time of arrest, and displayed very few problems with substance abuse compared to subjects with at least one elevated clinical scale. Likewise, Ray et al. (1983) discerned that a (MMPI) within-normal-limits group of law violators contained a larger percentage of first-time offenders arrested for shoplifting than the group with MMPI scale elevations.

Moderator variables may augment or suppress MMPI profile elevation just as they increase or decrease the altitude of a particular scale. In one study, Blanchard, Bassett, and Koshland (1977) administered the MMPI to male felons serving time on a state prison farm. Subjects earning within-normal-limits profiles had been arrested fewer times and had begun their criminal careers substantially later than subjects achieving more highly elevated profiles. However, race was found to moderate this relationship to the extent that white subjects achieving elevated scores on Scales 4 and 9 and blacks not registering such elevations had less of an ability to delay gratification than blacks with elevated scores on Scales 4 and 9 and whites not attaining this particular MMPI configuration. Walters (1986b) surveyed the relationship between MMPI profile elevation and diagnostic status as measured by a structured diagnostic interview (PDI). Concordance between MMPI elevation (at least one clinical scale ≥ T-score of 90) and the presence of at least two PDI diagnoses was higher in whites (96%) than blacks (71%), although both figures exceeded chance expectations. Interestingly, Green and Kelley (1988) discerned that racial variations on the MMPI correlated inversely with the apparent objectivity of the external criterion measure being used.

Special Scales: Special scales have been introduced in an effort to answer specific clinical and research questions. The development of special MMPI scales is deceptively easy, so easy in fact that Butcher and Tellegen (1978) lament that there are now more special MMPI scales than MMPI items. Hence, while myriad research and special scales have been derived, very few have been thoroughly investigated. Before these scales are ready for clinical use, it will need to be demonstrated that they provide information superior to that supplied by the standard MMPI validity and clinical scales, a test most special MMPI scales fail (Greene, 1980). We examine five special MMPI scales that seem particularly relevant to our discussion on criminal science assessment. One such scale has been reasonably well researched (Overcontrolled-Hostility), while the other four scales form the nucleus of what is commonly referred to as the MMPI Correctional Scales (Prison Adjustment, Recidivism, Escape, Homosexuality).

In an effort to distinguish between undercontrolled and overcontrolled assaultive individuals, Megargee, Cook, and Mendelsohn (1967) developed the 31-item Overcontrolled-Hostility (O-H) scale. The theory behind the O-H scale is that while undercontrolled assaultive individuals engage in aggressive action as a function of weak impulse control, overcontrolled individuals habitually constrict their emotions to where, given sufficient provocation, they periodically react in ways that are intense and highly destructive. Research studies plumbing the depths and theoretical underpinnings of the O-H scale are mixed. Lane and Kling (1979) reported that this scale successfully discriminated between overcontrolled and undercontrolled psychiatric patients, and Deiker (1974) noted that this scale was able to identify extremely assaultive male prisoners, although these differences were only on the order of two to three raw score points. What is more, several other investigations have failed to discern any *O-H* scale differences between groups of violent and nonviolent criminals (Hoppe & Singer, 1976; Mallory & Walker, 1972) and there is evidence of moderator effects for race and gender (Graham, 1987). Studies in which the behavioral correlates of the *O-H* scale have been explored are more supportive of the founding tenets of the theory which led Megargee et al. (1967) to develop the scale in the first place. Walters, Greene, and Solomon (1982) discovered hostility-anger, rigid denial, and a tendency toward behavioral overcontrol to be characteristic of high *O-H* subjects, while Quinsey, Maguire, and Varney (1983) note that high *O-H* murderers were rated as more unassertive on a role-playing task than low *O-H* murderers.

The Prison Adjustment Scale (Beall & Panton, 1956), in its original form, was 42 items in length, but Panton (1958b) shortened it to 36 questions and renamed it the Adjustment to Prison (*Ap*) scale. Initial validation of the *Ap* scale accurately identified 82 percent of a group of well-adjusted inmates and from 85 to 93 percent of several groups of poorly adjusted prisoners. A subsequent study carried out by Panton and his colleagues revealed the presence of high *Ap* scores in self-mutilating and recidivistic subjects (Panton, 1962b). However, validation research conducted outside North Carolina has been much more equivocal, with several investigators failing to find a meaningful connection between scores on the *Ap* scale and adjustment to incarceration (Jones et al., 1981; Stump & Gilbert, 1972; Sutker & Moan, 1977). Even in studies acknowledging the presence of a statistically significant correlation between *Ap* scores and prison adjustment, the obtained results are suspect from a clinical significance standpoint (Megargee & Carbonell, 1985) in large part because of the ground swell of false positive predictions that have been recorded (Pierce, 1972). Ambiguity is clearly illustrated in the outcome of studies on the proposed nexus between the *Ap* scale and performance in educational and vocational training programs, with two studies displaying concordance (Jaman, 1969; Levine, 1969) and a third study showing no association (Steuber, 1974).

Clark (1948) developed the Recidivism (*Rc*) scale by contrasting military prisoners who had a record of one AWOL with those charged with multiple AWOLs. Clark failed to cross-validate his 24-item scale, although it is included in several of the more popular MMPI computer-based scoring and interpretation systems. This should not be taken as evidence for the external validity of the scale, however. In fact, the few studies conducted on the *Rc* scale in nonmilitary samples have yielded largely negative outcomes (Freeman & Mason, 1952; Megargee & Carbonell, 1985; Panton, 1962a).

Beall and Panton (1956) devised a 42-item Escape (*Ec*) scale by contrasting the intake MMPIs of 103 state prisoners who eventually escaped with the intake MMPIs of 100 inmates without a history of escape. This scale accurately classified 77 percent of the escapees and 73 percent of the nonescapees in the derivation sample, and 77 percent of the escapees and 78 percent of the nonescapees in the cross-validation sample. Though Pierce (1971) determined that the

Ec scale correctly identified 80 percent of the escapees and 82 percent of the inmates without escape histories in his sample of state prisoners, several other investigators have failed to observe a connection between scores on this scale and escape history and/or behavior (Adams & West, 1976; Stump & Gilbert, 1972). There is also the corollary problem of trying to predict a very low base-rate behavior (Meehl & Rosen, 1955) in that more accurate results could probably be achieved if one were to assume that no subject would attempt to escape (which would correctly identify between 90 and 95% of the inmates in most samples) than by inspecting the scores of an MMPI scale, which at best can accurately classify no more than 80 percent of the subjects.

The final special scale to be considered in this section, the Homosexuality *(Hsx)* scale, was also developed in North Carolina. Panton (1960) constructed this 22-item scale by comparing the MMPI responses of confined homosexual prisoners and nonhomosexual inmates matched on age and IQ. The *Hsx* scale correctly identified 81 percent of the homosexuals and 87 percent of the non-homosexuals in the original sample, and 86 percent of the homosexuals and 81 percent of the nonhomosexuals in the cross-validation sample. Subsequent research has shown this scale to be effective in differentiating between chronic and situational homosexuals (Friburg, 1967), identifying prior-to-incarceration homosexuals (Panton, 1978), and achieving results that are relatively stable over a period of at least one year (Pierce, 1973). However, not all of the data are corroborative (Cubitt & Gendreau, 1972), and there is an expanding awareness that *Hsx* is not correlated with overall prison adjustment (Jones et al., 1981; Megargee & Carbonell, 1985; Panton, 1973).

The outcome of research on MMPI special scales applied to the question of criminal behavior demonstrates that while these scales may, in many cases, produce statistically significant findings, their clinical utility remains unproven and awaits verification. It would seem advisable, then, that we direct our attention toward thoroughly evaluating the standard and research scales that currently exist before moving into the development of even more specialized MMPI scales and indices.

California Psychological Inventory. The California Psychological Inventory (CPI) contains 480 true-false items similar to those found on the MMPI; in fact, approximately one-third of the items on the CPI are exact duplicates of MMPI items. Its founder, Harrison Gough (1957) conceived of the CPI as an alternative to the pathological leanings of the MMPI. As such, this instrument was designed to probe normal features of personality, with higher scores being associated with positive, rather than pathological, outcomes. The CPI is composed of 18 scales—Dominance *(Do)*, Capacity for Status *(Cs)*, Sociability *(So)*, Social Presence *(Sp)*, Self-acceptance *(Sa)*, Well-being *(Wb)*, Responsibility *(Re)*, Socialization *(So)*, Self-control *(Sc)*, Tolerance *(To)*, Good Impression *(Gi)*, Communality *(Cm)*, Achievement via Conformity *(Ac)*, Achievement via Independence *(Ai)*, Intellectual Efficiency *(Ie)*, Psychological-mindedness *(Py)*, Flexibility *(Fx)*, Femininity *(Fe)*—which, like the MMPI, are plotted using *T*-scores.

The Socialization scale (*So*) was assembled with the aid of an offender contrast group and has been found to be quite effective in identifying societal lawbreakers. Gough (1965) reports the presence of substantially lower *So* scores in offenders, as compared to nonoffenders, in 18 independent comparisons made in countries as diverse and disparate as the United States, Costa Rica, India, South Africa, and Switzerland. Low scores on this scale have been found to correlate with marijuana abuse (Hogan et al., 1970), dishonesty (Hetherington & Feldman, 1964), and an aggressive interpersonal style (Paterson et al., 1984) in college students. High *So* scores, on the other hand, tend to correspond with success on parole (Gough, Wenk, & Rozynko, 1965) and socialized, as compared to un-socialized, expressions of delinquency (Hindelang, 1973). It should come as no surprise that age (Grupp, Ramseyer, & Richardson, 1968), race (Fenelon & Megargee, 1971), and gender (Cross, Barclay, & Burger, 1978) variations have all been observed on this and several of the other CPI scales.

The Responsibility (*Re*) scale is also frequently depressed in criminal populations. Flanagan and Lewis (1974) determined that chronic juvenile delinquents scored significantly lower on the *Re* scale in comparison to a group of "first-time" adolescent offenders, while Megargee (1972) reports that low scores on both *Re* and Self-control (*Sc*) corresponded with delinquency in male and female juveniles. Cowden, Schroeder, and Peterson (1971) note that low scores on *Re* and several additional CPI scales (Well-being, Communality, Intellectual Efficiency) are associated with poor institutional adjustment. It has also been as-certained that exhibitionists who engage in a variety of different criminal activities tend to achieve significantly lower scores on Scales *So* and *Re* relative to individuals who have never been arrested for anything other than indecent exposure (Forgac & Michaels, 1982).

Other Objective Personality Measures. A variety of other objective measures of personality have been devised but little is known about their utility with criminal populations. Recently, however, Carlson (1982) published the Carlson Psychological Survey (CPS) in an effort to generate useful information for mental health professionals working in correctional settings. Composed of 50 items scored on a five-point scale—never, once in a while, some of the time, most of the time, all of the time—the CPS normally takes less than 30 minutes to complete and requires only a fourth-grade reading level. The CPS yields scores on five scales (Chemical Abuse, Thought Disturbance, Antisocial Tendencies, Self-Depreciation, Validity). In the test manual, Carlson (1982) references several studies of his instrument that hint that the CPS may be capable of differentiating between groups and categories of inmates. Though the CPS displays promise as an aid in identifying features of serious criminality, more research is required to determine the generalizability of Carlson's moderately impressive preliminary findings.

Projective Testing

In formulating the projective hypothesis, Frank (1939) argued that so-called projective techniques like the Rorschach and Thematic Apperception Test (TAT) provide a window through which one projects assorted proclivities and personality characteristics onto the stimulus material. Although many scholars take issue with Frank's notion of projection, there is evidence that we can learn how an individual structures and organizes his or her experiences by observing how he or she responds to an ambiguous stimulus situation, whether this is an inkblot, a picture, or a sentence stem (Exner, 1974). Maloney and Ward (1976) discuss ways in which projective techniques and objective personality measures differ. In general, projective techniques tend to be more unstructured, unquantified, global, disguised, and focused on latent features of personality than are objective assessment procedures. Projective techniques may therefore tap aspects of criminal thinking unavailable to clinicians relying exclusively on objective personality measures.

Lindzey (1959) divided projective techniques into five general categories: association, construction, completion, choice, and expressive. According to Lindzey, association techniques, like the Rorschach inkblot procedure, require that the individual respond to the eliciting stimulus with a word or percept. Construction techniques, on the other hand, ask the individual to formulate a narrative response to the stimulus material. The third category, completion techniques, solicits responses from the subject that complete or consummate the stimulus situation, such as the sentence stems that constitute sentence-completion procedures. Choice or ordering techniques apprise the subject that he or she must select or order a set of stimuli using a predetermined set of criteria. The final category, expressive techniques, advises the subject to draw, paint, or act out his or her response as exemplified by the Draw-A-Person technique.

Projective testing has never been particularly prolific in generating research outcomes relevant to our work with criminal offenders. This unfortunate state of affairs is largely a function of the ambiguous nature of the projective task itself, as well as a lack of consensus among scholars and clinicians as to what these procedures actually measure. Low specificity not only creates a quandary in terms of scoring and interpretation but also makes scientific study of the projective hypothesis difficult. Subjectivity, weak operationality, and limited standardization serve as obstacles to researchers wishing to investigate the projective test responses of criminal offenders. We must therefore carefully establish and define the boundaries of criminal science research on projective techniques, which in the present context is represented by the Rorschach Inkblot Technique.

Rorschach. The Rorschach was first introduced in a posthumously published book (Rorschach, 1921). The procedure itself commences with the presentation of ten ambiguous stimuli (inkblots), some of which are black-gray and others of which are chromatic. The subject is asked to provide associations to each of the ten Rorschach cards with the query, "What might this be?" (Exner, 1974). The examiner records the subject's responses, and then inquires into the blot features used by the subject to formulate his or her percepts. Scoring generally takes into account the location (whole blot versus part blot), determinants (form, movement, color, shading), and content (human, animal, blood, etc.) of the response. A number of Rorschach scoring systems have been proposed, although

Exner's (1974) Comprehensive System is probably the most widely utilized and thoroughly researched approach to Rorschach scoring and interpretation presently in use.

The location of Rorschach responses is concerned with that portion of the inkblot stimulus to which the subject attends in forming his or her response. Location is typically partitioned into whole responses, usual detail responses, unusual detail responses, and the white space response (Exner, 1974). Rapaport, Gill, and Schafer (1968) write that a small number of whole responses and an excessive number of usual detail responses are often found on the Rorschach protocols of delinquents and psychopaths. These authors speculate that this finding reflects impaired surveying ability and overly concrete thinking, although there is virtually no empirical data on this or other questions relating to the location of Rorschach responses in criminal populations.

Determinants are the blot features that contribute to the derivation of any particular Rorschach response and are a rich source of interpretive hypotheses. Form (utilizing the form or shape features of the blot) as the primary determinant in a Rorschach response portends behavioral control, while attention to chromatic color is said to be indicative of emotional responsiveness. In light of the fact criminal offenders tend to be impulsive and undercontrolled, we would anticipate a form:color ratio in favor of the latter, a possibility which finds some support in the empirical literature on Rorschachian correlates of criminal behavior (Exner & Weiner, 1982; Glueck & Glueck, 1968; Ostrov et al., 1972). Another measure of a subject's responsiveness to color, the Affective Ratio, has demonstrated an ascending slope on the Rorschach records of many juvenile delinquents (Curtiss, Feczko, & Marohn, 1979). There is also a general absence of movement responses (movement being associated with creativity and internalization tendencies) on the Rorschachs produced by delinquents and psychopaths (Rapaport et al., 1968). Research addressing the relationship between criminality and Rorschach determinants like texture, dimensionality, diffuse shading, and reflections is scarce.

By far, the most heavily investigated area with relevance to the Rorschach responses of criminal offenders concerns the content or subject of individual responses. Maitra (1985) contrasted 100 delinquent and 100 nondelinquent Indian male youth between the ages of 12 and 18 and found aggressive movement, aggressive content, and the perception of fire to be more prominent in the delinquent group. Gorlow, Zimet, and Fine (1952) used a content-based Rorschach scoring system designed to identify hostility (Elizur, 1949) to successfully discriminate between delinquents and nondelinquents. Rangaswami (1982) used this same scoring system to contrast groups of criminal and noncriminal schizophrenics, and discovered that the criminal schizophrenics obtained higher scores on this measure. Ostrov, Offer, and Marohn (1976) also witnessed a relationship between delinquency and scores on Elizur's procedure. Cooper, Perry, and Arnow (1988), however, were unable to demonstrate concordance between the

Rorschach Defense Scales, which rely almost exclusively on content categories, and a diagnosis of Antisocial Personality Disorder.

Popular responses tend to be quite common on the Rorschach records of criminal offenders and, like the criminal's focus on usual detail, reflect a trend toward concrete thinking (Rapaport et al., 1968). There is also evidence to suggest that prison inmates tend to produce a lower percentage of *H* (human content) responses than noncriminals (Walters, 1953). This seems to be a particularly significant finding in light of the fact that *H* responses are thought to reflect one's interest in meaningful human interaction (Exner, 1974). It is noteworthy that Endora (cited in Draguns, Haley, & Phillips, 1967) observed an inverse correlation between the percentage of *H* responses and the severity of crimes committed and propensity to re-offend.

The outcome of Rorschach research carried out on delinquents and criminals intimates that these individuals are impulsive, uncreative, and overly concrete. However, this knowledge might also be obtained through use of less expensive assessment procedures, most notably the MMPI and clinical interview. Consequently, we have yet to tap the full potential of projective techniques like the Rorschach, in part because the research in this area has been rather narrow and unsophisticated. It is conceivable that the Rorschach and other projective techniques may never contribute significantly to our understanding of crime and criminals (Rogers & Cavanaugh, 1983), although they may still have a place in certain specific diagnostic situations, to include assisting clinicians with certain differential diagnostic decisions (for example, psychosis versus malingering) or as part of a research project on, say, information processing and crime. Be this as it may, there is absolutely no evidence to support the recommendation of a former consultant to the National Commission on the Causes and Prevention of Violence that the Rorschach be administered to all six-year-olds as a means of identifying persons likely to become involved in criminal activity at some future date.

Rating Scales

A rating scale is an instrument used to assign subjects to groups or categories on the basis of ratings made by an observer or judge (Kerlinger, 1973). The Psychopathy Checklist (PCL) and Lifestyle Criminality Screening Form (LCSF) serve as two examples of rating scales with potential utility in criminal populations.

Psychopathy Checklist. In an effort to derive a reliable and valid measure of psychopathy (Cleckley, 1976) for use in research, Hare and Cox (1978) gave notice of having developed a seven-point global rating scale. By 1980 Hare had constructed a 22-item (for example, lack of remorse or guilt; proneness to boredom or low frustration tolerance; glibness or superficial charm) rating scale scored according to a three-point procedure: 0 = does not apply; 1 = item may apply;

2 = item definitely applies. This instrument, subsequently labeled the Psycho-pathy Checklist (PCL), was shown to possess a reasonable degree of inter-rater reliability (r = .91 to .95) and internal consistency (alpha coefficient = .83). Schroeder, Schroeder, and Hare (1983) cross-validated this checklist on 301 male prison inmates and obtained inter-rater reliability estimates of between .84 and .93, an alpha coefficient of .83 to .92, and correlation of .83 with the seven-item global rating scale that served as Hare and Cox's original measure of psychopathy.

After comparing several procedures designed to assess psychopathy, Hare (1985) discovered greater commonality between clinical-behavioral measures (PCL, global measure of psychopathy, DSM-III [*Diagnostic and Statistical Manual of Medical Disorders, Third Edition*—APA, 1980] diagnosis of Antisocial Personality Disorder) than between self-report measures (MMPI Scales 4 and 9, *So* scale of the CPI, self-report version of the PCL) and discerned a minimal degree of concordance between the two groups of measures. According to the results of this study the PCL correlated .80 with the global rating, .67 with the DSM-III diagnosis, .38 with the self-report version of the PCL, − .32 with the *So* scale, .27 with MMPI Scale 9, and .26 with MMPI Scale 4. Harpur, Hakstian, and Hare (1988) factor-analyzed PCL data in six different samples of prison inmates and found a two-factor solution that was replicated for all six samples. The first factor is said to assess the core features of psychopathy (superficiality; habitual lying; lack of guilt, remorse, and empathy), while the second factor features the chronically unstable and antisocial lifestyle commonly observed in psychopathic individuals. Harpur, Hare, and Hakstian (1989) report that Factor 1 is more closely aligned with the global rating scale and Cleckly's core criteria for psychopathy, while Factor 2 taps a domain normally appraised by self-report measures like the CPI's *So* scale or MMPI Scales 4 and 9.

The PCL's ability to identify psychopathy appears to be largely independent of intelligence and mental health effects. Newman (cited in Green, 1988) wit-nessed minimal concordance between the PCL and IQ test results (r = − .12), while Hart and Hare (1989) observed little relationship between the PCL and various indices of serious psychiatric and emotional disorder. Williamson, Hare, and Wong (1987) examined the most serious offense committed by 55 high-PCL and 46 low-PCL prison inmates and observed results largely supportive of Hare's ideas and formulations. In brief, the most serious crimes committed by subjects in the high-PCL group were not normally accompanied by a strong emotional response and the victims were typically strangers. By comparison, low-PCL subjects engaged in violent offenses that were often the result of a domestic argument, intense emotional arousal being an important precipitating factor.

Probing the external correlates of the PCL further, Hart, Kropp, and Hare (1988) compared the PCL scores of 231 white male offenders released from prison on parole or mandatory release with outcome (violation-nonviolation) one year later. The results of this study revealed that 65.2 percent of the high-PCL group, 48.9 percent of the moderate-PCL group, and 23.5 percent of the low-

PCL group had violated the conditions of their release, a highly significant difference. It was also discerned that the PCL scale predicted outcome at a level that was independent of the contributions made by such variables as age at time of release, type of release, and criminal history. The PCL's ability to predict recidivism was recently cross-validated in an independent sample of male inmates released from several different Canadian prisons (Serin, Peters, & Barbaree, 1990).

By way of summarizing nearly ten years of research on the Psychopathy Checklist, Green (1988, p. 187) states that "the PCL, although of only recent development, appears to provide a systematic and replicable approach to the assessment of psychopathy." This would appear to be a fair appraisal, although the PCL could benefit from further definitional refinements, exploration of its generalizability (Forth, Hart, & Hare, 1990), and a reduction in the amount of time required to administer and score this instrument.

Lifestyle Criminality Screening Form. Like the PCL, the Lifestyle Criminality Screening Form (LCSF) was conceived as a means of assessing a theoretical construct, in this case lifestyle criminality (see Fig. 2.1). Unlike the MMPI, which relies on information provided by the offender, or the PCL, which employs a replicable (but nonetheless subjective) approach to data collection, the LCSF was established as a chart review procedure. The LCSF can be completed without input from the offender, although it is dependent on the comprehensiveness of the pre-sentence report that normally serves as the data source for this instrument. A 14-item scale, which assesses the four behavioral domains of lifestyle criminality (irresponsibility, self-indulgence, interpersonal intrusiveness, social rule breaking), the LCSF yields a total score of between 0 and 22, with higher scores purportedly reflecting a lifestyle pattern of criminal conduct (see Walters, 1990).

In the initial validation of this instrument, the LCSF successfully discriminated between two groups of offenders hypothesized to contain differing proportions of lifestyle and non-lifestyle criminals—25 prisoners incarcerated in a maximum security federal penitentiary (high percentage of lifestyle criminals) and 25 inmates confined in a minimum security federal prison camp (low percentage of lifestyle criminals)—at a fairly impressive rate (R^2 = .82; Walters, White, & Denney, in press). The internal consistency of this instrument is acceptable (alpha coefficient = .84; Walters et al., in press) and the inter-rater agreement (total score) has been found to range between .93 and .96 (Walters, Revella, & Baltrusaitis, 1990; Walters et al., in press).

The lifestyle theory of criminal involvement contends that habitual felons function best when environmental structure is maximal. It would stand to reason, then, that if a relationship were to exist between lifestyle criminality and institutional adjustment, it might be moderated by the level of environmental structure. By way of evaluating this hypothesis, two separate analyses were conducted (Walters, 1991). In one of these analyses the LCSF served as the dependent measure and in a second analysis the LCSF served as the criterion measure. The results of both analyses revealed that no relationship existed between lifestyle

Figure 2.1
Lifestyle Criminality Screening Form

Directions: After reviewing a subject's background, complete this form by inserting the appropriate number (in parentheses next to the box) for responses suggested by information in the subject's file. If there is no information available for a particular question then leave the boxes blank, although more than one unanswered question per section may result in unreliable results. Once the evaluator has completed this form, numbers should be totaled for each of the four sections. A total section score of 2 indicates a probable diagnosis and a score of 3 a definite diagnosis of the lifestyle characteristic (i.e., irresponsibility, self-indulgence, interpersonal intrusiveness, social rule breaking) being measured by that particular section.

Section I. Irresponsibility

    A. Failed to provide support for at least one biological child.

        Yes..................................... ☐ (1)

        No...................................... ☐ (0)

    B. Terminated formal education prior to graduating from high school.

        Yes..................................... ☐ (1)

        No...................................... ☐ (0)

    C. Longest job ever held.

        Less than six months.................... ☐ (2)

        At least 6 months but less than 2 years.. ☐ (1)

        Two or more years....................... ☐ (0)

    D. Terminated from job for irresponsibility or quit for no apparent reason.

        Two or more times....................... ☐ (2)

        Once.................................... ☐ (1)

        None reported........................... ☐ (0)

    Total Irresponsibility   ☐

Section II. Self-Indulgence

    A. History of drug or alcohol abuse.

        Yes..................................... ☐ (2)

        No...................................... ☐ (0)

    B. Marital Background

        Two or more prior divorces.............. ☐ (2)

        One prior divorce/more than 1 separation. ☐ (1)

        Single but with illegitimate child....... ☐ (1)

        Married, no divorces/single, no children. ☐ (0)

Figure 2.1 (continued)

C. Physical Appearance (check only one box).

Tattoos on face or neck................... □ (2)

Tattoos up and down arms .... □ (2)

Presence of one or several tatoos

If black........................... □ (2)

If white........................... □ (1)

No tattoos............................. □ (0)

Total Self-Indulgence   □

Section III. Interpersonal Intrusiveness

A. Confining offense.

Intrusive (e.g., murder, rape, robbery,
breaking & entering, assault)........... □ (1)

Nonintrusive (e.g., drugs, embezzelment). □ (0)

B. History of prior arrests for instrusive behavior
(excluding the confining offense).

Three or more............................ □ (2)

One or two............................... □ (1)

None..................................... □ (0)

C. Use of weapon or threatened use of weapon during
commission of confining offense.

Yes...................................... □ (1)

No....................................... □ (0)

D. Physical abuse of significant others (primarily
family members).

Yes...................................... □ (1)

No....................................... □ (0)

Total Interpersonal Intrusiveness   □

Section IV. Social Rule Breaking

A. Prior arrests (excluding confining offense).

Five or more............................. □ (2)

Two to four.............................. □ (1)

One or none.............................. □ (0)

B. Age at time of first arrest.

14 years of age or younger............... □ (2)

Older than 14 but younger than 19........ □ (1)

19 years of age or older................. □ (0)

31

Figure 2.1 (continued)

```
C. History of being a behavioral/management problem
   at school.

        Yes.................................... ☐ (1)

        No..................................... ☐ (0)
                                              _____

   Total Social Rule Breaking                  ☐
```

Source: International Journal of Offender Therapy and Comparative Criminology, 33 (1989), 54–
    56. Used with permission.

criminality and disciplinary adjustment in the highly structured setting (maximum security penitentiary), but that high LCSF scores predicted poor institutional adjustment in the less structured environment (minimum security camp). The external structure provided by the maximum security penitentiary may therefore compensate for the lifestyle offender's lack of self-control and discipline.

Where the structure of the penitentiary may conceal the more destructive features of the criminal lifestyle, these characteristics surface with renewed vigor once the individual is removed from this highly controlled environment. It has been hypothesized that the lifestyle criminal should have particular difficulty functioning trouble free in the community where structure is low and temptation is high. This is exactly what Walters, Revella, and Baltrusaitis (1990) discovered when they examined the community adjustment of 79 federal parolees and probationers over a period of one year. Not only did the LCSF successfully predict future technical and criminal violations ($r = .36$), but it did so at a level independent of and superior to the individual contributions of such traditional indices as age and marital status. Viewed side by side, the results of the Walters (1991) and Walters et al. (1990) studies would seem to suggest that persons who rank high on the LCSF experience problems with self-control and self-discipline that may not fully manifest themselves until the individual is placed in an environment that is less than maximally structured.

Several additional research projects on the LCSF are currently in progress. The recent development of a self-report version of the LCSF (Walters, 1989) capable of generating results comparable to those obtained with the standard research form ($r = .72$) would appear to enhance future research applications. Unpublished data have shown that the LCSF correlates reasonably well with clinical diagnoses of Antisocial Personality Disorder. There may also be a link between the LCSF and the second factor of the PCL (for example, irresponsible behavior as a parent, frequent marital relationships, many different offenses), a possibility which warrants the attention of criminal science investigators. As future research projects come to fruition we will be in a much better position to judge the general utility of the LCSF as a measure of serious and repetitive forms of criminal conduct.

SITUATION-ORIENTED ASSESSMENT

While person-oriented assessment techniques are more popular than situation-oriented procedures, it is nevertheless possible to assess a person's environmental circumstances. Two general categories of situation-oriented assessment are identified for our purposes here. One category of situation-oriented assessment is physical or object-related procedures, of which the Correctional Institutions Environment Scale (Moos, 1974) is an example. The other category of situation-oriented assessment considers the social role and status of the individual, and will be referred to as social situation–oriented assessment. Techniques designed to measure social class and poverty capture the intent of social situation–oriented procedures.

Correctional Institutions Environment Scale

Rudolph Moos (1974, 1975) developed the Correctional Institutions Environment Scale (CIES) in an effort to measure the social and physical climate of selected correctional milieus and institutional programs. The CIES is a 90-item instrument comprising nine subscales. Moos groups these subscales into three primary dimensions or clusters: the Involvement, Support, and Expressiveness subscales forming the relationship dimension; the Autonomy, Practical Orientation, and Person Problem Orientation subscales forming the treatment program dimension; and the Order or Organization, Clarity, and Staff Control subscales subserving the system maintenance dimension. In addition to the 90-item long form, there is a 36-item short form, an "ideal" program form, and a form that assesses expectations.

Research depicts the test-retest reliability (one week interval) of the CIES as extending from .65 to .80 (Moos, 1974). Average internal consistencies have been shown to vary between .54 and .83, and item-subscale correlations between .38 and .56 in samples of male juveniles (Moos, 1975). Moos reports further that using the intraclass correlation as a measure of stability yields coefficients of .94, .95, and .91 for programs assessed with the CIES at one-week, one-month, and two-year intervals, respectively. Moos is quick to add, however, that despite its temporal stability, the CIES is surprisingly sensitive to changes occurring in the correctional environment. There is also evidence that the long and short forms of the CIES correlate reasonably well—that is, approximately .80 (Moos, 1975).

Wenk and Halatyn (1973) have determined that the CIES generates outcomes largely independent of such subject characteristics as age, length of sentence, time spent in confinement, and number of previous convictions. Moos (1975) cites a study in which the staff and residents of juvenile halls, ranches, and camps rated their institutions using the CIES. Outcomes indicated that the ranches and camps were rated higher than the juvenile halls on the relationship (Involvement, Support) and treatment program (Autonomy, Practical Orientation) dimensions. According to the results of studies comparing resident and staff impressions, staff in both adult and juvenile facilities view their institutions in more favorable terms than do residents—a finding reflected in higher ratings on all of the CIES subscales except Staff Control (Moos, 1974). Similarly, staff are considerably more positive and optimistic about the "ideal" correctional environment than are residents.

Summarizing the results of CIES research on adolescent correctional populations, much of which had never before been published, Moos (1975) offered several general conclusions. First, an increasing emphasis on the relationship and treatment program dimensions corresponds with a rise in the degree to which residents believe they can benefit from their correctional experience. Second, higher scores on the CIES have been shown to correlate with positive changes in the individual, as measured by the Jesness (1971) Inventory. Third, graduates normally hold their program environments in greater esteem than do nongraduates, scoring in the more positive direction on the Autonomy, Practical Orientation, Clarity, and Staff Control subscales. This effect was most pronounced when graduates were contrasted with residents who eventually absconded from custody. Fourth, rules violations are typically more prevalent in adolescents who score low on the Expressiveness, Practical Orientation, and Personal Problem Orientation subscales of the CIES.

Social Class and Poverty

It has been demonstrated that social class correlates with a number of factors, from intelligence (Whiteman & Deutsch, 1968), to mental illness (Hollingshead & Redlich, 1958), to emotional development (Zigler and Child, 1969). This has led several investigators to search for ways of quantifying the characteristics of social class. Probably the most frequently cited measure of social class is Hollingshead's Index of Social Position (Hollingshead & Redlich, 1958). This five-level system is based on estimates of occupation, education, and residence. Coleman and Neugarten (1971) designed a more sophisticated measure of social class using an eight-dimensional approach, each dimension rated on a seven-point scale. The descriptive utility of this instrument has been confirmed by research that shows a wide disparity in housing, employment, and income among the five social groups formed from this measure (Cartwright, 1974). It may go without saying, but a great deal more research is required before this technique can be seen as anything but experimental.

The primary limitation of multifaceted, global indices of social class like the Hollingshead Index is that they may confuse the issues by obscuring certain important relationships. Dunham, Phillips, and Srinivasan (1966), for instance, discerned that the educational accomplishments of schizophrenic men were generally congruent with the educational attainment of their fathers, but not very strongly correlated with their schizophrenic status. Occupational attainment, on the other hand, demonstrated a downward drift and revealed the presence of a robust relationship between schizophrenia and lower socioeconomic status. Similar findings have motivated some researchers to seek a more unidimensional definition of social position.

Poverty assumes a fundamental position in many estimates of social position. As such, Braithwaite (1979) and Messner (1982) have based their appraisals of social position on poverty thresholds provided by the Social Security Administration and adopted by the U.S. Bureau of Census. Loftin and Parker (1985), however, take issue with the poverty threshold procedure, arguing that it contains several forms of measurement error and propose use of the infant mortality rate instead. Rather than entering the debate at this juncture, I would simply like to state that the assessment of social position, whether it be through an estimate of poverty or a more sophisticated equation of socioeconomic status, is a thorny controversy that requires a great deal more attention than it has thus far received. This may all be academic for the purpose of this chapter, however, since measures like Loftin and Parker's are directed at aggregate-level data and appear to have little applicability to the assessment of individuals.

INTERACTION-ORIENTED ASSESSMENT

There is very little research, or even speculation for that matter, on how one might go about assessing the interaction of person and situation variables, although Bem and Funder (1978) demonstrate how this might be accomplished through the use of situational templates and a Q-sort (see Volume 1, Chapter 7). In explaining their procedure, Bem and Funder advocate the use of templates that describe a person's manner of reaction to a set of hypothetical ideal situations. By comparing these templates against the actual situation, one might then be able to predict the subject's behavior in a novel situation. Unfortunately, there has not been, to the author's knowledge, any attempt to apply Bem and Funder's methodology to criminal science assessment, although the possibilities abound.

CONCLUSION

In this chapter we have reviewed procedures with potential applicability to the third foundation of criminal science—that of evaluation and prediction. Although these various techniques differ on a number of important dimensions, they share a common purpose: to further our understanding of an often misunderstood group of individuals (criminals). The conclusion that some procedures are better equipped to answer particular questions than others may seem trite, but armed with this knowledge we should be able to make more effective use of those methods which are currently available to us. With this in mind, I recommend a three-tiered approach to criminal science assessment, with special concern directed at the bandwidth-fidelity dilemma (Cronbach, 1970).

Cronbach indicates that assessment procedures designed to survey a wide array of issues are normally less able to produce a fine-tuned analysis of an isolated event because of the width of the band they throw out. High-fidelity techniques, on the other hand, may provide detailed information on a specific issue but are applicable to only a small portion of the relevant questions. The first stage of the three-tiered approach to criminal science assessment is therefore dominated by wide band–low fidelity techniques like screening interviews and rating scales. Hence, use of the LCSF or Hollingshead's Index of Social Position can provide us with information for use in screening prisoners or classifying social groups into general categories, though these measures are too broad for the purpose of generating a detailed understanding of a specific offender or an isolated social situation.

Positioned on the second level of our three-tiered model are procedures that possess moderate bandwidth and moderate fidelity. The MMPI, structured interviews, and the CIES are examples of instruments likely to be used during this second stage in the assessment sequence. Though more expensive (in terms of administration, scoring, and interpretation) than most first-stage techniques, procedures like the MMPI are reasonably cost-efficient and provide information potentially capable of being both broad-based and moderately detailed. We might therefore administer these procedures with less regularity than we would a screening instrument like the LCSF, but more frequently than procedures native to the third level of criminal science assessment. Middle-stage assessment is normally conducted on a semiregular basis and might address such issues as custody classification, parole consideration, program evaluation, and the attitude of correctional officers toward a new institutional policy.

The third, and final, level of our three-tiered model of criminal science assessment encompasses techniques that exhibit a high degree of fidelity but narrow bandwidth. In the course of one's daily clinical practice, questions arise that, though rare, must be addressed. Under such circumstances, one would probably call upon a third-stage assessment technique. We would not, for instance, want to rely on a middle-stage method like the MMPI or SADS to answer a highly specialized person-oriented question like neuropsychological deficit, learning disability, or incipient psychosis. Consequently, we might utilize the Halstead-Reitan Neuropsychological Battery (Reitan & Davison, 1974) to address the first question, various educational and information-processing tests to address the second question, and the Rorschach to rule out the presence of a thought disorder in the third instance.

Assessment is normally the point at which criminal science intervention begins. It may also play a salient role in applied research on the criminal offender. For this reason, we need to make the assessment enterprise as organized, reliable, and cogent as possible. To this end, a three-tiered approach to assessment has been proposed and a number of specific assessment procedures reviewed. It should be kept in mind, however, that it will be contingent upon those of us charged with the responsibility of making ethical and meaningful use of these procedures, be it as part of one's routine clinical practice or as part of an ongoing research project, to realize the ideals espoused in this chapter and reiterated elsewhere (Cronbach, 1970).

3

Classification

Classification can be found in all walks of scientific life, be it within the context of a taxonomy of flora, a categorization of elements, or a systematic ordering of behavioral diagnoses. The classification of criminal science data is grounded in the knowledge that measurable differences, with implications for both treatment and management, do exist between individual offenders. Criminal science classification can therefore be defined as the process of identifying and grouping individual offenders in a manner that facilitates the placement of such persons in specific correctional institutions, housing units, job assignments, and treatment programs. It has the dual advantage of aiding in the management of a larger number of incarcerated offenders and making more efficient use of limited correctional resources. As such, the four primary goals of criminal science classification are treatment, management, prediction, and understanding (MacKenzie, Posey, & Rapaport, 1988).

The history of criminal classification can probably be traced back to the work of Caesar Lombroso, an Italian physician who in the late 1800s identified five categories of criminal. In forming his nascent system of classification, Lombroso made reference to "born criminals," "habitual criminals," "insane criminals," "occasional criminals," and "criminals of passion" (Megargee & Bohn, 1979). Of particular interest to Lombroso was the "born criminal," and it was from his research on this group of offenders that we have one of the first excursions into the genetics of criminal behavior. Since Lombroso, many classification systems have come and gone. Those that have taken as their primary focus specific categories of criminal offense have been particularly ineffective in cataloging society's lawbreakers, since criminal specialization is much less common than was once thought (Gibbons, 1988). Researchers subsequently turned their attention to alternative models of classification. Before reviewing these models, however, it is crucial that we explore the elements of a good system of classification.

The criteria of relevance to criminal science classification have been addressed by several authors (Gibbons, 1975; Megargee, 1977) and have received the attention of the National Advisory Commission on Criminal Justice Standards and Goals (1973). If we extrapolate from these sources, we can derive six primary criteria. First, a good system of classification should be comprehensive in the sense that it catalogs a large majority of offenders into one group or another (Gibbons, 1975; Megargee, 1977). Second, the categories should be mutually exclusive so that a subject falls into one, and only one, class (Gibbons, 1975). Third, the model should be consistent, reliable, and well operationalized (Gibbons, 1975; Megargee, 1977; National Advisory Commission on Criminal Justice Standards and Goals, 1973). Fourth, the system should be parsimonious to the extent that it comprises a manageable set of categories or groups (Gibbons, 1975). Fifth, it should be relatively inexpensive to operate and avoid reliance on highly trained personnel (National Advisory Commission, 1973). Finally, the classification system we select should be valid in the sense that it has implications for treatment and management that are meaningful and replicable (Megargee, 1977).

This chapter on models of classification is organized into the person-situation-interaction trichotomy that should be familiar to the reader by now. There are, however, other dimensions on which criminal science classification systems differ. Models falling into the person-centered category, for instance, can be either theoretical or empirical in nature. Theoretical classification systems, like Warren's (1966) I-level method, have their origin in theories of human development and behavior. In direct contrast to the theoretical paradigm is the empirical or atheoretical model, of which Quay's (1984) Adult Internal Management System (AIMS) and Megargee's MMPI typology (Megargee & Bohn, 1979) are examples. Situation-centered classification can also be partitioned into two categories: physical and social. Arranging for the categorization of correctional institutions is an example of physical or object-related situation-centered classification, while grouping subjects on the basis of their early home environments reflects social situation–centered concerns. Over the course of the next several sections, person-, situation-, and interaction-centered models of criminal science classification are discussed and contrasted relative to the six criteria of a good categorization system.

PERSON-CENTERED CLASSIFICATION

As the term suggests, person-centered classification is primarily concerned with the identification and categorization of individual offenders. These procedures consequently build on several of the assessment techniques reviewed in the person-oriented section of Chapter 2.

Objective Classification Models

In a survey of state correctional systems, Megathlin, Magnus, and Christiansen (1977) discovered that while a wide assortment of different assessment procedures were utilized, nearly all states embraced a maximum-medium-minimum classification scheme. During the past several years state correctional systems have become increasingly more interested in objective models of classification. In contrast to traditional correctional classification procedures, which depend on the reliability and validity of clinical judgments and subjective impressions in assigning inmates to facilities, objective classification schemes are concerned with the systematic application of a more objective methodology designed to predict future institutional adjustment and assess an inmate's need for higher or lower levels of correctional supervision. Propelled by the Ramos v. Lamm (1979) decision, which holds that classification systems must be coherent, consistent, and nondiscriminatory, the objective approach to inmate classification has found its way into nearly every correctional system in the United States.

Austin (1983) groups objective procedures into two principal categories: risk assessment and equity-based techniques. Risk assessment utilizes a combination of clinical, criminal, and socioeconomic characteristics to forecast the individual's future institutional adjustment, potential risk of escape, and chances of success in the community. Equity-based models, on the other hand, shy away from the use of individual characteristics for empirical (Monahan, 1978), as well as legal or ethical (Clements, 1980), reasons and base their classification decisions on a small number of explicitly defined legal criteria. However, as Austin points out, these two models often utilize the same variables, the main difference being the manner in which these models are conceptualized and derived. Whereas risk models are formed through statistical and empirical analysis, equity models make use of a consensus-building procedure wherein the opinions and judgments of practitioners and classification "experts" are pooled. Consequently, many equity instruments are as subjective as the traditional classification systems they were designed to replace.

Objective classification is often conceptualized as a two-tiered process: initial classification, followed by reclassification. Buchanan, Whitlow, and Austin (1986) argue that reclassification is a check against mistakes sometimes made during the initial classification phase. Variables that frequently find their way into initial classification decisions may include a subject's criminal record, prior commitments, escape history, detainers, and previous institutional adjustment. Factors considered in reclassifying offenders normally emphasize in-custody behavior (for example, disciplinary infractions, general institutional adjustment) and practical necessity (for example, release date).

Applying three objective classification schemes (Federal Bureau of Prisons, California State, National Institute of Corrections) to inmates in the Nevada state prison system, Austin (1983) ascertained a high degree of congruence in classificatory outcome despite the fact that these systems often rely on divergent measures and assign differing weights to the variables they do have in common. Further analyses revealed that this consistency was principally attributable to the fact that criminal history and current offense data explained between 87 and 92 percent of the total variance in classification scores for each of the three systems (Austin, 1983). Previous institutional adjustment had minimal impact, and social variables virtually no impact, on a subject's overall classification score.

Empirical evaluation of objective classification models has yielded mixed outcomes. Thus, while Wright (1988) witnessed a relationship between scores on a risk-assessment measure and subsequent disciplinary infractions in a large sample of New York State inmates, the association was actually minuscule ($R^2 = .02-.06$). Buchanan et al. (1986) determined that objective classification procedures developed in California, Illinois, and Wisconsin reliably predicted future disciplinary problems, with age, prior criminal convictions, and previous prison behavior accounting for the largest share of systematic variation. As with the Wright study, however, a major portion of the variance in disciplinary adjustment could not be explained by these objective systems ($R^2 = .10$). Where Hanson et al. (1983) report that custody classification was superior to both an equation of demographic variables and the Megargee MMPI-based classification system in predicting institutional adjustment, as measured by the number of disciplinary reports accrued, amount of time spent in segregation and work performance ratings, this study has been criticized on both conceptual and methodological grounds (Zager, 1988).

Levinson (1980) evaluated a six-level objective classification scheme adopted by the Federal Bureau of Prisons in 1979, and determined that it resulted in an increased percentage of inmates assigned to lower security and less expensive facilities without compromising the custody and security of inmates. Hence, the proportion of prisoners housed in minimum security facilities rose from 23 to 33 percent, while the percentage of inmates confined in maximum security institutions fell from 38 to 20 percent and the escape rate dropped from 14 per 1,000 inmates to 6 per 1,000 inmates. The Bureau of Prisons' security classification program reduced costs even further by slashing the number of interinstitutional transfers and providing case managers with information that was current, coherent, and timely. It would seem that objective classification systems have a place in corrections, although their role may need to be more clearly defined.

While objective classification procedures have been employed primarily with persons confined in institutions, they may also have a place in community corrections. The Level of Supervision Inventory, or LSI (Andrews, 1983), is a 58-item checklist that considers criminal history, education and employment background, alcohol and/or drug usage, peer associations, and several other variables designed to predict the behavior of offenders in halfway house and community placement settings. The LSI has been found to correlate significantly with future institutional (Andrews et al., 1984), halfway house (Bonta & Motiuk, 1985), and community (Andrews et al., 1985) adjustment. In one study the LSI surpassed the Wisconsin Risk and Salient Factor scales in predicting halfway house in-program rules violations and post-program recidivism (Andrews et al., 1985), and in a second study it outperformed the MMPI in prognosticating halfway house and community adjustment in an independent sample of offenders (Motiuk, Bonta, & Andrews, 1986). Since the LSI is primarily an instrument conceived and tested in Canada there is the need for cross-validation in the United States.

Interpersonal Maturity Level

In tracing the origins of the Interpersonal Maturity Level (I-level) system of classification it is important to understand that this system began as a general theory of personality and ego development. Sullivan, Grant, and Grant (1957) proposed that as a person develops he or she progresses from a state of minimal perceptual discrimination to levels of increasing perceptual differentiation, integration, and complexity. A person's I- (interpersonal maturity) level, of which there are seven, is a reflection of their world view. Consequently, individuals at level I–2 tend to perceive the world in concrete, black-or-white terms, while I–3 is populated by individuals whose world view revolves around a given set of rules and who are motivated to seek power and control over others. Persons situated at I–4 are more likely to possess an internalized value system and greater self- and other awareness than individuals at the lower I-levels. It is worth noting that I-levels 2 through 4 are the ones most often encountered in delinquent populations, the primary focus of Warren's (formerly Grant) I-level system of correctional classification.

Working with delinquents, Warren (1966) soon realized that the I-levels would need to be subdivided in order to more accurately reflect the behavior of these individuals. Level I–2, labeled primitive egocentricity, was subsequently partitioned into the asocial aggressive (*Aa*) and asocial passive (*Ap*) types. Level I–3, which holds to power-oriented concerns, is subclassified into the immature conformist (*Cfm*), cultural conformist (*Cfc*), and manipulator (*Mp*) types. The internalized group, I–4, is divided by Warren into four types: neurotic acting out (*Na*), neurotic anxious (*Nx*), cultural identifier (*Ci*), and situational-emotional reaction (*Se*). The validity of the I-level system is difficult to evaluate directly because it is so closely tied to differential treatment (Gibbons, 1970). However, Warren (1971) reports that treatment efficacy varied as a function of I-level in a large sample of California delinquents.

Warren's system relies on interview-based classification. This interview takes approximately 90 minutes to administer and is normally videotaped and rated by a second trained professional. The inter-rater reliability of this interview technique has been shown to range between 67 and 86 percent for level and between 37 and 74 percent for subtype (Harris, 1983; Jesness, 1974; Palmer & Werner, 1972). Test-retest estimates have also been less than fully satisfactory:

84 to 93 percent for level and 74 to 80 percent for subtype (Palmer & Werner, 1972). In an effort to save time and augment reliability, Jesness developed the Jesness Inventory, or JI (Jesness & Wedge, 1985), a 155-item true-false instrument which yields age-normed T-scores for 11 personality and attitude scales and an I-level classification. Although there are many advantages to be found in using the JI, it is still an open question whether the results observed with this measure are any more stable or reliable than those obtained with Warren's original interview procedure (Harris, 1988). Moreover, in one study using JI-generated diagnoses, it was determined that only 65 percent of the subjects fit into a single I-level category, while 34 percent were dual classified, and 1 percent were unclassifiable (Jesness & Wedge, 1984).

Though Gibbons (1970) maintains that the I-level system is not amenable to direct analysis, it has received a fair amount of empirical attention. I-level has been found to correlate with age, socioeconomic status, locus of control, intelligence (Warren, 1978), tolerance, independence, flexibility (Werner, 1975), ego development, cognitive complexity (Jesness, 1974), self-concept (Jesness & Wedge, 1983), and behavioral problems at school (Jesness & Wedge, 1983; Warren, 1978). Following a sample of 1,133 California Youth Authority (CYA) wards, Jesness and Wedge (1984) ascertained that juveniles achieving higher I-level scores were less likely to be in conflict with the law four to five years later. A longitudinal follow-up of 1,626 junior high school students by Jesness (1986) identified subtype differences in school achievement, classroom behavior, confidence, responsibility, behavior at home, self-reported delinquency, and school disciplinary problems consistent with Warren's original formulations.

One of the primary goals of I-level theory is to match people with situations. Warren (1966) postulates that persons falling at the lower end of the I-level continuum will respond best to more highly structured environments, while persons scoring at the upper end of this level are more liable to accept the responsibilities associated with a less structured housing situation, job, or treatment program. In testing this hypothesis, Palmer (1973) found better results for youth enrolled in therapy with workers whose treatment approach matched the therapeutic ''ideal'' of that particular I-level categorization. Similarly, Jesness (1974) observed fewer disciplinary infractions in delinquents living in quarters where counselors assumed an interactive style that matched the juvenile's own developmental level. Unfortunately, this matching had no appreciable effect on recidivism. There would seem to be at least guarded support, then, for Warren's (1971) initial findings from the Community Treatment Project (CTP); that is, that an optimal match between the individual and his or her environment will yield a better outcome than a less optimal match.

Even though the I-level system was developed for use with adolescents, it has been employed with adults as well. In a pilot project comparing five classification systems, Van Voorhis (1988) failed to witness a relationship between I-level and subsequent disciplinary adjustment in a sample of adult federal prisoners, although she did note that inmates earning lower I-level scores were more inclined to request protective custody than persons scoring higher on the I-level continuum. Van Voorhis speculates that because they are less cognitively sophisticated, persons scoring at I-level 2 or 3 may have greater difficulty coping with the correctional environment than persons at I-level 4. Though the I-level system of classification appears to have garnered a fair amount of empirical support with respect to youthful offenders, a great deal more research is required before we can determine its applicability to adult felons.

The Quay Classification Systems

Taking an empirical approach to the issue of criminal science classification, Quay (1965) factor-analyzed a large reservoir of behavioral data on incarcerated juvenile offenders. From his analyses, Quay isolated three primary factors or patterns (unsocialized-psychopathic, subcultural-socialized, neurotic-disturbed) and identified a fourth factor (inadequate-immature) that accounted for only a small fraction of the variation in behavioral ratings. The unsocialized-psychopathic group contains aggressive, assaultive, manipulative adolescents who experience minimal levels of guilt and anxiety relative to their rule-breaking activities. Where the criminal actions of subcultural-socialized youth are normally followed by guilt, their behavior is nonetheless repetitive because of the strong ties these juveniles have with delinquent peers. Neurotic-disturbed youth, on the other hand, are anxious and withdrawn, and they perceive themselves as inferior to others.

By way of developing a typology for older inmates, Quay (1984) identified five dimensions along which he believed adult offenders varied. Inmates were hypothesized to differ along each of these dimensions, and the dimension on which they scored highest was the group to which they were assigned. Group I comprises adult male offenders who own a history and/or currently display evidence of aggressive, hostile, or violent behavior. These persons are easily bored, readily enter into conflict with authority figures, frequently exhibit poor disciplinary adjustment, and regularly prey on "weaker" inmates. Group II is composed of inmates who, while less outwardly violent than Group I subjects, use deception and subterfuge to obtain their goals. These individuals also experience problems with authority figures and encounter disciplinary problems of moderately high severity. The rather large reservoir of offenders who neither prey on others nor are themselves the targets of predation fall into Group III. Reliable, industrious, and cooperative, these persons rarely have problems with disciplinary adjustment. Group IV inmates are characteristically withdrawn, dependent, and unhappy. Frequently taken advantage of by Group I and II inmates, these individuals experience a moderate to low rate of disciplinary maladjustment. Group V inmates are also regular victims of predation and come across as tense, depressed, worried, and potentially explosive under stress. These persons display a moderate level of disciplinary intractability.

Quay and his colleagues have developed several measures by which classification might be accomplished. The History Review Form, Behavior Problem Checklist, and Personal Opinion Study (Quay & Peterson, 1975) were developed for use with juveniles, while the Life History Checklist and Correctional Adjustment Checklist (Quay, 1984) were designed for use with adults. Though these measures provide reasonably reliable and stable results (Levinson, 1988; Megargee & Bohn, 1970; Quay, 1984), they are not without their shortcomings. For one, the system requires a solid foundation of accurate historical information, not to mention commitment and competence on the part of the correctional staff who complete the rating forms. Further, the dimensional approach used by Quay sometimes makes it difficult to assign a subject to one specific category. As such, if one desires "pure" groups the number of unclassifiable cases will be relatively high.

Validational research, though conducted mostly by Quay and his associates, has been generally corroborative of the system. Research carried out relative to the juvenile classification system has been particularly supportive of Quay's hypotheses. Borkovec (1970), for instance, discovered that psychopathic delinquents pursued higher levels of sensory stimulation than neurotic and "normal" delinquents, a finding which is consonant not only with Quay's classification system but also with his stimulation-seeking theory of criminal conduct. Hetherington, Stouwie, and Ridberg (1971), and Skrzypek (1969) also obtained results that confirmed major aspects of Quay's theory of criminal conduct and his behavioral system for classifying juvenile offenders. Just how the adult version of the Quay classification system fares when subjected to empirical examination is less clearly understood.

In an early investigation on his adult classification system, Quay (1973) found relatively small but statistically significant and theoretically congruent differences on age, race, income, academic achievement, and arrest history for the five groups that constitute his adult classification system. A survey of federal inmates classified under the Quay system revealed that Group I inmates received the largest number of disciplinary reports of any of the five groups and twice as many as Group III inmates (Quay, 1984). Follow-up analyses of these same inmates demonstrated that Group I subjects released from confinement had the highest rate of re-arrest (39%) and Group III subjects the lowest (33%). Although these differences may seem microscopic, it is well to keep in mind that out of the 20 cases re-arrested for violent offenses, 12 (60%) were from Group I and none were from Group III. Van Voorhis (1988) also found the Quay system to be useful in predicting the disciplinary adjustment of adult federal prisoners, although it was generally ineffective in identifying inmates who subsequently sought protective custody because of their inability to cope with the prison environment.

Levinson (1988) argues that Quay's system is well suited to the task of internal classification. Where external classification is directed at placing an individual in a particular facility (maximum-medium-minimum), internal classification is used to assign inmates from a single institution to a specific dorm, tier, or unit.

Levinson recommends that Groups I and II be placed in one unit, Group III in a separate unit, and Groups IV and V in a third unit, and that officer personalities be matched with inmate classification (for example, authoritarian, by-the-book officers assigned to the unit with Groups I and II, and the more flexible, talk-oriented officers manning the unit in which Groups IV and V are housed). The Quay system might also be of benefit to administrators searching for ways to efficiently assign inmates to institutional jobs. Levinson (1988) maintains that inmates in Groups I and II are better suited to jobs that are physically demanding and stimulating, Group III to positions of responsibility, and Groups IV and V to repetitive tasks capable of providing these subjects with a sense of accomplishment and self-worth.

Following implementation of the Quay system, staff at the United States Penitentiary in Lewisburg, Pennsylvania, reported that assaults on inmates fell by one-third and assaults on staff by two-thirds (cited in Levinson, 1988). Moreover, where there had been an inmate-on-inmate homicide once a month prior to implementation of the Quay system, there were no inmate-on-inmate homicides over a period of 13 months post-implementation. A second study conducted in a state prison in South Carolina revealed that serious incidents fell by as much as 18 percent after the Quay classification system for adults was set into place (cited in Levinson, 1988).

Whereas the Quay system of juvenile classification has received a fairly substantial base of support, much less is known about the adult system. It would be interesting, therefore, to explore how adult inmates in Groups I and II, III, and IV and V response to different institutional programs and therapeutic approaches. Of even greater concern, however, is the atheoretical nature of empirically derived models of classification like the Quay system. It is reasonably well accepted that persons strongly committed to criminal goals, whether they are called unsocialized offenders (Quay, 1984), psychopaths (Hare, 1980), or lifestyle criminals (Walters, 1990), are characteristically more violent (Williamson, Hare, & Wong, 1987), experience significantly greater problems with institutional adjustment (Walters, 1991), and are at increased risk for violating the conditions of their release (Hart, Kropp, & Hare, 1988; Walters, Revella, & Baltrusatis, 1990) than persons less committed to a criminal way of life. This knowledge alone, however, does little to assist us in our efforts to more effectively manage the behavior of these individuals. Accordingly, greater effort needs to be directed at clarifying and developing theoretical underpinnings for the Quay typology.

An MMPI-Based Classification System

Edwin Megargee, a professor of psychology at Florida State University, set out to construct an MMPI-based correctional classification system using a large sample of MMPIs generated by inmates at the Federal Correctional Institution in Tallahassee. With several thousand MMPIs at their disposal, Meyer and

Table 3.1
MMPI-Based Classification System

Group	1 Profile Config.	Distribution range median		3 Behavioral Description
Able	4-9/9-4	7-28	16	dominant, extroverted, self-assured
Baker	4-2	0-7	3	constricted, passive, unassertive
Charlie	8-6-4	4-19	7	hostile, isolated, misanthropic
Delta	Spike 4	1-18	9	active, antagonistic, impulsive
Easy	3-4/4-3	1-17	5	nonaggressive, well-adjusted
Foxtrot	4-9-8	3-16	7	aggressive, egocentric, insolent
George	2-4/4-2	2-13	6	fairly dependable, opportunistic
How	high elevation	5-26	10	anxious, disturbed, withdrawn
Item	low elevation	14-32	19	adaptable, friendly, reliable
Jupiter	8-9-7	0-8	2	awkward, guarded, introverted

Sources: (1) Megargee & Dorhout (1977); (2) Based on Zager's (1983) review of 19 different studies—numbers are actually percentages; (3) Megargee & Bohn (1979).

Megargee (1977) subjected three samples of 100 subjects each to a hierarchical profile analysis. The outcome of these three analyses showed the presence of nine factors or clusters that were sequentially labeled Able, Baker, Charlie, Delta, Easy, Foxtrot, George, How, and Item. A tenth pattern (Jupiter) was subsequently added to the model and specific inclusory rules were later devised in order to make the model more amenable to computer scoring (Megargee & Dorhout, 1977). The configural pattern, frequency, and behavioral correlates of each of these ten profile types can be found in Table 3.1.

The Megargee MMPI-based classification system has been cross-validated in several different clinical settings. Edinger (1979), however, was the first investigator to replicate the Megargee system on an independent sample of prison inmates. Applying the Megargee system to 2,063 male federal prisoners and 1,455 male and female state offenders, Edinger discovered that 85 percent of the federal sample, 86 percent of the male state sample, and 87 percent of the female state sample could be classified into one of the ten Megargee types. Additional analyses revealed that the ten types differed according to current offense and disciplinary record. The Megargee MMPI-based classification system has also been cross-validated in military offenders (Walters, 1986a), sentenced state incarcerates (Booth & Howell, 1980; Nichols, 1979), violent federal prisoners (Edinger, Reuterfors, & Logue, 1982), death row inmates (Dahlstrom et al., 1986), jail detainees (Cassady, 1978), and halfway house residents (Mrad, Kabacoff, & Duckro, 1983).

Assessing the correlates and predictive capabilities of a classification system are two ways by which the validity of Megargee's procedure has been probed. Appraising the correlates of the Megargee system, Zager (1988) noted that the Adjective Checklist (compare Megargee, 1984), Bipolar Inventory (compare Booth & Howell, 1980), Sixteen Personality Factor (16 PF) (compare Mrad, 1979), and various self-report and behavioral measures (compare Walters, 1986a) have all generated corroborative support for the system's concurrent validity. The predictive utility of this MMPI-based classification model has also attracted the attention of investigators. It has been discerned, for example, that the ten types vary in terms of future disciplinary adjustment (Van Voorhis, 1988; Walters, 1986a), self-reported problems with stress (Wright, 1988), and success in a work release program (Howell & Geiselman, 1978) in ways congruent with Megargee's initial formulations. Bohn (1980) employed a combined Megargee-Quay classification scheme to assign a sample of federal inmates to different housing units and discerned a significant drop in violent incidents following implementation of the program.

Of course, not all of the research on the Megargee system affirms its authors' original intentions. On the basis of a series of studies conducted at the federal penitentiary in Lompoc, California, a group of researchers (Hanson et al., 1983; Moss, Johnson, & Hosford, 1984) concluded that the Megargee system could not be used to effectively predict the future adjustment of maximum security prison inmates. Zager (1988), however, finds serious methodological fault with these studies, noting sampling bias, reliance on incorrect or suspect classification procedures, and utilization of a criterion measure (violence) with a very low base rate of occurrence.

Though the validity of the Megargee system has been reasonably well established with young adult male offenders, much less is known about its ability to assess and predict the behavior of juvenile, female, and nonwhite lawbreakers. Veneziano and Veneziano (1986) obtained MMPIs from 251 adolescent offenders and determined that 79.3 percent of the sample could be categorized into one of the ten Megargee types using adult MMPI norms, and 81.2 percent of the sample could be categorized into one of the ten types when adolescent MMPI norms were employed. Application of adult norms resulted in a higher incidence of Charlie and How profiles than is characteristically found in adult samples, and use of adolescent norms culminated in a larger proportion of Item profiles and a lower percentage of Able and Delta profiles in comparison to what is normally observed with adults. Doren, Megargee, and Schreiber (1980) ascertained that 44 percent of a group of adolescent probationers were classified into Item, 15 percent into Able, and less than 8 percent into all other categories when adult MMPI norms were employed. Further research is necessary in order to determine, first, whether adult or adolescent norms are more useful for the purpose of scoring the MMPIs of juvenile respondents and, second, whether the adult-adolescent discrepancies noted in previous studies reflect meaningful differences between adult and juvenile offenders or simply demarcate the outer limits of validity for MMPI-based classification.

Reviewing the MMPI profiles of state prison female incarcerates, Schaffer et al. (1983) determined that the Able, Charlie, Delta, Easy, How, and Item groups were fully replicated and the George group partly replicated; however, the Baker, Foxtrot, and Jupiter groups could not be replicated in this particular sample of subjects. Moreover, two clusters of profiles were found to fit the How group. The Megargee system may also be differentially effective depending upon the racial status of subjects under investigation, since Carey, Garske, and Ginsberg (1986) report that the MMPI-based classification system successfully predicted prison adjustment in whites but not blacks. Studies conducted by Edinger, Reuterfors, and Logue (1982) and Walters (Walters, Mann, Miller, Hemphill, & Chlumsky, 1988; Walters, Scrapansky, & Marrlow, 1986) document the presence of a higher than normal rate of How and Charlie profiles in seriously disturbed populations of state, federal, and military prisoners. Such a relationship makes sense, however, in light of DiFrancesca and Meloy's (1989) observation that mild to moderate levels of thought disturbance can be observed in offenders whose MMPI performance places them in the How or Charlie group. It is evident that more research is required before the Megargee system can be extended to populations other than young adult male offenders, for whom the system was originally conceived, designed, and instituted.

The possible limitations of MMPI-based classification with adolescent, female, and nonwhite subjects aside, the Megargee system appears to possess a number of positive features. In addition to a solid base of empirical support (at least where young adult male felons are concerned), the system receives high marks for reliability. Inter-rater agreement for the ten types classified clinically has been found to range between 76 and 90 percent (Dahlstrom et al., 1986; Van Voorhis, 1986), while the comparability of clinician- and computer-generated diagnoses has been shown to vary between 68 and 84 percent (Carey et al., 1986; Mrad, 1979). Simmons et al. (1981), however, question the system's stability over time and contend that this may diminish the utility of the model for the purposes of clinical decision making. Zager (1988), on the other hand, finds methodological fault with the Simmons et al. study and argues that classification decisions may fluctuate over time for reasons other than instability (for example, a genuine change in behavior). There is, nevertheless, a need to evaluate the temporal stability of the Megargee system since research studies show that the majority of MMPI scales are reasonably stable over periods lasting up to one year (Greene, 1980).

SITUATION-CENTERED CLASSIFICATION

In contrast to person-oriented classification, situation-centered strategies take as their focus characteristics of the environmental situation. As we saw in Chapter 2, assessment is, to a large extent, person oriented. Much the same could be said of classification; like situation-oriented assessment, there are two general categories of situation-centered classification: procedures that are object related

Table 3.2
Levinson and Gerard's Institutional Classification Scheme

Feature	Maximum	Classification Level Medium	Minimum
Mobile Patrol	constant	intermittent	none
Gun Towers	staffed continuously	staffed part-time	none
Perimeter Barriers	double fence/ wall	single fence	none
Detection Devices	camera, high- mast lights	one camera	none
Internal Security	sally port/ corridor grills/ secure building	sally port/ secure building	minimal
Housing	cells	dorms and/or cells	dormitories
Inmate/Officer Ratio	3.5/1 or less	7.1-3.6/1	7.1/1 or more

Source: Levinson & Gerard (1986).

and procedures that are oriented to social groups or phenomena. Levinson and Gerard's (1986) institutional classification approach serves as our example of an object-related situation-centered system, while Rubenfeld's (1965) home environment scheme captures the essence of social situation-centered procedures.

Classifying Institutions

In a survey of state and federal correctional systems, Buchanan et al. (1986) discerned that the security ratings of over three-quarters of the systems were based on such object-related features as perimeter security, housing configuration, and staff:inmate ratio. Incidentally, the vast majority of correctional administrators reported to these investigators that their systems relied on three primary levels of classification: maximum, medium, and minimum. Levinson and Gerard (1986) offer a framework by which institutional security classifications might be better understood. Seven fields or dimensions are considered within the context of this institutional classification system: mobile patrol, gun towers, perimeter barriers, detection devices, internal security, housing, and the inmate:officer ratio. The basic model is outlined in Table 3.2.

Even though the Levinson and Gerard (1986) procedure seems to accurately represent the manner in which the federal prison system and several state systems classify institutions, it remains to be seen whether this scheme stands up under empirical scrutiny. A more objective analysis of the model and each of its dimensions is most assuredly the next step in evaluating this procedure. Levinson and Gerard note that each dimension can be weighted and the security classifications of specific institutions manipulated. Unfortunately, there is a dearth of published research on how this or any other manipulation of the correctional environment affects the behavior (for example, escape attempts, violent assaults, involvement in programs) of persons confined in these facilities.

Classifying the Home Environment

Rubenfeld (1965) devised a four-category system by which the social class of one's home of origin might be classified. At one end of the continuum we find the lower-class matriarchal Negro home. The upper-lower second- or third-generation ethnic patriarchal working-class home is positioned on the next peg of this classification scheme. The lower-middle-class white-collar home falls on the next rung of Rubenfeld's conceptual ladder, while the upper-middle-class materialistic establishment home is situated at the upper end of Rubenfeld's classificatory scheme. In addition to the problems this system has with comprehensiveness, operationality, and reliability (Megargee & Bohn, 1979), it has failed to generate much in the way of empirical support. Hence, the model remains at any early stage of development, awaiting further exposition, analysis, and clarification.

INTERACTION-CENTERED CLASSIFICATION

Matching the person to his or her environmental situation, the marrow of interaction-centered procedures, is a core goal of criminal science classification. A correctional administrator might pair a person-oriented objective model with Levinson and Gerard's situation-based institutional classification system to marry a particular offender to a specific correctional environment. Likewise, Interpersonal Maturity Level might be measured in an effort to identify an inmate's optimal treatment, learning, or vocational environment, while the Quay system has been used to match an offender with a specific housing unit. In this section we critique two classification schemes with implications for interaction-centered classification.

Prison Preference Inventory

Toch (1977) argues that there are eight environmental factors for which inmates express varying degrees of preference. These eight factors, which serve as the foundation for the Prison Preference Inventory (PPI), are activity, emotional feedback, freedom, privacy, safety, social stimulation, structure, and support. Toch postulates that these dimensions can be used to match inmates with institutions. He also proposes that the PPI be used to identify prisoners with special needs. Distress, frustration, conflict, and violence are said to result when preference and environment are incongruous. This hypothesis is contaminated, however, by the fact that research finds variation in the perception-of-environment factor reflective of the status of the person providing the rating. As such, studies reveal that staff and inmates differ markedly when asked to evaluate specific correctional environments (Enyon, Allen, & Reckless, 1971; Moos, 1974), a finding which makes it difficult to properly test Toch's formulations.

In a recent study Wright (1988) evaluated the efficacy of the Toch system and failed to find a relationship between the PPI and objective indices of institutional adjustment (for example, number of disciplinary infractions accrued, frequency of sick call usage). On the other hand, a nexus was observed between the PPI and subjective indices of institutional adjustment. The Freedom scale of the PPI identified inmates who experienced greater anger, fear, and/or anxiety in prison than in the community. Freedom and structure dissonance, on the other hand, distinguished inmates who perceived themselves as having more problems relating to others inside the penitentiary than out. Finally, the Privacy, Safety, and Structure scales established which inmates experienced greater difficulty with physical ailments inside, as opposed to outside, a correctional institution. The outcome of Wright's study suggests that "objective" and perceived problems of adjustment are not one and the same and that Toch's system does a better job of identifying the latter.

Lifestyle Criminality Screening Form

In Chapter 2 of this volume we reviewed research on the Lifestyle Criminality Screening Form, or LCSF (Walters, White, & Denney, in press). As we discussed previously, this instrument can be used to classify subjects into two categories: lifestyle and non-lifestyle offenders. Walters (1991) compared scores obtained on the LCSF with the number of disciplinary reports received over a period of six months for minimum and maximum security federal inmates. Although there was no apparent connection between LCSF scores and disciplinary adjustment in the highly structured confines of a maximum security penitentiary, higher scores on the LCSF (indicative of lifestyle criminality) corresponded with a rising rate of disciplinary infraction in the less structured milieu of a minimum security prison camp. Thus, a person characteristic (lifestyle criminality) was shown to interact with a situation variable (environmental structure) in their influence on the dependent measure of disciplinary adjustment.

Two primary limitations of the lifestyle approach to classification are oversimplicity and improper operationality of several key concepts. In order to become a truly viable system of classification the lifestyle scheme must break the non-lifestyle category down into several different patterns. This, in fact, was the rationale behind development of a multi-pattern theory of criminal involvement (see Chapter 10 of Volume 1). This model appears to possess the potential for further application, although the eight patterns require continued study and increased operationalization. The environmental (structural) factor in the Walters (1991) study also suffers from poor precision. Perhaps use of a measure like the Correctional Institution Environment Scale or CIES (Moos, 1975), particularly

Table 3.3

Assessing Eight Systems of Criminal Science Classification

System	Source	Criteria					
		1	2	3	4	5	6
Person-Centered							
Objective	Austin (1983)	H	M	M	H	M	M
I-Level	Warren (1966)	M	M	L/M*	M	L/H*	M
Quay Systems	Quay (1984)	M	L	M	H	L	M
MMPI-Based	Megargee & Bohn (1979)	M	M	H	M	H	H
Situation-Centered							
Institutional Classification	Levinson & Gerard (1986)	H	H	H	H	M	M
Home Environ.	Rubenfeld (1965)	L	M	L	H	L	L
Interaction-Centered							
Toch System	Toch (1977)	M	M	M	M	M	L
Lifestyle	Walters (1990)	H	H	L	H	M	M

Key: Criteria: 1 = comprehensiveness, 2 = mutual exclusiveness, 3 = operationality, 4 = parsimony, 5 = inexpensiveness, 6 = validity. Ratings: L = low, M = moderate, H = high.

*Initial rating found under criteria 3 and 5 (left side of slash) represents Warren's original interview procedure, while the second rating (right side of slash) represents the Jesness Inventory.

the Autonomy, Clarity, and Staff Control subscales (see Chapter 2, this volume), would augment the operationality of the lifestyle scheme for the purpose of interaction-centered classification.

CONCLUSION

Though classification finds its primary expression in corrections, it has a berth in other areas of criminal science endeavor as well. The multi-pattern theory of criminal involvement discussed in the previous volume is one way by which this might be realized. The multi-pattern model provides the prospect of wide-spectrum application, although at this point operationalized measures have only been developed for the lifestyle pattern. Of course, this system would need to be designed in such a manner as to be congruent with the four classification goals (management, prediction, treatment, understanding) and six criteria of a good classification system (comprehensiveness, mutual exclusiveness, operationality, parsimony, inexpensiveness, validity). We can see from Table 3.3 just how the eight classification schemes reviewed in this chapter fare when measured against our six classification criteria.

Exploring person-centered procedures first, we notice that objective classification systems are strong on comprehension (nearly 100% of all subjects can be categorized) and parsimony (three categories in most cases), and adequate in terms of operationality, mutual exclusiveness, expense, and validity. The interpersonal maturity approach to classification does not fare quite as well as the objective model on our six criteria. Although Warren's I-level approach to classification is rated as moderately strong on comprehensiveness, mutual exclusiveness, parsimony, and validity, it falls short of the mark on operationality and inexpensiveness. Use of the Jesness Inventory, however, is potentially capable of improving precision and controlling costs with no discernable reduction in validity. The Quay system can also be expensive to operate and is less than fully mutually exclusive, since the dimensional scheme used in defining the adult system can lead to unacceptably high rates of multiple classification. Alternately, the system's comprehensiveness, operationality, and validity are adequate while its parsimony is high. Megargee's MMPI-based typology does as well as any of the person-centered approaches on the six criteria. In addition to being rated moderately strong on comprehensiveness, mutual exclusiveness, and parsimony, it receives high marks for operationality, inexpensiveness, and validity.

Turning our attention to situation-centered approaches to classification, we notice that Levinson and Gerard's institutional classification scheme does very well on four of the criteria and moderately well on the other two. First, the system is comprehensive in that nearly all correctional institutions can be classified into a small number of mutually exclusive categories. Second, a review of Table 3.2 reveals that this system is well operationalized. Levinson and Gerard's approach to criminal science classification is also as parsimonious (three categories) as any of the models reviewed in this chapter. Where it receives less than maximum marks are on expense and validity. Depending upon how the institutional ratings are accomplished they can be moderately expensive to generate, and while this system seems valid on the surface, it has yet to be adequately evaluated from an empirical standpoint. In direct contrast to the institutional classification system, Rubenfeld's home environment scheme, though parsimonious and moderately strong on the mutual exclusiveness rule, falls well short of adequacy on the other four criteria. Rubenfeld's model is particularly weak on operationality and empirical support.

Surveying the two interaction-centered systems of classification (Toch, Walters), we find mixed outcomes. While Toch's model is adequate on five of the six criteria, its empirical validity has been shown to be less than fully adequate in predicting "objective" estimates of institutional adjustment. It may, however, have a role in evaluating "subjective" adjustment. Walters' lifestyle model of classification receives somewhat higher grades than the Toch model on comprehensiveness, operationality, and validity, but is not without certain problems of its own. With its two-category format (lifestyle/non-lifestyle) the system is parsimonious yet overly simplistic, and its operationality suffers when it is utilized as an interaction-centered approach owing to a lack of precision in the environmental measures, as represented by the 1991 investigation on the relationship between lifestyle criminality and disciplinary adjustment in high- and low-structured correctional settings.

While we might be able to offer a reasonably objective analysis of the major systems of criminal classification, it is crucial we recognize that no single classification system is equipped to answer all the questions confronting researchers, clinicians, and administrative policymakers on issues relevant to criminal science classification. Where an objective model might be more appropriate for the purposes of external classification (assigning offenders to a particular institution), the Quay and Megargee systems are better suited to internal classification (assigning inmates in a single institution to a particular housing unit or domicile). In a related vein, Wright (1988) notes that certain classification schemes (for example, Toch) are more sensitive to subjectively experienced adjustment difficulties, while other models are in a better position to predict "objective" estimates of prison maladjustment (for example, Megargee). This clearly reflects the necessity of considering more than just one system in establishing a program of criminal science classification.

In light of what we learned about assessment in the previous chapter, I would like to point out that while various procedures can be used to assess, evaluate, and arrange persons into a finite number of categories, important individual differences nonetheless exist. This awareness is, in reality, a critical linchpin in the organization of the knowledge that is psychology and serves as one of the five foundations (assessment/prediction) of criminal science endeavor. Individual differences are therefore phenomena that should be studied rather than ignored or denied. The value of considering individual differences within specific groupings and categories of people will become increasingly more apparent in our discussions on mental health evaluation (Chapter 4) and prediction (Chapter 5).

4

The Crime–Mental Health Nexus

Hollywood has seemingly portrayed a clear and vibrant association between serious emotional disorder and significant criminality. In the spirit of movies like *Psycho*, *Halloween*, and *Fatal Attraction*, filmmakers have taken liberties to depict psychiatrically disturbed individuals as substantially more violent and appreciably more dangerous than the rest of society, and seem of the opinion that mental illness and crime go hand-in-hand. However, the proposed nexus between mental disorder and crime is, at this point, an open question for which there is no ready answer. Governmental, law enforcement, and correction officials nonetheless rank mental illness near the top of the list of problems confronting the criminal justice system at the present time (National Institute of Corrections, 1985). As such, this chapter explores the putative link between crime and mental disorder in four sections: deinstitutionalization and the criminalization of mentally disordered behavior; arrest rates in psychiatric populations; mental illness in criminal populations; and forensic evaluation.

DEINSTITUTIONALIZATION AND THE CRIMINALIZATION OF MENTALLY DISORDERED BEHAVIOR

In a survey of data from 18 European nations, Penrose (1939) noted a connection between asylum and prison populations. Specifically, as the asylums became less crowded the prison population rose, and vice versa. This led Penrose to formulate what has become known as the hydraulic model of population shift, in which a change in the population of one system (for example, psychiatric hospitals) creates an inverse change of equal magnitude in another system (for example, jails and prisons). Some 33 years later, Abramson (1972) used the hydraulic model to explain how public laws mandating deinstitutionalization of mental health cases from hospitals to the community were responsible for a rise in the prison population. He postulated that many persons previously hospitalized in mental institutions were now being confined in jails and prisons because they could no longer be committed to a mental health facility. Abramson disparagingly referred to this as the "criminalization" of mentally disordered behavior.

Whereas Abramson believes that persons exhibiting signs of psychiatric decompensation would be better served by the mental health delivery system than by the criminal justice network, Monahan (1973) is of the opinion that a mental health diagnosis may be more damaging than a criminal record. In a rejoiner entitled "The Psychiatrization of Criminal Behavior," Monahan alleges that Abramson's assumptions about there being less stigma in a mental health diagnosis than a criminal record, and more treatment opportunities in mental hospitals than in jail or prison, are without merit or solid empirical support. Data on the criminalization hypothesis are sparse and what is available can be divided nearly in half as to the corroboration they provide for the antagonistic positions of Abramson and Monahan. Perhaps Teplin (1983, p. 64) sums it up best: "The available empirical evidence provides only tentative support for the speculation that the mentally ill have been criminalized."

There are several methodologies by which the criminalization hypothesis might be studied. One would be to examine the rate of psychiatric disorder in prison populations before and after deinstitutionalization. Bonovitz and Guy (1979), for instance, witnessed a 20 to 100 percent rise in the number of requests for psychiatric consultation following a decision by Pennsylvania lawmakers to implement a more stringent civil commitment procedure. Treffert (1981) observed a similar outcome in criminal observation cases confined in Wisconsin state forensic facilities. In support of Monahan's position on the criminalization hypothesis, Steadman et al. (1984) calculated the number of offenders with previous histories of psychiatric hospitalization admitted to correctional facilities in six states (Arizona, California, Iowa, Massachusetts, New York, Texas) and concluded that the rapid growth in prison populations between 1968 and 1978 could not be attributed to a shift in patients from the mental health system to various correctional institutions. Borzecki and Wormith (1985) also failed to uncover support for the criminalization argument in their review of studies conducted in several Canadian prisons.

The criminalization hypothesis holds that mental patients, who in the past would likely have been admitted to a psychiatric facility after engaging in a minor or trivial offense, were now being processed through the criminal justice system in ever-increasing numbers. Logically, then, we should see a post-deinstitutionalization rise in the number of emotionally disturbed offenders arrested for minor infractions. In support of the criminalization hypothesis, Bonovitz and Guy (1979) determined that a group of prison psychiatric ward inmates had committed fewer and less serious crimes in the past and present relative to residents who had inhabited the ward prior to deinstitutionalization. Reviewing the cases of defendants adjudged incompetent to stand trial before and after deinstitutionalization in California, Massachusetts, and New York, however, Arvanites (1988) noticed an increase, rather than decrease, in crime seriousness.

Such an outcome is inconsistent with the contention that deinstitutionalization has led to an accelerated rate of incarceration for nondangerous mental patients who in the past would have been housed in psychiatric hospitals.

A third methodology commonly used to explore the possibility that mentally disordered behavior has been criminalized as a result of the more stringent commitment procedures introduced in the late 1960s and early 1970s relies on reviews of police decision making. Whereas Bittner (1967), in an article published prior to the advent of widespread deinstitutionalization, commented that police officers frequently rely on informal techniques in dealing with mental health–related matters, Matthews (1970) asserted that the standard operating procedure in many jurisdictions was to arrest persons who engaged in disruptive behavior and appeared mentally ill. Teplin (1984) studied the arrest practices of police in Chicago and discovered that persons displaying bizarre behavior or other actions suggestive of mental illness were more apt to be arrested than persons failing to exhibit such symptomatology. Though provocative, these findings are far from conclusive owing to the fact that a direct linkage between the arrests and a subject's mental status cannot be demonstrated on the basis of these results. There is also the possibility that in a smaller community, where the police are familiar with a larger portion of the citizenry, officers may be more tolerant of the type of behavior that, if observed in the city, would likely result in the subject's arrest.

Bonovitz and Bonovitz (1981) recorded an increase of 228 percent in the mental health–related incidents reported to police between 1975 and 1979, but add that of the 200-plus mental health–related incidents studied, only 13 percent were cleared by arrest. While such an outcome seems inconsistent with the criminalization hypothesis, the Bonovitz study suffers from poor operationalization of terms and omission of a non–mental health comparison group (Teplin, 1983). Monahan, Caldeira, and Friedlander (1979) also failed to generate support for the criminalization hypothesis in a study in which the authors interviewed 100 police officers from Orange County, California. Monahan et al. report that 70 percent of all the cases handled by the police officers in this study were perceived by the officers as wholly inappropriate for one disposition or the other (arrest vs. hospitalization) and in only 6 percent of the cases were they sufficiently concerned about an individual's behavior to arrest the person when commitment proceedings could not be initiated. Whereas Teplin (1983) asserts that mental health difficulties augment one's risk of arrest, deinstitutionalization has apparently not led to an appreciable elevation in the number of former mental patients being processed through the criminal justice system, as proponents of the criminalization hypothesis first predicted.

ARREST RATES IN PSYCHIATRIC POPULATIONS

The possibility of a nexus between crime and mental disorder can also be explored by examining the rate of arrest in psychiatric patients. Early research on state hospital populations in New York (Ashley, 1922; Brill & Malzberg, 1962; Pollock, 1938) and Connecticut (Cohen & Freeman, 1945) revealed that psychiatric patients released from inpatient mental health facilities experienced lower rates of subsequent arrest than the general public. Problems such as biased sampling, faulty operationalization of terms, incomparability of general population estimates of arrest with psychiatric samples, and ambiguous reporting of procedures and results served to limit the significance of these findings, however. It was obvious that this issue required increased attention of a more methodologically rigorous nature.

Rappeport and Lassen (1965) responded to the challenge by conducting a systematic review of male patients released from Maryland psychiatric facilities in 1947 and 1957. Subsequent analyses of these data revealed that the psychiatric patients were more frequently arrested for certain aggressive categories of crime (for example, rape, robbery) compared to persons in the general population. They further ascertained that female patients discharged from these same psychiatric facilities exhibited a higher rate of arrest for aggressive assault compared to the female population base rate for assault (Rappeport & Lassen, 1966). Giovannoni and Gurel (1967) observed levels of disruptive and criminal behavior in male psychiatric patients released from a VA Medical Center in excess of that found in the general population. Studies directed by Zitrin (Zitrin et al., 1976) and Sosowsky (1978) revealed much the same outcome in psychiatric patients discharged from facilities in New York and California, respectively. Whereas Durbin, Pasewark, and Albers (1977) determined that the cumulative (ten-year) arrest records of male psychiatric patients admitted to a Wyoming state hospital were longer than the summative arrest records of the general population of Wyoming males, female psychiatric patients did not differ from the general female population on this measure.

Although studies conducted since 1965 insinuate the possibility of a connection between crime and psychiatric disorder, factors other than a direct causal link may explain the increased rate of criminal behavior observed in psychiatric patients upon their release from the hospital. It may be that these patients are arrested more frequently because their mental instability brings them a great deal more attention than the average citizen, or it could be that such difficulties serve to make patients less proficient in carrying out specific criminal acts, thereby enhancing the probability of their being apprehended. It is also important to note that assigning someone a psychiatric label does not always imply the presence of serious psychopathology, for as Guze, Woodruff, and Clayton (1974) comment, felony convictions are found principally among patients with diagnoses of sociopathy, alcoholism, and drug abuse, while felonious behavior is much less common in patients receiving more serious diagnoses (for example, schizophrenia, major affective disorder). There is also the possibility that the connection presumed to exist between crime and mental disorder is actually a function of their common association with some third variable.

A group of investigators under the guidance of Henry Steadman, director of research for the New York State Department of Mental Hygiene, reports that patients owning prior records of arrest were subject to a much higher rate of subsequent arrest following their release from New York State psychiatric facilities compared to the general population base rate for arrest, but that patients absent previous police contact experienced lower rates of post-release arrest than the general population (Steadman, Cocozza, & Melick, 1978; Steadman, Vanderwyst, & Ribner, 1978). Rabkin (1979), among others, reasons that the escalating rate of arrest observed in psychiatric populations between 1922 and the present is due largely to an increase in the number of persons with prior histories of arrest. Comparing 1954 New York State estimates (Brill & Malzberg, 1962) with data collected in 1968 and 1975 (Steadman, Cocozza, & Melick, 1978), Monahan and Steadman (1984) observed an ascending rate of patients with prior histories of arrest—from 15 percent, to 32 percent, to 40 percent—confirming Rabkin's suspicions and leading Monahan and Steadman to conclude that a change in system input (proportion of patients with prior arrests) rather than a change in system output (deinstitutionalization) was responsible for the observed increase in arrest for psychiatric patients. While Klassen and O'Connor (1988) discerned a strong relationship between prior psychiatric hospital admissions and subsequent arrest, the sample of psychiatric patients they studied had been preselected for violence proneness.

Sosowsky (1980) reanalyzed his Napa (California) state hospital data and noticed that patients previously arrested did, in fact, demonstrate a much higher percentage of subsequent arrest than patients without a prior history of arrest, although the latter group still displayed a significantly higher rate of arrest than the general county population. Monahan and Steadman (1984) take issue with Sosowsky's choice of San Mateo County as the site for development of base-rate estimates of arrest, however, since this county contains a much higher proportion of middle and upper-class persons than the Napa state hospital catchment area. In a self-report study on this issue, Steadman and Felson (1984) discerned that ex-mental patients were typically no more violent than general population subjects and substantially less violent than ex-offenders. The weight of evidence, therefore, suggests that the mental health status of psychiatric patients does not significantly raise their risk of future criminal violence, although there is a subgroup of emotionally disturbed individuals for whom antisocial inclinations and mental illness apparently co-exist (Rabkin, 1979).

MENTAL HEALTH DIFFICULTIES IN PRISONERS

It has frequently been stated that a significant number of incarcerated persons have prior histories of psychiatric hospitalization. Scrutinizing the backgrounds of Denver (Colorado) County jail inmates, Swank and Winer (1976) discovered that 14 percent had been hospitalized in one or more psychiatric facilities in the past. Of 102 male country jail inmates referred for psychiatric evaluation, Lamb and Grant (1982) determined that 75 percent possessed at least one prior felony arrest and 90 percent had one or more previous psychiatric hospitalizations, leading them to postulate, much like Rabkin (1979), the existence of a subgroup of individuals with features of both mental illness and criminality. Examining the records of persons admitted to the Philadelphia prison system, Guy et al. (1985) espied that 17 percent had a past record of psychiatric hospitalization. Monahan and Steadman (1984) uncovered a prior hospitalization rate of between 2.2 percent (Arizona) and 16.7 percent (Iowa) in a six-state analysis of psychiatric hospitalization records. At Winchester Prison in England, Faulk (1976) identified a prior psychiatric hospitalization rate of 26 percent in the 72 male prisoners whose records he reviewed.

While prior hospitalization rates suggest that up to one-fourth of the jail or prison population suffers signs of serious emotional disorder, there are at least three problems associated with using psychiatric hospitalization as the sole indicator of serious psychopathology. First, previous hospitalization does not always correlate well with other measures of psychopathology (Bonovitz & Guy, 1979). Second, there are no good base-rate estimates of psychiatric hospitalization in the general population (Monahan & Steadman, 1984). Third, hospitalization has been used for evaluative purposes and by some defense attorneys as a pre-trial strategy, particularly in cases where the offense was especially violent or heinous (Cooke, Johnston, & Pogany, 1973), and so may tend to overestimate the rate of serious psychopathology present in correctional populations. As a result, several investigators have endeavored to provide individual diagnoses for incarcerated offender groups.

Investigations furnishing psychiatric diagnoses for randomly or consecutively sampled correctional populations are outlined in Table 4.1. As one can readily surmise, the volume of serious psychopathology (that is, psychotic-level diagnoses like schizophrenia, major affective disorder, and paranoia) falls somewhere in the neighborhood of 1 to 15 percent, with a modal value of 5 percent. Comparing this figure with general base-rate estimates, Monahan and Steadman (1984) contend that serious emotional disorder does not appear to be any more prevalent in correctional populations than it is in community samples of comparable social status. There is also evidence to suggest that the jail experience itself may temporarily inflate the expression of psychiatric symptomatology— depression, anxiety, somatic concern, and obsessive-compulsive features in particular (Gibbs, 1987). Consequently, it is imperative that investigators wait at least one week before interviewing newly admitted offenders, since transient symptom expression begins to subside within four to five days.

A logical question at this juncture is whether emotionally disturbed offenders are any more violent or dangerous than nondisturbed criminals. Quinsey and Boyd (1977) argue that there is no evidence to support the contention that psychiatrically disordered offenders are any more dangerous than other of society's lawbreakers, while Valdiserri, Carroll, and Hartl (1986) discerned that psychiatrically impaired persons confined in the Berks County, Pennsylvania, jail were normally charged with relatively minor offenses compared to the indictments facing nonimpaired inmates. Ashford (1989), in Arizona, and St. Croix, Dry, and Webster (1988) in Alberta, Canada, on the other hand, indicate that the emotionally disturbed offenders in their studies were typically charged with more serious and violent crimes than their nondisturbed counterparts. Evaluating a sample of U.S. military offenders, Walters, Scrapansky, and Marrlow (1986) discovered a greater percentage of emotionally disturbed inmates serving time for person crimes relative to the number of person crimes committed by a group of matched nondisturbed military incarcerates. Finally, Adams (1983) observed post-prison differences in the adjustment of emotionally disturbed and nondisturbed inmates in which the mentally disturbed group experienced greater problems of adjustment; although interpretation of this finding is clouded by the fact that emotionally disturbed subjects presented a more extensive history of prior criminal conviction.

Where the data are ambiguous on the question of whether disturbed inmates commit more violent and serious crimes than their nondisturbed jailmates, the problems these persons encounter while confined are well documented and rarely contested. In general, mentally ill offenders encounter many more problems of adjustment than nondisturbed inmates, whether they are housed in a county jail, prison work camp, or maximum security penitentiary. This has been documented in state (Adams, 1986; Walters et al., 1988), federal (Adams, 1983; Walters et al., 1988), and military (Walters, Scrapansky, & Marrlow, 1986) correctional populations. Therefore, while it seems improbable that emotional disorder is any more prevalent in jails or prisons than it is in community at large, persons demonstrating problems of both a criminal and psychiatric nature experience significant adjustment difficulties, even in the highly structured milieu of a penal institution.

FORENSIC ISSUES

Nowhere is the presumed nexus between crime and mental disorder any more critical than in the courtroom. However, problems abound in cases where legal and mental health concerns co-exist. The adversarial nature of the U.S. system of jurisprudence is foreign to many clinicians, while those trained in the legal profession have trouble appreciating the subtle nuances of human experience and emotion. Alexander (1985, p. 358) tersely describes the problems indigenous to a domain in which legal and mental health issues overlap: ''Trying to describe human emotion in the language of the law is like trying to dissect a butterfly with a meat ax, and in the courtroom, at least, the two professions have scant respect for each other.'' There is insufficient space in this chapter to adequately address the full spectrum of issues pertinent to the imbricating relationship among crime, mental disorder, and the law. However, it would seem advisable that we at least touch upon three pivotal forensic matters: competency, responsibility, and transfers to mental health facilities.

Table 4.1
Prevalence of Serious Psychiatric Symptomatology in Prisons and Jails

Study	Subjects[1] N S P Description	Diagnostic Measure	Rate of Disorder
Glueck (1918)	680 M C state prisoners	clinical interview	12%-psychotic
Shands (1958)	1720 C state prisoners	clinical interview	3.5%-psychotic
Guze et al. (1962)	223 M T parole/probationers	structured interview	6.0%-major aff. dis. 1.5%-schizophrenic
Bluglass (1966)	300 M R Scottish prisoners	clinical interview	1.9%-psychotic
Cloninger & Guze (1970)	66 F T parole/probationers	structured interview	1%-schizophrenic
Bolton (1976)	1084 T county jail inmates	clinical interview	6.7%-psychotic
Faulk (1976)	72 M C British prisoners	structured interview	3%-schizophrenic
Jones (1976)	1040 M T state prisoners	clinical interview/ chart review	4%-psychotic

	Subjects	Method	Description
Swank & Winer (1976)	100 M C county jail inmates	clinical interview	5%-psychotic
Schuckit et al. (1977)	199 M R county jail inmates	structured interview	3%-major aff. dis.
Good (1978)	11 M C state prisoners 89 F	structured interview	10%-major aff. dis.
Gunn et al. (1978)	106 M R British prisoners	clinical interview	1%-schizophrenic 1%-major aff. dis.
James et al. (1980)	174 M R state prisoners	clinical interview/ self-report	5%-schizophrenic
O'Keefe (1980)	995 C county jail inmates	clinical interview	4.6%-seriously dis.
Guy et al. (1985)	486 C city jail inmates	clinical interview	11.5%-schizophrenic 4.2%-major aff. dis.
Walters et al. (1988)	100 M C state prisoners 218 M C federal prisoners 55 M R military prisoners	structured interview structured interview structured interview	10%-seriously dis. 8.7%-seriously dis. 7.3%-seriously dis.

[1]*Subjects: N* = number of subjects in sample; *S* = sex of subjects; *P* = sampling procedure (C = consecutively sampled, R = randomly sampled, T = total subject population) used; *Description* = type of population from which subjects were sampled.

Competency

The Constitution of the United States assures persons accused of a crime legal counsel and a fair and speedy trial. An individual must therefore be mentally competent to appreciate the objective and nature of the court proceedings and participate in his or her own defense. The modern-day competency standard is grounded in British common law and derives from the Supreme Court's landmark decision in Dusky v. United States (1960). The Dusky decision holds that an individual must have a rational and factual understanding of the proceedings against him or her and possess the capacity to consult with his or her attorney in a rational and effective manner before he or she can be tried. Recently, the Supreme Court ruled that prisoners condemned to die must also be competent—that is, be able to rationally understand their sentence and the punishment they are about to receive and have the ability to aid in their continuing defense—before they can be executed (Ford v. Wainwright, 1986). This decision demonstrates not only the transient nature of competency but also the impact forensic psychologists and psychiatrists can have on the legal decision-making process.

Although the criteria for mental competency seem fairly straightforward, an alarming number of mental health professionals are without even a rudimentary understanding of competency as it pertains to a person's capacity to stand trial. Hess and Thomas (1963), for instance, discovered that the psychiatrists they interviewed often confused competency with responsibility, while Robey (1965) writes that many of the psychiatrists he spoke with were embarrassingly ignorant of the criteria used to assess competency. McGarry (1965) adds that mental health professionals often adopt the untenable position that a psychotic person is, by definition, incompetent to stand trial. Rosenberg and McGarry (1972) reviewed court-ordered reports prepared by psychiatrists and interviewed a group of lawyers, from whence they discovered that many of the professionals in both groups lacked a precise understanding of the criteria for competency. These findings intimate that many mental health and legal professionals need to be educated on the competency standard.

In order that he might provide mental health professionals with greater guidance and structure for conducting competency evaluations, Robey (1965) offered readers a simple checklist comprising three sections. The first section, "comprehension of court proceedings," probed the defendant's understanding of court procedure, basic legal principles, charges, possible verdicts and penalties, and one's legal rights. In the second section, entitled "ability to advise counsel," facts, pleas, legal strategies, the waiver of rights, one's relationship with one's attorney, the consistency of one's defense, and one's ability to interpret witness statements were surveyed. "Susceptibility to decompensation while awaiting trial" was covered in the third section of Robey's checklist, a section that considered a subject's propensity for violence and the presence of acute psychosis, organic deterioration, regressive withdrawal, and suicidal depression.

Bukatman, Foy, and DeGrazia (1971) labored to revise and update this checklist, dividing their checklist along the lines of factual and inferential items. Although both measures, and the Robey checklist in particular, were widely disseminated, there is no published research on their reliability or validity (Steadman & Hartstone, 1983).

The Competency Screening Test (CST) is a 22-item sentence-completion instrument developed by a team of researchers from the Harvard Medical School under the direction of Louis McGarry (Lipsitt, Lelos, & McGarry, 1971). The CST is the most widely investigated competency measure presently available to clinicians and researchers. Each of the 22 items on the CST (for example, "The lawyer told Bill that _____ "; "If the jury finds me guilty, I _____ .") are scored on a three-point scale: 2 = appropriate response; 1 = borderline response; 0 = inappropriate response. The CST yields a total possible score of 44 and scores of 21 or higher are said to be indicative of a competent mental state. Inter-rater reliability estimates have been shown to range between .88 and .95 (Lipsitt et al., 1971; Randolph, Hicks, & Mason, 1981), the alpha coefficient figures out to be .85, and the mean inter-item correlation is .20 (Nicholson, Briggs, & Robertson, 1988).

Validating the CST in a group of 43 persons referred for competency evaluations at Bridgewater State Hospital in Massachusetts, Lipsitt et al. (1971) learned that 71 percent of the defendants rated by staff as competent and 84 percent of those rated incompetent were correctly identified by the CST for an overall hit rate of 76 percent. The validity of the CST has been replicated in state hospital populations in Illinois (Randolph et al., 1981), Mississippi (Nicholson et al., 1988), New York (Shatin & Brodsky, 1979), North Carolina (Roesch & Golding, 1980), and Virginia (Nottingham & Mattson, 1980) with the overall level of accuracy falling somewhere between 70 and 82 percent. Chellsen (1986), on the other hand, discovered that the CST failed to adequately identify incompetency in 25 mentally retarded (IQ = 47–77) patients.

Short forms of the CST have been developed, with five- and seven-item variations receiving the greatest level of empirical attention. Shatin (1979) constructed a five-item version of the CST and observed that it correctly identified 17 of 21 patients (81% hit rate) referred for competency evaluations. Nicholson (1988) also accumulated evidence for the validity of this short form, but added that the reliability was lower than that achieved with the full CST. Paramesh (1987) reported on a seven-item version of the CST, which generated outcomes comparable to the full scale and superior to Shatin's five-item alternative in a study examining the competency evaluations of 260 males admitted to the Kansas state security hospital in Larned, Kansas. The advantages of CST short forms are obvious, although more research is required before they can be considered interchangeable with the full 22-item version.

Whereas the CST would appear to be both reliable and valid, there are several problems with this instrument. One liability is that the CST yields a rather high percentage of false positive determinations (15 to 30%). Consequently, two to three times as many competent defendants will score below 20 on the CST (false positives) as incompetent defendants who score above 20 (false negatives). Another hindrance is that portions of the CST scoring manual are ambiguous, which in turn limits the reliability of one's findings (Melton et al., 1987). Lastly, there are problems with the construct validity of the CST because of the nebulous nature of the test's internal structure (Nicholson, Briggs, & Robertson, 1988). Therefore, while the CST apparently does an adequate job of screening out incompetency (Melton et al., 1987), it should be supplemented with other measures to guard against the possibility of a high rate of false positive determinations.

Other instruments designed to assess competency include the Competency Assessment Instrument, Georgia Court Competency Test, and Interdisciplinary Fitness Interview. The Competency Assessment Instrument or CAI (McGarry, 1973) is a semistructured interview rated on a five-point Likert-type scale that can be used in conjunction with the CST in making competency determinations. The Georgia Court Competency Test, or GCCT-MSH (Wildman et al., 1978) is an orally administered test that asks the defendant 17 questions about his or her knowledge of courtroom procedure, the charges against him or her, possible penalties, and ability to communicate rationally with his or her attorney. Two studies conducted by Robert Nicholson and his colleagues (Nicholson, Briggs, & Robertson, 1988; Nicholson et al., 1988) demonstrate both the predictive validity and robust internal consistency of this procedure, although a great deal more research is required. Utilizing the decision-making strategies of a panel of forensic experts, Golding and Roesch devised the Interdisciplinary Fitness Interview or IFI (Golding, Roesch, & Schreiber, 1984), a semistructured interviewing technique that allows for ratings of 0 (minimum incapacity) to 2 (substantial incapacity) for knowledge of the legal procedure, presence of psychopathology, and overall evaluation of competency. While preliminary data (Golding et al., 1984) suggest that the IFI is a time-efficient procedure that possesses high reliability, there is insufficient research to evaluate its overall level of validity at this time.

In Pate v. Robinson (1966) the Supreme Court ruled that the judge, prosecutor, and defense attorney have an obligation to raise the issue of competency if there is any doubt about a defendant's ability to understand the nature and objective of the legal proceedings against him or her or assist in his or her own defense. Under such circumstances the court will refer the defendant for evaluation by a psychologist, psychiatrist, or social worker who will then report his or her findings to the court. Although the court is responsible for determining a defendant's competency, judges normally act on the recommendations of mental health professionals in nine out of ten cases (McGarry, 1965; Roesch & Golding, 1980; Steadman, 1979). The combined results of ten studies reviewed by Roesch and Golding (1980) reveal that only 30 percent of those referred for competency evaluations are actually found incompetent to stand trial. When we consider these findings, in light of the knowledge that only 10 to 47 percent of those referred for evaluation actually display psychotic symptomatology (Cooke, 1969;

Russell, 1971) and that referral rates are higher for certain offenses (serious, violent, atrocious crimes) than others (petty crimes), we see the value in Cooke, Johnston, and Pogany's (1973) statement that strategies other than legitimate concern about mental pathology sometimes motivate referrals for competency examinations.

After reviewing the characteristics of persons found incompetent to stand trial, Steadman (1979) noted that incompetent defendants were more often black, unmarried, less well educated, and lacking in occupational skill than defendants deemed competent. These individuals also possessed more extensive histories of past psychiatric hospitalization and criminal arrest than the competent group. In a like manner, Roesch and Golding (1980) relate that the incompetent defendants in their study were younger, less well educated, and more likely to be black, unmarried, and diagnosed psychotic than were competent defendants. Cooke (1969), on the other hand, was unable to identify any reliable psychometric or diagnostic differences between patients classified as competent or incompetent by staff working on the forensic unit of a Pennsylvania state hospital. It would appear, then, that persons eventually found incompetent to stand trial are more poorly adjusted than those found competent, although these differences are often difficult to detect using standard psychometric procedures like the MMPI.

Defendants adjudicated incompetent to stand trial are normally hospitalized in an effort to restore competency and bring the individual to trial. As Hess and Thomas (1963) point out, however, only 20 to 30 percent of all persons initially found incompetent to stand trial (IST) are ever returned to court. They estimate that nearly half the sample of ISTs they studied will spend the remainder of their lives in a mental institution. At first glance this would appear to be a violation of these defendants' due process rights, a sentiment echoed by the Supreme Court in Jackson v. Indiana (1972). The Jackson decision holds that a defendant found incompetent to stand trial should be detained no longer than is reasonable to determine whether competency can ever be restored. Unfortunately, the high court failed to specify what it meant by a "reasonable" length of time and approximately half of the jurisdictions in the United States can still hold an individual found incompetent to stand trial for an indefinite period of time.

According to the results of two more recently conducted investigations, however, incompetent detainees are rarely hospitalized any longer than five or six years. Steadman (1979), for example, determined that incompetent defendants in New York State charged with crimes of lesser severity spent an average of one year, while persons charged with more serious crimes normally spent two years, in a state mental hospital before being returned to court or released back into the community. Roesch and Golding (1980) report that the average length of hospital stay for IST patients in North Carolina is 2.6 years, the high group in this sample being defendants charged with murder (mean hospital stay = 3.7 years).

Of cardinal concern to those professionals tasked with making decisions about IST defendants is whether these patients are at increased risk for arrest once they are released from the hospital. In one of the first published studies to address this issue, McGarry (1971) observed that IST patients recorded a slightly lower rate of recidivism (48%) during a four-year period of observation than felons released from prison (60%). Utilizing data on IST patients released from Michigan psychiatric hospitals, Mowbray (1979) reports that 32 percent of her sample had committed one or more crimes within five years of their release from a psychiatric hospital, the average length of time between release and arrest being 17 months. Similarly, Steadman (1979) witnessed re-arrest and re-hospitalization rates of 44 percent each in a group of 411 IST patients released from New York State hospitals and followed an average of 18 months. Although both the Mowbray and Steadman studies suggest that many persons found incompetent to stand trial continue to experience problems of both a criminal and psychiatric nature, very few of these individuals are subsequently arrested for violent criminal offenses.

Responsibility

The notion that an individual should not be punished for unlawful acts for which he or she was not mentally responsible goes back at least as far as the Bible. The first recorded case of a jury acquitting a defendant on the basis of mental nonresponsibility occurred in 1505 (Robitscher & Haynes, 1982), although modern formulations of the insanity defense have their roots in mid-nineteenth-century English law. It was in 1843 that a young Scotsman by the name of Daniel M'Naghten shot and killed Edward Drummond, the personal secretary of British Prime Minister Robert Peel. M'Naghten was exonerated on the basis of testimony from physicians that he suffered from delusions of persecution and was not mentally responsible for his actions at the time he attacked Drummond. This decision stimulated both popular and scholarly debate, and led the House of Lords to establish an advisory board composed of selected legal and medical experts tasked with establishing guidelines for cases where the insanity issue was raised. The board's answers to two of the questions posed to it soon became known as the M'Naghten rules and were subsequently adopted as the standard for insanity determinations in England and the United States:

To establish a defense on the ground of insanity, it must be clearly proved that, at the time of the committing of the act, the party accused was labouring under such a defect of reason, from disease of the mind, as not to know the nature and quality of the act he was doing; or if he did know it, that he did not know he was doing what was wrong. (M'Naghten case, 1843)

Dissatisfaction with the M'Naghten rules came from experts in both the medical and legal communities. One common criticism directed at the nascent criteria asserted that these rules only took into account one's cognitive understanding of the wrongfulness of a particular criminal act and failed to address whether the person possessed the capacity to exert control over his or her actions. There was also a growing sense on the part of certain scholars that the M'Naghten rules were overly rigid in their consideration of mental illness as an explanation for crime (Melton et al., 1987). These and other disapprobations spurred development of alternative conceptualizations of the insanity defense.

Forty years after M'Naghten, Parsons v. State (1886) encouraged ratification of the "irresistible impulse" test for insanity in several U.S. jurisdictions. According to this rule, a person cannot be prosecuted for criminal acts over which he or she has no volitional control. The next major development in the insanity defense took place in 1954, when Judge David Bazelon introduced into law the "product test" for insanity. As set forth in Durham v. United States (1954), the "product test" contends that a person should not be held culpable from a legal standpoint for unlawful acts that are "the product of mental disease or defect." The principal limitation of the "product test" is that if we define mental disease or defect as disorders recognized by various mental health organizations, it is foreseeable that it could be used to exonerate the criminal activities not only of persons with psychoses but with personality and character disorders (for example, psychopathy) as well.

The Durham decision was overturned in 1972, and the District of Columbia Court of Appeals replaced it with a version of the insanity test drafted by the American Law Institute (ALI). According to the ALI formulation, "a person is not responsible for criminal conduct if at the time of such conduct, as a result of mental disease or defect, he lacks substantial capacity either to appreciate the criminality [wrongfulness] of his conduct or to conform his conduct to the requirements of law" (Model Penal Code, 4.01, [ALI, 1955]). The ALI conceptualization of mental responsibility is presently the most popular strategy for determining insanity in the United States (see Figure 4.1).

Recently the American Bar Association (ABA) and American Psychiatric Association (APA) jointly recommended a narrowing of the insanity test to where "a person is not responsible for criminal conduct if, at the time of such conduct, and as a result of mental disease or defect, that person was unable to appreciate the wrongfulness of such conduct" (APA, 1983). It would appear that we have come full circle, from M'Naghten and back again, and like M'Naghten, the Appreciation Test proposed in the ABA-APA reformulation and adopted by the federal courts has raised some concern because it restricts itself to the cognitive prong of the ALI test.

A great many myths have sprung up around the issue of insanity as a legal defense. It has been assumed, for example, that the insanity defense is a common occurrence in most courtroom situations. Pasewark and his associates determined that college students and state legislators estimated use of the insanity plea in 37 percent (Pasewark & Seidenzahl, 1980) and 20 percent (Pasewark & Pantle, 1979) of all criminal cases tried in the state of Wyoming between 1971 and 1973, when in fact only .46 percent of the cases tried during that period actually relied on this defense (Pasewark & Lanthorn, 1977). Studies conducted in Mich-

Figure 4.1
The Insanity Defense in the United States

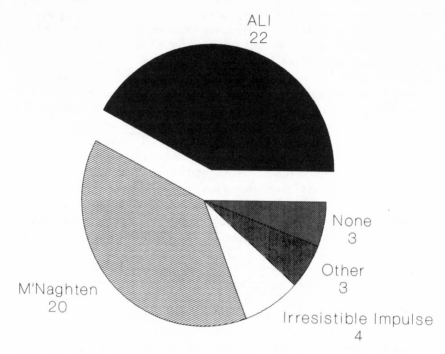

ALI = American Law Institute Criteria (AL, AR, CT, DE, DC, HI, IL, KY, ME, MD, MA, MI, MO, ND, OH, OR, RI, TN, VT, WV, WI, WY).

M'Naghten = variations on the M'Naghten rule (AK, AZ, CA, FL, IA, KS, LA, MN, MS, NE, NV, NJ, NY, NC, OR, PA, SC, SD, TX, WA).

Irresistible Impulse (CO, GA, NM, VA).

Other = Product (NH) and Appreciation (Federal Courts, IN) tests.

None = states that have abolished the insanity defense (ID, MT, UT).

igan (Cooke & Sikorski, 1975), Missouri (Petrila, 1982), and Virginia (Bonnie & Slobogin, 1980) note an insanity plea rate of between .1 and .5 percent. The degree to which the insanity defense results in acquittal has also been over-estimated. Thus, where college students projected a success rate of 44 percent (Pasewark & Seidenzahl, 1980) and state legislators a rate of 40 percent (Pasewark & Pantle, 1979) in cases where the insanity issue was raised, the actual acquittal rate was only 1 percent (Pasewark & Lanthoin, 1977). The success of insanity defenses in New York (Steadman et al., 1982) and New Jersey (Rodriguez Statement, 1982) is somewhat higher, with acquittal rates of 25 and 30 percent, respectively, being reported.

Another common misconception is that experts regularly disagree on the sanity of specific defendants. Investigating the insanity plea in Missouri, Petrila (1982) noted that this defense was rarely contested, while in Oregon, Rogers, Bloom, and Manson (1984) determined that four out of every five successful insanity defenses never made it to trial because the prosecutor was unwilling to litigate. A reasonably high degree of concordance has been reported for experts asked to evaluate the mental responsibility of defendants in Hawaii (Funkunaga et al., 1981), New Jersey (Singer, 1978), and Erie County, New York (Steadman, Keitner, Braff, & Arvanites, 1983). It would appear, then, that the insanity defense is used sparingly, unsuccessful more often than not, and in cases where it is successful, rarely contested by the prosecution because it is obvious to everyone involved that the defendant lacked the mens rea, or intent, to commit the unlawful act in question.

Reliability and validity are of critical consequence when evaluating a person's responsibility for a given criminal act. Concerning the reliability of insanity determinations, agreement among mental health professionals asked to evaluate the issue of responsibility varies between 64 percent, for evaluators selected alternately by the defense and prosecution (Raifman, 1979), and 97 percent, for evaluators working in the same forensic center (Stock & Poythress, 1979). In an effort to improve upon the reliability and validity of responsibility evaluations, Slobogin, Melton, and Showalter (1984) developed a brief mental-status exam designed to screen out nondisturbed defendants. Rogers and associates comment that another structured diagnostic procedure, the Schedule for Affective Disorders and Schizophrenia (SADS), is capable of discriminating between sane and insane defendants (Rogers, Thatcher, & Cavanaugh, 1984). Measuring responsibility continues to be a problem, however, in part because those conducting the evaluations often base their decisions on a limited range of information (Smith & Graham, 1989).

The Rogers Criminal Responsibility Assessment Scales, or RCRAS (Rogers & Cavanaugh, 1981b) were born of a desire to develop systematic indices of criminal responsibility. The RCRAS consists of 25 psychological and situational variables organized into five summary scales: reliability (absence of malingering), organic factors, psychopathology, cognitive control, and behavioral control. Decision rules based on scores for the five scales are available for the ALI and M'Naghten rules. A series of studies run on the RCRAS revealed inter-rater reliability estimates (kappa coefficient) of between .73 and .80 (Rogers, Dolmetsch, & Cavanaugh, 1981; Rogers, Wasyliw, & Cavanaugh, 1984). These same studies unearthed wide discrepancies on all five RCRAS scales in subjects judged sane and insane using the RCRAS decision rules. However, none of the studies employed an external measure of insanity against which the RCRAS might be more properly evaluated. Further, since Rogers' items rely on the subjective impressions of the appraiser, it is questionable whether the RCRAS commands a significant advantage over the traditional interview approach to responsibility evaluations (Melton et al., 1987).

Once a defendant is found Not Guilty by Reason of Insanity (NGRI) he or she is normally committed to a psychiatric facility for a period of evaluation and treatment. The length of hospitalization has been shown to vary by crime and jurisdiction. Hence, Pasewark, Pantle, and Steadman (1979) remark that male NGRI defendants charged with murder spent twice as long in the hospital as male defendants charged with manslaughter. Though some studies suggest that NGRI defendants may be released after spending an average of only 9½ (Criss & Racine, 1981) to 14 (Pasewark et al., 1979) months in a psychiatric facility, the results of one study (State of Illinois, 1982) intimate that these averages may underestimate the amount of time these individuals actually spend in mental hospitals, since almost three-quarters of the Illinois sample had previously been adjudicated Incompetent to Stand Trial with a mean length of time between competency determination and NGRI acquittal of 38½ months.

In Bolton v. Harris (1968) it was determined that insanity acquittees could not be held in the hospital without benefit of a civil commitment hearing. Subsequent to this decision, however, the Supreme Court ruled in Jones v. United States (1983) that it is constitutional to confine a NGRI defendant longer than if he had been convicted and sentenced to prison provided the appropriate civil commitment procedures have been followed. In actual practice, states differ markedly in how long they detain NGRI acquittees. Connecticut, for instance, has mandated that NGRI defendants can be held no longer than the maximum prison term they could have received had they been convicted and many are released before expiration of the maximum prison term. As a result, NGRI defendants in Connecticut are released an average of 19 months earlier than prisoners incarcerated for the same offense (Phillips & Pasewark, 1980). New Jersey, on the other hand, holds insanity defendants twice as long as comparable groups of prison inmates (Rodriguez Statement, 1982), while Pasewark, Pantle, and Steadman (1979) detected no difference in the length of hospitalization for NGRI defendants in New York and the length of imprisonment for same-offense prison inmates.

The correlates of hospital stay in patients found NGRI have also been explored. Examining the records of 167 NGRI patients, Cooke and Sikorski (1975) determined that sex, education, marital status, residence, offense, previous mental hospital internments, and results from the MMPI corresponded with length of hospitalization. As such, females, more highly educated persons, individuals who were married or widowed, and those having lived in urban areas recorded significantly shorter hospital stays, while acquittees with previous mental hospital admissions, charges of murder, or more highly elevated MMPI profiles were subject to longer hospital stays. Pantle, Pasewark, and Steadman (1980) also observed that sex and offense category correlated with length of hospitalization and that males and defendants charged with homicide remained in the hospital significantly longer than the average NGRI acquittee. Though Steadman, Pasewark, Hawkins, Kiser, and Bieber (1983) identified significant gender, severity of index crime, and marital status correlates of length of hospital stay in their study of 255 NGRI acquittees, they were unable to find a meaningful predictive equation that accounted for any more than 11 percent of the total variance in hospitalization.

Contrary to popular belief, NGRI acquittees do not generate an excessive amount of serious criminality upon release. In one of the first investigations to address this issue, Morrow and Peterson (1966) observed recidivism rates of 16 percent after one year, 43 percent after three years, and 52 percent after five years in a group of NGRI releasees—arrest figures comparable to those obtained in a large sample of federal prisoners. A study by Steadman and Cocozza (1974) registered a much lower rate of recidivism in NGRI releasees than had been predicted by staff, while Pasewark, Pantle, and Steadman (1982) surmised that persons acquitted NGRI were no more likely to be arrested upon release than other offender groups. Similarly, Quinsey, Pruesse, and Fernley (1975) observed an arrest rate of 5.4 percent and a re-hospitalization rate of 42.9 percent in groups of Canadian IST and NGRI defendants released an average of 30 months earlier. A one-year follow-up of NGRI acquittees released from St. Elizabeth's Hospital in Washington, D.C., revealed a moderately low rate of ensuing criminal involvement (12.8%) and a reasonably low rate of serious antisocial activity (8%; Seitz & Baridon, 1982).

The insanity defense has always been shrouded in controversy, and during the past three decades many voices have called for its abolition. These dissenting voices have been as divergent as those of Richard Nixon (Dershowitz, 1973), Abraham Halpern (1977), Thomas Szasz (1979), and the American Medical Association (1984). There are multifarious examples of the insanity defense being used by unscrupulous attorneys for their own personal convenience or by crafty criminals attempting to evade prosecution for their unlawful acts (Halpern, 1977). These and other concerns have led to proposed changes in the insanity defense and the development of alternative conceptualizations like the Guilty But Mentally Ill plea, although the latter has its own set of faults and potential abuses (Robey, 1978). After John Hinckley was acquitted by reason of insanity in his attempt on the life of then-president Ronald Reagan the debate grew even more intense. Following the Hinckley verdict the U.S. Congress introduced into law a revised standard for the insanity defense—the ABA-APA model with the provision that the burden of proof was on the defense rather than on the prosecution.

There is no realistic hope of ever deriving a definitive answer to the question of insanity defense propriety since it is as much a moral issue as it is an empirical or legal one. Monahan (1973a), nonetheless, makes a strong case in favor of preserving the insanity plea. He skillfully argues that the insanity defense reinforces the average citizen's belief in personal responsibility by bringing into clearer focus the issue of free choice and the necessity of considering the consequences of one's actions. Monahan asserts further that the insanity defense buttresses our long-held belief in personal choice, one of the pillars of our Anglo-American approach to law. Thus, while I am sympathetic to the concerns expressed by those opposed to the insanity defense, and am certainly in concert with parties wishing to see its scope restricted, I agree wholeheartedly with Monahan that the insanity defense is necessary, not only to highlight the role of free choice in our daily lives but also as a way of instilling a clear sense of personal responsibility in society as a whole.

Mental Hospital Transfers

Issues involved in transferring patients from prisons, jails, and other correctional facilities to psychiatric hospitals revolve around two court decisions, commonly referred to as the Baxstrom and Vitek decisions. The court in Baxstrom v. Herold (1966) ruled that authorities could not retain mentally disordered offenders in mental health facilities past the maximum date called for by their sentence without benefit of a civil commitment proceeding. Fourteen years later the protections provided by Baxstrom were extended to prison inmates. In this decision the Supreme Court ruled that an inmate must be afforded an administrative hearing to determine the appropriateness of a mental health transfer before such a transfer could be instituted (Vitek v. Jones, 1980). In the next several paragraphs research addressing the Baxstrom and Vitek decisions is reviewed.

In the wake of the Baxstrom decision nearly 1,000 New York State inmates were transferred from institutions for the criminally insane to civil mental hospitals. Despite fears by hospital administrators that these individuals would present a danger to staff and other patients, very few serious incidents were noted after an initial period of adjustment lasting several weeks (Hunt & Wiley, 1968). Only 26 of the 967 (2.7%) so-called Baxstrom patients were returned to state institutions for the criminally insane because of disruptive behavior occurring within five years of their transfer (Steadman, 1973), and of those patients released to the community (approximately 27% of the sample), only 7 percent were convicted of crimes during a follow-up period which lasted an average of two and one-half years (Steadman & Keveles, 1972). Similar results have been recorded in Pennsylvania (Thornberry & Jacoby, 1979), Ohio (Beran & Hotz, 1984), and Great Britain (Dell, 1980). It would appear that most NGRI acquittees can be effectively handled in civil mental health facilities without appreciably increasing the risk to staff and other patients or of reducing the acquittees' chances of success in the community.

Less is known about the effect of the Vitek decision on the daily running of the criminal justice system since it is only a little over ten years old. In a national survey of correctional administrators, Steadman et al. (1982) determined that 3.9 percent of the prison population in the United States is transferred to mental health facilities each year. They further ascertained that the most popular transfer options were the forensic units of civil mental hospitals and maximum security hospitals run by the state department of mental health. A question that begs further examination is whether a hearing is required if an inmate is to be transferred from a prison to a department of corrections mental health facility. In-depth interviews with officials from six states revealed that none held a due process hearing before transferring an inmate to a department of corrections mental health institution; however, the interviews predated Vitek by two years (Steadman et al., 1982).

Despite increased usage of civil hospital facilities for the more seriously disturbed inmates, problems persist. Dell (1980), for one, reports marked reticence on the part of civil hospitals in England to accept mentally disordered prison inmates, with an average waiting period of 9 months for mentally ill persons and 18 months for mentally retarded individuals. The hesitancy of civil hospitals to accept emotionally disturbed prison inmates stems in part from fears that such individuals will disrupt the orderly running of the hospital and in part from what many hospital administrators perceive to be a burgeoning number of inappropriate referrals for mental health placement. The first concern seems unfounded on the basis of the Baxstrom data and the second concern can best be handled by implementing specific referral guidelines (Gearing, Heckel, & Matthey, 1980). Given the controversy generated by the Baxstrom decision and the recentness of Vitek, a great many more legal and empirical questions will need to be answered before we are able to gauge the full impact of these decisions on prison-to-hospital transfer policies.

CONCLUSION

A query commonly voiced when crime and mental disorder are considered in combination is whether the emotionally disturbed offender is mad (psychiatric) or bad (criminal). What the results of the current review confide is that the emotionally disturbed offender is both. He or she is both in the sense that research studies have recorded evidence of behavioral and psychiatric maladjustment in the background and current behavior of emotionally disordered felons that frequently parallel patterns observed in criminal (Morrow & Peterson, 1966) and psychiatric (Steadman & Cocozza, 1974) populations. There are features of this profile that serve to distinguish this group of individuals from their nondisturbed criminal (Walters, Mann et al., 1988) and noncriminal psychiatric (Sosowsky, 1980) counterparts. It remains an open question whether the dual presence of criminality and mental disorder makes one more dangerous, although research studies probing the adjustment of NGRI acquittees indicate that such individuals are no more a threat to the orderly running of a civil mental hospital than noncriminal psychiatric patients (Hunt & Wiley, 1968; Steadman, 1973), and no more likely to engage in serious criminal conduct upon release than nondisturbed offenders (Morrow & Peterson, 1966; Pantle et al., 1980).

Statements concerning the relationship between crime and mental illness appear to have been greatly exaggerated. While it is true that the two occasionally overlap, the rate of serious antisocial behavior in psychiatric populations and the rate of emotional disorder in criminal populations are no higher than would be expected if nonpsychiatric or noncriminal groups of comparable social status were surveyed. There are several salient issues involved in the interface of legal and psychiatric concerns that warrant further investigation—competency, responsibility, and mental hospital transfers, among others—although these questions are raised in but a small fraction of all cases appearing before the bench each year. The results of the present review suggest that it is time we put the proposed nexus between crime and mental health concerns in its proper perspective, in that most criminals do not exhibit signs of serious emotional disorder and most psychiatric patients do not engage in significant criminality. Moreover, where the presence of mental health symptomatology may put one at increased risk for arrest in certain jurisdictions, it does not seem to appreciably elevate one's chances of becoming involved in future criminal acts.

5

Prediction

Predicting human behavior is a painstaking task that presents problems for both clinician and researcher. Initially, we are faced with the dilemma of defining, in precise terms, the behavior we are hoping to predict. Then, we must identify our predictors from the large reservoir of measures available at any one point in time. Since it is the rare situation that finds single variables sufficiently robust to effectively predict criterion behavior at clinically meaningful levels, we should consider combining several different measures as a way of maximizing our prognostic capabilities. Finally, in order that prediction might be advanced scientifically, it is essential that we direct ourselves to the theoretical analysis of empirical relationships. This search for conceptual meaning is indispensable to our scientific aspirations, since the ultimate goal of criminal science prediction is to identify variables capable of assisting us with the management and understanding of criminal offenders.

Prediction encompasses two principal sets of variables, alternately referred to as predictors and criteria. Clinical prognostication involves forecasting a criterion behavior (for example, dangerousness, recidivism) from a set of previously measured predictor variables (for example, age, criminal history), a procedure which generates four categories of outcome: true positives, false positives, true negatives, and false negatives. A true positive prediction is recorded when a projected outcome is observed during our period of follow-up. Conversely, a false positive prediction is observed when we offer a projection that fails to occur during the follow-up period. If we were to correctly presage the absence of a particular future outcome, then we would have registered a true negative prediction, while failing to predict an outcome that eventually occurs is labeled a false negative prediction.

The primary goals of clinical prognostication are to maximize the true positives and true negatives, minimize the false positives and false negatives, and control for as much extraneous variance as possible. Since any steps taken to reduce the false positive rate will tend to increase the number of false negative predictions and vice versa, we must weigh the cost of making a false positive decision against the cost of making a false negative prediction. Therefore, if our main objective is to minimize unnecessary incarcerations and hospitalizations, we would want to minimize the false positive rate. If, on the other hand, our principal aim is to avoid releasing persons from prisons and hospitals who may still pose a threat to others, then we would want to keep the false negative rate as low as possible. Where the false positive rate in the first instance and the false negative rate in the second instance will be reduced, the converse error (false negatives in the first instance and false positives in the second) will tend to rise in corollary fashion.

Prediction does not necessarily portend a future orientation. Kerlinger (1973) refers to prediction in more general terms as a way of correlating a phenomenon with external criteria. The external criteria that attract our attention in this chapter, however, will be future oriented. In an attempt to forecast features of criminal adjustment, we consider both person and situation variables, armed with the knowledge that the best predictor of future behavioral outcomes is often past behavioral patterns. The present chapter is organized around three primary prediction themes: decisions leading up to confinement (dangerousness), behavior during the course of incarceration (institutional adjustment and dangerousness), and the probability of re-offense following release (recidivism and dangerousness).

DANGEROUSNESS

Definitional Issues

Clinicians are often asked to make difficult decisions, one of the more troublesome being predictions of violence and dangerousness. A shift in the criteria for civil commitment that saw the need for treatment replaced by predictions of imminent dangerousness, as well as the introduction of indeterminate sentencing, focused increased attention on the validity of clinical predictions of dangerous behavior (Monahan, 1984). National Institute of Mental Health analyst Saleem Shah (1978) writes that there are at least 15 separate instances in which the issue of dangerousness might be raised, from civil commitment to institution of the death penalty in capital cases. Our concern at this point, however, is with the precision and specificity of conventional definitions of dangerous behavior.

The problems associated with defining dangerousness have been widely recognized (Megargee, 1976; Monahan, 1981; Shaw, 1973). Both Monahan (1981) and Megargee (1976) prefer the term dangerous or violent behavior to that of dangerousness, since they believe the latter carries with it connotations of violence as a trait. The definition of dangerous behavior advanced by Shah (1978, p. 22) guides our present discourse: "Acts that are characterized by the application of or the overt threat of force and that are likely to result in injury to other persons." Dangerousness, a term which will also find its way into our discussion, is viewed by Shah as nothing more than the propensity to engage in dangerous behavior.

It is a safe bet that our manner of defining dangerous behavior likely will influence the final outcome. We are therefore left with the problem of how to go about operationalizing dangerous behavior. Which criteria yield the most powerful or useful results: official arrests for "violent" crimes, self-reported acts of aggression, or an observer's ratings of a subject's tendency to engage in interpersonally destructive behavior? In a large-scale analysis of published research (1945 to 1983 inclusive) addressing the racial, gender, and social-class correlates of violent behavior, Bridges and Weis (1989) failed to discern a significant data-source (self-report vs. official records vs. victim statements vs. observational techniques) effect. This does not mean, however, that the manner in which dangerous behavior is defined does not influence one's results—just that it may have less of an impact than was once thought. The long-term solution to the problem of differing definitions of dangerousness is to include several different criteria of dangerousness in one's investigation.

Common Errors in the Clinical Prediction of Dangerousness

Clinicians asked to forecast dangerous behavior are subject to errors of both omission and commission. Several of the more common errors committed by clinical decision makers are: (1) criterion-related problems; (2) incomplete understanding of the effect cultural differences can have on clinical judgment; (3) illusory correlation; (4) ignorance of statistical base rates; and (5) failure to incorporate environmental and situational considerations into one's evaluation.

Criterion-related Problems. Accuracy of prediction has been shown to vary according to the scope of a study's definitional criteria (Monahan, 1981). In one study, Pfohl (1979) determined that staff judgments of dangerousness were based on differing and idiosyncratic definitions of future violence, and that the final determination of dangerousness often came down to a compromise among several members of the mental health team. Unsynchronized definitions are especially problematic in studies comparing the prognostic accuracy of clinician- and research-generated judgments. Consequently, it is contingent upon investigators to specify their criteria for dangerousness and effectively identify measures that accurately assess this behavior.

Cultural Effects. It would appear that some mental health professionals may have difficulty understanding certain client groups because of cultural differences. Given the fact that most mental health professionals were raised in middle- or upper-middle-class home environments, many such individuals have difficulty relating to young urban blacks who have grown up in the ghetto. The ideals, interests, and language of urban black youth may be as foreign to some psychologists and psychiatrists as German and Spanish are to the average American. Levinson and Ramsay (1979) addressed this issue as it pertains to presaging violence, and discovered that cultural and experiential differences between evaluators and their subjects may indeed result in major errors of prediction.

Illusory Correlation. Chapman and Chapman (1969) have discussed the issue of illusory correlation as it relates to behavioral science data. Illusory correlation occurs when an observer assumes the existence of a correlation between two or more events on the basis of clinical lore or prior experience, when, in fact, such a relationship does not exist or exists at a substantially lower level. Hence, while some police dispatchers genuinely believe they receive significantly more calls when the moon is full, empirical investigations do not support this supposition (Wagner & Almeida, 1987). Sweetland (1972) examined illusory correlation in predictions of dangerous behavior and surmised that even when there was no empirical relationship between dangerousness and six characteristics traditionally thought to portend violence, nonprofessional judges continued to respond as if there were a connection between these two sets of variables.

Statistical Base Rates. If 90 percent of the subjects in a study fail to display the criterion behavior, the accuracy of our predictions will need to exceed 90 percent to be useful. Low base-rate behaviors like violence and dangerousness are therefore exceedingly difficult to predict because of their low rate of occurrence. Low population base-rates are also a major cause of an unacceptably high rate of false positive determinations, something which has plagued both clinical and statistical studies on dangerousness prediction. Livermore and Mill (cited in Monahan, 1981) estimate that even with a highly accurate procedure (for example, 95% level of accuracy), correct identification of 95 dangerous patients would result in 495 nondangerous persons being misclassified as dangerous.

Research has shown that many clinicians fail to incorporate base-rate information in their judgments, even when it is provided as part of the experimental procedure (Kahneman & Tversky, 1973; Walters, White, & Greene, 1988). Part of the problem may lie in the way in which this information is presented. Carroll (1980), for one, comments that clinicians are more inclined to consider statistical base-rate information when the data are expressed in individualized rather than group or population terms. Shapiro (1977) interjects that the statistical base rate can be used to "anchor" predictions along a range of scores and that patient-specific information can be helpful in pinpointing a subject's score within this range. However, until clinicians recognize the value of population base-rate information in making decisions and predicting behavior, recommendations such as those offered by Carroll and Shapiro will remain largely academic.

Environmental and Situational Considerations. Along the lines of conceptualizing dangerousness as a trait, mental health practitioners have been known to focus on clinical signs, symptoms, and diagnoses. There is evidence that the availability of a victim, presence of a weapon, and use of mood-altering substances may have just as much (if not more) of an effect on future displays of violence as do personality, impulse control, and emotional reactivity (Monahan, 1981). Research addressing victim and third-party behavioral correlates of serious assault has also shown that situational considerations are important (Felson,

Ribner, & Siegel, 1984; Felson & Steadman, 1983). As such, we need to be cautious not to overlook environmental and situational factors in our haste to find effective predictors of violent behavior.

Person-Variable Predictors of Dangerous Behavior

Age. It should come as no surprise that age and dangerous behavior are negatively or inversely correlated. It is likely the reader can recall, from either personal experience or newspaper accounts, many more violent episodes involving juveniles and young adults than older individuals. To guard against the possibility that the observed association between age and dangerousness is nothing more than illusory correlation, we must examine this relationship empirically. The preponderance of evidence on this subject reveals that age is inversely correlated with acts of violent criminality (Gunn, 1973) and recidivism (Steadman & Cocozza, 1974). Zimring (1978) writes that where 15- to 20-year-olds constitute only 8.5 percent of the total population of the United States, they account for 35 percent of all arrests for violent crime. The age-dangerousness connection has also been replicated in research conducted in the Federal Republic of Germany (Hafner & Boker, 1973), Great Britain (Farrington, 1979), and Israel (Shavit & Rattner, 1988). In fact, an inverse relationship has been noted in virtually every study carried out on the age-dangerousness connection, with but one or two possible exceptions (for example, Heller & Ehrlich, 1984).

Explanations of the age-violent criminality nexus are more elusive than demonstrating the presence of an empirical link between these two variables. Several of the more viable interpretations of the age effect for dangerousness and violent criminality are similar in kind to explanations of the general relationship between age and crime (see Volume 1, Chapter 5). Developmental changes created by a reduction in sensation-seeking motivation (Baldwin, 1984) and a shift in personal priorities (Levinson et al., 1978) figure prominently in attempts to clarify how age augurs lower levels of violence and dangerous behavior. Choice may also play a significant role in this relationship since an increasing number of persons exit crime as they get older (Cusson & Pinsonneault, 1986). Consequently, the distribution of persons engaged in crime, violent or otherwise, is heavily skewed in favor of youthful offenders. Whether these suppositions fully account for the prognostic value of age relative to predictions of dangerous behavior awaits further analysis, it is hoped with the aid of longitudinal-type surveys.

Race. Curtis (1985) writes that more than half of all violent crime is perpetrated by minority members of society and that the victims of these crimes are often other minority members. Studies show that blacks and Hispanics exhibit higher rates of violent criminality than whites (Heller & Ehrlich, 1984; Wenk, Robison, & Smith, 1972), although these comparisons have traditionally failed to control for the fact that blacks or Hispanics and whites differ on more than just the color of their skin (early family environment, social class). Though Wolfgang and his associates discovered that lower-class blacks engaged in more violent criminality than lower-class whites (Wolfgang, Figlio, & Sellin, 1972), the experiences of lower-class blacks and whites are hardly identical. It is possible, then, that these experiences are what subserve the relationship that persists between race and aggressive criminality.

Gender. Males would appear to engage in a great deal more violent criminality than females (Hafner & Boker, 1973; Heller & Ehrlich, 1984). As has been noted with both age and race, there is no conventionally accepted explanation for the empirical link between gender and dangerous behavior. Scrutinizing longitudinal data on females in 31 countries, Simon and Baxter (1989) determined that women played only a minor role in the violent crimes observed in these nations. Their analyses nonetheless reveal that the female crime rate does, in fact, correspond with general indices of societal economic opportunity. More research is required to determine whether rising economic opportunities for women may explain the observed increase in serious female criminality that occurred during the mid-1960s.

Marital Status. The verdict on marital status as a predictor of violent behavior is still undecided. Thus, while there are studies supporting the proposition that unmarried persons are prone to higher levels of violence than married persons (Gunn, 1973), other studies fail to confirm a connection between these two variables (Hafer & Boker, 1973). There is also the possibility that outcomes such as those recorded by Gunn (1973) arose because of the intervening influence of a variable like age; that is, single people tend to be younger than married persons.

Early Childhood Behavior. Guided by psychoanalytic theory, MacDonald (1963) found that enuresis, fire setting, and cruelty to animals were commonly observed in the early histories of 100 psychiatric patients hospitalized for making homicidal threats against others. Hellman and Blackman (1966) examined this triad of early childhood behaviors in a forensic population and discerned that defendants charged with violent person crimes recorded a higher incidence of bedwetting, fire setting, and cruelty to animals than defendants charged with nonviolent crimes. In this study, 74 percent of the violent patients reported a full or partial triad in comparison to 28 percent of the nonviolent patients. Several other investigators have also uncovered support for the prognostic value of this triad of negative childhood behaviors (Felthous & Bernard, 1979; Marcus & Conway, 1969).

With the exception of the studies previously mentioned, most researchers have failed to establish a relationship between the triad of enuresis, fire setting, and cruelty to animals and later violence, or else have observed that this association can be accounted for solely on the basis of the cruelty to animals measure (Felthous, 1981; Langevin et al., 1983; Lewis, Shanok, Grant, & Ripvo, 1983). Therefore, while support for the triad as a predictor of adult criminality is equivocal, childhood cruelty to animals may, in fact, be associated with, or even prognostic of, later episodes of dangerous and violent behavior (see Felthous & Kellert, 1986; Kellert & Felthous, 1985).

Criminal History. Mischel (1973) writes that the best predictor of future behavior is past behavior. Nowhere is this more evident than in studies attempting to predict dangerous behavior. The results of research conducted in several different jurisdictions and countries indicate that past violence is not only prognostic of future dangerousness but may actually be the single most powerful harbinger of violent behavior. Investigators have documented, time and again, that persons owning more extensive records of violent criminality (Heller & Ehrlich, 1984; Kozol, Boucher, & Garofalo, 1972; Rappeport & Lassen, 1965; Shah, 1978; Wenk et al., 1972) and who have been arrested from an early age (Heller & Ehrlich, 1984; Wolfgang et al., 1972) are at substantially increased risk for future episodes of dangerous behavior. The authors of one study estimated that 80 percent of their subjects with four or more arrests would be arrested at least one more time and that 90 percent of their subjects with ten arrests would be arrested an eleventh time (Wolfgang et al., 1972).

Even when studies fail to identify a statistically significant association between past and present criminality or violence, the observed trends are generally consistent with the hypothesis that past behavior predicts future behavior. Lewis and associates, for instance, found family and psychiatric variables to be more successful than juvenile violence in predicting adult violent crimes (Lewis et al., 1989). However, a trend was noted in which more persons possessing histories of juvenile violence evidenced adult arrest records (77%) compared to persons absent such a history (61%). It would appear, then, that past criminal history is at least as effective as age and gender in predicting future violence.

Mental Illness. It has often been assumed that mental illness is a powerful predictor of future dangerousness. However, findings from most studies surveying this issue reveal that mental health status is generally inadequate for the task of differentiating between those who will and will not engage in future episodes of violent criminality (Hafner & Boker, 1973; Mullen, 1984; Rubin, 1972). The belief that mental illness is prognostic of violence, held even by some mental health professionals, therefore, seems largely based on illusory correlation.

Psychometric Indices of Personality. Research studies exploring the strengths and weaknesses of personality assessment measures relative to the prediction of dangerous and violent behavior are too numerous to be reviewed here. Suffice it to say that while a handful of studies have documented a relationship between personality test scores and future violence, most have not (Megargee, 1970, 1976; Megargee & Mendelsohn, 1962). Furthermore, of the few studies implicating a possible linkage between personality test results and future dangerousness, most have produced false positive rates that have been prohibitive (McGuire, 1976). These findings are succinctly summarized by Megargee (1970, p. 145), who concludes that "no test has been devised which will adequately postdict, let alone predict, violent behavior."

Intelligence. Like most research on person-oriented predictors of dangerous behavior, the outcome is mixed with regard to intelligence as a predictor of future violence. Whereas an inverse correlation appears to exist between intelligence and general indices of criminality (Hirschi & Hindelang, 1977), Gunn (1973) recorded a direct or positive link between IQ scores and dangerous behavior and several other investigators have failed to witness a relationship between these two variables (Hafner & Boker, 1973; Lewis et al., 1979). Heilbrun (1979), on the other hand, accrued evidence of an interactive effect between intelligence and a personality test score (Scale 4 of the MMPI) in his research on violent criminality. Where Heilbrun was unable to discern a relationship between Scale 4 and crimes of violence in white male prisoners achieving IQ scores of 95 or higher, Scale 4 scores did correspond with higher levels of violence in prisoners earning IQ scores below 95. Ultimately, the clinical significance of these findings will need to be evaluated if they are to find their way into the daily decisions of mental health practitioners charged with determining whether a subject is dangerous or not.

Situation-Variable Predictors of Dangerous Behavior

Social Class. There is evidence that social class may be associated with a tendency to engage in violent and interpersonally aggressive behavior (Elliott & Voss, 1974; Gunn, 1973; Wolfgang et al., 1972). However, the effect appears to be relatively weak (Bridges & Weis, 1989; Tittle, Villemez, & Smith, 1978). As such, it is improbable that social class measures will ever be sufficiently powerful to effectively predict future episodes of dangerous behavior.

Substance Abuse. Studies on the alcohol and drug use habits of incarcerated state felons indicate that approximately one-half of those confined for violent crimes acknowledge having been under the influence of alcohol (Bureau of Justice Statistics, 1983a) and one-third report having been under the influence of illegal drugs (BJS, 1983b) at the time of the instant offense. In research utilizing a history of substance abuse to portend future violence, the results are equivocal with regards to drugs like heroin and marijuana but much more supportive of an association between alcohol and future episodes of violence (Gunn, 1973; Heller & Ehrlich, 1984; Wenk et al., 1972). Alcohol, by virtue of its inhibition-lowering properties, may heighten the predilection of persons predisposed to aggressive displays of emotion to react in a violent manner when confronted with a frustrating set of circumstances. It is also possible that the alcohol-influenced behavior of these persons greatly increases their chances of becoming involved in violent confrontations with others.

Situational Context. It is important for us to keep in mind that violence does not occur in a vacuum but is as much a function of the situational context as it is of the personal characteristics of the protagonist, a fact traditionally overlooked by clinicians attempting to predict dangerous behavior. Richard Felson and his colleagues have sought to understand how victim and bystander behavior affect violent outcomes. In one study, Felson and Steadman (1983) reviewed 159 violent incidents perpetrated by males subsequently incarcerated in New York State correctional facilities and discovered that homicide victims were more often intoxicated, verbally or physically aggressive, and likely to have displayed, threatened to use, or actually used a weapon relative to victims of nonhomicidal assault. From the results of this study Felson and Steadman concluded that the outcome of a potentially violent scenario is determined by a complex interplay of behaviors exhibited by both the antagonist and his or her victim.

Felson has also studied the effect of bystander behavior on violence (Felson, Ribner, & Siegel, 1984). A path analysis of these data revealed that offenders delivered significantly more blows to a victim when third parties (who were often friends and family) displayed greater aggression than when these parties attempted to serve as mediators. It is worth noting that age played an intervening role in these results, since the younger the antagonist, the more probable it was that third parties would aggravate, instigate, or encourage violence rather than mediate the situation (possibly because they too were younger). The results of Felson's work demonstrate the necessity of adopting a wide-spectrum approach to dangerousness prediction in which both the characteristics of the individual and the situational context are taken into account.

Selecting Variables for Prediction

Judges and parole examiners often base their decisions about dangerousness on the recommendations of mental health professionals (Webster & Menzies, 1987). For this reason, the reliability and validity of clinical determinations of dangerousness are of prime significance. However, Quinsey and Ambtman (1979) observed minimal levels of concordance between psychiatrists and teachers asked to predict dangerous behavior. Similarly, Quinsey and Maguire (1983) witnessed only modest consensus among psychiatrists, psychologists, and social workers striving to presage future episodes of violence within the context of their duties as members of an interdisciplinary review board. Though Sepejak et al. (1983) found the prognostications of psychiatrists, psychologists, and correctional officers to be superior to those provided by social workers and nurses, none of these groups was able to produce results likely to instill much confidence in the reliability or validity of clinical predictions of violent behavior. In a related vein, Werner, Rose, and Yesavage (1983) disclosed that only 2 of the 30 psychiatrists and psychologists they studied were able to predict dangerous behavior at a level that exceeded chance expectations. It would appear that clinical predictions of dangerous behavior are of low reliability and dubious validity, and that professional status does little to enhance either.

Although several investigators have ascertained that empirically demonstrated variables like age (Williams & Miller, 1977) and criminal history (Menzies, Jackson, & Glasberg, 1982) are sometimes considered by clinical decision makers pondering the issue of dangerousness, many other studies show clinical determinations of dangerous behavior to be based on unverified and spurious predictive variables and schemes. The results of a study administered by Aaland and Schag (1984) indicate that the decision to release an inmate from a sex offender program was predicated on such unproven predictors as the individual's diagnosis (psychosis versus nonpsychosis) and response to therapy, while previously validated predictors like age, marital status, and prior criminal history were largely ignored. Cocozza and Steadman (1978) observed much the same outcome when they contrasted groups of defendants identified by a psychiatric examination as dangerous and nondangerous. Thus, where the groups in the Cocozza and Steadman study failed to differ on age, race, marital status, and past criminal history, mental illness and the severity of the current charges were central to the recommendations of evaluating psychiatrists.

Experimental studies also show clinical decision making to be based on less than fully validated predictors of dangerous behavior. Monahan and Cummings (1974) presented undergraduate college students with the characteristics most commonly associated with dangerous conduct and then instructed them to assess the dangerousness of subjects portrayed in 22 case vignettes. The outcome revealed that subjects were more likely to consider a person dangerous if such a decision was for the purpose of hospitalization than if it was for the purpose of incarceration, thereby lending credence to the hypothesis that dangerousness predictions are influenced by the perceived consequences of these predictions. In a more recently conducted investigation, Jackson (1986) discerned that judges, psychiatrists, and lay persons relied heavily on negative information, even if this information was irrelevant to the dangerousness criterion, in predicting dangerous behavior. Physical attractiveness has also been found to be a factor in such determinations, with less attractive subjects rated as more dangerous and more attractive subjects rated as less dangerous (Esses & Webster, 1986).

Though the studies reviewed in this section reflect the influence of unsubstantiated and oftentimes irrelevant factors in formulating estimates of future dangerousness, there are indications that the more idiosyncratic aspects of such predictions are minimized in situations where the decision task is sufficiently structured (Esses & Webster, 1986; Jackson, 1988). Menzies, Webster, and Sepejak (1985) introduced the Dangerous Behavior Rating Scheme (DBRS) with the intent of providing the requisite structure by which prognostic decisions might be made more reliable and accurate. Preliminary results suggest that this instrument is strong on inter-rater reliability and accuracy, and that it yields a relatively low percentage of false positive determinations (Menzies et al., 1985). However, since the DBRS relies on ranges and cutting scores instead of binary judgments (yes-no), it leaves a great many cases unclassified. Procedures such as the DBRS would appear to be of potential utility, although they have yet to be sufficiently cross-validated to be of much use to contemporary clinical decision makers.

Clinical Prediction of Dangerous Behavior

The inaugural attempt to empirically assess the ability of mental health professionals to predict dangerousness was initiated by a team of researchers from the

Center for the Diagnosis and Treatment of Dangerous Persons in Bridgewater, Massachusetts (Kozol, Boucher, & Garofalo, 1972). These authors report that over the course of their study 592 offenders were evaluated. Of this number, 435 were released, 386 with staff ratings of nondangerous and 49 with staff ratings of dangerous. A five-year follow-up of this sample revealed that 8 percent of the nondangerous group subsequently committed a serious criminal act in comparison to 34.7 percent of the dangerous subjects. Though these results seem moderately impressive, we should keep in mind that 65 percent of those rated dangerous did not commit a single serious criminal act during the follow-up period, a finding which signifies a fairly high rate of false positive predictions. Additionally, subjects recommended for release (nondangerous group) were at risk in the community for a shorter period of time than patients recommended for retention (dangerous group) but released by the courts anyway (Cocozza, 1973).

The next major study to address the ability of clinicians to predict dangerous behavior was conducted at the Patuxent Institute in Maryland (State of Maryland, 1973). Of 421 patients receiving three or more years of treatment at Patuxent, staff recommended the release of 135 and opposed the release of 286. Between 71 and 81 percent of the persons released against the advice of staff were subsequently arrested for one or more (not necessarily violent) crimes during a three-year follow-up, while 37 percent of the patients recommended for release by staff were arrested during the follow-up period. There was a built-in bias to this study, however, since the recommended group received up to three years of community-based parole supervision before being included in the follow-up, while the recidivism count began for nonrecommended subjects the moment they were released to the community. Steadman (1977) reanalyzed the Patuxent data using a more methodologically sound design and discovered only a small difference in the violent recidivism of recommended and nonrecommended patients (31% versus 41% over three years).

Release of the Baxstrom patients in New York State also provided researchers with the opportunity to evaluate clinical predictions of dangerousness. Although forecasting dangerousness was never an issue with the Baxstrom patients, the stated purpose for their detention was based loosely on a criterion of dangerousness to self and others. Results from the Baxstrom studies indicate that only 20 percent of the patients in this group had been assaultive to persons in the hospital or community during a period of four years following their release from a New York State maximum security mental health facility (Steadman & Cocozza, 1974). Similar findings were reported by Thornberry and Jacoby (1979) in their research on a group of 438 Baxstrom-like patients released from Pennsylvanian hospitals, only 14 percent of whom were eventually arrested or rehospitalized for an assaultive criminal offense within four years of their release. These outcomes indicate that for every correct dangerousness determination there are at least four or five persons who will be labeled dangerous but demonstrate no subsequent violent criminal activity.

Table 5.1

Studies on the Clinical Prediction of Dangerous Behavior

Study	1 Sample N Sex Des.			2 Criterion Behavior	3 Follow- up	Overall Accuracy	4 False Pos Ratio
Kozol et al. (1972)	592	M	Dangerous Sex Offenders	Serious Criminal Act	5 yr.	89.0%	1.9:1
State of Maryland (1973)	421	M	Defective Delinquents	Arrest for Any Crime	3 yr.	58.9%	1.4:1
Steadman & Cocozza (1978)	257	M	IST Defendants	Assaultive in Hospital	3 yr.	54.1%	1.3:1
				Arrest or Rehospital.	3 yr.	36.6%	23.0:1
Levinson & Ramsey (1979)	53	M&F	Community Residents	Arrests for Behavior of a Violent Nature	1 yr.	62.3%	2.4:1
Thornberry & Jacoby (1979)	438	M	Max. Sec. Forensic Patients	Arrest or Rehospital. for Assault	4 yr.	-	5.9:1
Rofman et al. (1980)	59	M&F	Civilly Committed Patients	Violent Act in Hospital	40 days	66.5%	1.5:1
Steadman & Cocozza (1980)	98	M	Max. Sec. Forensic Patients	Arrest or Rehospital. Assaultive Behavior	3.5 yr.	-	5.7:1
Mullen & Reinehr (1982)	165	M	Max. Sec. Forensic Patients	Arrest for Violent Offense	4 yr.	62.4%	7.7:1
Sepejak et al. (1983)	596	M&F	Pretrial Detainees	Arrest or Rehospital.	2 yr.	59.6%	0.8:1
Clanon & Jew (1985)	573	M	Correct. Releasees	Arrest for Violent Offense	2 yr.	61.1%	6.9:1

[1]Sample: N = sample size; Sex = male (M) or female (F); Des = description of sample group.

[2]Criterion Behavior: definition of dangerous behavior utilized.

[3]Follow-Up: period of time over which criterion behavior measured.

[4]False Positive Ratio: ratio of false positives to true positives.

The results of more recently conducted studies corroborate further the earlier observations of investigators that clinical predictions of dangerous behavior typically result in two to eight times as many false positive determinations as true positive ones (see Table 5.1). From Steadman and Cocozza's (1978) research on IST defendants to Clanon and Jew's (1985) survey of inmates released from the Stress Assessment Unit at Vacaville, support for the validity of clinical predictions of dangerous behavior has been scant and the false positive rate has been shown to range between 54 and 99 percent. Furthermore, studies producing positive results have, in many cases, been compromised by defective designs. Take, for instance, Rofman et al.'s (1980) investigation of hospital-based violence in civilly committed patients. Although Rofman and his associates observed a relatively low rate of false positive predictions, the study is limited by the fact that dangerous-rated patients spent 50 percent more time in the hospital than patients rated nondangerous.

If we tally up the results of studies on the clinical prediction of violent behavior (Table 5.1), we see that in most cases this behavioral outcome is overpredicted by clinicians addressing themselves to the dangerousness question (Monahan, 1981). Though a simple solution to this problem is unlikely, increased sensitivity to the low population base rate of dangerous behavior and the potential utility of statistical models of prognostication (the subject of our next section) may aid efforts to make the clinical prognostication of violent behavior more accurate.

Actuarial Prediction of Dangerous Behavior

In 1972, the same year Kozol et al. (1972) published the first large-scale study on clinical prognostications of dangerous behavior, Wenk, Robison, and Smith reported results of an actuarial study examining statistical predictors of future dangerousness. Using data collected by the California Department of Corrections, Wenk et al. (1972) identified a small group of offenders (3% of the entire population) who exhibited a significantly higher rate of violent recidivism (14%) than the remaining subjects (5%). A 15-month follow-up identified a past history of violence as the single best predictor of future violence, although there were 19 false positive classifications for every true positive prediction. In a similar vein, a multivariate equation comprising several of the more effective predictors was able to achieve reasonably accurate results, but at the cost of eight false positive determinations for every true positive determination.

Studying a group of psychiatric inpatients admitted to four Missouri state mental health centers, Hedlund et al. (1973) constructed a stepwise discriminant analysis designed to predict dangerousness defined three ways: attempts to harm others, actual harm to others, and a combined measure. The level of accuracy obtained by these measures was impressive (90%, 94%, and 90%, respectively), although the equations were never cross-validated nor were they able to improve upon the base-rate prediction that all individuals would be nonviolent. Heller and Ehrlich (1984) also examined the capacity of a large number of variables to identify the more violent members of a group of 1,525 defendants undergoing court-ordered evaluations. They observed significant violent-nonviolent differences on 30 variables, although half of these findings may have surfaced simply by chance, since the authors failed to correct for the increased rate of experimentwise error that occurs when multiple comparisons are made.

Analyzing data on 98 of the Baxstrom patients released to the community,

Cocozza and Steadman (1974) constructed the Legal Dangerousness Scale (LDS), a measure comprising four items—presence of a juvenile record, number of previous arrests, violent crime convictions, and severity of the Baxstrom offense—and a total score that ranges between 0 and 15. Cocozza and Steadman discovered that a prediction equation composed of age (under 50 years old) and LDS score (equal to or greater than 5) correctly identified 11 of 14 (78.6%) patients who, during a three and one-half-year period of follow-up, were either arrested or re-hospitalized for a violent act, and misclassified 25 of 84 (29.8%) patients as dangerous who remained violence free during the follow-up period. In the end, the age-LDS composite achieved an overall hit rate of 71.4 percent and a false positive–true positive ratio of 2.3:1. Koppin (1977) was able to successfully cross-validate the LDS in a group of Colorado state hospital patients, although the LDS was unable to improve upon the population base rate of 70 percent nondangerous.

The results of research on actuarial and statistical models of prediction indicate that they frequently produce as many false positives as do clinicians. Furthermore, multivariate statistical models of prediction must be cross-validated since the multiple regression analyses upon which they are based are known to capitalize on chance fluctuations in the data. Therefore, the amount of variance explained by a multivariate equation normally shrinks upon cross-validation. Unfortunately, most statistical models of dangerousness prediction have yet to be adequately cross-validated, thereby making it difficult to meaningfully compare the results of actuarial and clinical models of prognostication.

Clinical and Statistical (Actuarial) Prediction

Research in the field of clinical psychology is reasonably consistent in showing that actuarial models of prediction are superior to clinical ones (Meehl, 1954; Sawyer, 1966; Walters, White, and Greene, 1988). The outcome of research pitting clinical against actuarial models of dangerousness prediction has reached this same general conclusion (Gottfredson & Gottfredson, 1988). Steadman and Cocozza (1978) contrasted a statistical equation composed of seven variables with the clinical judgments of mental health professionals in an effort to identify dangerous behavior in 257 defendants undergoing IST evaluations. Against a criterion of hospital-based assaultive behavior, the statistical equation achieved an overall hit rate of 63 percent (false positive ratio of 0.9:1) as compared to 46 percent (false positive ratio of 1:1) for the clinicians. With a shift in criterion to arrest for violent crimes in the community, the gap between the actuarial and clinical models grew even wider. Employing arrest as the criterion measure of dangerous behavior, the statistical equation attained 75 percent accuracy with a false positive ratio of 2.2:1. In contrast, clinical judges were only able to accurately identify 43 percent of the cases while visiting a false positive ratio of 6.4:1 on their outcomes. Comparing the LDS and clinical judgment, both Thornberry and Jacoby (1979) and Steadman and Cocozza (1978) detected only a small reduction in the rate of false positive determinations when moving from clinical judgment to the LDS.

Much of the problem with research on clinical and actuarial models of prediction is that we have traditionally asked the wrong questions. Instead of limiting ourselves to an examination of the relative merits of clinical and statistical models of prediction, criminal science might be better served by directing its investigative efforts at identifying ways in which these two approaches might be productively combined. In one of the few studies to address itself to this issue, Hoffman et al. (1974) presented parole examiners with statistical risk estimates derived from actuarial tables and discerned a correlation of .74 between actuarial and clinical predictions when statistical tables were provided and .53 when they were not. There were also indications that less favorable statistical risk estimates were more likely to influence the judgments of parole board members than more favorable statistical risk estimates. Further research is required in order to determine whether actuarial and clinical models of prognostication can be efficiently combined to produce outcomes superior to those obtained with either model separately.

Comment

The results of research on the prediction of dangerous behavior divulge the presence of a high rate of false positive determinations. This is due largely to the fact that dangerous behavior, with its low population base rate, is overpredicted by both clinicians and statistical formulae. With concerns about liability mounting, it is easy to understand why clinicians frequently overpredict dangerousness (Morris & Miller, 1987). However, we must find ways to protect society from those who would be violent without unduly restricting the freedom of those who would not. This delicate balance might possibly be struck by considering the following changes in the way dangerousness predictions are construed. First, prognosticators need to offer their predictions ever mindful of the low base-rate nature of dangerous behavior. Second, prognosticators must avoid relying exclusively on traits and personality characteristics in making dangerousness predictions and recognize that situational and environmental factors are at least as important as person variables. Third, it is essential that we abandon the antiquated either-or thinking of clinical versus statistical prediction, and search for points of commonality, integration, and synthesis.

INSTITUTIONAL ADJUSTMENT

Definitional Issues

Defining precisely what is meant by institutional adjustment is the first hurdle confronting researchers wishing to enter into the scientific study of the predictability of confinee behavior. Does the number of disciplinary infractions recorded over a period of several months adequately capture the essence of institutional adjustment? Would work supervisor ratings, sick call usage, or a composite measure do a more satisfactory job? These and other questions have yet to receive the attention they deserve. What is known, however, is that these measures do not all assess institutional adjustment in the same way. Carbonell, Megargee, and Moorhead (1984) cross-tabulated six measures commonly employed in research on institutional adjustment (rules infractions, time spent in segregation, sick call usage, domicile officer ratings, work supervisor ratings, evaluations by educational staff) in a large-scale study of youthful federal offenders, and witnessed inter-correlations in the neighborhood of .04 to .45 (mean $r = .17$). At this point there is no universal definition of institutional adjustment, although disciplinary reports (Wolf, Freinek, & Shaffer, 1966), sick call usage (Twaddle, 1976), and officer or work supervisor ratings (Carbonell et al., 1984) are the measures most commonly encountered in research on institutional adjustment.

Besides appreciating the definitional parameters of institutional adjustment, we must consider that the data source may also influence our findings. Officially recorded institutional documents, inmate self-report, and observations by staff are among the more popular sources of information upon which estimates of institutional adjustment are based, and like the various definitions of institutional adjustment, they frequently yield divergent outcomes. Accordingly, Hewitt, Poole, and Regoli (1984) compared the type and number of infractions reported by correctional officers, acknowledged by inmates, and recorded in official files, and discovered that guards and inmates acknowledged substantially more incidents than were recorded in official disciplinary reports. Also, the guards reported a larger volume of property destruction, fighting, theft, and weapon possession infractions relative to inmates, who themselves acknowledged a higher rate of sex-code violations.

We have thus far considered only the criterion side of the predictor-outcome equation. There are, however, features of the predictor that should also be contemplated. Paralleling prediction research on dangerousness, objective or statistical methods are generally superior to subjective or clinical models in forecasting institutional adjustment. In a representative study, Holland and Holt (1980) found decision makers' predictions to be substantially less effective than objective measures in accounting for the eventual institutional adjustment of 293 men housed in a minimum security state prison facility in California. Cooper and Werner (1990) also observed minimal concordance between individual judges' predictions of institutional violence and actual episodes of violent behavior occurring during the first six months of incarceration, but did note a reasonably strong association between composite predictions of violence and subsequent violent behavior.

There are no easy answers or hard and fast rules when it comes to measuring institutional adjustment. In fact, Twaddle (1976) asserts that optimal measures of institutional malfeasance may vary depending upon how long the inmate has been confined. On the basis of data collected in a large prison hospital, Twaddle and Geile (1976) postulated that sick call usage may provide an accurate estimate of institutional adjustment during the first year of incarceration, but that disciplinary reports eclipse sick call usage as the optimal measure of institutional adjustment after the first year. Likewise, Wright (1988) comments that where scores on the Salient Factor Scale were more strongly associated with objective measures of institutional adjustment (infractions, sick call usage) than either Toch's Prison Preference Inventory (PPI) or Megargee's MMPI classification system in a study of incarcerated offenders, the Toch and Megargee systems were superior to the Salient Factor Score in forecasting self-reported adjustment difficulties. It would appear, then, that institutional adjustment is a multidimensional phenomenon that is properly assessed using disparate measures generated by several different sources.

Person-Variable Predictors of Institutional Adjustment

Age. Chronological age is probably the strongest single correlate of institutional adjustment. From the very first studies (Wolfgang, 1961) to investigations conducted just recently (Toch, Adams, & Greene, 1987), increased age has been shown to augur good institutional adjustment. This has been observed in studies where the criterion of institutional adjustment has been the number of disciplinary reports received (Flanagan, 1983; Petersilia & Honig, 1980; Porporino & Zamble, 1984), inmate-on-inmate assaults (Ekland-Olson, Barrick, & Cohen, 1983), inmate-on-staff assaults (Wright & Smith, 1985), sick call usage (Twaddle, 1976), or a composite measure (Moss & Hosford, 1982), and in studies where the data source was derived from objective records (Brown & Spevacek, 1971; Flanagan, 1983), self-report measures (Jensen, 1977; Wright & Smith, 1985), or staff nominations (Myers & Levy, 1978). Age is a powerful predictor of institutional adjustment, even when its range is severely restricted. Consequently, the disciplinary infraction rate of young offenders entering the Texas Department of Corrections for crimes occurring prior to their seventeenth birthday was substantially higher than that observed in youthful offenders serving time for crimes committed between the ages of 17 and 21 (McShane & Williams, 1989).

It would seem that no matter how we approach the age issue, it is one of the more reliable predictors of institutional adjustment. Less is understood, however, about the theory behind the relationship. Several criminologists have suggested that age promotes a heightened sense of caution or fear (Ellis, 1984), while others reason that older inmates, by virtue of a growing sense of social investment, believe they have more to lose by involving themselves in institutional infractions than younger offenders (Greenberg, 1985). Conversely, MacKenzie (1987) observed something other than a direct linear drop in the relationship between age and the disciplinary infraction rate of adult men sampled from correctional institutions in Connecticut, Minnesota, and Illinois. She noted that misconduct incidents peaked during the teenage years, dropped, and then leveled off after age 30, while interpersonal conflict climaxed during a subject's early

20s and then declined from here. McKenzie interprets her findings as evidence of an age-mediated attitudinal shift in incarcerated offenders; that is, older inmates learn to deal with interpersonal conflict in ways that do not bring punishment from the administration. Whatever the explanation, age is a strong correlate of many important criminal science criteria, be it criminal involvement, crime seriousness, or institutional adjustment.

Race. It has been observed that nonwhite inmates typically accumulate more disciplinary reports than white subjects (Flanagan, 1983; Myers & Levy, 1978) and demonstrate other signs of negative institutional adjustment, to include increased sick call usage (Twaddle, 1976). This effect may vary as a function of both geographic location and data source. Petersilia and Honig (1980), for instance, noticed an amplified rate of disciplinary infraction for black inmates in Texas and white inmates in California, but failed to identify a racial effect for subjects sampled from Michigan prisons. Hewitt et al. (1984) determined that while twice as many blacks as whites received incident reports for rules violations, white inmates acknowledged a slightly higher rate of infraction than black inmates. If we can assume an equivalent degree of candor on the part of black and white inmates, Hewitt et al.'s findings suggest that blacks and whites contribute proportionally to violations of institutional rules, but that the negative actions of black inmates are more frequently written up by correctional staff.

Gender. Based on the knowledge that crime is much more common in males than females, a logical assumption would be that females are less apt to engage in institutional misconduct. Unfortunately, there is a paucity of data on this issue since the vast majority of studies on prison-based adjustment have been conducted on all-male prison populations. In one of the few studies to address the issue of male-female differences in disciplinary adjustment directly, Hewitt et al. (1984) failed to identify any significant variations between male and female inmates in terms of the number of incident reports incurred or the rate of self-reported institutional intractability.

Marital Status. Studies scrutinizing the marital status of incarcerated offenders report that incorrigible inmates are more often single and corrigible prisoners more frequently married (Flanagan, 1983; Myers & Levy, 1978). There is a good possibility, however, that marital status owes a portion of its prognostic power to its common association with chronological age; that is, younger offenders are more frequently single than older ones. This interpretation of the observed relationship between marital status and institutional adjustment receives confirmatory support in the outcome of at least one stepwise discriminant analysis (Flanagan, 1983).

Criminal History. As was mentioned in the introductory section of this chapter and reiterated in our discussion on dangerousness, the best predictor of future behavior is past behavior. This is also true, albeit to a somewhat lesser degree, of institutional disciplinary problems (Myers & Levy, 1978). Where Myers and Levy advise that a greater number of prior police contacts and an early entrance into a criminal lifestyle were associated with poorer institutional adjustment, several other studies suggest that disciplinary infractions are more common in prisoners possessing less criminal and prison experience (Brown & Spevacek, 1971; Toch et al., 1987). This outcome could be construed as lending support to the hypothesis that unlike experienced convicts, novice inmates have a great deal to learn about managing jail-house conflict.

Mental Illness. Although the Baxtrom experience suggests that many emotionally disturbed prisoners can be managed effectively in a civil hospital setting, these persons may experience significant problems adjusting to the harsher penal environment. Adams (1983), for one, has determined that inmates with prior histories of psychiatric hospitalization tend to incur a proportionally larger number of prison disciplinary write-ups while engaging in more seriously assaultive behavior than nondisturbed inmates (although the latter finding seems inconsistent with research that shows mental illness to be inadequate for the purposes of predicting dangerousness). Adams (1986) witnessed a positive relationship between mental illness and disciplinary intractability even after statistically controlling for age, criminal history, and incarceration experience. Walters and his associates (Walters et al., 1988; Walters, Scrapansky, & Marrlow, 1986) have determined that emotionally disturbed offenders classified by means of a structured diagnostic interview encountered subsequent problems with psychiatric hospitalization, disciplinary reports, and poor work or domicile evaluations to a significantly greater degree than nondisturbed inmates.

By way of explaining the inverse association between mental illness and institutional adjustment some criminal scientists have implicated the negative effect of labeling (Toch & Adams, 1986), while others have pointed to a lack of coping skill on the part of emotionally disturbed offenders (Walters et al., 1988). Little can be deduced at this point without taking into account how mental health status fits within a wider intercorrelational network of variables. Toch et al. (1987) in one study observed an interaction between mental illness and race in their effect on the disciplinary adjustment of 9,103 male inmates released from the New York State penal system between July 1982 and September 1983. In this study, black and Hispanic inmates, who over the course of their incarceration had been hospitalized for psychiatric reasons, recorded a significantly greater number of disciplinary reports than nonpatient black and Hispanic prisoners, while white patients and nonpatients failed to differ on this measure. It is hoped that additional mental health status will be initiated since the institutional adjustment of emotionally disturbed incarcerates will probably never be fully understood without such research.

Personality Measures. Early studies examining the ability of structured personality measures like the MMPI and CPI to forecast institutional incorrigibility produced equivocal results. Though adjustment-related effects may occur on one or two scales (Cowden, Schroeder, & Peterson, 1971; Driscoll, 1952; Sutker & Moan, 1973), personality measures rarely account for more than 30 to 35 percent of the variance in institutional adjustment (Jones, Beidelman, & Fowler, 1981; Snortum, Hannum, & Mills, 1970). Moreover, nearly a third of the early studies failed to uncover a single significant finding (Jaman, 1969; Panton, 1962b). Not only are these outcomes less than impressive but the studies from whence they derive are replete with methodological errors and oversights, from the use of extreme groups (Driscoll, 1952), to the practice of collecting concurrent, rather than future, criterion estimates (Jones et al., 1981), to the failure to cross-validate initial findings (Panton, 1973).

Carbonell et al. (1984) have conducted the most elaborate and methodologically sophisticated analysis of structured personality correlates of institutional adjustment to date. Employing multiple measures of institutional adjustment (disciplinary reports, time spent in segregation, sick call usage, dormitory ratings, work performance ratings, educational evaluation), Carbonell et al. administered the MMPI and CPI to 1,345 young adult male federal prisoners and followed them for a period of several months to several years. Although the MMPI and CPI scales were shown to correspond with various indices of subsequent institutional adjustment, only a handful of correlations exceeded .20 and none was higher than .30. This same group of investigators (Megargee & Carbonell, 1985) discerned that a series of special MMPI scales designed to appraise prison adjustment, escape risk, and recidivism also demonstrated a low to low-moderate degree of concordance with subsequent measures of institutional adjustment and behavior. It would seem that while structured personality measures are capable of generating statistically significant findings, these results are not particularly useful from a clinical or managerial decision-making standpoint.

Situation-Variable Predictors of Institutional Adjustment

Prison Crowding. Between 1980 and 1985, a 52 percent increase in the sentenced prison population took place, thereby forcing 150,000 additional inmates into the nation's already burgeoning correctional monolith (Bureau of Justice Statistics, 1986). Studies addressing the impact of prison crowding on the institutional adjustment of confined prisoners have produced mixed outcomes. Hence, whereas Megargee (1976) observed a link between prison overcrowding and misconduct in a medium-security federal facility, Paulus et al. (1975) witnessed a rise in the rate of institution-based misfeasance which corresponded with an increase in the population density of several state prisons, and Jan (1980) detected the presence of a moderate correlation between crowding and disruptive behavior in four state prisons, other investigators report no such relationship when examining institutional maladjustment and prison crowding in Texas (Ekland-Olson, Barrick, & Cohen, 1983), Connecticut (Harris & Parke, 1980), and Ontario, Canada (Bonta & Nanckivell, 1980). The possibility that age may moderate the prison crowding-institutional adjustment relationship is suggested in the outcome of studies carried out by Nacci, Teitelbaum, and Prather (1977) and Carr (1980). Both investigations, the former conducted in federal correctional institutions and the latter in Michigan state facilities, demonstrated that a crowding-adjustment connection occurred only in facilities inhabited by juveniles.

Gaes and McGuire (1985) set out to test the possibility of an interactive relationship between age and prison crowding in a more precise manner. Surveying data collected in 19 Federal Bureau of Prisons facilities over a 33-month period, they ascertained that the effect of age was less than what had been documented previously and that this effect was overshadowed by the contributions of institutional crowding. In fact, after such variables as crowding level, institutional size, staff-inmate ratio, and criminal history were taken into account, age was implicated in only one of the four categories of assaultive infraction studied. Conversely, crowding correlated directly with three of the four measures (inmate-on-inmate assaults with and without a weapon; inmate-on-staff assaults without a weapon) at a statistically significant level, although all of the correlations were nonlinear. Interestingly, the interaction between crowding and assault in this particular study revealed that institutions inhabited by older offenders were more affected by crowding than institutions housing younger offenders.

Whereas the relative contributions of age and crowding require further study, it would appear that prison crowding has an influence on the adjustment of a significant portion of the prison population. How might this effect be explained? Schmidt and Keating (1979) speculate that prison crowding promotes a sense of loss of personal control over the external environment, a state which Walters (1990) contends is a cardinal cognitive feature of lifestyle patterns of criminal conduct. Dy (1974) theorizes that anxiety and fear drop off as one adapts to the prison environment and that this is why inmates with less prior correctional experience typically incur a greater number of disciplinary write-ups, particularly when the prison census approaches peak capacity. Fear and anxiety would therefore appear to be two of the more likely candidates in explicating the nature of the crowding-adjustment relationship.

Ambient Temperature. Research findings show that crime, violent crime in particular, is associated with higher ambient temperatures (Anderson, 1987; Rotton & Frey, 1985). It would stand to reason, then, that elevated temperatures in institutional cell houses and dormitories might lead to a rising incidence of interpersonal conflict and subsequent disciplinary intractability, a possibility which finds support in the results of studies conducted by the Federal Bureau of Prisons during the early 1970s (J. Prather, Federal Bureau of Prisons, Office of Research, personal communication, March 24, 1990). More recent Bureau of Prisons' data reveal that inmate-on-staff assaults in 1988 and 1989 peaked slightly during the warmer months of the year (July, August) and fell to their lowest levels during the cooler months (January, February). There is also the possibility that ambient temperature and crowding interact in their effect on aggressive outcomes (see Matthews, Paulus, & Baron, 1979).

Institutional Structure and Policy. A common observation is that higher security level institutions have higher rates of disciplinary infraction than lower security institutions (Gaes & McGuire, 1985). There is, then, the prospect of an interaction between institutional characteristics and various person variables. Walters (1991), for instance, examined the connection between a measure of lifestyle criminality (which contains a large number of criminal history items) and disciplinary adjustment in offenders incarcerated in a maximum security federal penitentiary and minimum security federal prison camp. The outcome of this investigation revealed that while there was no relationship between scores on the lifestyle criminality measure and disciplinary adjustment in the maximum security prison, higher scoring inmates in the minimum security camp had accumulated a significantly larger number of disciplinary write-ups than lower scoring camp inmates. Walters interprets this finding as confirming the ameliorative and controlling effects of environmental structure on persons displaying lifestyle patterns of criminal conduct.

Stone-Meierhoefer and Hoffman (1982) from the U.S. Parole Commission surveyed data assessing the influence of various parole conditions and practices on institutional adjustment. Providing inmates with a presumptive parole data during the early stages of incarceration is a practice utilized not only by the federal parole board but by several state parole boards as well. What Stone-Meierhoefer and Hoffman observed was that the frequency and severity of subsequent rules violations were no greater in federal prisoners assigned a presumptive parole date than a control group containing inmates without a presumptive parole date. In fact, presumptive parole subjects tended to incur fewer infractions than control subjects. A great deal more research is required, however, before we can understand the full impact of institutional structure and policy on the institutional adjustment of prison inmates.

Comment

Age, mental health status, and prison crowding appear to display the most consistent and reliable associations with indices of institutional adjustment. Multivariate analyses have also been carried out in an effort to maximize our ability to predict the future adjustment of prison inmates. Even at their best, however, these equations are rarely able to account for more than 35 percent of the variance in institutional adjustment (Myers & Levy, 1978) and most estimates are appreciably lower than this (Carbonell et al., 1984; Flanagan, 1983). The situation is similar to the one involving predictions of dangerous behavior. We have a relatively low base-rate behavior (using official records, 5–25%), which lends itself to overprediction and a higher rate of false positive prognostications (Holland & Holt, 1980). Accordingly, we need to focus on the strongest predictors (age, mental health status, prison crowding), attempt to explain why these are more successful than most other measures in forecasting institutional adjustment problems, work to develop and cross-validate multivariate equations composed of the strongest variables, and tailor our predictions to specific indices of institutional maladjustment—mindful, of course, that most such indices have a low base rate of occurrence.

RECIDIVISM

Definitional Issues

As with dangerousness and institutional adjustment, the manner in which recidivism is defined will have an important bearing on the results obtained. For the purposes of this text *recidivism* is defined as that portion of a previously identified offender population that experiences a given negative future outcome during a specified period of time. We must therefore clearly demarcate the offender population (adult versus juvenile; prison versus probation; federal versus state) to which we would like to generalize our findings, the negative outcome (arrest, conviction, reincarceration) which serves as our criterion measure, and the period of time accommodated by our follow-up (for example, 6 months, 1 year, 10 years). The results of several of the larger recidivism studies carried out over the past two decades are summarized in Table 5.2.

As Table 5.2 illustrates, recidivism is normally measured in one of three ways: arrest, conviction, or commitment. While Klein and Caggiano (1986) report minimal levels of variation in their findings when going from one criterion definition to another, a more frequent observation has been that outcomes fluctuate as the definition of recidivism changes (Hoffman & Stone-Meierhoefer, 1980). Griswold (1978) compared three data sources—self report, state department of corrections files, FBI records—and recorded estimates that varied by data source, the self-report measure yielding the highest estimates by a wide margin. Other studies also suggest that self-reported estimates of recidivism are characteristically higher than those calculated on the basis of official records (see Table 5.2, Guze et al. (1970) for a self-report estimate of the recidivism rate). This is one reason why Monahan (1978) recommends that investigators consider multiple measures of re-offending in their research on recidivism and advises against the use of a unidimensional approach to the recidivism question.

Follow-up periods have ranged anywhere from six months (Heilbrun, Knopf, & Bruner, 1976) to 18 years (Kitchener, Schmidt, & Glaser, 1977). Within the same study the period of follow-up should remain uniform across subjects, a procedure which has not always been adhered to by researchers investigating recidivism rates in offender populations. Post-release time frames in three of the studies reviewed in Table 5.2 (Cloninger & Guze, 1973; Grunfeld & Noreik, 1986; Guze et al., 1970) were averaged so that in one study (Grunfeld & Noreik) follow-up varied by as much as five years between subjects. Obviously, the recidivism rate will grow as the follow-up period is lengthened. There has been speculation, however, that this increase is not uniform across time and that the highest rate of re-offending occurs one to two years post-release. This is an issue to which we now turn our attention.

Table 5.2
Recidivism of Released Offender Populations

Study	N	Sample Sex	Des	Follow-up Period	ARR	Outcome CON	COM
Guze et al. (1970)	176	M	State Releasees	8-9 yr	85.0%	49.0%	41.0%
Cloninger & Guze (1973)	66	F	State Parolees	29 mo	33.0%	21.0%	-
Kitchener et al. (1977)	903	M	Federal Releasees	1 yr	-	15.0%	-
				3 yr	-	42.0%	-
				5 yr	-	51.0%	-
				10 yr	-	59.0%	-
				18 yr	-	63.0%	-
Hoffman & Stone-Meierhoefer (1980)	1806	M&F	Federal Releasees	1 yr	29.0%	15.4%	12.6%
				2 yr	43.7%	25.7%	21.0%
				3 yr	51.4%	32.2%	26.4%
				4 yr	54.9%	36.4%	30.3%
				5 yr	57.4%	39.4%	32.7%
				6 yr	60.4%	41.7%	34.3%
Holland (1983)	343	M	State Releasees	32 mo	57.0%	52.0%	37.0%
Petersilia et al. (1985)	1672	M	State Probationers	40 mo	65.0%	51.0%	34.0%
Romero & Williams (1985)	231	M	Sex Off. Probationers	10 yr	11.3%	-	-
Grunfeld & Noreik (1986)	541	M	Scandinavian Sex Off.	12 yr	12.8%	-	-
Beck & Shipley (1987)	3995	M&F	Youthful State Parolees	1 yr	32.0%	-	19.0%
				6 yr	69.0%	53.0%	49.0%
Beck & Shipley (1989)	108,580	M&F	State Releasees	3 yr	62.5%	46.8%	41.4%

[1]Sample: *N* = number of subjects; *Sex* = male (M) or female (F); *Des* = description of sample: state or federal, parole or all forms of release.

[2]Outcome: *ARR* = arrests; *CON* = convictions; *COM* = commitments.

Time Patterns in Recidivism

Early research on recidivism noted the presence of a critical period for re-offending that extended from six months to a year after release (President's Commission on Law Enforcement and Administration of Justice, 1967). Unfortunately, the validity and generalizability of these early findings were limited by a plethora of methodological problems. Take, for instance, an investigation carried out by Bennett and Ziegler (1975). After examining recidivism patterns in a large sample of parolees, Bennett and Ziegler unveiled evidence of a sharp decline in the return rate after the first year. However, because Bennett and

Ziegler limited their investigation to parolees, it is difficult to generalize these findings to all released offenders, since parolees are characteristically less likely to re-offend than persons released on expiration of sentence (Flanagan, 1982). There is also evidence that the definition we decide on may greatly influence our results, since arrest data show a sharper temporal decline than conviction data (Hoffman, Stone-Meierhoefer, & Beck, 1978).

In an early study examining the proposed link between time and the severity of recidivism, Mannheim and Wilkins (1955) discovered that English youth re-offending within four months to a year of their release from a juvenile facility were more likely to have engaged in a violent criminal act, as measured by the severity of the sanctions received, than youth re-offending a year or more after release. The primary flaw in this study concerns the assumption that sanction severity plainly reflects crime severity. This assumption may be unfounded, however, since sanction severity in this study may represent nothing more than the court's frustration with persons committing a new criminal offense shortly after their release from confinement. Hoffman and Stone-Meierhoefer (1979) probed the relationship between re-offending and crime severity in a large group of federal releasees and discovered that offenses committed during the first year of freedom were no more serious or violent than offenses committed later in the post-release period.

Several studies inspecting temporal recidivism patterns and trends can be faulted for failing to take into account the decreasing number of persons "at risk" for re-arrest or re-conviction over time. Accordingly, when studying the influence of time on the failure rate of released felons it is essential that the recidivism rate be calculated on the basis of the number of persons "at risk" during the period in question (first year, second year, and so on), rather than at the beginning of the study (Berechochea, Himelson, & Miller, 1972). Even the authors of a recent Bureau of Justice Statistics study showing re-arrest rates of 25 percent after six months and 39 percent after one year in released state prisoners (Beck & Shipley, 1989) apparently overlooked the necessity of recalibrating their instrument to account for the drop in "at risk" persons over time. The results of studies correcting for changes in the number of "at risk" offenders show that recidivism is highest during the first two years of follow-up (Forst et al., 1983; Hoffman & Stone-Meierhoefer, 1979; Kitchener et al., 1977).

A final consideration in research on time patterns in recidivism is that these patterns vary as a function of certain characteristics of the individual. The most commonly studied characteristic in this regard is criminal history. Hoffman and Stone-Meierhoefer (1979) discerned that the Salient Factor Score (SFS) loses its ability to discriminate between successful and unsuccessful releasees after the third year. Likewise, Flanagan (1982) ascertained that time and criminal history variables exerted an interacting effect on the recidivism noted in a group of offenders paroled from state prison. Hence, the failure rate of a priori "low risk" parolees rose steadily, peaked at 24 months, and then gradually fell off after this. "Medium risk" parolees, on the other hand, demonstrated a failure rate that achieved its zenith at 21 to 23 months and evidenced a graduated decline over the next several years. Parolees in the "high risk" category demonstrated a failure rate that rose sharply, peaked at 12 months, and then plunged dramatically from here.

Person-Variable Predictors of Recidivism

Age. Research suggests that age is as strongly prognostic of recidivism as it is of dangerousness and institutional adjustment. Gottfredson (1967) reviewed the early prediction research on parole failure and age, and concluded that parole violations decline proportionally with age. Research studies conducted since the Gottfredson review have also confirmed the presence of an inverse relationship between age and recidivism (Beck & Shipley, 1989; Forst et al., 1983; Gottfredson, Mitchell-Herzfeld, & Flanagan, 1982; Grunfeld & Noreik, 1986; Romero & Williams, 1985; Roundtree, Edwards, & Parker, 1984; Schmidt & Witte, 1980). In combining age with estimates of criminal history, Beck and Shipley (1989) discovered that 94 percent of the offenders in a large sample of state prison releasees between the ages of 18 and 24 with 11 or more prior arrests were re-apprehended within three years as compared to a base rate of 62.5 percent for the entire sample.

A two-year follow-up of 6,287 released federal prisoners revealed a robust inverse relationship between age at time of release and subsequent commitments of at least 60 days or return to prison as a parole violator (Hoffman & Beck, 1984). These authors asseverate further that this relationship retained its significance even after adjustments were made for prior criminal history as measured by the Salient Factor Score. Hoffman and Beck conclude that these findings afford empirical support to the notion, often expressed in clinical lore, that offenders characteristically "burn out" with age. Such burn-out would appear to have physical, as well as psychological, concomitants (Walters, 1990), both of which warrant further investigation.

Race. The relationship between race and recidivism is less consistent than that observed between age and recidivism. While several large-scale studies have recorded increased rates of re-offending among black (Beck & Shipley, 1987, 1989) and Hispanic (Beck & Shipley, 1989) prison releasees, several other studies have failed to uncover support for the presence of a link between race and recidivism (for example, Roundtree, Edwards, & Parker, 1984). Moreover, Kitchener et al. (1977) comment that while recidivism was slightly more common in nonwhites than whites during an 18-year period of follow-up (71% vs. 60%), a smaller percentage of the nonwhite group failed during the first several years than was the case with subjects in the white group. This led Kitchener et al. to speculate that post-release assistance may be more beneficial to minority, as opposed to white, subjects. Further support for this contention can be ascertained from the results of a subsequent study directed by Beck (1981), in which it was determined that release through a community treatment center reduced the long-term recidivism of nonwhite offenders, but failed to affect the failure rate of white offenders.

Gender. Just as males account for more crime than females, they are also responsible for a larger share of the re-offending that occurs following release. Probing the post-release adjustment of a group of juvenile offenders, Sawyer (1975) noted that males were more likely to recidivate than females. Investigators from the Bureau of Justice Statistics report similar outcomes in 17- to 22-year-old offenders released on parole (Beck & Shipley, 1987) and adults released from 11 state correctional systems (Beck & Shipley, 1989). Roundtree et al. (1984), on the other hand, failed to uncover the presence of a gender-recidivism connection in a group of 100 adult probationers.

Marital Status. Recidivism has also been found to be more prominent in single persons (Cloninger & Guze, 1973; Gottfredson et al., 1982; Schmidt & Witte, 1980). The problem with marital status correlates of recidivism is that offenders who have never before been married are often younger than felons who are either married, divorced, or widowed. This makes it difficult to tease out the individual contributions of age and marital status as each relates to patterns of re-offending.

Criminal History. As we discovered in our review of research on the dangerousness issue, the best predictor of future behavior is past behavior. This also appears to hold true with recidivism. An increased rate of release failure has been observed in parolees possessing an above-average number of prior arrests, convictions, and incarcerations (Roundtree et al., 1984; Schmidt & Witte, 1980). Beck and Shipley (1987) report that 93 percent of the young adults in a large sample of state prison releasees with six or more prior arrests re-offended, compared to 59 percent of those with no previous history of arrest. The age at first arrest also appears to be an important correlate of recidivism. Kitchener et al. (1977) witnessed a discrepancy of nearly 60 percent between felons whose initial arrest took place prior to age 14 (78% recidivism) and felons who were 35 years of age or older at the time of their inaugural police contact (19% recidivism) and Beck and Shipley (1987) observed a re-arrest rate of 79 percent in persons arrested prior to age 17 compared to 51 percent for persons whose first arrest occurred after age 19.

Criminal history is prominent in the career criminal and lifestyle criminal conceptualizations of Greenwood (1982) and Walters (1990), respectively. Based on findings that show a large portion of serious criminality being committed by a relatively small group of offenders (Chaiken & Chaiken, 1982; Hamparian, et al., 1978; Wolfgang, Figlio, & Sellin, 1972), Greenwood set out to develop a measure that could identify career criminals for reasons of selective incapacitation. The end result was a scale comprising seven items: prior convictions for the same offense; incarcerated for more than half of the preceding two years; conviction prior to age 16; commitment to a state juvenile authority; use of narcotic drugs as a juvenile; narcotic drug use two years prior to present commitment; unemployment 50 percent of the time for two years preceding the present commitment.

Whereas Greenwood (1982) asserts that his instrument is effective in identifying career criminals, von Hirsch and Gottfredson (1984) argue that this instrument is beset with manifold problems, most notably a high false positive rate. Decker and Salert (1986), on the other hand, report that the Greenwood scale produces a relatively high rate of both false positive and false negative determinations. Though the lifestyle approach to understanding criminal involvement has yet to receive wide empirical attention, the results of one study indicate that a measure of lifestyle criminality was able to correctly identify a moderately high percentage of federal offenders who eventually violated the conditions of their parole or probation, and did so at a level which exceeded such traditional measures as age, education, and marital status (Walters, Revella, & Baltrusaitis, 1990).

Personality and Psychodiagnostic Measures. For some reason few studies have been initiated on the personality test correlates of recidivism. Gough, Wenk, and Rozynko (1965) note that higher scores on the Social Presence scale of the CPI and lower scores on the Socialization and Self-Control scales were associated with poorer parole outcomes, but add that the CPI was much less effective than a simple measure of criminal background in identifying those parolees who eventually violated the conditions of their release. Hall (1988) states that MMPI Scales 1 (*Hs*), 2 (*D*), 4 (*Pd*), and 5 (*Mf*) were prognostic of sexual and nonsexual forms of re-offending, although the effect was relatively weak. Gendreau and associates also found social history variables to be superior to the MMPI in forecasting future release failures, but add that when the MMPI and social variables were combined, results surpassed that which could be attained using the social history variables alone (Gendreau, Madden, & Leipciger, 1980). There is some evidence that releasees with psychopathic or sociopathic diagnoses are more apt to re-offend than persons receiving non–character-disorder diagnoses (Cloninger & Guze, 1973; Guze et al., 1970).

Intelligence. The relationship between intellectual level and recidivism is ambiguous and uncertain. Therefore, while most studies spotlight an inverse relationship between intelligence test scores and recidivism (Ganzer & Sarason, 1973; West & Farrington, 1973; Wolfgang et al., 1972), one investigation unveiled a positive correlation (Hartman, 1940) and another no association at all (Merrill, 1947) between IQ and recidivism. At this time the most we can say is that a mild inverse relationship may exist between intellectual ability and re-offending, although it is probably not strong enough to serve as the basis for decisions about individual offenders.

Situation-Variable Predictors of Recidivism

Family Background. Recidivists are more likely to come from broken homes than first-time offenders (Monahan, 1957) and to have had fathers who themselves were diagnosed sociopathic (Cloninger & Guze, 1973). Other potentially fruitful areas of inquiry include family atmosphere, parental abuse, and sibling relationships, although these remain largely unexplored at this point.

School and Work. Dropping out of high school prior to graduation has been shown to correlate reliably with recidivism (Beck & Shipley, 1987, 1989; Roundtree et al., 1984; Schmidt & Witte, 1980). However, just as the marital status–recidivism relationship may arise from age differentials across marital status categories, so may the education-recidivism link owe its existence to the intervening effect of the criminal history variable. This is because offenders with extensive histories of prior criminal involvement typically drop out of school more frequently than offenders with less prodigious criminal records (Walters, 1990). For this reason, failure to complete high school may be nothing more than a symptom of an evolving criminal lifestyle, the latter of which is appreciably more prognostic of re-offending in previously convicted persons. The same could be said of the moderately strong association between employment history and recidivism (Kitchener et al., 1977; Myers, 1983) since habitual criminals have been shown to exhibit poorer work habits than noncriminals and persons who engage in crime on a more sporadic basis (Walters, 1990).

Institutional Atmosphere. As part of the Camp, Ranches, and Schools Study conducted by the California Youth Authority, it was determined that certain features of juvenile probation camps were more conducive to reductions in recidivism than others. More "successful" camps were constructed along the lines of single living units, provided residents with greater opportunities for work and educational activities, and permitted youth to be present at team meetings in which their cases were being reviewed. Youth enrolled in camps that had all or most of these features experienced a 24-month recidivism rate of 54 percent compared to the 92 percent rate recorded by juveniles matriculated through camps possessing few or none of these characteristics (Palmer & Wedge, 1989).

Substance Abuse. Though the Greenwood (1982) scale, Lifestyle Criminality Screening Form (Walters, White, & Denney, in press), Salient Factor Score (Hoffman & Beck, 1974), and Wisconsin Risk Screening Instrument (Baird, 1981) were developed for different reasons and normed on divergent populations, they all consider past drug abuse to be prognostic of poor outcome. Recent studies addressing the issue of substance abuse and release failure concur that past drug misuse diminishes one's chances for post-release success (Beck & Shipley, 1989; Forst et al., 1983; Petersilia et al., 1985). Though the drug-recidivism nexus, like those linking school and employment history with recidivism, may be influenced by the common association noted between substance abuse and high-rate criminality, it is also possible that drug usage exerts a more direct effect on re-offense rates (individuals who have abused drugs in the past will tend to do so in the future, and this will make it more difficult for them to maintain regular employment while at the same time encouraging their involvement in future criminal activity).

Instruments Designed to Predict Recidivism

Salient Factor Score. The United States Parole Commission established the Salient Factor Score (SFS) in an effort to identify variables that might predict recidivism and separate good-risk from poor-risk parolees (Hoffman & Beck, 1974). Originally constructed as a seven-item scale, the SFS was modified in 1981 and inquires into an offender's prior criminal convictions, prior commitments, age at time of present offense, time between last commitment and current offense, parole/probation/escape status at time of current offense, and past heroin dependency. This measure has been successfully cross-validated in several groups of federal inmates released from prison on parole, mandatory release, and expiration of sentence (Hoffman & Beck, 1980, 1985; Hoffman, Stone-Meierhoefer, & Beck, 1978). Though research addressing the utility of this measure in state prison samples is lacking, Hoffman (1982) found the SFS effective in forecasting how a group of female prisoners fared following their release from custody.

The SFS yields four primary categories of predicted release outcome—very good (8–10), good (6–7), fair (4–5), and poor (0–3)—and research conducted by Hoffman and colleagues suggests that recidivism rates vary accordingly—9 to 12 percent in the very good-risk category, 18 to 25 percent in the good-risk category, 29 to 39 percent in the fair-risk category, and 40 to 49 percent in the poor-risk category (Hoffman, 1983; Hoffman & Beck, 1985). Hoffman writes further that the SFS 81 is not only more reliable, valid, and stable than its predecessor (SFS 76), but is also more congruent with what von Hirsch and Hanrahan (1979) refer to as the "modified just desert" model of criminal sanctioning, for just as the "modified just desert" conceptualization emphasizes the extent and recency of an offender's criminal behavior, so does the SFS 81.

Wisconsin Risk Screening Instrument. Whereas the SFS was designed for use with federal prisoners, many states have adopted their own risk assessment procedures. The Wisconsin Risk Screening Instrument (WRSI) is possibly the most widely researched of these procedures. Analyzing the outcome of 2,200 Wisconsin inmates released on parole in 1971, Baird (1981) conducted a multiple-regression analysis of 350 different variables. Splitting this sample in half, Baird derived a scale comprising eight weighted variables (age, prior criminal behavior, prior correctional placements, drug abuse, alcohol abuse, parental control, school behavior, peer relationships) on one-half of the sample and then successfully cross-validated the scale on the other half. Scores on the WRSI range from 0 to 35 (higher scores being prognostic of poorer outcomes) and are organized in a ranking scheme that can be used to determine a youthful offender's risk for violating the conditions of his or her parole (Clear & Gallagher, 1983).

Though the WRSI has been found useful for the purposes of parole decision making in Wisconsin (Baird, 1985), research has shown this instrument to be much less effective in predicting recidivism in youthful offenders in Arizona (Ashford & LeCroy, 1988) and New York (Wright, Clear, & Dickson, 1984). It is noteworthy that the only WRSI variable capable of distinguishing between re-offending and nonrecidivistic juveniles in the Arizona study was age (Ashford & LeCroy, 1988). It would be interesting to test whether the WRSI's prognostic value rests largely with its use of age as one of its primary variables or whether it possesses additional redeeming qualities.

Clinical and Statistical Models of Prediction

In studies comparing clinical and statistical or actuarial approaches to re-offense prognostication, statistical models have traditionally come out ahead (Hall, 1988; Wormith & Goldstone, 1984). A group of researchers at the California Institution for Men in Chino, however, advise that they observed differential outcomes as a function of the definition of recidivism employed (Holland et al., 1983). Thus, while statistical procedures outperformed clinical measures in forecasting general recidivism, clinical decision makers were more effective in predicting violent recidivism leading to arrest. Mirroring research findings on clinical and statistical models of dangerousness prediction, actuarial models are normally superior to clinical ones in auguring recidivism, although the statistical models are themselves only modestly prognostic of this outcome (Gottfredson & Gottfredson, 1980), while being subject to significant levels of shrinkage upon cross-validation (Van Alstyne & Gottfredson, 1978).

Comment

In this review of the literature on recidivism we see that similar to research findings on dangerousness, age and criminal history are the best predictors of future offending. Unlike the dangerousness criterion, however, recidivism has a much higher base rate of occurrence and is therefore more amenable to prediction. The trick is to refine our forecasting efforts, minimizing but not eliminating nonactuarial input, maintaining a proper balance between protecting society from recalcitrant criminals and providing opportunities for release to deserving inmates, and continually updating our models as new information becomes available. We must also include person × situation interaction variables in our analyses, since research suggests that they provide a rich source of information on recidivism (Gottfredson & Taylor, 1986). In accomplishing these goals it is crucial for us to realize that the actuarial format is far less important (Gottfredson & Gottfredson, 1980) than the variables we include in our formulae—variables which should be meaningful, measurable, and reasonably stable over time.

CONCLUSION

While the predictions of dangerous behavior, institutional adjustment, and recidivism have been treated separately, they are actually part of a wider network of variables that predict how a person responds to societal norms, rules, and values. The interrelated nature of the dangerousness, institutional adjustment, and recidivism questions is revealed in research showing that selected variables (for example, age, criminal history) are strong predictors of all three criterion behaviors. There are, of course, salient differences among the three, although sometimes these differences are more apparent than real. It has traditionally been assumed, for instance, that a subject's level of institutional adjustment provides us with few clues as to how he or she might adjust to the demands of community life (von Hirsch & Hanrahan, 1979). However, the results of a study directed by Gottfredson and Adams (1982) confide that a subset of institutional adjustment items (assaultive infractions, escape history) may, in fact, have prognostic value in predicting future patterns of re-offending.

A question paramount on the minds of clinicians and researchers asks how might we improve predictions of dangerous behavior, institutional adjustment, and recidivism. It is probably unrealistic to expect to completely eliminate the subjective features of prognostication without also removing the human observer from the decision-making process. That is not only impractical but will likely result in a significant loss of diagnostic information since the human observer provides knowledge and insights that are unavailable in most statistical equations and formulae. The clinician must learn, however, to make more efficient use of base-rate information and consider variables other than trait characteristics in offering judgments on such critical predictive issues as dangerousness, institutional adjustment, and recidivism. These nontrait variables would include not only situational and environmental factors but interactive (person × situation) ones as well.

Critics of the prognostic approach to parole and sentence decision making argue that clinical and statistical models of prediction are generally incapable of forecasting future behavior at reasonably accurate levels. Though this would appear to be an overly pessimistic reading of the data on prediction, there is evidence that dangerousness, institutional adjustment, and recidivism prognostication have a great many limitations. As a means to overcoming these limitations we must embrace alternatives to the clinical versus statistical rivalry that has dominated our thinking on prediction. Instead of forcing ourselves into an artificial dichotomy of dangerous versus nondangerous or poor prognosis versus good prognosis, the science of criminal investigation might be better served by a model that conceives of dangerousness and prognosis as continuums with dangerous and nondangerous or poor prognosis and good prognosis at the poles. We could enlist statistical base-rate information to locate a circumscribed range within our continuum from whence we might implement a more individualized analysis, the eventual goal being to anchor our predictions within this range (Shapiro, 1977).

It should come as no surprise to persons familiar with the clinical decision-making enterprise that predictions of dangerous behavior, institutional adjustment, and recidivism raise a number of delicate ethical issues. Few people would advocate use of predictors like gender and race in making confinement, release, or custody decisions, regardless of how impressively they may correlate with the outcome of interest. This does not mean, however, that we ignore the relationships that surface. Though it is highly unlikely, for instance, that blacks are inherently more criminal or dangerous than whites, there does appear to be something about growing up black in America that portends higher rates of violent crime, recidivism, and institutional maladjustment. We certainly want to avoid making unfounded statements about such serious issues, but to evade our responsibilities by ignoring these issues does society and its citizens a grave disservice. Ethical issues are discussed with a great deal more specificity in the final chapter of this volume.

PART III

INTERVENTION

6

Person-Oriented Intervention

Person-oriented interventions feature treatment programs aimed at the individual offender. While such interventions may be conducted in a group or family setting, they share a common interest in procedures capable of promoting behavioral change in individual offenders. Interventions directed at the environmental correlates of crime and the interaction of person and environmental factors (most notably, the criminal justice system) are reviewed in separate chapters. The present chapter is concerned with establishing meaningful change through modification of individual offender behavior. Before surveying the major systems of person-oriented intervention, we examine Martinson's "nothing works" hypothesis and several of the more prominent methodological issues affecting research on treatment interventions directed at the individual offender.

EXPLORING THE MARTINSON CONTROVERSY

In 1966 the New York State Governor's Committee on Criminal Offenders commissioned Douglas Lipton, Judith Wilks, and Robert Martinson to direct a review of treatment program efficacy. In the 1,400-page manuscript which followed, Lipton, Wilks, and Martinson surveyed 231 studies on offender rehabilitation published prior to 1968. Intervention strategies considered included educational or vocational training, individual and group counseling, environmental manipulation, medical treatment, and parole or probation supervision. Summarizing the results of this review, Martinson (1974, p. 46) argued that "perhaps education, at its best, or psychotherapy at its best, cannot overcome or even appreciably reduce, the powerful tendency for offenders to continue in criminal behavior." There are, however, several serious problems with Martinson's position on offender rehabilitation that require our attention.

Martinson (1974) originally deduced that there was no good evidence in the research literature to support the efficacy of treatment interventions with criminal offenders. What is left unsaid, however, is that he was also unable to uncover any solid evidence rebutting the arguments of rehabilitationists. The problem is that the studies upon which the Martinson review was based were in many cases so methodologically flawed that they defied meaningful analysis and interpretation. Reviewing the quality of early research on the rehabilitation hypothesis, Bernstein (1975) notes that of 236 studies published prior to 1975, 59 percent enlisted random samples of subjects, 25 percent utilized experimental or quasi-experimental designs, and fewer than 35 percent reported the outcome of statistical analyses. With studies of such low quality it is no wonder Lipton, Martinson, and Wilks (1975) failed to unearth support for the efficacy of offender rehabilitation programs.

Surveying offender rehabilitation research published between 1973 and 1987, Gendreau and Ross (1979, 1987) restricted themselves to studies that possessed experimental or quasi-experimental designs, reported the results of data analyses, and encompassed a follow-up of at least six months. The outcome of these reviews has confirmed that treatment-based interventions with criminal offenders can be effective in reducing future episodes of antisocial behavior. Gendreau and Ross report further that well-designed programs and studies typically yield more positive outcomes than more poorly designed programs and studies. In truth, the better constructed programs have been shown to reduce recidivism by as much as 30 to 60 percent (Alexander & Parsons, 1973; Lee & Haynes, 1980; Phillips et al., 1973) for periods spanning three to fifteen years (Blakely et al., 1980; Shore & Massimo, 1979).

Quantitative analyses of the rehabilitation literature following a meta-analytic framework (Glass, McGraw, & Smith, 1981) have also found support for the efficacy of person-based interventions in criminal populations. In direct contrast to the pessimistic leanings of Martinson, meta-analyses of rehabilitation research have consistently recorded modest but significant treatment effects (Davidson et al., 1984; Garrett, 1985; Izzo & Ross, 1990). The only negative outcome obtained in meta-analyses of the rehabilitation literature to date was recorded by Whitehead and Lab (1989). Incorporating studies published between 1975 and 1984, Whitehead and Lab observed minimal support for the rehabilitative hypothesis, more rigorous tests of the hypothesis yielded poorer outcomes than less rigorous tests. Andrews et al. (1990) reanalyzed 45 of the 50 studies examined by Whitehead and Lab, and added a second sample of 35 studies. This group of investigators subsequently determined that appropriate correctional services, as defined by the principles of risk, need, and responsivity (see pages 136–138 of this chapter), achieved results that were superior to nonrehabilitative criminal sanctions or treatment interventions that failed to adequately address the principles of risk, need, and responsivity (see Figure 6.1).

There would appear to be little objective evidence in favor of Martinson's "nothing works" hypothesis. In fact, just five years after publishing his negative review of the rehabilitation literature, Martinson (1979) recanted and willingly

Figure 6.1
Mean Phi Coefficients Obtained in a Meta-Analysis of Criminal Sanctions,
Inappropriate Correctional Services, and Appropriate Correctional Services

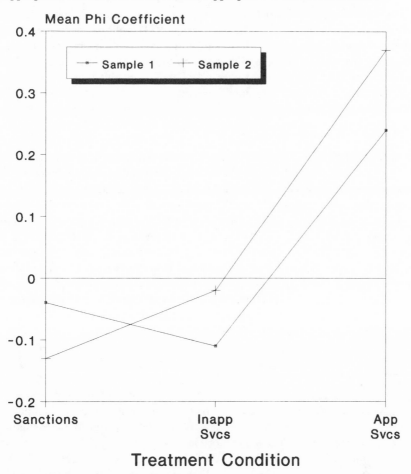

Source: Data from Andrews, Zinger, et al., 1990.

acknowledged that under specific circumstances successful rehabilitation was possible. Unfortunately, this paper is cited much less frequently than the "nothing works" article, the latter still being quoted by researchers, administrators, and politicians looking to remove rehabilitation from the criminal justice agenda. Nonetheless, available data are reasonably congruent in showing that if the programs are well conceived, adequately staffed, and properly evaluated, and if participants are appropriately motivated for change, then rehabilitation is possible.

METHODOLOGICAL ISSUES IN RESEARCH ON PERSON-ORIENTED INTERVENTION

The methodological limitations of early research on rehabilitation were probably partly responsible for leading Martinson (1974) to the erroneous conclusion that nothing can be done to effect change in criminal offenders. It is therefore essential that we identify several of the more common threats to the internal and external validity of research studies on offender rehabilitation. These threats revolve around conceptual, sampling, treatment, outcome, and statistical issues.

Conceptual Issues

In the past many investigators addressing the rehabilitation question have failed to provide a theoretical rationale for their interventions and predictions. The absence of an organizing conceptual framework has probably contributed immeasurably to the inconsistent and oftentimes puzzling results reported in reviews by Martinson and other early critics of rehabilitative programming. According to Gendreau and Ross (1979, 1987), effective programs are often more strongly conceptualized than less effective ones, since robust conceptualizations not only guide development of treatment goals but also help clarify targets for intervention and evaluation. In their recent meta-analysis of the rehabilitation literature on adolescents, Izzo and Ross (1990) observed that studies based on an articulated theoretical rationale yielded stronger effects than studies employing procedures devoid of a clear theoretical infrastructure.

Sampling Issues

Control and randomization are two critical features of research endeavor. Competent scientific inquiry demands that an appropriate control or comparison group be formulated and that subjects be randomly assigned to conditions. Though the ideal research situation is one in which subjects are randomly assigned to a treatment or control group, this is not always possible. Researchers therefore bear the responsibility of identifying alternative means of experimental control. This might involve matching subjects on one or more relevant dimensions, although this procedure can inspire systematic group differences on characteristics and variables not matched (Kerlinger, 1973). Another procedure enlists the use of prediction tables by which the experimental effect is contrasted with base-rate estimates derived statistically from data known to be predictive of the outcome in question (Mannheim & Wilkins, 1955). The problem with this procedure is that it fails to account for nonspecific treatment effects as might be found in studies where experimental subjects have received more attention than control subjects (placebo and Hawthorne effects).

Random assignment of subjects to a treatment condition and one or more control conditions (at least one of which is a placebo-attention group) is the preferred route of subject assignment in treatment studies on the rehabilitation hypothesis. Randomization will not guard against all possible methodological improprieties, however. Take, for instance, subject attrition patterns in the Cambridge-Somerville Project (Powers & Witmer, 1951). Though this project began with random assignment of subjects to treatment and control conditions, the intervening effect of several program changes and a world war eventually rendered the groups nonequivalent. Consequently, researchers need to guard against the threat of differential mortality in their studies on treatment interventions with adult and juvenile offenders, particularly when these treatments and follow-ups span several years.

Treatment Issues

Treatment may be adequately conceptualized, but if it is not properly implemented the integrity of studies investigating its efficacy will be compromised. In such well-known therapeutic initiatives as the California Community Treatment Project (Palmer, 1975) and Cambridge-Somerville Study (Powers & Witmer, 1951), treatment planned and treatment received were not necessarily one and the same (Rutter & Giller, 1984). Kassebaum, Ward, and Wilner (1971) conducted what, on the surface, appeared to have been a tightly conceptualized intervention study that failed to find evidence of a treatment effect. However, a careful reading of the methods section of this report shows that the counseling was unevenly applied, counselors were poorly trained, staff were skeptical about the value of treatment, and many of the participants lacked sincerity in enrolling themselves in the program (Quay, 1977). In a related vein, Zivan (1966) notes that staff hostility toward a vocational/occupational training program frustrated the outcome before the program had a chance to get off the ground.

Besides support, program and inmate characteristics may also impact on the success of rehabilitation programs. Hence, Gearhart, Keith, and Clemmons (1967) observed a positive outcome in a survey of vocational training programs but only when the training was reasonably relevant to the kinds of jobs subjects were likely to obtain upon release. There are also indications that grouping all treated offenders in a single category may obscure important intervention effects. Thus, while subjects judged to have been "successfully treated" (Persons, 1967) or "amenable to treatment" (Adams, 1961) have demonstrated positive outcomes relative to control estimates, the community adjustment of "unsuccessfully treated" or "unamenable" subjects is no better (and in some cases worse) than that achieved by control subjects. These factors need to be considered in implementing and evaluating offender rehabilitation programs.

Outcome Issues

In the past, researchers have relied extensively on single-outcome measures, the most common standard being recidivism. However, re-arrest or re-conviction rates may not be as sensitive to treatment effects as, say, self-report outcome measures. Several investigators, for example, have determined that a fair number of offenders may continue engaging in criminality but remain free of legal scrutiny. The necessity of following subjects for a reasonable length of time would appear to be self-evident, although problems continue with regard to defining the proper length of follow-up. Consequently, while Quay and Love (1977) ascertained a substantial treatment effect in a study of offending male delinquents, the fact that they followed the control group an average of 139 days longer than the treatment group (450 days versus 311 days) calls into question the validity of their results. For the purpose of achieving interpretable research findings it is recommended that researchers consider employing multiple-outcome measures (encompassing both official and self-report sources) collected for a period of one year or longer with a comparable follow-up for treatment and control subjects.

Statistical Issues

A final issue concerns the statistical analysis stage of the research enterprise. In many of the earlier studies data were either not statistically evaluated or the data analyses were not reported (Bernstein, 1975). It is essential that such analyses be conducted, that they be reported, and that they be appropriate to the level of data used. With the advent of multiple sources of outcome data, multivariate statistical techniques are being observed more frequently in studies embracing the offender rehabilitation issue. Efforts need to be initiated to ensure that these procedures are appropriately applied and their limitations and assumptions noted.

PERSON-ORIENTED TREATMENT MODALITIES

There are several models of treatment intervention that have been utilized with a fair degree of regularity in person-oriented interventions with criminal offenders. The five modalities discussed in this section include biomedical models, psychodynamic models, behavioral models, cognitive models, and moral models.

Biomedical Models

Surgical Procedures. O'Callaghan and Carroll (1987) reviewed studies probing the utility of psychosurgery in the treatment of sexual offenders and violent criminals, and exhumed no compelling support for the efficacy of this form of treatment intervention. Furthermore, the few positive effects that have been recorded have often been shown to be transient. As a case in point, take Narabayashi's (1979) follow-up of 18 patients who had received amygdalectomies because of seriously violent behavior. While 61 percent of the patients demonstrated marked improvement, 17 percent some improvement, and 22 percent no improvement immediately after surgery, the rate of marked improvement dropped to 39 percent and the rate of no improvement rose to 39 percent 5 to 22 years post-treatment.

The Quasimodo Complex is a term used to describe crime resulting from physical deformity. Studies assessing the effect of cosmetic surgery on recidivism rates in criminal samples have met with equivocal outcomes. Hence, while some studies reveal a positive effect on recidivism (Kurtzberg et al., 1969; Lewison, 1965; Spira et al., 1966), one study uncovered a negative effect (Lehman & Conklin, 1973) and several other studies failed to find evidence of any relationship, positive or negative, between cosmetic surgery and recidivism (Meyer et al., 1973; Schuring & Dodge, 1967). In a recent review of plastic surgery programs for prison inmates, Thompson (1990) concluded that we still do not know if disfigurement is a cause or an effect of criminal behavior, adding that we must be careful not to view plastic surgery as a quick fix for the serious underlying behavioral problems of the criminal offender.

A study of prisoners released from the Texas Department of Corrections (Freedman et al., 1988) revealed that 253 offenders undergoing cosmetic surgery during confinement displayed recidivism rates that were 58, 52, and 70 percent of the Texas Department of Corrections baseline one, two, and three years post-release, respectively. These investigators reasoned that cosmetic surgery exerted its counter-recidivism effect by enhancing the self-esteem, interpersonal relationships, and confidence of treated offenders, although such a conclusion is premature without benefit of an adequate control group. Research studies examining the outcome of surgical approaches to offender rehabilitation have been flawed to the point where they are difficult to interpret; and while it may well be that cosmetic surgery provides some solace to offenders beset with severe facial deformities, it remains to be seen whether this impacts on future criminal involvement.

Psychotropic Solutions. Lithium carbonate is the treatment of choice for bipolar, also known as manic-depressive, disorders. However, it has also been used to treat adult and juvenile offenders. The outcome of one study demonstrated that 25 to 33 percent of a group of offenders administered lithium carbonate for anxiety, paranoia, aggressive hyperactivity, and emotional liability displayed remission of symptomatology (Tupin et al., 1973). In a later study it was determined that hospitalized children with DSM-III diagnoses of conduct disorder administered lithium carbonate and haloperidol (a neuroleptic) displayed significant improvement on a global measure of clinical status, although there were no differences on ratings provided by the children's parents or teachers (Campbell et al., 1984). Despite the fact this was a randomized double-blind study, the follow-up period was only six weeks. Surveying the literature on the use of lithium carbonate with offender populations, Cloninger (1987) remarked that this form of treatment is effective only in reducing offender impulsivity and aggressiveness, and that antisocial behaviors unrelated to these two characteristics do not normally respond to lithium-based interventions.

Neuroleptics like fluphenazine have been found effective in reducing aggression in some cases (Itil & Wadud, 1975) but well-designed research studies addressing the efficacy of neuroleptics in the treatment of criminal behavior are lacking. Minor tranquilizers, particularly the benzodiazepines (Valium, Librium), have been shown to result in increased as well as decreased levels of aggressiveness, depending upon previously measured intervals of anxiety, hostility, and the subject's premorbid personality (Azcarate, 1975; Brown, 1978). Physicians report success with stimulant drugs in the treatment of childhood hyperactivity (Allen, Safer, & Covi, 1975; Wender, Reimherr, & Wood, 1981) and speculate that stimulants might also be beneficial in reducing hyperactivity in some youthful adult offenders (Wender et al., 1981). However, their abuse potential, like that of the benzodiazepines, limits their utility for widespread clinical use in criminal populations. It would appear, then, that while psychotropic agents may prove useful in the symptomatic treatment of offenders experiencing serious emotional problems, the practice of administering them routinely as a means of alleviating criminal or aggressive conduct cannot be endorsed on the basis of empirical studies conducted up to this time.

Diet Management. Hippchen (1976) comments that diet modification can be of great benefit in managing offender populations. Diet modification advocates argue that lowering the intake of food additives and preparing meals low in sucrose and high in complex carbohydrates (particularly fruit juice and vegetables) will not only aid digestion but also lead to better behavioral outcomes in juvenile offenders. Using a double-blind methodology, Schoenthaler (1983) determined that institutional misconduct and acts of violence in several juvenile facilities declined by 21 to 54 percent after diets were revised along the lines recommended by Hippchen. Schauss, working out of the American Institute for Biosocial Research in Tacoma, Washington, contrasted offenders receiving nutritional counseling with persons enrolled in traditional psychotherapy and witnessed recidivism rates of 14 and 34 percent, respectively (Lewis, 1985). Although a great deal more research needs to be conducted on this matter, of the various programs of biomedical intervention discussed in this section diet management may perhaps have the most to offer a science of offender rehabilitation.

Psychodynamic Models

Psychoanalytic interpretations of criminal behavior rest on assumptions about psychic determinism, psychosexual development, and the unconscious. Since Freud did not spent much time interviewing or writing about criminals, it was left to several of his followers to formulate psychoanalytic theories of crime and criminal behavior. Alexander and Staub (1931, p. 73) contend that the goal of psychoanalytic therapy with offenders is to "gain the upper hand over the unconscious by means of the conscious part of the personality." Glover (1960) adds that projection and guilt are central to both the development and the treatment of criminal behavior, a sentiment reiterated in the writings of Dixon (1986) and Hofer (1988). However, where descriptions of psychoanalytic treatment with criminal offenders may be interesting and sometimes invective, they are rarely empirical. Opinions on this issue run strong, but interpretable data and solid research designs are infrequent, and those which exist are often discordant with the claims of psychodynamic scholars. Perhaps the most consistent observation made about the psychoanalytic approach to criminal behavior is that because it was originally devised with neurotic patients in mind, it is generally inappropriate for use with criminal and delinquent populations.

Behavioral Models

Behaviorists focus on the specific actions of the individual and the consequences of these actions (reinforcement, punishment). Three behavioral intervention strategies that have been used rather extensively in the treatment of criminal and delinquent activity are surveyed in this section: contingency management, behavioral contracting, and family interventions.

Contingency Management. A token economy is a program, normally established in institutional settings, wherein subjects earn tokens for good behavior—tokens which can then be exchanged for goods and privileges at a later time. Studies carried out with groups of delinquent offenders tend to corroborate the hypothesis that token economies promote behavioral control as long as the individual remains in an institutional setting (Kazdin & Bootzin, 1972; Phillips et al., 1973; Ross & McKay, 1978). Once the individual is released from the institution it is not uncommon to find gains made in confinement gradually disappearing (Rutter & Giller, 1984). Furthermore, whether token economies are institution or community based, frequently there are many problems associated with their implementation.

Community-based programs in which contingency management has assumed a prominent role frequently yield efficacious results. Take, for instance, a community-based program reviewed by Davidson and Robinson (1975), in which hard-core male delinquents served as subjects. The fruits of this program included increased school attendance, improved achievement test scores, and a declining rate of arrest (from 3 arrests per year to .46 arrests per year). Residential group homes, such as Achievement Place in Lawrence, Kansas, are run on contingency management principles but also emphasize self-control, social skills development, and responsibility within the context of a family-style living arrangement. Behavioral control and social functioning have been shown to improve as a result of enrollment in programs like Achievement Place (Philips et al., 1973), although the jury is still out on whether such programs significantly reduce long-term recidivism (Rutter & Giller, 1984).

Behavioral Contracting. The behavioral contract is a written agreement between the delinquent and his or her caretakers outlining the responsibilities of each and the consequences of not living up to these responsibilities. Doctor and

Polakow (1973) monitored a behavioral contracting program in which juvenile offenders were awarded reduced probation time for appropriate behavior. Analysis of follow-up data revealed that employment time increased, probation violations decreased, and new arrests plummeted as a result of involvement in this program. The outcome of a second program in which behavioral contracting played a major role indicated that the experimental subjects experienced 31 percent fewer arrests and more dramatic improvements at home, school, and in the neighborhood relative to control subjects (Douds, Engelsjord, & Collingwood, 1977). Finally, Seidman, Rappeport, and Davidson (1980) report that the behavioral contracting component of a multifaceted treatment program contributed strongly to the program's counter-recidivism effect.

Family Interventions. Perhaps the most noteworthy attempt to treat delinquency through behavioral family management techniques can be found in the work of Gerald Patterson and his associates at the Oregon Social Learning Center. Patterson's (1980) goal in intervening with the parents of delinquents is to teach them how to more effectively interact with their children through an unambiguous system of positive reinforcement predicated on helping the child develop self-control and problem-solving skills. Patterson and Fleischman (1979) discerned a declining rate of aggressive behavior in children identified as delinquent that persisted to the time of follow-up one year later. Since that time the Patterson group has provided additional support for the efficacy of its system with delinquent populations (Patterson, 1985; Patterson, Chamberlain, & Reid, 1982). The utility of behaviorally oriented family interventions has also been documented by a group of investigators from Salt Lake City, Utah (Alexander et al., 1976; Alexander & Parsons, 1973).

While behaviorally oriented family intervention strategies have generated impressive empirical outcomes, there are several problems with these procedures that beg further discussion. Moore, Chamberlain, and Mukai (1979), for instance, found immediate success with delinquents whose parents were instructed in parenting skills, but add that these gains had all but disappeared by the time they conducted a follow-up one year later. An additional problem with the Patterson program is that there is a general paucity of studies utilizing random assignment of subjects to conditions. Additionally, the program's effectiveness is circumscribed in that success has been clearly documented only in cases of adolescent aggressiveness (Rutter & Giller, 1984). There are also indications that the Oregon program is more efficacious with first-time offenders than with hard-core delinquents (Wade et al., 1977). Finally, since initial treatment effects sometimes diminish after a year or two, therapists should consider employing booster sessions in order to reinforce embryonic treatment gains.

Cognitive Models

It is fairly well documented that successful forms of offender rehabilitation typically include a cognitive component (Davidson et al., 1984; Garrett, 1985;

Izzo & Ross, 1990; Ross & Fabiano, 1985). Ross and Fabiano, for instance, relate that 94 percent of the cognitive programs they surveyed were effective compared to 29 percent of the noncognitive programs. Kazdin (1987) laments, however, that efforts to construct effective programs of rehabilitation and intervention (cognitive or otherwise) for use with juvenile conduct disorders have been slow to develop. The three cognitive or social learning interventions reviewed in this section include modeling, rational analysis, and cognitive skills training.

Modeling. The actions of others can serve as a source of information about the world and a stimulus for learning new behaviors. As such, modeling can be important in changing a person's actions (Bandura, 1969). Aiken, Stumphauzer, and Veloz (1977) note that youth living in high-crime areas often learn to avoid trouble by modeling the actions of law-abiding older siblings. Vorrath and Brendto (1974) examined the efficacy of a training school program that emphasized modeling and guided group interaction. Although a two-year follow-up revealed a lower rate of recidivism in program participants relative to the reoffense rates of former training school students who had not gone through the program, the presence of a large number of uncontrolled variables leaves this study vulnerable to several criticisms and exposes the obtained results to the scrutiny of viable rival hypotheses.

In one of the better designed investigations on the utility of modeling as a treatment for delinquency, Sarason and Ganzer (1973) randomly assigned first-time offenders incarcerated in a juvenile facility to one of three conditions: modeling, group discussion, or no-contract control. Subjects not only expressed greater satisfaction with the modeling group but also demonstrated better postrelease adjustment, with 23 percent of the modeling subjects recidivating within five years compared to 48 percent of the controls (Sarason, 1978). It would appear, then, that the modeling of prosocial behaviors might very well be important in fostering positive change in youthful offenders, although more research needs to be conducted on the use of modeling with adult felons.

Rational Analysis. Based on the work of Ellis (1962), Beck (1976), and Maultsby (1975), the rational perspective holds that feelings and actions are a direct consequence of one's interpretation of events. Negative feelings and actions are therefore the result of negative or irrational thinking. Erroneous self-talk is intrinsic to Yochelson and Samenow's (1976) work on the criminal personality and Walters' (1990) work on the criminal lifestyle. The few research studies that have addressed the issue of criminal thinking have found support for the suppositions of these authors. Kipper (1977), for instance, determined that a group of habitual criminals displayed more rigid, concrete, and stereotypic patterns of thought than noncriminal controls, while Evans and Picano (1984) report that poorly adjusted prison inmates harbored many more irrational beliefs than better adjusted prisoners. Perseveration (Newman, Patterson, & Kosson, 1987), poorly developed cognitive skills (Polonski, 1980), and a poverty of "internal" speech (Camp, 1977) have also been implicated in research probing the possible cognitive roots of criminal behavior. In an investigation addressing itself to this issue, Garvin and Goldstein (1990) constructed a 64-item instrument designed to measure six of Yochelson and Samenow's (1976) criminal thinking errors, and found their instrument capable of discriminating between delinquent and nondelinquent juveniles.

Research on the long-term efficacy of rational approaches to treatment intervention with criminal offenders has been far less abundant than studies addressing the utility of cognitive interpretations of criminal behavior. In the few studies that have been conducted, though, the results have been encouraging. Goodman and Maultsby (1974), for example, employed a rational approach with alcoholic felons confined at the federal correctional institution in Lexington, Kentucky, and discerned a significant drop in disciplinary reports during confinement and a strong post-release effect in which only 13.3 percent of the subjects had their paroles revoked during the first six months. However, the authors of this investigation failed to include a control or comparison group. Utilizing a more methodologically sound research design, Lee and Haynes (1980) instructed university students in the use of rational counseling and role playing with delinquent adolescents. Findings indicated that juveniles enrolled in the college student-facilitated treatment groups engaged in 50 percent fewer criminal acts than a group of untreated controls, and that these differences persisted for 24 months post-treatment (Piercy & Lee, 1976). The rational approach to treatment intervention would therefore appear to warrant further study.

Cognitive Skills Training. Robert Ross and his colleagues instituted the Reasoning and Rehabilitation Project in an effort to teach high-rate adult probationers emotions management, assertiveness, social communication, creativity, problem solving, and negotiation skills (Ross, Fabiano, & Ewles, 1988). Subsequent arrests were appreciably lower for project subjects (18.1%) compared to persons exposed to regular probation (69.5%) or a life skills group (47.5%) during a nine-month period of follow-up. Moreover, as opposed to reincarceration rates of 30 percent in the regular probation condition and 11 percent in the life skills group, none of the subjects enrolled in the Reasoning and Rehabilitation Project served time in jail or prison during the follow-up. Ross and Fabiano (1985) recorded similarly positive outcomes in juvenile offenders instructed in basic cognitive skills, the implication being that offenders lack the cognitive or social abilities most of us take for granted.

Problem-solving training is known to decelerate disruptive behavior on the part of institutionalized delinquents (D'Zurilla & Goldfried, 1971), improve family communication in homes of predelinquent children (Kifer et al., 1974), and retard recidivism in acting-out youth (DeLong, 1978). Platt et al. have successfully utilized problem-solving techniques with groups of juvenile and adult offenders. In one study carried out by the Platt group it was determined that over the course of a two-year follow-up, 18 percent of the problem-solving subjects had been reconvicted compared to 30 percent of a group of untreated controls (Platt, Labate, & Wicks, 1977). Kazdin et al. (1989) randomly assigned children (ages 7–13) referred for antisocial behavior to one of three conditions: problem-solving skills training, problem-solving skills training with in vivo practice, or relationship therapy. Children in both problem-solving groups exhibited reductions in deviant behavior and accentuated prosocial behavior that exceeded levels attained by children enrolled in relationship therapy all the way up to the one-year follow-up. Although the in vivo group accrued outcomes superior to those attained by the problem-solving group immediately after treatment, these differences were no longer significant at follow-up.

While problem solving is perhaps the most popular cognitive skill taught to offenders, training in other cognitive skills has also served to suppress recidivism and promote prosocial activity in adult and juvenile offenders. Alexander and Parsons (1973) report that the delinquent members of families trained in ways of negotiating conflict experienced a reduction in recidivism in the neighborhood of 21 to 47 percent. Likewise, Maskin (1976) notes that offenders instructed in interpersonal problem solving and communication skills re-offended at a rate of 2 percent, which compares favorably with the 20 percent figure achieved by a group of matched control subjects. Chandler (1973) used both untreated and placebo control groups to evaluate the efficacy of role-taking training with chronically delinquent youth, and found a positive effect that remained significant 18 months post-treatment. Juveniles participating in a 12-session social-cognitive intervention program for aggressive offenders displayed an increase in their social problem-solving skills, a decrease in their endorsement of aggressive beliefs, and reduced levels of aggressive or impulsive behavior relative to youth enrolled in a placebo control or no-treatment control group (Guerra & Slaby, 1990). There would appear to be a great deal cognitive treatment in general and cognitive skills training in particular have to offer a science of criminal rehabilitation.

Moral Models

William Glasser, possibly more than anyone else, is responsible for bringing moral issues to the forefront in interventions involving delinquents and criminals. In describing his approach to treatment, which he terms reality therapy, Glasser (1965) has stressed the role of irresponsibility in the genesis of antisocial forms of behavior, and he directly attacks the ''sickness'' and pathology models that were in vogue at the time he first introduced his theory. The goals of interventions emanating out of a moral philosophy of treatment intervention are to educate the offender about his or her obligations to him or herself and exhort the individual to accept greater responsibility for his or her actions. At present, there exist juvenile institutions run largely on the basis of principles derived from reality therapy. The William Roper Hull Progressive Education Center in Alberta, Canada, and the Ventura School for girls in Southern California are two such examples. Use of reality therapy principles at the Ventura School, for instance, may be responsible for the lowered rate of recidivism noted by officials at the school, although the methodology of the ''Ventura studies'' (Glasser & Zunin,

1979) is open to criticism. While very few properly designed studies have been carried out on reality therapy, available data are moderately supportive of this moral approach to offender rehabilitation (Cohen & Sordo, 1984; Goldstein & Stein, 1975).

Possibly the greatest contribution made by moral theories has been their assertions of responsibility and choice. This would seem to make them particularly compatible with cognitive models of intervention. Czudner (1985) offers an integrated cognitive-moral approach to treatment intervention that follows a five-step format. Personal responsibility is emphasized and excuse making confronted in the first of these five steps. Next, the offender is educated as to the effect criminal thinking has on his or her behavior and how the individual's actions have caused others, particularly victims and family members, to experience emotional and physical pain. Third, guilt and self-disgust are enlisted to bridge the gap between thinking and behavior. After this, the individual is encouraged to make a personal commitment to stop hurting others and start embracing prosocial behavior. Finally, the offender is instructed to immerse him or herself in activities incompatible with crime, the emphasis being on aiding and assisting others.

SPECIAL OFFENDER GROUPS

Substance-Abusing Offenders

Innes (1988) reports that 35 percent of a large group of state prisoners admitted they had been using drugs at the time they engaged in the crime for which they were currently incarcerated. Another 43 percent acknowledged regular usage of drugs within a month of their arrest for the instant offense. Estimates originally derived ten years ago suggest that drug abuse costs society close to $50 billion annually, one-third of which is directly tied to the crime-related features of drug dependency (Harwood et al., 1984). Alcohol has also been implicated in a large portion of the violent and nonviolent crimes committed each year in the United States (Bureau of Justice Statistics, 1983a). Drug and alcohol abuse would therefore appear to be important targets for intervention.

The results of an 11-city survey of drug use and crime revealed that nearly three-quarters of a group of male arrestees voluntarily agreeing to submit to urinalysis tested positive for illegal substances (Wish, 1988). It would stand to reason that this figure may underestimate the level of drug usage in criminal populations, since drug-imbibing offenders are probably less willing to submit to a drug screen than nonusing offenders. It should also be noted, however, that subjects in Wish's sample had been arrested for more serious offenses, and so the three-quarters figure may apply only to offenders involved in serious criminality. Chaiken (1989) advises that in 1979 approximately 4.4 percent of all inmates in the 50 state correctional systems were involved in drug treatment. By 1987 this figure had more than doubled so that 11 percent of the total state prison population was now enrolled in drug treatment programs. As a way of charting the progress of drug treatment for substance-abusing felons we explore three principal modes of intervention: outpatient programs, therapeutic communities, and methadone maintenance.

Outpatient Programs. Research on the use of outpatient treatment with alcohol-abusing felons offers mixed outcomes. Ross and Lightfoot (1985) conclude that there is little evidence for the efficacy of outpatient alcohol treatment programs with criminal offenders in the half-dozen or so reasonably well-designed studies available on this subject. Miller and Hester (1986), however, report that behavioral and cognitive-behavioral strategies may be moderately efficacious for the purpose of intervening with certain categories of alcohol-abusing offender— covert sensitization, behavioral self-control, stress management, and social skills training being among the more successful in this regard.

Outpatient treatment with drug-abusing offenders has centered on community-based programs like Treatment Alternatives to Street Crime (TASC). The TASC program was designed with the intent of bridging the gap between the criminal justice system and treatment opportunities available in the community. This is typically accomplished by identifying, assessing, and referring nonviolent offenders to various community-based treatment programs. These programs, inpatient as well as outpatient, are made available to offenders who would otherwise find themselves in jail or prison. The TASC approach to treatment shows promise in reducing costs by diverting nondangerous offenders into community programs, thereby reserving prison and jail cell space for the more dangerous criminals.

Like research on alcohol-related programs for offenders, the outcome of studies examining the long-term efficacy of TASC is equivocal. A study conducted by System Sciences Incorporated (1978) found that TASC offered a cost-efficient alternative to criminal justice sanctioning in drug-abusing felons. A review of the results of TASC programs in ten U.S. cities directed by Hubbard et al. (1988) determined that criminal justice clients enrolled in substance-abuse treatment were no more likely to engage in future drug use than other substance-abusing TASC enrollees. Though these authors report that treatment did not appear to suppress future episodes of criminality, they acknowledge that the full impact of TASC could not be properly evaluated from the data available at that time.

Therapeutic Communities. The therapeutic community approach to treatment with the drug-abusing felon has its roots in the Synanon movement that began in California in 1958. Early reviews of research conducted on the efficacy of therapeutic communities for the treatment of drug-abusing felons revealed that pre- to post-program reductions in arrest ranged anywhere from 24 to 53 percent (Mandell, Goldschmidt, & Grover, 1973; Nash, 1973). Inspecting a large reservoir of data from 24 therapeutic communities, System Sciences Incorporated (1973) noted a 59 percent decrease in arrests after 4 to 6 months of treatment and an 81 percent drop after 10 to 12 months. Studies contrasting subjects enrolled in therapeutic communities with matched controls (Platt, Perry, & Metzger, 1980) and counseling-comparison controls (Wexler, Lipton, & Foster, 1985) have also corroborated the efficacy of the therapeutic community approach to intervening with substance-abusing offenders. A recent review of the therapeutic community literature describes moderately favorable outcomes in approximately half the clients enrolled in such programs, with follow-up periods lasting up to five years (De Leon, 1988).

Multivariate studies document that the amount of time spent in a therapeutic community is normally the strongest predictor of positive outcome (De Leon, 1984; Simpson & Sells, 1982). However, this may reflect the tendency of more highly motivated and self-disciplined subjects to terminate treatment less often and remain crime free in the community more often than less motivated or highly impulsive subjects. A case in point can be found in Field's (1989) evaluation of the Cornerstone therapeutic community for drug-abusing felons in Oregon. Field reports that program graduates were significantly less likely to be involved in criminal activity during a three-year period of follow-up than nongraduates who spent at least six months, two to five months, or less than two months in the program. However, this outcome may have had little to do with the program and everything to do with preexisting differences in the personal characteristics of participants who successfully completed the program versus those who dropped out prior to completion.

Evaluating New York's Stay'n Out program, which takes a therapeutic community approach to treatment with drug-abusing criminals, Wexler, Falkin, and Lipton (1990) noticed that a 12-month enrollment resulted in the most favorable outcome. In a manner of speaking, persons remaining in the program more than 12 months experienced less success than persons released at 12 months. Though Wexler and his associates argue that this finding may be a result of increased levels of frustration on the part of persons who remained in the program longer than most participants, the study fails to account for the possibility that the decision to retard a person's release date beyond the 12-month standard may have been based on the realization that they were poor risks for release in the first place.

As a means of controlling crime and drug use in offenders, the therapeutic community approach to intervention is appealing from both a practical and empirical standpoint. Studies have shown therapeutic communities to be effective in ameliorating chemical-abuse problems in a group normally unreceptive to intervention—the habitual criminal (De Leon, 1984; De Leon, Wexler, & Jainchill, 1982), although such individuals are characteristically less responsive to the therapeutic community approach than less serious offenders (Ogloff, Wong, & Greenwood, 1990). More effort needs to be directed at evaluating these therapeutic systems. The Stay'n Out program, for instance, is highly structured, emphasizes client responsibility, offers group and individual counseling, and is staffed almost entirely by ex-addicts. There is little research, however, appraising which program components are most strongly correlated with future success. By identifying the more salient features of this particular intervention strategy, such analyses would add immeasurably to our level of accumulated knowledge on the efficacy of treatment interventions with drug-abusing offenders.

Methadone Maintenance. Introduced as a treatment for heroin addiction in 1965, methadone is a synthetic narcotic agent that satisfies the craving for heroin without producing tolerance or the euphoria normally associated with heroin use. Though there are a number of legal, moral, and political questions centered around the practice of dispensing methadone to heroin addicts, we focus attention in this section on the validity of methadone maintenance as a treatment for opiate-abusing criminals. As is the case with much of the research conducted on person-oriented intervention strategies with criminal offenders, studies probing the efficacy of methadone maintenance are replete with various methodological faults and deficiencies. Faupel (1981) surveyed the results of 31 studies on methadone maintenance and witnessed mixed outcomes, though the lack of methodological rigor in many of the studies confounded the results obtained. A series of quasi-experimental investigations conducted in New York City, however, suggested that methadone maintenance had been successful in reducing crime in persons previously addicted to heroin (Dole & Joseph, 1978). Joseph (1988) comments that between 1971 and 1973, a twofold increase took place in the number of persons enrolled in methadone-maintenance programs in New York City and that this corresponded with a drop in the rate of arrests for drug offenses and crimes typically associated with addiction (burglary, larceny, robbery). Similar results were observed in Hong Kong between 1976 and 1980 (Joseph, 1988), although the presence of a correlation between methadone maintenance and crime, no matter how dramatic, cannot be taken as bona fide evidence of a causal nexus between these two variables.

It is probably unrealistic of us to consider methadone maintenance a cure for heroin addiction, despite the fact it may be capable of reducing the frequency and intensity of subsequent periods of both addiction and criminality (Anglin, 1988; Anglin, Brecht, & Maddahian, 1989). Ball and Corty (1988) found methadone maintenance to be effective in alleviating problems associated with drug use and crime in a three-city study conducted in New York, Baltimore, and Philadelphia, but attrition was, in some cases, extreme (81% of the compulsory patients in one 12-month period). These authors conclude their paper by broaching the differential treatment issue. They argue that the confusion that obfuscates research on treatment strategies with drug-abusing offenders is partly a consequence of studies failing to take differential treatment effects into account. Their point is well taken, since a research agenda guided by differential treatment concerns will likely contribute immeasurably to the development of our fifth foundation of criminal science endeavor.

Comment. Whenever this issue of drug programming for offender populations is broached, the question of compulsory versus voluntary treatment invariably comes to the forefront—a question for which there is no simple answer. De Leon (1988) reviewed this issue and concluded that legal referral (compulsory versus voluntary) is rarely a predictor of post-treatment success and that while there may be a small trend in favor of better outcomes for voluntary patients, this effect can probably be attributed to preexisting differences in criminal background, a variable which correlates with both legal referral and post-treatment success. A study of 296 heroin addicts matriculating through a methadone maintenance program in southern California failed to identify noticeable variations in outcome for persons legally coerced versus those voluntarily entering treatment (Anglin et al., 1989). Though a person may be ''coerced'' into treatment by more than just the criminal justice system (a spouse, family member, or employer), legal-based compulsory admission does not appear to detract appreciably from eventual outcome, at least where methadone maintenance programs are concerned.

The results of research on the treatment of substance-abusing offenders suggest that while therapeutic communities may produce a positive outcome, particularly in highly motivated participants, methadone maintenance may be a more cost-efficient alternative for heroin addicts less committed to making major changes in their lifestyle. However, shifting program priorities, financial constraints, space requirements, and staff and inmate resistance have hindered the proper development, implementation, and evaluation of drug-abuse programming for criminal offenders (Chaiken, 1989). Besides improving the methodology of future research in this area, we would also do well to direct more of our investigative resources to studying differential treatment effects and proactive interventions. Regarding this last point, data generated by McAuliffe (1990) show that heroin addicts participating in an outpatient program emphasizing relapse prevention and self-help training demonstrated significantly lower levels of opioid involvement and a higher rate of employment upon follow-up one year later relative to a group of nonparticipating addicts. In expanding our treatment options with drug-abusing felons we should take heed of research showing behavioral and cognitive skill therapies to be particularly effective with offender populations.

Sex Offenders

The sex offender is not only scorned by society but by his or her fellow inmates as well. Where sex offenders constitute 10 percent of the total prison population in the United States and Canada, and upwards of 20 percent in some facilities (Borzecki & Wormith, 1987), their special treatment needs are frequently overlooked. This, in light of studies showing treatment to be effective in selected groups of child molesters (Lanyon, 1986) and rapists (Abel, Blanchard, & Becker, 1978), speaks to the necessity of sex-offender programming. The development of selection criteria is important, however, since excessively violent, sadistic, and seriously psychopathic sex offenders do not normally respond to treatment (Hobson, Boland, & Jamieson, 1985). Two of the more popular treatment approaches employed with sex offenders—biomedical and behavioral models—are major topics of discussion in this section.

Biomedical. Medroxyprogesterone acetate (depo-provera) is a drug that stimulates the release of a hormone in the pituitary gland that in turn suppresses production of sperm in the testes. Some medical experts believe that depo-provera reduces the male sex drive and, as such, can be effective in reducing sexually aberrant behavior. The departments of corrections in Maryland, Montana, and Oregon have approved the use of depo-provera in the treatment of sexual offenders. Walker and Meyer (1981) report that pedophiles and exhibitionists are better candidates for this type treatment than voyeurs, rapists, and incestuous fathers, although there are no long-term outcome studies presently available (Dougher, 1988). Moreover, depo-provera treatment is associated with several annoying, and in some cases, potentially serious, side effects (headaches, nausea, lethargy, irritability, weight gain) and seemingly ignores research showing that rape and sexual assault characteristically reflect themes of anger, control, and violence, the act itself often being viewed as sexually unsatisfying by the offender (Groth & Hobson, 1983).

Behavioral Treatment. Knopp, Rosenberg, and Stevenson (1986) identified 297 programs for adult sex offenders in the United States and determined that behavioral techniques played a substantial role in the treatment strategies of 64 percent of these programs, with 32 percent of the programs employing counterconditioning principles. Counterconditioning entails pairing an adverse stimulus (for example, shock) with the target behavior (visualizing or acting out the sexual deviation). Uncontrolled clinical studies denote that counterconditioning procedures are effective in reducing the aberrant behavior of exhibitionists (Evans, 1967), voyeurs (Bancroft, Jones, & Pullan, 1966), and pedophiles (Rachman & Teasdale, 1969). Studies in which greater experimental control has been achieved have shown counterconditioning to be superior to brief psychotherapy (Feldman & MacCulloch, 1971), muscular relaxation (Rooth & Marks, 1974), and placebo conditioning (Birk et al., 1971), but not desensitization (Bancroft, 1970), in the treatment of various forms of sexual deviation.

Covert sensitization (Cautela, 1967) is an imagery-based counterconditioning procedure in which the subject is instructed to visualize him or herself engaging in the deviant act (for example, sexual molestation) followed by images of an adverse consequence (for example, nausea followed by vomiting). This technique has been found effective in reducing recidivism in a wide spectrum of cases where sexual offending was the target behavior (Barlow & Abel, 1981; Kelly, 1982; Lanyon, 1986; Laws & Osborn, 1983). Maletzky (1974) recorded positive outcomes with 10 to 12 bimonthly sessions of assisted covert sensitization (use of an actual noxious odor to help promote the nausea response) and booster sessions after six months.

Arousal reconditioning involves pairing masturbation with an appropriate sexual stimulus (for example, picture of a naked adult female). Davison (1968) advises that because sexual offenders often have difficulty becoming aroused when exposed to an appropriate stimulus, subjects should commence by masterbating to deviant stimuli (for example, picture of a male or female child) but then shift to a more appropriate stimulus once arousal has been achieved. Reviewing the literature on arousal reconditioning, Conrad and Wincze (1976) raised several methodological questions about research showing this particular form of behavioral intervention to be an effective adjunct in the treatment of sexual deviations. Attempting to overcome these problems, Abel et al. (1975) recommended that fantasy alternation (shifting from an inappropriate target to an appropriate one) occur between sessions rather than within sessions. Only time and further research will tell whether these recommendations prove fruitful.

A variety of other behavioral techniques, among them masturbatory satiation (Abel & Annon, 1982), verbal satiation (Laws & Osborn, 1982), desensitization (Annon, 1971), and shaping (Annon, 1975), have been successfully employed in the treatment of sexually aberrant behavior. Davidson (1984) compared 36 incarcerated sex offenders enrolled in a behaviorally oriented treatment program with 36 control subjects and found recidivism in the control group to be five times higher than that observed in treated subjects over a five-year follow-up period. Utilizing penile plethysmographic readings as a measure of sexual arousal, investigators from the Pines Residential Center in Portsmouth, Virginia, determined that adolescent molesters of prepubescent children witnessed substantial reductions in arousal to deviant cues after participating in a treatment program employing covert sensitization, satiation training, and a variety of cognitive-behavioral techniques (Hunter & Santos, 1990). The general consensus, then, is that behavioral techniques are more effective than psychodynamic, eclectic, and biomedical approaches in promoting change in rapists (Abel, Rouleau, & Cunningham-Rathner, 1985), exhibitionists (Blair & Lanyon, 1981), and the molesters of young children (Kelly, 1982).

Though more widely effective than drug and traditional psychotherapeutic interventions, behavior modification and counterconditioning techniques are inadequate to the task of effecting long-term change in sex offenders unless supplemented by other procedures (social education, cognitive skills training, relapse prevention, post-release reinforcement). This is clearly apparent in the early results obtained from the Vermont Treatment Program for Sexual Aggressors (VTPSA). Effective integration of behavioral and nonbehavioral modalities and procedures by VTPSA staff has served to limit re-offense rates on the part of treated offenders to 4 percent after one year, with a five-year controlled comparison currently being conducted (Turkington, 1987).

Comment. Reiterating a sentiment expressed numerous times in this chapter, we must find ways to identify which programs and procedures are most effective with which categories of sexual offender. Groth's trichotomy of anger, power, and sadistic forms of rape may be of assistance in this regard. Anger rapists are said to be more physically aggressive and their acts more impulsive and episodic than power or sadistic rapists (Groth & Hobson, 1983). Therapeutic inroads with anger rapists might well be carved with educational and rational-emotive interventions. Power rapists are characterized as anxious, consumed with sexual fantasy, and likely to engage in sexual assault as a means of achieving a sense of power and control over others (Groth & Hobson, 1983). Stress management, cognitive skills training, and social/assertive skill development may well aid treatment efforts directed at the thinking and behavior of power rapists. Finally, the sadistic rapist eroticizes physical force, power, and control and is said to engage in rape as an expression of compulsive, ritualistic, and oftentimes bizarre sexual fantasies. Counterconditioning and drug therapies would appear to be the interventions of choice with sadistic rapists. However, in the absence of well-designed studies in which subjects are randomly assigned to treatment and placebo control conditions, we remain largely ignorant of these possible subtype-treatment relationships.

Violent Offenders

Agee (1986) has designed a treatment program for violent recidivists that borrows liberally from the therapeutic community and team-management approaches. Though the program seems to possess potential, controlled outcome studies have yet to be conducted. Fagan (1990) has evaluated the results of the Violent Juvenile Offender (VJO) project instituted in four cities: Boston, Detroit, Memphis, and Newark, New Jersey. The VJO was established for the purpose of preparing young institutionalized offenders for the difficult task of integrating back into society by teaching them how to avoid future episodes of violent and nonviolent criminality. This is accomplished with the assistance of social networking techniques, identification of subject needs, and interventions conducted from a social learning perspective. In two of the cities studied (Boston, Detroit) implementation of VJO principles was strong, while in the other two cities (Memphis, Newark) implementation was weak. Outcomes were in the predicted direction for the two cities exhibiting strong implementation; a converse pattern was noted in the two cities displaying weak implementation. This study benefits from the fact subjects were randomly assigned to the experimental program (VJO) or a control condition (mainstream juvenile corrections), although experimental subjects may have benefited from the augmented attention they received as a result of their participation in this project.

Emotionally Disturbed Offenders

With interest in the emotionally disturbed offender growing, one would think that treatment programs for mentally disordered felons would also be on the rise. Other than traditional mental hospital care, however, there are relatively few innovative programs directed at the emotionally disordered offender and even fewer that have been adequately and thoroughly evaluated. Rogers and Cavanaugh describe the development of an outpatient program for emotionally disturbed offenders at the Issac Ray Center, Rush-Presbyterian-St. Luke's Medical Center in Chicago. The goals of this program are threefold: (1) reduce offenders' potential for future violence; (2) stimulate the remission of psychiatric symptomatology; (3) foster more positive interpersonal relationships. After 20 months none of the 50 program participants had been arrested for a violent crime, although two had been apprehended and charged with disorderly conduct (Rogers & Cavanaugh, 1981a).

Approximately one-fourth of Rogers and Cavanaugh's sample had been re-hospitalized during the 20-month follow-up period, but the majority of hospitalizations were for relatively brief stays. Case study material intimates that approximately half the treatment sample showed signs of significant improvement over the course of this 20-month period. Goldmeier, Sauer, and White (1977) followed 42 persons released from a halfway house for mentally disordered offenders and discovered recidivism to be low (4.7%) and re-hospitalization moderate (24%) for a period of three years. Where the results obtained by Rogers and Cavanaugh and Goldmeier et al. are interesting, both studies lacked appropriate control groups and methodological rigor that, in turn, may have confounded the results and made interpretation all but impossible.

DIFFERENTIAL TREATMENT EFFECTS

The necessity of considering differential treatment effects and the possibility that research studies on person-oriented treatment interventions have typically fallen short of providing clinicians with fully useful treatment information suggests that we must find a mechanism by which we might understand and identify differential treatment-offender effects. A major impediment to the development of knowledge on differential treatment effects is that, of the few studies probing this issue, there has been minimal effort directed at cultivating a theoretical superstructure useful in formulating hypotheses and working models of treatment-offender interaction. A paper published recently by Andrews, Bonta, and Hoge (1990), however, might well span the conceptual chasm that has too long blemished the integrity of research and practice on person-oriented intervention. The Andrews model considers four classification principles, three of which are discussed here.

Risk

Risk factors are measurable characteristics, attributes, and circumstances that possess demonstrable prognostic value in the prediction of future criminal outcomes. Andrews et al. (1990) explored the possibility of an interaction between risk factors and level of service or treatment. Whether one's subjects are juveniles (Byles & Maurice, 1982) or adults (Andrews & Friesen, 1987), the intervention is aimed at the individual (Byles & Maurice, 1982) or the community (Kirchmer et al., 1980) level, or the outcome is measured by arrests (Byles & Maurice, 1982) or scores on a probation success inventory (Andrews et al., 1986), the relationship between antecedent risk variables and level of service is remarkably consistent. Persons and circumstances evaluated to be at high risk for criminal involvement benefit from increased intensity of service while lower-risk persons and circumstances either do no better or actually end up doing worse when the service level is increased (Andrews et al., 1990).

Needs

Criminogenic needs are conceptualized by Andrews et al. (1990) as a sub-category of risk factors. In defining criminogenic needs Andrews et al. comment that needs are characteristics that may change over time, and as a result, either enhance or diminish an offender's chances of becoming involved in future criminal conduct. Scores on the Level of Supervision Inventory, or LSI (Andrews, 1983) were used by Andrews et al. to demonstrate how comprehending criminogenic needs can facilitate our ability to detect differential treatment effects. Andrews and Wormith (1984) ascertained that six-month retest scores on the LSI were more predictive of post-probation recidivism than LSI results obtained at intake. Accordingly, high-risk offenders whose LSI scores had for some reason dropped to below average after six months experienced a substantially better outcome than offenders whose LSI scores remained high. It also must be kept in mind that various offenders present with different treatment needs and that while a change in an attribute may portend a positive treatment effect in one group, a similar change may presage poor outcome in a second group (Andrews et al., 1990).

Responsivity

Offenders differ according to their abilities and learning styles. Responsivity involves matching models and styles of intervention with offender characteristics and abilities (Andrews et al., 1990). The PICO and Camp Elliot projects (Grant, 1965) are two early examples of responsivity research on offender populations. Inmates in the PICO project were judged either amenable or unamenable to treatment based on their verbal skills, anxiety level, and motivation for change. Results indicated that amenable subjects assigned to psychodynamic casework experienced better outcomes than psychodynamic casework–exposed unamenable subjects; however, no amenable-unamenable outcome differences were noted in the untreated group (Grant, 1965). In the Camp Elliot study military inmates judged to be more mature (perceptive, reflective, anxious) responded better to a less structured treatment regime, while less mature inmates responded better to a more structured milieu (Grant, 1965). Similar findings have been recorded in studies comparing offender groups classified according to criminal history (Walters, 1991), expressed anxiety (Andrews, 1980), or conceptual level (Reitsma-Street & Leschied, 1988).

Anxiety, sensation seeking, social support, and motivation for change are all person variables cited by Andrews et al. (1990) as possible theoretical links in the concatenated chain of events that make up the responsivity process. However, in keeping with the spirit of studies implicating cognitive skills training as particularly effective in reducing future episodes of criminal involvement, cognitive skill level may be one of the more powerful determinants of responsivity. As a case in point, Simons et al. (1985) surmised that subjects entering treatment with good self-management skills faired better in cognitive therapy while less skilled subjects responded best to drug therapy. Likewise, Arbuthnot and Gordon (1986) discerned that not all of the subjects enrolled in an intervention program designed to improve moral reasoning skills responded to the treatment regime. The authors speculate that unimproved subjects lacked the cognitive skill necessary to benefit from the moral reasoning component of this program. Consequently, the principles of risk, need, and responsivity should be taken into account when attempting to match offenders with various treatment modalities.

CONCLUSION

In this initial chapter on intervention, the fifth of our five foundations of criminal science, two things are clear. First, the vast majority of studies addressing themselves to the issue of treatment efficacy in criminal populations can be faulted on methodological and conceptual grounds. Though investigators have improved the methodological rigor of their studies since Martinson (1974) announced his "nothing works" verdict nearly 20 years ago, the field still lacks the effulgence of a meaningful theoretical superstructure by which to organize and buttress future research projects and effectively apply current research findings. Second, the data reviewed in this chapter find the "nothing works" hypothesis to be weak and unconvincing. Not only do the results of recent meta-analyses of the rehabilitation issue indicate that treatment can be efficacious (Andrews, Zinger et al., 1990; Davidson et al., 1984; Garrett, 1985; Izzo & Ross, 1990), but narrative reviews of the literature suggest that more methodologically sound studies show more of an effect than less methodologically sound ones (Gendreau & Ross, 1979, 1987). More important, the "nothing works" argument has helped steer us away from more theoretically and conceptually fertile ground, differential treatment questions in particular.

The results of this admittedly brief survey of person-oriented strategies of intervention connote that cognitive and behavioral procedures are generally superior to most other forms of therapeutic intervention, at least where criminal populations are concerned. The moral model, however, holds promise of effectively infusing such issues as choice and personal responsibility into mainstream cognitive and behavioral thought. The theoretical underpinnings that are so sorely lacking in person-oriented forms of treatment intervention with adult and juvenile offenders might very well be found in behavior, thought, and moral reasoning. This, in fact, has already been accomplished to a degree in the general writings of Beck (1976), Maultsby (1975), and Meichenbaum (1977) and in the offender-specific writings of Czudner (1985) and Walters (1990), though it awaits further evaluation and exposition.

Research studies scrutinizing the efficacy of person-based intervention strategies with criminal populations could be improved if researchers would consider but a few points. First, random assignment of subjects to conditions is necessary if we wish to boost confidence in the internal and external validity of our findings. Use of a control or comparison group (preferably one designed along attention-placebo lines) is a second factor that should be routinely assimilated into future research investigations on person-oriented interventions with criminals and delinquents. Finally, a sufficiently long period of follow-up, one to two years at a minimum, is required in order to provide investigators with the opportunity to review the stability of a particular outcome. Of the research findings reviewed in this chapter, few studies have addressed all three, or even two, of these issues, Sarason (1978) and Kazdin et al. (1989) being two notable exceptions to this general rule.

Of overriding necessity in advancing criminal science research on person-oriented interventions is the development of a theoretically meaningful and methodologically sound system of inquiry. Component analyses of global programs will help identify those factors responsible for a major portion of the variance in outcome measures and should aid us in devising more cost-efficient intervention strategies. Where there are now only a handful of studies on the differential treatment issue, we must take steps to expand their number so that we are in a better position to answer newly formulated questions on rehabilitation; for example, ''which specific interventions work to bring about change in which type offenders under which sets of circumstances?'' Should researchers choose to make a concerted effort to tighten up their research designs, ground their investigations in coherent theory, and examine such issues as component analysis and differential treatment effects, then the next 20 years of research inquiry promise to offer a great deal more than have the past 20.

7

Situation-Oriented Intervention: Prevention

We have been told that an ounce of prevention is worth a pound of cure. Nowhere is this more evident than with criminal science interventions. If we could find ways to effectively avert crime before it had an opportunity to wield its destructive influence we would be well on our way to becoming the architects of a truly sophisticated science. Reducing the financial and emotional costs of crime is therefore a major objective of investigations probing the fifth foundation of criminal science: intervention. Whether our efforts are directed at preventing crime, venereal disease, or forest fires, valid procedures are essential. This is because, unlike interventions taking place ex post facto, preventive efforts are capable of interceding before a potentially explosive situation has a chance to materialize and adversely effect others. This is why we must subject the techniques and procedures of crime prevention to hard empirical fact, scrutiny, and exposition.

Prevention can be conceptualized as existing in one of three forms: primary, secondary, and tertiary. Primary prevention is aimed at reducing the incidence and general prevalence of crime through modification of certain criminogenic conditions, whether these conditions be psychological, physical, or interpersonal. In contrast, secondary prevention is concerned with the early diagnosis and treatment of nascent criminal behavior. Tertiary prevention, on the other hand, encompasses rehabilitation efforts directed at long-term criminal cases. All three levels of prevention need to be addressed if there is to be any hope of impeding crime by way of a comprehensive system of crime prevention.

Although the primary-secondary-tertiary trichotomy is central to any discussion on prevention, the present chapter is organized conceptually. According to formulations derived from rational-choice theory, preventive efforts are designed to influence the costs, benefits, incentives, and opportunities for future criminal activity. The goals of crime prevention include raising the cost of crime as well as decreasing its benefits, incentives, and opportunities. In corresponding fashion, prevention seeks to enhance the benefits, incentives, and opportunities for noncrime while lowering the cost of prosocial activities. In the discourse that follows we find ourselves perusing the efficacy of preventive interventions engineered to influence not only the relative costs and benefits of criminal and prosocial forms of behavior, but also the relative incentives for crime versus noncrime and opportunities for lawbreaking conduct. First, however, we take a moment to reflect on the methodology of research studies addressing the crime prevention issue.

METHODOLOGICAL ISSUES IN RESEARCH ON CRIME PREVENTION

The preceding chapter ably demonstrated that studies on person-based intervention strategies are replete with myriad methodological errors, oversights, and omissions. This unfortunate state of affairs is an even more potent problem in research on crime prevention. The cream of the prevention crop are quasi-experimental studies that compare treatment or target groups with one or more presumably equivalent control conditions. Because most investigations on crime prevention have failed to achieve true experimental control—that is, subjects are not randomly assigned to experimental (target) and control (comparison) conditions—alternative explanations of the relationships observed in these studies abound. It would therefore appear that research addressing the issue of crime prevention is flawed to the point of defying meaningful analysis and interpretation. However, it is still possible to identify significant patterns and trends that, with the development of a more sophisticated methodology, might then be subjected to rigorous empirical evaluation.

Before proceeding with our review of crime prevention strategies it seems advisable that we examine one particular methodological issue in some detail: the problem of defining outcome. Traditionally, crime rates have served as the sole outcome measure for research on crime control and prevention. This is an overly narrow conceptualization in light of the fact that crime prevention is duty-bound to eliminate resident fear, improve community solidarity, and reduce the rate of crime. Rosenbaum (1988), in fact, advises assessing the relative merits of crime prevention programs to incorporate measures of intermediate outcome, such as increased membership in community action groups and changes in the behavior of targeted persons and organizations (landlords, local businesses). Therefore, while crime rates remain the most frequently cited measure of outcome, attitudinal change, fear of crime, and various intermediate measures are considered as they appear in the literature.

ALTERING THE INCENTIVES FOR CRIMINAL AND NONCRIMINAL BEHAVIOR

Modification of incentives for crime and noncrime can be a particularly effective means of situation-based intervention aimed at the primary and secondary prevention of crime. As such, this section explores interventions occurring in the home, in the school environment, in the neighborhood and general community, and in the mass media.

Family Interventions

Owing to the fact that family and parental factors have been shown to correlate meaningfully with later behavior, one form of which is criminal conduct (see Chapter 6 of Volume 1), it is reasonable to assume that changing parenting strategies and family interactive patterns may prove fruitful in preventing future criminal outcomes in selected family members. Short of an Orwellian government program where people are required to demonstrate their parental competence before being granted permission to have children, we must resign ourselves to a world where people produce children for whom they are unable, unwilling, or ill equipped to provide adequate care and guidance. This does not mean, however, that ameliorative programs designed to instruct the parents and families of delinquents and predelinquents in more effective child management strategies do not exist.

The majority of anticriminal family interventions have secondary prevention (working with the families of delinquents), rather than primary prevention (working with families before delinquency problems appear), goals in mind. A study conducted in Tucson, Arizona, showed that teaching parents and children various behavioral contracting techniques led to improved behavior, augmented grades, and reduced delinquency on the part of treated children (Tharp & Wetzel, 1969), although the implications of these results are limited by the fact that the investigators failed to include a control group. Alexander and Parsons (1973, 1982) in Salt Lake City and Patterson (1980) at the Oregon Social Learning Center have developed two of the more popular and widely researched behavioral management programs for families of problem and delinquent children and adolescents. The intent of these programs is to train parents and families in how to establish clear rules, monitor behavior, and make reinforcement contingent upon approved behavior and punishment contingent upon disapproved behavior.

At the Oregon Social Learning Center, Patterson, Chamberlain, and Reid (1982) offered the parents of highly aggressive children and teenagers 17 hours of training in behavioral management techniques. Targeted youth in the ten treated families demonstrated reductions of 60 percent in aggressive behavioral outcomes compared to a 15 percent drop in the acting-out behavior of youth in untreated control families. Other studies also highlight the efficacy of this approach to primary and secondary prevention when experimental-control comparisons are made (Patterson, 1985; Patterson et al., 1982; Patterson & Fleischman, 1979), although there is a dearth of experimentally controlled investigations on this topic. A one-year follow-up of a study in which random assignment of subjects to experimental and control conditions was accomplished revealed that while treated juveniles spent significantly less time in youth de-

Table 7.1
The "Ten Beliefs" of Toughlove

1. Family problems have roots and supports in the culture.

2. Parents are people too.

3. Parents' material and emotional resources are limited.

4. Parents and kids are not equal.

5. Blaming keeps people helpless.

6. Kids' behavior affects parents. Parents' behavior affects kids.

7. Taking a stand precipitates a crisis.

8. From controlled crisis comes the possibility of positive change.

9. Families need to give and get support in their own community in order to change.

10. The essence of family life is cooperation, not togetherness.

Source: York & York (1990).

tention centers than untreated controls (indicating a treatment effect for severity of offending), there were no experimental-control differences in the frequency of offending (Marlowe et al., 1986).

The Salt Lake City group (Alexander & Parsons, 1973, 1982) has also documented the efficacy of family-oriented behavioral interventions with the families and parents of delinquent and predelinquent youth. This program has been shown to be effective in modifying the behavior of first-time offenders (Klein, Alexander, & Parsons, 1977) as well as hard-core delinquent recidivists (Barton et al., 1985). Comparing youth treated with the family intervention program designed by Alexander and Parsons with youth placed on probation, Gordon, Arbuthnot, Gustafson, and McGrew (cited in Gendreau & Ross, 1987) observed that six times as many probationers as treated subjects (67% versus 11%) were subsequently adjudicated during a two-and-one-half-year follow-up period. Similar outcomes were observed in a California study on parent training and delinquency (Berkowitz & Hazlewood, 1973).

Self-help programs like Toughlove have also been developed to assist parents and others embroiled in a negative relationship with an out-of-control family member. The underlying philosophy of programs like Toughlove is that through support, information, and action change is possible. This philosophy is summarized in the "Ten Beliefs" that buttress the Toughlove model of intervention (see Table 7.1). Toughlove comprises numerous local chapters, each providing participants with skills, knowledge, and emotional support in a highly structured group atmosphere. The central organization, Toughlove International, is funded by contributions, membership fees, the sale of program materials, and workshop honorariums (York & York, 1990). Though there is testimonial support for the efficacy of Toughlove, there are, to the author's knowledge, no experimental outcome studies addressing the efficacy of this particular approach to secondary prevention.

The findings of research conducted on interventions with the families of delinquents and nondelinquents suggest that clearly defined and behaviorally oriented intercessions can reduce future occurrences of delinquency and contribute to the secondary prevention effort. However, less is known about the use of family- and parent-based interventions as a primary prevention strategy, although there is evidence that parent training programs are capable of producing favorable reactions in delinquent children as well as in their nontargeted siblings (Humphreys et al., 1978; Klein et al., 1977). Baumrind (1971) reports that the sons of authoritarian parents (rigid, aloof, dictatorial) tend to be mistrustful, rebellious, and hostile, but that boys raised by authoritative parents (structured, warm, democratic) tend to be friendly, cooperative, and successful. Since parenting style may be as much an effect as a cause of child hostility (Bell & Harper, 1977), longitudinal research is needed to address the causal direction of the frequently observed relationship between parenting style and offspring behavior.

In closing this section it is important to point out that the rising rate of divorce and looming significance of single parenthood have led to what some people believe to be the demise of the nuclear family in America. If this is true it makes it that much more difficult to intervene through the identified client's family or parents. It may therefore be necessary to explore additional ways by which we might alter the incentives for crime and noncrime as well as find alternatives to the traditional nuclear family. Perhaps school- and community-based interventions or the adoption of a more communal approach to child-rearing philosophy (such as is practiced on the Israeli kibbutz) might eventually fill the void left by the apparent disintegration of nuclear family values in American society, although additional research is required in order to evaluate this possibility.

School-Based Interventions

Some parents would argue that schools were established to instruct students in academic matters and that social learning matters should be left to the parents and various community organizations. This is a point well taken, but not all parents take the time to instruct their children in the social amenities and not all children participate in community activities like scouts, Little League, or the YMCA/YWCA. The school can therefore serve a vital function in socializing youth by educating pupils in interpersonal relations, problem solving, and social negotiation in a setting that provides students with the opportunity to interact with peers and authority figures. Though school-based social learning is no substitute for family-based instruction, it can serve a useful adjunct function by providing the individual with an array of learning opportunities on which to hone their decision-making and problem-solving skills.

Unlike research on family interventions, school-based studies have considered the issue of primary prevention. Rose and Marshall (1974) examined the results of a study in which social workers intervened with elementary-level pupils in northern England by way of a social casework approach. Results indicated that students exposed to the program were slightly less likely to end up in legal trouble than were untreated students. In one of the better designed studies on school-based intervention as a primary prevention tool, the Perry Preschool research team (Berreuta-Clement et al., 1984) evaluated 123 black children randomly assigned to a Head Start program at three to four years of age. By age 19 approximately one-fourth of the preschool subjects had experienced legal trouble as adults in comparison to 40 percent of the controls, with 74 adult arrests per 100 people in the preschool condition and 160 adult arrests per 100 people in the control condition.

It seems reasonable that sufficiently intense programming aimed at preschoolers would have a significant impact on later social adjustment, but what about less intense interventions aimed at older pupils? Englander-Golden (1983) followed such a procedure in designing the Say It Straight (SIS) program for the treatment of adolescent drug use. Borrowing from interpersonal communications theory, family sculpturing, and various role-playing procedures, SIS instructs students in how to communicate with others, in hopes of helping them form better peer relations and a more positive self-image. A school in which fifth to eighth graders were exposed to a five-day SIS training program witnessed lower rates of alcohol- and drug-related problems and a drop in vandalism-related repair bills over time (Englander-Golden, Elconin, & Satir, 1986). Extending SIS training to 352 high school students, Englander-Golden and colleagues followed trained and untrained pupils for a period of one-and-one-half years and discovered a five-to-one ratio of subsequent offenses for untrained versus trained subjects (Englander-Golden et al., 1989). However, because the untreated group comprised students who had entered the ninth grade a year after training had been completed, the obtained outcomes are far from conclusive.

School-based interventions have also been utilized with secondary prevention aims in mind. Bry (1982), for instance, randomly assigned high-risk students to experimental and control conditions, and determined that programs designed to teach high-risk adolescents behavioral management and self-efficacy skills were effective in reducing the percentage of students engaged in a chronic pattern of rule-violating behavior during a five-year follow-up period. Several additional studies have also shown school-based programs to be effective in reducing the level of ensuing criminality experienced by high-risk or actively delinquent youth (Chandler et al., 1984; Johnson & Breckenridge, 1982). Although the effect of school-based prevention may not be as puissant as family-oriented procedures, it seems sufficiently robust to warrant further study and inclusion in a comprehensive program of crime prevention.

Community-Based Programs

Community-oriented prevention programs also appear to be reasonably effective in reducing the frequency and intensity of future delinquent behavior (Bry,

1982; Chandler et al., 1984; Johnson & Breckenridge, 1982). The belief that community-based programs can impact on the relative incentives for crime and noncrime can be traced back to the Chicago school of criminology (Shaw & McKay, 1942), which held that high-crime areas were characterized by social disorganization and a lack of community cohesion. Skogan (1987) supplies evidence of augmented levels of social disorder and crime in neighborhoods beset with low community solidarity and less frequent social interaction, while such behavior tends to be much less common in areas where residents show affinity for their neighbors (Taub, Taylor, & Dunham, 1984), exude a sense of responsibility for activities going on in the community (Taylor, Gottfredson, & Brower, 1981), and display a willingness to intervene in situations where crime is occurring (Newman & Franck, 1980). Though it is difficult to determine whether social disorganization or alienation is a cause or an effect of criminal activity, the implication of cross-sectional analyses of this topic is that community-based interventions may be capable of aiding the primary and secondary prevention efforts.

Studies show that witnesses are more likely to provide police with information if they know the victim, other witnesses, or are familiar with the environment in which the crime took place (Gills & Hagan, 1982; Moriarity, 1975). Lavrakas and Bennett (1988) reviewed the preliminary outcome of ten urban neighborhood anticrime self-help programs that had been in existence for approximately five years. Findings from this study indicate that the programs had little impact on official crime statistics, victimization rates, or fear or crime, though there may have been some effect on an individual level (Fischer, 1988). The use of community-based programs to increase surveillance and decrease criminal opportunities is a major topic in the next section of this chapter.

Whereas community-based programs may be of dubious value in influencing the incentives for crime and noncrime from a primary prevention standpoint, they appear to be more useful as secondary prevention measures. The Argus Community Program in the South Bronx (Sturz & Taylor, 1987) and the House of Umoja in Philadelphia (Fattah, 1987) provide extended-family support for high-risk and adjudicated adolescents, and have been shown to be effective in curbing recidivism when compared with outcomes achieved by youth released from juvenile facilities (Curtis, 1987). Smith, Farrant, and Marchant (1972) intervened with 54 predelinquent and delinquent males residing in an English slum by way of community meetings and individualized casework, and noted that program youth did better than matched controls living in another slum in the same general area. However, the effect was moderate and largely transient. Moreover, interpretation of these results is confounded by the fact that control subjects were sampled from a different area than were program participants. In a study providing better experimental control, Fo and O'Donnell (1974) paired troublesome youth with adult companions who used verbal reinforcement and small monetary rewards that were either contingent on approved behavior or dispensed independent of the juvenile's actions. Consistent with their main hypothesis, Fo and O'Donnell reported that the contingent group experienced better outcomes during a three-year follow-up than youth in the noncontingent condition or subjects in a no-treatment control group.

Media-Based Programs

The media explosion of the past several decades provides us with one more avenue through which we might modify incentives for criminal and noncriminal action. Whether it be television, movies, newspapers, or magazines, the prospects seem limitless. The average American household watches seven hours of television a day (Comstock, 1980), and it would be naive of us to think this has no effect on behavior. Recently the American public has been exposed to television commercials informing us of the dangers of drugs and extolling the virtues of drug-free living. As creative and poignant as these campaigns might be, whether they promote behavioral change is an empirical question for which there is no definitive answer at this time. Nevertheless, in a recent review of the Partnership for a Drug-Free America media campaign, Black (1991) of the Gordon S. Black Research Corporation of Rochester, New York, discerned that attitudes toward and self-reported use of marijuana and cocaine declined more in high, as opposed to low, media-exposed areas. This issue demands further attention, though, since the differences between high and low media-exposed areas were only on the order of two to four percentage points.

Past research studies on media-based medical education campaigns suggest that such promotions rarely effect long-term behavioral change (Hu & Mitchell, 1981; Vuylsteek, 1979). Supplementing these media campaigns with additional information, however, may yield more positive results as were observed in an Australian study investigating a television commercial on controlled drinking. This commercial was effective in reducing alcohol consumption in viewers, but only if accompanied by a form letter announcing initiation of the campaign (Barber, Bradshaw, & Walsh, 1989). Consequently, it may be necessary to alert viewers to the commencement and purpose of an anti-crime, anti-drug, or controlled-drinking advertising campaign before we can expect our efforts to yield positive outcomes.

The mass media not only reflect the national attitude but help shape it as well. It is therefore possible that the media may exert an unintended counterprevention effect by glamorizing certain criminals (for example, organized crime figures) or making it appear that crime is rampant and beyond our control. Gorelick (1989) reviewed a four-month crimefighters campaign conducted by the New York *Daily News* in 1982. In addition to discovering that the newspaper overrepresented the incidence of serious crimes like rape, robbery, and burglary, the language used by the paper conveyed the impression that crime was random, unpredictable, and without realistic remedy. Unintended antiprevention media effects were also observed in an experimentally conducted investigation of citizens in the city of Amsterdam (Winkel, 1987). Therefore, while the mass media might very well provide a useful adjunct to incentive-modifying primary preventive interventions with families, schools, and communities, they are generally ineffective as a stand-alone procedure (Nuttall, 1989; Sacco & Silverman, 1981).

By way of conclusion, more research is required to ascertain the potential utility of media-based interventions as incentive-altering crime-prevention strategies, and care needs to be exercised so that we might avoid the unintended antiprevention effects that sometimes accompany media campaigns. A study constructed from data provided by the National Crime Survey showed evidence of a complex relationship between media exposure and people's fear of crime (Liska & Baccaglini, 1990). At the sake of oversimplification, the main effect observed by Liska and Baccaglini was that certain categories of coverage (for example, a local homicide) elicited increased fear in respondents while other crime stories (for example, a nonlocal homicide) seemed to correlate with a diminution of fear.

DECREASING CRIMINAL OPPORTUNITIES

Crime is encouraged by minimal levels of surveillance in public places and discouraged by a willingness to supervise youth, challenge strangers, and testify as a witness (Goodstein, 1980). That most reported crimes are normally restricted to a relatively small number of areas, so-called hot spots of crime (Sherman, Gartin, & Buerger, 1989) demonstrates the potential utility of opportunity-reducing prevention techniques. Rarefying opportunities for crime by marking possessions, increasing surveillance, or agreeing to serve as a witness in a particular criminal case is covered in this section.

Target Hardening

Target hardening involves establishing physical (locked doors, alarms, marking possessions) and psychological (leaving house lights on, halting mail delivery, posting a "Beware of Dog" sign in a prominent place) barriers designed to deter crime. Research suggests that burglarized homes have fewer physical barriers and fences, fewer symbolic and psychological barriers, and fewer signs of occupancy (Brown & Altman, 1983). Installing new locks in an inner-city housing project (Arthur Young Inc., 1978), burglar alarms in schools (Cedar Rapids Police Department, 1972), and high-intensity street lights in a neighborhood (Lavrakas & Kushmuk, 1986) have all been shown to correspond with diminished levels of criminal victimization. Psychological barriers and occupancy status, however, are normally even more powerful deterrents to property-oriented crimes like burglary (Bennett & Wright, 1984; Winchester & Jackson, 1982).

Target hardening has been used to fight public telephone vandalism, deter bus robberies, and reduce automobile theft. Vandalism from public telephones in England declined substantially after aluminum coin boxes were replaced by sturdier steel boxes (Clarke, 1983). The rate of bus robberies in New York City plummeted after flat-fare automatic collection procedures were instituted (Hough, Clarke, & Mayhew, 1980). Auto theft in the Federal Republic of Germany fell dramatically after all automobiles were fitted with locking steering columns (Mayhew et al., 1976). When these steering-column locks were installed in new automobiles in England a reduction was noted in the number of new vehicles stolen, although the overall rate did not change owing to the fact that there was an increase in the number of older vehicles (which had not been fitted with the steering-column locks) being pilfered (Mayhew et al., 1976).

Target hardening also occurs when persons mark their valuables with a name, number, or code. It has been estimated that one in four households engrave valuables as a crime-prevention measure, the most commonly utilized procedure in most surveys (Bureau of Justice Statistics, 1985). Households participating in property-marking schemes in Seattle, Washington (Seattle Law & Justice Planning Office, 1975), and St. Louis, Missouri (Schimerman, 1974), experienced reductions in home burglaries of 33 and 25 percent, respectively. A longitudinal analysis of this issue revealed that displaying property-marking stickers in the window of a home dramatically lessened that home's chances of being burglarized (Wilson & Schneider, 1978). On the other hand, property marking is viewed by property offenders themselves as a generally ineffective means of crime prevention (Figgie Corporation, 1988) and has little impact on city-wide burglary rates (Mattick et al., 1974). The logical explanation is that, like auto thefts diverted by steering-column locks in England, burglars deterred by the property-marking practices of one home likely shift their attention to a more vulnerable target in that same neighborhood. Consequently, while participating homes may experience lower rates of victimization, there is a corresponding increase in the number of nonparticipating homes burglarized, which in the long-run eliminates any community-wide effect.

Defensible Space

In a 1972 book entitled *Defensible Space*, architect Oscar Newman outlined ways by which the physical design of a housing project might be modified to discourage criminal victimization. Defensible space is founded on the principles of territoriality and surveillability. By creating perceived zones of territorial influence through augmentation of a resident's sphere of personal space, and by maximizing the opportunity for surveillance through various architectural design modifications, theorists like Newman reason that crime can be substantially reduced. Probing the relationship between physical space and crime in several New York City housing projects, Newman uncovered data that verified aspects of the defensible space theorem. Though Newman's early work was severely criticized for failing to account for household density and the characteristics of persons living in these housing areas (Mawby, 1977; Mayhew, 1979), more recent investigations have also found general support for defensible space formulations (Newman & Franck, 1980; Sommer, 1987).

It has been observed that criminals prefer areas that are open and public and avoid areas that are closed and private (Brown & Altman, 1983). Accordingly, residences and businesses located near parking lots, streets, and recreation areas are subject to higher crime rates (Brill, 1972). White (1990) determined that differences in the permeability of neighborhoods to heavily traveled throughways accounted for 34 percent of the variation in officially recorded burglary rates. It has also been noted that vandalism is more common in semipublic areas where surveillance and a sense of ownership or territoriality are low (Wilson, 1978). In further support of defensible space theory, burglary rates are two times higher in blocks that border a neighborhood and in apartments that sit on the outer perimeter of a block than ones located interiorly (Brantingham & Brantingham, 1975; Greenberg & Rohe, 1984). Similar outcomes have been observed with stores and business located near the boundaries of a neighborhood or block (Luedtke & Associates, 1970).

The territoriality function of the defensible space doctrine holds that diminished social cohesion and interaction will lead to increased levels of neighborhood crime (Skogan, 1987). As public areas are made more private, so say defensible space theorists, residents achieve a superior sense of ownership and an inclination to defend their territory through increased vigilance and willingness to report crime. However, research studies addressing this issue show that architectural modifications designed to encourage territoriality are less reliably correlated with reductions in the crime rate than modifications directed at expanding surveillance (Greenberg & Rohe, 1984; Rosenbaum, 1988; Winchester & Jackson, 1982). MacDonald and Gifford (1989) presented a group of convicted burglars with 50 photographs of single-family dwellings and unraveled support for the surveillability function of defensible space theory but not the territoriality function.

Whereas the surveillability function of the defensible space approach to crime prevention has received far greater support than the territoriality function, the former is not above reproach, largely because of the methodological frailty of the studies upon which it rests. Take, for instance, a study of surveillance modifications made in a chain of convenience stores. Sixty 7-Eleven stores were altered to increase surveillance and reduce opportunities for crime (installation of high-intensity outdoor lighting, removing advertising from the front window, relocating the cash register to the front of the store). Although these 60 stores experienced 30 percent fewer robberies than 60 nonmodified stores (Krupat & Kubzansky, 1987), this study, like many of those conducted on defensible space theory, lacked adequate experimental control.

While a national evaluation of 41 street-lighting projects (Tien et al., 1979) disclosed that street-light augmentation correlated with reduced levels of citizen fear, there was little overall reduction in crime. A more recent investigation administered by Lavrakas and Kushmuk (1986) disclosed that the installation of high-intensity street lights in Portland, Oregon, was followed by a dramatic attenuation of crime, although interpretation of these findings is made difficult by the fact that several other physical and social preventive measures also went into effect around the same time. Musheno, Levine, and Palumbo (1978) note that closed-circuit television cameras installed in the lobbies and elevators of three buildings in a public housing project in New York City failed to affect crime, possibly because only 14 percent of the residents used the system regularly. Results obtained in studies of vandalism in school as a function of visibility and location (Pablant & Baxter, 1975), crime victimization as a function of pedestrian traffic (Luedtke & Associates, 1970), and property crime as a function of doorman-guarded residences (Repetto, 1974) have generated support for the surveillance prong of the defensible space model of crime prevention.

In sum, defensible space theory provides for several interesting possibilities, but studies addressing its founding tenets have been correlational and cross-sectional in nature (Rubenstein et al., 1980) and the theory itself suffers from conceptual and definitional problems (Mayhew, 1979). With these caveats in mind, I would like to offer the following observations. First, there appears to be moderate support for the surveillance function of defensible space theory but minimal support for the territoriality function. Second, the characteristics of residents living in the housing units targeted for intervention have typically been superior to architectual modifications as a means of predicting crime (Wilson, 1978; Taylor, Gottfredson, & Schumaker, 1984), although taking into account the architectual features of a particular housing situation may enhance the accuracy of forecasts predicated on resident characteristics (Sommer, 1987). Based on findings such as were revealed in Merry's (1981) 18-month analysis of a multiethnic housing project, the University of Illinois at Chicago's Dennis Rosenbaum (1988, p. 20) concluded that "physical design may establish the preconditions for citizens to exercise social control ('defensible space') but it cannot guarantee such behavior ('defended space')."

Policing

Expanding surveillability through police action, private security, and community patrols and watches provides an avenue through which criminal opportunities might be reduced, and in the case of community patrols and watches, could potentially promote increased investment in behavioral displays of social control ("defended space"). In this section we inspect public policing, private policing, and community-based policing.

Public Policing. When the issue of policing is broached, local, state, and federal law enforcement agencies typically come to mind. In fact, many of us view policing to be the personal province of the public law enforcement establishment. However, research suggests that without community support, stepped-up law enforcement has little effect on crime (Clarke & Hough, 1980; Eck & Spelman, 1987; Kelling, 1988). Eck (1982) estimates that a two- to threefold increase in the number of detectives hired by a local police department in the absence of any additional assistance from the community would do little to improve the clearance rate for felony crimes, because detection is highly dependent on leads and information provided by citizens. Steenhuis (1980) adds that patrolling as a deterrent to crime is only effective if conducted in concert with positive police-community relations. Consequently, traditional public policing interventions like motorized police patrols (Kelling et al., 1974), stepped-up criminal investigations (Eck, 1982), and rapid police response (Spelman & Brown, 1984) have been found to be ineffective in curbing crime when police-community relations are ignored.

Even when police-community relations are addressed, the impacts of policing interventions on crime rates are equivocal and relatively mild. Foot patrols instituted in Flint, Michigan (Trojanowicz, 1986), and Newark, New Jersey (Pate, 1986), have generated mixed outcomes as to crime attenuation, although citizen fear of crime did drop and police-community relationships did, in fact, improve. A security program initiated in Oakland, California, in 1982 proved more fruitful, however. The Oakland program called for an increase in the number of officers on foot, motorbike, and motorscooter patrols and added a mounted patrol. Not only did strong-arm robbery, commercial burglary, and auto theft fall precipitously during a one-year period of follow-up, but there was also a corresponding enlargement in feelings of security on the part of persons living and working in the center city (cited in Stewart, 1986). One possible explanation for why the Oakland program enjoyed a greater measure of success than the Flint or Newark programs is that the Oakland procedure received greater community support.

Sherman (1983) described initiation of a program in Houston, Texas, wherein several police officers were assigned to a commercial zone in an effort to establish better community relations. Though the cost of program implementation was substantial, so was the reduction in reported fear. Corollary results were observed in Baltimore, Maryland (Cordner, 1986), and community-sensitive police patrols in Newport News, Virginia, recorded a 39 percent reduction in personal robberies, 35 percent decline in home burglaries, and 53 percent abatement in theft from automobiles (Eck & Spelman, 1987). However, neither study included a control group and so the findings may reflect the influence of a variety of factors external to the policing campaigns themselves, to include the effect of history (Campbell & Stanley, 1966). A research group headed by George Kelling analyzed the results of a program of "proactive patrolling" in Kansas City, Missouri, that called for increased visibility of motorized police patrols in selected areas. However, there was no difference in the rate of recorded criminal activity between proactive patrol and control areas, and citizen fear was actually higher in the experimental zones (Kelling et al., 1974).

At this point it appears that our reliance on public law enforcement as a solution to the problem of crime is naive, fallacious, and short-sighted. While instilling public confidence in the police department by way of integrating officers into the community (Sherman, 1983) or increasing the number of officers on foot patrol (Pate, 1986) may reduce the fear of crime, it is questionable, even under the best of circumstances, whether this takes a noticeable bite out of crime. There are indications from studies conducted in both Baltimore (Furstenberg & Wellford, 1973) and Seattle (Smith & Hawkins, 1973), however, that police-citizen relations can be substantially improved if investigating officers take the time to explain procedures and follow up initial contacts with victims and witnesses. For this reason we must not lose sight of the fact that building good police-community relations should be a major goal of public law enforcement, and that supplementing these efforts with private and community policing programs may enhance, rather than detract from, the efficacy of public systems of law enforcement.

Private Policing. It may come as a surprise to the reader but there are actually more people employed in the private sector of the security industry than in public law enforcement (Cunningham & Taylor, 1985). A rising fear of crime has given birth to expanding private security opportunities. Assigned to protect businesses, office buildings, and apartment complexes, these individuals serve a crucial policing function in a nation that has become increasingly fearful of and preoccupied with dangerous criminal action. Unfortunately, there has been very little empirical research published on private policing as a deterrent to crime. In one of the few studies addressing this issue, Donovan and Walsh (1986) note that crime was lower and feelings of security higher in a middle-class housing development in Brooklyn, New York, patrolled by a private security firm compared to the reports of residents living in housing areas not under private patrol. A great deal more research is needed to properly evaluate the role of private policing in the wider law enforcement effort, particularly as this relates to increasing surveillance and reducing opportunities for crime.

Community-Based Policing. It has sometimes been reported that the police are unsupportive of community volunteer groups because they resent having to share their authority with "amateurs" (Marx & Archer, 1973). Be this as it may, research investigators and law enforcement administrators concur that public policing is generally ineffective without support from persons in the community. It would stand to reason, then, that responsible use of community-based intervention may be helpful in the primary prevention of certain forms of criminal activity. Community patrols, to include vigilante groups like the Guardian Angels, and neighborhood watches are the focus of this discourse on community-based surveillance-enhancing, opportunity-reducing interventions.

Community Patrols: Anecdotal evidence suggests that forming community patrols may be effective in reducing crime and helping residents experience a superior sense of safety and empowerment (Yin et al., 1977). Though there have been reports of vigilantism in several of these community patrol programs, such occurrences are relatively infrequent as long as youth factions are not a major component of the patrol. Walking patrols initiated in Columbus, Ohio, and on the campus of Drake University in Des Moines, Iowa, served to reduce burglary and auto theft (Latessa & Allen, 1980) and vandalism (Troyer, 1988), respectively, in patrolled areas. A Canadian study also revealed diminutions in targeted crimes after implementation of a citizen-based policing program (Engstad & Evans, 1980).

Given the moderate success of community-based policing efforts it might behoove police to expend greater resources instructing citizens in crime-prevention strategies. A car security campaign encouraging car owners to lock their cars in order to avert future episodes of auto theft was largely unsuccessful, however, because it had little effect on people's propensity to lock their cars (Riley, 1980). Contingency contracts, on the other hand, have been found effective in encouraging community-based policing of public areas. Youth in an English study were promised a disco show (Taylor, 1978) and juveniles in an American study a sum of money (Clarke, 1978) in exchange for reduced vandalism and window breakage, with positive results in both cases. Providing tangible incentives and instilling a sense of community responsibility may therefore be essential preconditions for the development of an effective system of community-based policing.

Vigilante groups have also played a role in the community-policing effort. The most visible of these vigilante groups is the red-bereted Guardian Angels. The Guardian Angels patrol the streets, parks, and subways of over 50 American and Canadian cities as a deterrent to crime. In telephone interviews conducted with residents of Toledo, Ohio, it was determined that citizens were more supportive of the group's plans to start a new chapter in Toledo than either the police or city fathers (Perry & Pugh, 1989). Pennell and colleagues surveyed crime rates in San Diego, California, after the Guardian Angels began patrolling there. Results indicated that citizen fear plunged sharply and property crimes fell modestly, but that violent crime rates were untouched by the patrols (Pennell et al., 1989). Outside groups like the Guardian Angels appear to have an impact on the communities they patrol, particularly when it comes to reducing fear of crime; however, community-based policing by local residents seems to be even more efficacious in bringing about increased surveillance and decreased opportunities for crime.

Neighborhood Watch: Another form of community-based policing involves increasing surveillance through implementation of a Neighborhood Watch (NW) program. Seven percent of the households in the United States (Whitaker, 1986) and 10 percent of the households in England (Hope, 1988) belong to a NW. The characteristics of neighborhoods with NW programs are outlined in Table 7.2. As this table denotes, NW programs are most commonly found in predominantly white, middle-income neighborhoods composed of single-family dwellings. NW programs hold the advantage of being relatively inexpensive, promoting an attitude of community solidarity and self-efficacy, and since most neighborhood watches are sponsored by the police, fostering positive police-community relations.

In a national survey of Neighborhood Watch programs, Garofalo and McLeod (1989) ascertained that 61 percent of the programs held regularly scheduled

Table 7.2

Characteristics of 550 Neighborhood Watch Programs

	Percentages
Type Housing	
Apartments	5.8%
Single-family houses	79.2%
Townhouses/Condominiums	5.4%
Mobile homes	5.8%
No predominance	3.8%
Proportion of Home Owners and Renters	
Owners	79.3%
Renters	20.7%
Racial/Ethnic Composition of Neighborhood	
White	75.1%
Black	4.4%
Hispanic	3.5%
No predominance	17.0%
Income Level of Residents	
Under $10,000	3.7%
$10,000–$29,999	38.5%
$30,000 or more	40.1%
No predominance	17.7%
Mean Length of Residence	
One to two years	8.1%
Three to five years	23.1%
More than five years	68.8%

Source: Garofalo & McLeod (1989).

meetings, 54 percent distributed crime-prevention newsletters, and 40 percent did both. The outcome of such programs, according to Garofalo and McLeod, is modest and exerts its primary effect on residential burglaries and property theft. Several uncontrolled survey studies strongly support the efficacy of the NW approach to crime prevention. Reductions of 58 percent in all crime in the Crary–St. Mary section of Detroit; of 77 percent in residential burglaries in Lakewood, Colorado; and of 45 percent in theft in Cypress, California, were detected following the development of large-scale NW programs (National Crime Prevention Council, 1987). However, the better designed quasi-experimental investigations delving into the question of NW program validity have been significantly less supportive of this approach to crime prevention (Rosenbaum, 1988).

The four strongest quasi-experimental studies were conducted in London, England (Bennett, 1987); Seattle, Washington (Cirel, Evans, McGillis, & Whitcomb, 1977); Minneapolis, Minnesota (Pate, McPherson, & Silloway, 1987);

and Chicago, Illinois (Rosenbaum, Lewis, & Grant, 1986). Dependent measures included the aggregate community crime rate, fear of personal crime, fear of property crime, and community cohesion. Only 4 of the 30 measured effects generated by these four investigations confirmed the efficacy of NW programming (a marginal decrease in crime rate in Cirel et al. [1977] and a marginal decrease in crime in one of four target areas studied in Rosenbaum et al. [1986]; a decrease in fear of property crime and an increase in social cohesion in Bennett [1987]). On the other hand, 17 effects were nonsignificant and 9 effects showed that NW-covered areas experienced worse outcomes than control zones.

Since only slightly more than one-third of all households in watch neighborhoods participate in NW programs (Rosenbaum, 1988), negative outcomes may reflect less than maximum watch involvement on the part of persons in the community. There are at least two ways by which the relationship between participation in NW programs and such characteristics as fear of crime might be explained. The Durkheimian position, for one, postulates that a rising fear of crime will stimulate collective action on the part of residents in order to meet the perceived threat to community solidarity. Not surprisingly, there are studies that show that participants in NW programs express a stronger fear of crime than nonparticipants (Lavrakas & Herz, 1982). Conversely, there are those theorists who believe that increased fear of crime will interfere with a community's ability to take effective action; this position can also point to corroborating evidence, which in this case takes the form of research demonstrating a negative relationship between NW participation and fear of crime (DuBow & Podolefsky, 1982).

Examining the fear-participation issue further, Hope (1988) proposed a curvilinear relationship in which moderate levels of concern were posited as ideal for community-based programming, on the premise that low levels fail to sufficiently motivate the neighborhood and high levels lead to behaviors (suspicion and social withdrawal) antithetical to the evolution of effective community crime prevention. Further consideration of the participation issue by Bennett (1989) revealed high levels of both fear and community involvement in persons participating in two English NW programs. This outcome was interpreted by Bennett as confirming the supposition that persons electing to participate in NW programs must not only be sufficiently concerned about crime to invest the necessary time and effort in developing such programs, but must also feel confident in the community's ability to take effective action.

The consensus of researchers examining surveillance and watch programs is that better designed studies show less of an effect than more poorly designed investigations. Rosenbaum (1988) interprets this finding as evidence that watch programs are inadequate as stand-alone crime-prevention strategies. There is also the corollary problem of stimulating and maintaining community resident interest in NW programs. Perhaps the recent work of investigators like Hope (1988) and Bennett (1989) may be of some assistance in encouraging program participation. Though there is no evidence that NW programs inspire community solidarity, feelings of self-efficacy, or greater behavioral surveillance, research needs to contrast neighborhoods exhibiting different levels of participation before and after implementation of NW programming.

By way of conclusion, it is important to note that the efficacy of community-based programming depends in large measure on the financial and technical support supplied by public law enforcement agencies (Bennett, 1989; Lewis, Grant, & Rosenbaum, 1988; Troyer, 1988). Previously, we observed that public policing was dependent on the support of citizen groups. We can now see that the converse also applies: the effectiveness of community-based policing varies with the amount of support and guidance provided by local law enforcement. This points out the necessity of creatively blending formal and informal sources of social control in constructing an integrated model of primary and secondary crime prevention.

Media-Based Surveillance

Crime-Stoppers. Given that television has become a major source of information and entertainment in this country, it is not surprising that the media have assumed an increasingly vital role in the crime-prevention efforts of American society. The Crime Stoppers (CS) program is an example of such an approach to tertiary (and to a lesser degree, secondary) prevention. Enlisting the joint cooperation of mass-media, law enforcement, and community agencies, CS programs offer cash rewards as inducements and assure anonymity in exchange for information leading to the arrest and conviction of suspected criminals. The first CS program was established in Albuquerque, New Mexico, in 1976 but interest grew at such a rate that the number of programs ballooned to over 600 in just ten years (Figure 7.1). Funding to pay for these programs and the contingent financial rewards have derived largely from the contributions of local businesses, while national surveys reveal that CS programs have been well received by news executives, law enforcement officials, and the general public (Rosenbaum, Lurigio, & Lavrakas, 1986).

CS programs are fairly uniform in that each has a coordinator (who is normally a police department employee), detectives (who investigate cases), a board of directors (who represent the community), one or more media outlets, and persons providing the tips and information. Program coordinators estimate that 25 percent of the calls to CS programs come from known criminals, another 41 percent are placed by persons who regularly associate with offenders, and just 35 percent are made by regular citizens (Rosenbaum, Lurigio, & Lavrakas, 1989). A national survey of CS programs indicates that the best predictors of program success are the coordinator's level of effort and job satisfaction, the amount of energy expended by the board of directors, the quality of information relayed to detectives, and the presence of good media-police-community relationships. It was also determined that areas blessed with lower crime rates and medium-size

Figure 7.1
The Growth of Crime Stopper Programs in the United States, 1980–1986

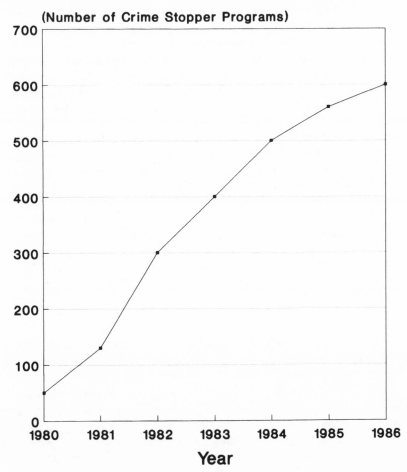

(Number of Crime Stopper Programs)

Source: Rosenbaum et al. (1986).

populations had more successful CS programs than areas sporting higher crime rates and small or larger populations (Rosenbaum et al., 1989).

Collectively, the 570 programs scrutinized by Rosenbaum and his associates have reportedly solved 213,000 felony crimes, convicted more than 43,000 criminals, and recovered more than $1.3 billion in stolen property and narcotics. The cost-effectiveness of CS programming is highlighted by the observation that solved cases net callers an average of $77 in reward money but yield an average take of $6,593 in recovered stolen property and narcotics per case (Rosenbaum et al., 1989). Interestingly, the results of a controlled investigation conducted in Lake County, Illinois, revealed that the size of the monetary reward (low = \$100, moderate = \$250, high = \$400) had no bearing on caller satisfaction or willingness to participate in the program in the future. This outcome suggests that the cost-effectiveness of CS programs might be enhanced further by examining the degree to which rewards can be reduced without adversely affecting program participation.

National Crime Stopper Programs. Crime Stopper programs have traditionally been directed by local law enforcement and aired on local television stations, using funds from local businesses. However, the CS philosophy has also been extended to nationally televised programs like "America's Most Wanted" (AMW). Of the 215 fugitives profiled on AMW between February 1988, when it was first aired, and January 1990, 136 were in custody, 86 as a direct consequence of tips provided by viewers (Breslin, 1990). As with local CS programs, anecdotal evidence is strong, although we still require more experimentally elegant studies in order to properly evaluate the efficacy of national CS programs. The anecdotal evidence is nonetheless impressive, and while it could be argued that some of the criminals profiled on AMW may have been apprehended without the aid of the program, it should be kept in mind that many of these profiled individuals had been wanted by the legal authorities several years prior to their appearance on AMW. A particularly dramatic case was that of New Jersey's John List, who after 17 years on the run was apprehended within a week of being featured on AMW.

Crime Stopper programs are not without certain limitations. Critics argue that these programs may invade the privacy or violate the civil rights of an individual who has been accused but not convicted of a crime. There are also those who contend that CS programs teach people to report crime for profit rather than out of a sense of civic duty. A criticism leveled against national programs like "America's Most Wanted" is that they may unwittingly perpetuate violence through their graphic depictions of crime scenarios. The reenactments, however, may be part of the show's appeal and popular acceptance. The apparent success of this show can also probably be traced to the fact that it informs viewers when a profiled criminal has been apprehended, thereby producing feelings of self-efficacy and reinforcing the notion that citizens can play an important role in apprehending dangerous criminals. Empiricism demands, however, that we experimentally investigate whether programs like AMW have a positive, negative, or neutral effect on viewers' fear of crime. Though we must address these sundry issues and empirically probe the efficacy of CS programming before we can exude confidence in these various outcomes, preliminary findings are promising.

INCREASING OPPORTUNITIES FOR AND BENEFITS OF PROSOCIAL BEHAVIOR

In setting our sights on behaviors incompatible with crime we find ourselves focusing on four preventive strategies designed to enhance prosocial opportunities and the benefit of noncriminal activity. These four procedures include the social problems approach to intervention, employment and financial assistance, challenge programs, and early release from prison.

The Social Problems Approach

The founding philosophy of the social problems approach to primary and secondary prevention is that certain social conditions cause youth to become involved in delinquency and that crime can be eradicated by attending to these conditions. Several of the more popular social problem–based interventions include augmented youth activities, crime-focused community meetings, and efforts to improve physical-environmental conditions (Podolefsky & DuBow, 1981). Bennett and Lavrakas (1989) surveyed ten community crime-prevention projects in nine cities and determined that these programs relied on youth-oriented activities like athletics, social clubs, literacy drives, drug awareness, and educational enrichment to achieve their goals.

Though social problem–based programs appear to have intuitive appeal, empirical research in the United States has failed to enlist support for their use in preventing crime. A national evaluation of the Eisenhower Foundation's Neighborhood Program (Bennett & Lavrakas, 1989), for instance, revealed that the opportunity-reduction features of neighborhood programs were significantly more effective than the social welfare and causes-of-crime features in reducing crime and abating the fear of becoming a victim of crime. In a more general review of the social welfare literature, Murray (1984) comments that U.S. social welfare policies have had a detrimental effect on poverty and related social problems like crime, although several scholars take exception to Murray's conclusions (Jencks, 1985).

Whereas the social problems approach to crime prevention has met with limited success in the United States, there are several isolated examples of successful application in Europe. A six-month follow-up of a program in The Hague, Netherlands, which offers predelinquent youth referrals for parent-child, school, interpersonal, emotional, leisure time, and criminal law problems, found positive effects for family communication, school attendance, and subsequent delinquent behavior, although school achievement, relationships with teachers and other pupils, peer-group involvement, and leisure time activities did not change as a function of involvement in the program (Scholte & Smit, 1988). French authorities also emphasize social problems in their approach to delinquency prevention, and King (1989) reports that there was a 12 percent reduction in crime in the French city of Lille after implementation of a social problems program of crime prevention. Though these two studies provide circumscribed support for a social problems approach to secondary prevention, in both instances the treated and control groups were of questionable comparability and the follow-up periods were noticeably brief. Furthermore, other studies indicate that social welfare interventions may exhibit short-term benefit but rarely are effective in the long run (Frazier & Cochran, 1986; McCord, 1978).

Employment and Financial Assistance

The adult analogue of the social problems approach to delinquency prevention is the employment or financial assistance model of tertiary intervention. This approach to crime prevention is based on research hinting at a possible connection between unemployment and criminal recidivism (compare Seiter, 1977). Rossi, Berk, and Lenihan (1980) evaluated the efficacy of the Transitional Aid Research Project (TARP), which provides funds to released offenders while they find employment. TARP subjects who found work were less subject to future arrest, although employment rates were significantly lower in the TARP condition, possibly because the unemployment insurance payments served as a disincentive to work. A similar program, known by the acronym LIFE (Living Insurance for Ex-Offenders), provides job placement services and monetary grants to ex-felons in an effort to enhance the community adjustment of persons released from prison. The results of one study assessing the LIFE program imply that while financial aid apparently helped retard recidivism, it had no appreciable effect on work performance (Maller & Thornton, 1978). Other studies have found positive employment effects for the Probation Employment Guidance Program (PEGP), but no group differences in recidivism (Greenwood, Lipsett, & Norton, 1980; Lightman, 1982).

In contrast to the mixed results obtained with monetary assistance programs, employment and job training programs for ex-offenders have consistently shown few positive effects. Piliavin and Gartner (1981) randomly assigned 2,311 ex-felons to either an experimental or a no-training control condition. Subjects in the experimental condition were guaranteed placement in various jobs (mostly construction and service industries) and after 36 months 59 percent of the experimental group was employed as compared to 58 percent of the control group. Contrasting recidivism rates, Piliavin and Gartner surmised that 44 percent of the experimental group and 35 percent of the control group had been convicted of a new criminal code violation during this 36-month period. After reviewing the literature on employment and training programs for ex-offenders and delinquents, McGahey (1986) concluded that the large-scale government training programs of the 1960s and 1970s failed to influence either the labor market or recidivism. A notable exception to this general rule can be found in Job Corps training, although the positive outcomes recorded by subjects enrolled in this program may simply have been a function of the fact that the Job Corps succeeded in physically and socially removing at-risk youth from high-crime neighborhoods (McGahey, 1986).

While funding a newly released offender may delay this individual's reentry into crime long enough to allow him or her the opportunity to find legitimate employment and build a noncriminal lifestyle, these programs enjoy only modest success in facilitating the long-term adjustment of treated offenders. Job training programs for ex-offenders appear to have an even more dismal prognosis if reducing recidivism is the aim. Perhaps part of the problem is that many of these financial and employment programs were conceived as tertiary prevention measures and implemented with chronic offenders who strongly identified with criminal goals and had no genuine interest in legitimate employment. Maybe these programs would be more effective if conceptualized along primary or secondary prevention lines. Or perhaps we need to take into account factors such as prisonization and self-esteem, as has been suggested by Homant (1984), or the relevance of prison-based job training, as has been discussed by Callison (1989), in designing employment programs for ex-felons. Whatever the explanation, it is apparent that social problem and employment models of crime prevention have yet to demonstrate their utility, possibly because social factors like poverty, education, and employment have been oversold as causes of crime and delinquency (Walters & White, 1988a).

Challenge Programs

The rationale for exposing delinquent youth to challenge programs follows the logic that presenting young offenders with physical and mental challenges fosters self-confidence, internal discipline, and increased respect for authority. Originally conceived during World War II as a way of teaching survival skills to English merchant seamen, the Outward Bound program was transported to the United States in 1960. With an emphasis on self-control, choice, group cohesion, and wilderness training, Outward Bound is the most popular of the challenge programs currently used with delinquent populations (Logan, 1989).

A controlled investigation of Outward Bound by Kelly and Baer (1971) uncovered moderately positive results. These authors compared 60 Massachusetts delinquent boys who had been enrolled in a 26-day Outward Bound experience with 60 delinquents who had been treated in a routine manner by the youth correctional system, and determined that 20 percent of the experimental and 34 percent of the control subjects had been committed to juvenile facilities or adult prisons within nine months of release. At one year the confinement rates were 20 and 40 percent, and at five years 38 and 58 percent, respectively (Kelly, 1974). Further analysis of these Massachusetts data revealed that boys who enrolled in the program after age 14, had never before been confined, or had committed property-related offenses had better outcomes than boys who had been enrolled before turning 14, had a history of running away from home or group home placements, or were rated by Outward Bound staff as "stubborn."

Winterdyk and Roesch (1981) of Simon Fraser University in Canada scrutinized the effects of Outward Bound in 13- to 16-year-old juvenile offenders randomly assigned to a 21-day program or regular juvenile probation. Though immediate improvements in self-confidence and interpersonal relations were noted for subjects participating in Outward Bound, these effects were barely discernible at follow-up four to six months later. The authors of this report also failed to identify significant experimental-control differences in future reconvictions, although this may have been partly a function of the relatively low base rate of reconviction after four to six months. Murray and Cox (1979) also failed to unearth support for the superiority of wilderness camps over traditional confinement in probing the community adjustment of a group of recalcitrant juvenile offenders exposed to one or the other of these two forms of intervention.

Encouraged by the apparent success of the Outward Bound experience in their state, Massachusetts authorities established the Homeward Bound program. Utilizing a randomized experimental-control comparison, Wellman and Chun (1979) witnessed recidivism rates in treated juveniles that were half that of control subjects. Vision-Quest is another wilderness program found to be moderately effective with juvenile delinquents as revealed by a one-year follow-up in which 55 percent of the program graduates were re-arrested compared to 71 percent of a group of juveniles placed in a conventional treatment facility (Criminal Justice Newsletter, 1988). In reviewing research available on challenge programs at that time, Shore (1977) remarked that the evidence was consistent but not conclusive that such programs were effective in improving self-esteem and reducing recidivism in juvenile offenders. This same conclusion would appear to apply today; though there is a need for more controlled comparisons of youth randomly assigned to participant and nonparticipant groups, there is room for guarded optimism in the use of challenge programs as a means of averting future criminal and delinquent outcomes.

Early Release from Prison

Releasing offenders from prison prior to completion of their sentences has always generated controversy. The news media are quick to report violent incidents perpetrated by persons released early from prison, but much less inclined to feature felons who, when released, never commit another serious crime. We do not normally find photos of the latter plastered on the front page of the newspaper, televised on the evening news, or profiled in a national magazine. This preoccupation with the violent few at the expense of the conforming many can also serve a political purpose, as we saw in the 1988 presidential campaign when the Willie Horton case was put on center stage. Is there any actual evidence, however, that offenders released from confinement before completion of their sentences present any more of a threat to the general public than persons discharged on expiration of sentence?

As a means of addressing the question of relative dangerousness, research conducted in Colorado (Malak, 1984) and Illinois (Austin, 1986) denotes that inmates released early from prison on the basis of accrued "good time" were no more likely to re-offend than inmates released upon expiration of sentence. A review of the Michigan penal system, in fact, revealed that inmates not entitled to "good time" credit were more likely to be involved in disciplinary infractions (to include participating in riots) than inmates covered by "good time" policies, although the authors are quick to point out that this outcome may have been affected by initial group differences on offense and time period measures (Em-shoff & Davidson, 1987). It is unknown, however, whether the practice of rewarding "good time" credit for acceptable behavior in prison aids the community adjustment of released felons or just introduces dangerous persons back into the community that much sooner (Weisburd & Chayet, 1989).

Parole serves many diverse, and in some cases contradictory, functions, but one thing that it clearly accomplishes is the early release of prison inmates. Lerner (1977) examined the utility of parole with misdemeanant offenders, and Sacks and Logan (1979) probed this same issue with persons convicted of minor felonies, and both deciphered support for the efficacy of parole supervision. However, Sacks and Logan noted that the antirecidivism effect of parole seemed to disappear once supervision was terminated. After controlling for preexisting differences in parole and control subjects, state (Gottfredson, Mitchell-Herzefeld, & Flanagan, 1982), federal (Gottfredson, 1975), and Canadian (Waller, 1974) prisoners discharged to parole supervision were found to experience significantly lower rates of re-arrest than inmates released on expiration of sentence.

Even more critical than ascertaining the relative dangerousness of discharged felons is identifying ways by which their temerity might be tempered, since nearly all prisoners will eventually be released from prison (Rogers, 1989). Planning and support, both before and after release, appear crucial to the community adjustment of persons who may have spent many years behind bars. Danesh (1989) describes the development of a clearinghouse in Baton Rouge, Louisiana, designed to assist recently liberated offenders with counseling, employment, medical, and other specialized services. Only 1 of the 31 program graduates who remained in Louisiana was subsequently arrested during an unspecified period of follow-up. Unfortunately, there was no control group by which to evaluate the significance of these findings, and as often happens with funded projects, political considerations came into play and the program was discontinued.

It is clear that unless we plan to confine persons who commit felonies indefinitely, we must search for ways to ease the prison-to-community transition. Parole still seems a viable option, though we need to develop useful models of parole decision making (see Hoffman & Beck, 1974, 1980, 1985 for an example), and be willing to expand the number of pre- and post-release programs available to offenders.

INCREASING THE COST OF CRIME

The cost of crime to offenders might be elevated by strengthening the probability of apprehension or bolstering the penalties associated with a particular criminal act. Whether we inspect official data (Wilson, 1983) or victimization rates (Wilson & Boland, 1978), jurisdictions displaying higher conviction and confinement rates characteristically experience less crime than jurisdictions exhibiting lower rates of conviction and confinement. The problem is that because these studies were cross-sectional in nature, causal inferences cannot be drawn. A longitudinal analysis of British crime statistics (1894 to 1967), on the other hand, revealed the possibility of a causal connection between sanction probability and the rate of crime (Wolpin, 1978a). Though augmenting the probability of apprehension may affect the behavior of the average citizen, it typically has little impact on habitual offenders. Therefore, in one study it was ascertained that doubling the odds of arrest diminished the number of incarcerated auto thieves who believed their crime was worth the risk by only 26 percent, the number of burglars by only 29 percent, and the number of robbers by less than 1 percent (Figgie Corporation, 1988).

Raising the penalty for a particular criminal act is a second avenue through which the cost of crime might be influenced. Elevating the penalty for drunk driving in Finland during the 1960s and in Chicago during the 1970s seemingly had no effect on the number of alcohol-related accidents in these jurisdictions, although raising the risk of arrest wielded a modest incident-reducing impact (Ross, 1981). As with research investigating manipulation of the probability of apprehension, however, one needs to take into account the characteristics of the individual offender when exploring the effect of penalty severity on behavior. The Bartley-Fox law was passed in Massachusetts in 1974, and stipulated that possession of an unregistered firearm would be punished by a mandatory one-year jail sentence. Results indicated that while this law apparently led to a reduction in the number of crimes involving unplanned use of a firearm, it had no effect on crimes committed by professional criminals (Wilson & Herrnstein, 1985). Therefore, while sanction certainty and severity may influence the behavior of most people, they appear to have little effect on the actions of persons who account for the majority of serious crimes committed in this country (the career or lifestyle criminal; see Walters, 1990).

Situation-oriented interventions designed to raise the cost of crime have been utilized primarily for secondary and tertiary prevention purposes. However, research scrutinizing sanction certainty and severity suggests that increasing the costs associated with crime may be most effective if employed as a primary prevention measure (deterring the noncriminal from engaging in criminal behavior). In the next section we explore three primary forms of crime cost manipulation: incarceration, probation, and intermediate forms of punishment like community service, intensive probation supervision, and shock incarceration. We begin with a cost-inflating form of situation-oriented intervention that has become increasingly popular in this country over the past 20 years, incarceration.

INCARCERATION

Confinement is a criminal justice sanction upon which officials in this country have become increasingly dependent. Even when population-age shifts are taken into account, available evidence suggests that the per capita rate of incarceration more than doubled between 1880 and 1980 (see Figure 7.2). A review of ad-

Figure 7.2
Rate Per 100,000 Population and Rate Per 100,000 Population Aged 20–44
Confined in State and Federal Prisons Between 1880 and 1980

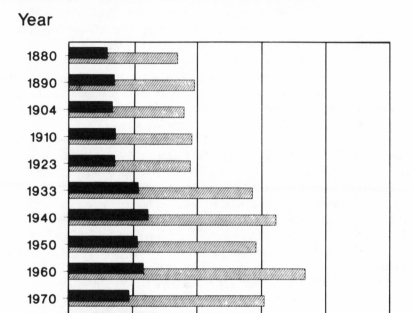

Year

(Rate Per 100,000 Population)

■ Entire Population   ▨ Aged 20 to 44

Source: Cahalan (1986).

ditional information indicates that it is the rate of incarceration, not the rate of crime, that has risen precipitously in recent years (Glazer, 1989). In 1980 the courts remanded 196 of every 1,000 persons arrested for serious crimes (murder, rape, robbery, burglary, aggravated assault) to the custody of state or federal correctional authorities. By 1987 this figure had climbed to 301 incarcerations for every 1,000 arrests for serious crime, a jump of 54 percent in just eight years (Bureau of Justice Statistics, 1989). While a consummate review of the penological literature is beyond the scope of this chapter, it seems advisable that we at least peruse several of the more prominent issues and problems associated with incarceration as a form of criminal science intervention.

It is convenient to blame this nation's formidable crime rate on its penal system, but in reality we must all share responsibility for the general state of ineffectualness that envelops the United States' response to crime. Modern-day corrections may not be a solution to the problem of crime, but it is a practical necessity in a highly industrialized nation like ours. The question then becomes not whether prisons are necessary but the degree to which we want to rely on incarceration as a means of secondary and tertiary prevention. Although confinement may be an unfortunate fact of industrialized life, we should not allow this to divert us from identifying alternative avenues of reasoned social control. Nor should we allow the reality of prison to blind us to the serious problems facing correctional administrators in the years to come.

Of the crisis presently confronting U.S. corrections, none is more pressing than the issue of prison overcrowding. On January 1, 1988, occupancy exceeded rated capacity by 14 percent nationwide (Camp & Camp, 1988), a figure which is certain to grow larger in coming years. The American Correctional Association and the U.S. Department of Justice recommend 60 square feet (80 square feet in situations where inmates inhabit cells for more than 10 hours a day) per inmate (Rogers, 1989). A review of 694 prisons, however, reveals an average square footage of only 57.3 square feet per inmate, a mean of 11.3 hours in unit confinement, and multiple occupancy in 66 percent of all cases (Innes, 1986). By 1985 only eight states were not fettered by some form of judicial review because of complaints about unconstitutional or inadequate prison conditions (Taggart, 1989). The problem of prison overcrowding will only intensify if we continue along our present course of relying almost exclusively on prison as a way of managing crime.

One solution to the overcrowding problem is to build more prisons. This, however, creates a second problem: the growing expense of correctional construction projects. Over the course of the past 50 years construction costs have risen even more dramatically than has the confinement rate. Erecting a new prison facility carried a price tag of $28.5 million per institution in 1987. The cost of new construction in 1987 was $49,554 per bed, while the expense of renovation was $30,640 per bed (Camp & Camp, 1988). Accounting for inflation and the skyrocketing expense of new prison construction, it would not be unrealistic to expect these figures to double over the next 15 to 20 years. Considering that it costs an average of $15,892 to maintain an inmate in prison for one year (Camp & Camp, 1988), we can understand the significance of growing expenditures as prison rolls expand.

A third crisis confronting American corrections is the prospect of long-term incarceration and the graying of the U.S. prison population. Wilson and Vito (1988) acknowledge an increase in the average prison sentence, a recent trend exemplified by congressional passage of the Federal Crime Control Bill of 1984. Modification of parole eligibility guidelines, enactment of career offender statutes, and a growing focus on determinant and mandatory sentencing has increased the number of persons committed to prison and substantially inflated the number of prisoners serving sentences of seven or more years (Rogers, 1989). As the length of confinement swells so will the average age of prison inmates, a state of affairs which presents a unique challenge to prison officials accustomed to dealing with populations skewed toward the youthful side of the spectrum. These challenges include the need for expanded bed space, specialized and incremental housing, augmented medical and mental health services, increased security, and development of recreational and programming activities to fill time voids created by an influx of older inmates (Wilson & Vito, 1988).

Correctional officer stress is a fourth crisis confronting prison officials as we move into the twenty-first century. Corrections consistently rates near the top when occupational stress is measured (Philliber, 1987). However, because of overcrowding and the aging of U.S. correctional population, correctional officer stress appears to be on the rise. A number of studies have documented the debilitating effects of stress on the personal adjustment and occupational performance of correctional personnel (Crouch & Alpert, 1982; Lasky, Gordon, & Srebalus, 1986). Philliber (1987) surveyed the literature on correctional officer stress and discovered that the manner in which officers handle stress has a direct bearing on both staff and inmate welfare. The development of in-house stress management programs and administrative remedies designed to get correctional officers more involved in institution-level decision making may help combat the mounting levels of correctional officer stress and turnover threatening the already tenuous structure of the American correctional system.

I would like to bring to the reader's attention one final issue challenging the American correctional assemblage in the coming years: developing a coherent philosophy of corrections. With the demise of rehabilitative programming in the late 1970s, incapacitation and deterrence replaced rehabilitation in the hearts and minds of many correctional administrators. An unfortunate side effect of this policy is that under such circumstances incapacitation may serve to encourage the warehousing of large numbers of inmates. Rehabilitation, as it was conceptualized 20 years ago, may have been a failed experiment, but this does not justify the wide-scale abandonment of change as a principal goal of correctional intervention. We must come to realize that incarceration does not raise the cost of crime for many habitual offenders, because it is viewed by many such individuals as nothing more than an inconvenience or occupational hazard (Walters, 1990). Walters and White (1988b) have elaborated on ways in which the correctional experience might be modified to raise the cost of crime and provide offenders with opportunities to learn prosocial forms of behavior (responsibility in particular). Several of these recommendations are examined in greater detail in Chapter 9 of this volume.

Probation

Whereas incarceration is at the more restrictive end of the criminal sanctions continuum, probation anchors the less restrictive pole. As Figure 7.3 clearly

Figure 7.3
Persons on Probation, Parole, and Custody in the United States on January 1, 1988

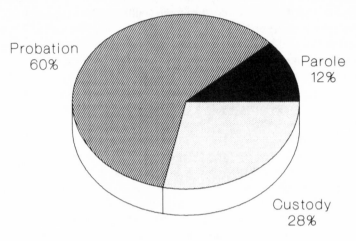

Source: Data from Camp & Camp (1988).

displays, probation is the most common sanction imposed by modern-day U.S. courts. In California, which can boast of the largest correctional population in the nation, 70 percent of all convicted felons are granted probation, a figure fairly representative of most states. A 40-month follow-up of probationers in California betrayed a re-arrest rate of 65 percent, re-conviction rate of 51 percent, and re-incarceration rate of 31 percent (Petersilia et al., 1985). A 20-state inquiry into the adjustment of probationers under supervision disclosed that between 66 and 95 percent of all adults granted probation were successfully discharged from supervision (Bureau of Justice Statistics, 1984b). The logical assumption, then, is that offenders adjust reasonably well (or at least avoid violating the conditions of their probation) while under supervision, but experience significant problems upon being released from supervision.

Empirical studies comparing probation with other forms of intervention and nonintervention have yielded equivocal outcomes (Erwin, 1986; Gottfredson et al., 1982; Jackson, 1983). However, the methodological rigor of many of these investigations has tended to be weak and there is a trend that finds the effect of probation strongest in studies where the integrity of the intervention has been maintained (Gendreau & Ross, 1987). One of the better designed investigations on this topic contrasted the recidivism rates of matched groups of Australian juveniles alternately assigned to probation or detention, and the effects were more generally supportive of probation (Kraus, 1974).

According to one investigation, 9 percent of a group of first-time misdemeanant offenders granted probation were re-convicted (three-year follow-up) compared to 20 percent of first-time misdemeanants receiving fines and 34 percent of first-time misdemeanants sentenced to jail (Wheeler & Hissong, 1988). A similar pattern was observed with previously convicted misdemeanants—33 percent of the probationers, 44 percent of the finees, and 59 percent of the jailees recidivating within three years. Survival analysis established that probationers had an 88 percent chance of not re-offending during a two-year period at risk compared to 77 percent of the fined misdemeanants and 55 percent of the incarcerates (the probation-incarceration difference being statistically significant). Since randomization of subjects to conditions was not possible in this particular study, these findings need to be treated as speculative, although available research would seem to indicate that probation is at least as effective as incarceration and benefits from a tenfold increase in savings (Camp & Camp, 1988). Of course, there are persons who because of the seriousness of their current charges or past criminal record are simply not appropriate for probation. For this reason intermediate forms of punishment have been proposed.

Intermediate Punishment

Sandwiched between probation and incarceration are intermediate-level sanctions. Morris and Tonry (1990) have co-authored a book on intermediate sanctions that sheds light on several critical issues in the use of this particular form of punishment. Morris and Tonry argue that intermediate-level sanctions are not alternatives to confinement but have their own set of goals and procedures that helps bridge the gap between probation and incarceration. This method of sanctioning is therefore no more a substitute for incarceration than it is a proxy for probation, existing as a mid-level step in a three-tiered model of criminal accountability. Intermediate-level punishments reviewed in this section include fines, community service, intensive probation supervision, awareness programs, house arrest, and therapeutic communities.

Fines. Fines are the oldest form of punishment, predating Hammurabi by centuries. Research studies intimate that over $1 billion in fines are collected in the United States each year, although in only 10 percent of the cases where fines were levied were they the sole sanction imposed on an offender (Hillsman et al., 1987). Whereas judges in the United States rely more extensively on mixed sentences (fines combined with probation or incarceration), European courts make greater use of simple fine sanctions. Germany, for example, demonstrates a fine-only to mixed-sanction sentence ratio of four to one (Gillispie, 1980). This has led to a significant decrease in the use of short-term incarceration in this nation of 65 million people.

Day fines are a concept born in Scandinavia and utilized rather extensively in several Western European nations. This procedure allows for calculation of the number of fine units by the severity of the instant offense, while the monetary value of each unit is based on an offender's ability to pay. In the event of default, the length of time spent in jail will not vary as a function of affluence, since the number of fine units is based on the severity of the crime, not on the defendant's ability to pay. Where offenders fail to meet their financial obligations to the courts, research carried out in England and Germany demonstrates that prompt notification often brings about a positive response (Hillsman et al., 1987). A study conducted in Georgia shows that a bureaucracy motivated by self-interest to collect court-sanctioned fees can be highly effective, although it may be necessary to enlist the aid of private collection agencies in situations where the governmental bureaucracy is not motivated to collect fines (Morris & Tonry, 1990).

Community Service. Community service is another common form of inter-mediate sanctioning. Here the individual is instructed to provide a specified number of hours of community service. This might include cleaning up a park, providing baby-sitting services, or lecturing a group of high school students on the dangers of drugs. McDonald (1986) comments that surveys administered in 1977 and 1978 identified 58 organized community service programs for adults and 70 community service programs for juveniles. Though community service has been promoted as a way of reducing prison crowding, research conducted in New York (McDonald, 1986) and England (Pease, 1985) suggests that less than half of all persons sentenced to community service would have entered prison. There is, obviously, a substantial savings in cases where community service is granted to persons who would otherwise have been imprisoned, al-though this number is too small to support the argument that community service can substantially ease the pressure of prison overcrowding.

The Vera Institute of Justice in New York City makes use of community service in its interventions with repeat property offenders and reports favorable preliminary outcomes (Morris & Tonry, 1990). A lack of experimental control and randomized assignment of subjects to conditions, however, hinders the few studies that have been conducted on community service as an intermediate-level sanction. Uncontrolled comparisons have shown that the recidivism rate of of-fenders sentenced to a period of community service tend to be lower than that attained by persons released from jail and prison (Morris & Tonry, 1990), although we should keep in mind that no more than half the persons granted community service would likely have been sentenced to jail. Accordingly, com-munity service recipients are no less likely to re-offend than persons sentenced to probation or whose sentences had been suspended (McDonald, 1986; Pease, 1985). Future studies on this issue need to expand the definition of outcome beyond the narrow scope of re-arrest or re-conviction to include the benefits afforded the community as a result of the services provided.

Intensive Probation Supervision. Dissatisfaction with traditional probation has led to the development of substitute forms of supervision. One of the more frequently utilized alternatives is something known as Intensive Probation Su-pervision (IPS). There are three primary methods of IPS: "front door" programs, "back door" programs, and community-based programs. "Front door" pro-grams, as represented by the Georgia IPS, divert offenders from the prison system to community-based supervision. In contrast, New Jersey employs a "back door" methodology in which lower-risk prison inmates with good institutional adjustment records are discharged early to IPS. Massachusetts takes still another approach to IPS, channeling high-risk probationers, rather than persons scheduled for admission to or release from prison, into their intensive supervision program.

The Georgia IPS program, which began in 1982, consists of five face-to-face contacts per week, mandatory curfews, weekly review of local arrest records, and 132 hours of mandatory community service. Preliminary evaluation of this project has shown that following implementation of the IPS program the number of felons in Georgia sentenced to prison declined by 10 percent, while the number of offenders on probation rose by 10 percent. It has also been noted that IPS subjects are more similar to prison-bound offenders than they are to persons granted regular probation and that IPS subjects commit fewer and less serious offenses than persons released from prison (Erwin & Bennett, 1987). Of 2,322 offenders sentenced to the Georgia IPS program between 1982 and 1985, 16 percent were terminated from program participation for technical violations or the commission of a new offense, although less than 1 percent had been convicted of a violent crime. The cost-effectiveness of the Georgia IPS is clearly verified when the relative expense of IPS is compared vis-à-vis that of incarceration ($984.66 per year versus $7,759.65 per year), IPS providing a savings of nearly $6,800 (Erwin & Bennett, 1987).

Pearson (1988) has presented data on the New Jersey IPS program that holds to a "back door" philosophy in establishing program admissions. The New Jersey IPS requires 12 face-to-face encounters, 7 curfew visits, and 4 random urinalyses each month. The stated purpose of the program is to help offenders reintegrate into society. As such, all participants must either be employed full time or enrolled in a vocational training program. The New Jersey IPS also provides each participant with a community sponsor who is responsible for furnishing the offender with support and guidance. A follow-up of 600 offenders enrolled in the New Jersey IPS program denoted that slightly more than a third of the sample returned to prison for technical violations before completing the 18-month program—10 percent for the commission of a new crime, half of which were felonies (Pearson, 1988). The cost of the New Jersey IPS ($13,693), though appreciably higher than that of the Georgia program, is still cheaper than incarceration in a New Jersey state correctional facility ($19,958–$20,851).

The Massachusetts case management IPS program was reviewed by Byrne and Kelly (1989). These authors note that more frequent contact between the parole officer and offender portends decreased levels of recidivism when interventions are proactive (high rate of visits before the appearance of any problems) but not when they are reactive (high rate of visits only after problems arise). The cost-effectiveness of IPS is apparent, and studies addressing its utility are encouraging. However, a great deal more investigative attention needs to be directed at the individual components of each program, and recidivism rates need to be measured several years post-treatment. In this regard we might ask why the Georgia program seems to yield more positive results than the New

Jersey version. Perhaps this "proves" the superiority of "front door" approaches to IPS or perhaps this verifies the utility of the Georgia practice of dividing IPS duties between two individuals, a probation officer who handles treatment and management issues and a surveillance officer who conducts home visits, drug tests, and arrest checks.

Tonry (1990) argues that IPS programs have failed to achieve their stated objectives: reduce prison crowding, save public funds, and lower the recidivism rate. This conclusion may be somewhat premature, however. While it may be true that the IPS movement has done little to reduce prison crowding, this was probably not a realistic goal to begin with, since intermediate sanctions are designed to supplement, not replace, incarceration. Cost containment, on the other hand, will vary as a function of the number of offenders diverted from prison versus those diverted from probation, and there is nothing to say that Tonry's estimate of prison divertees (50%) is any more valid than traditional estimates (80%).

While it is true that studies carried out in California (Petersilia & Turner, 1990), Ohio (Noonan & Latessa, 1987), and Washington (Fallen et al., 1981) have failed to identify meaningful IPS-comparison differences in the rate of recidivism, questions have been raised about the appropriateness of the comparison groups utilized in these studies. Moreover, data supplied by Latessa and Vito (1988) on Lucas County, Ohio, shock probationers revealed that while enrollment in an IPS program did not significantly reduce the level of recidivism experienced by their subjects, it did appear to have a positive effect on employment status. In a field renowned for fads and shortsighted solutions to long-term problems, the IPS program, Tonry's concerns aside, stands out as a truly innovative approach to intermediate punishment, which deserves continued administrative support and empirical scrutiny.

Awareness Programs. Youth and adult awareness programs are intermediate forms of punishment that seek to deter adolescents and young adults from engaging in future criminality by installing a sense of fear and trepidation through implementation of a short-term, intensive program of intervention.

Juvenile Awareness—Scared Straight: Developed at New Jersey's Rahway State Prison and depicted in a 1969 documentary film, the New Jersey Scared Straight program was initiated by a group of hardened conflicts who spoke with visiting delinquent youth about the graphic realities of serving time in a maximum security prison. Finckenauer (1982) of Rutgers University studied juveniles participating in the Rahway Scared Straight program and discerned that 41.3 percent were subsequently involved in some form of delinquent activity during a six-month follow-up, in comparison to 11.9 percent of a group of nonparticipants. Lewis (1983) evaluated a Scared Straight program run by inmates at the California State Prison in San Quentin and found little evidence of a positive treatment effect, although less delinquent youth appeared to benefit more from the program than high-rate delinquents. Research also failed to support the efficacy of a Michigan program modeled after the New Jersey Scared Straight technique, 20 percent of the participants and 19 percent of the controls re-offending within three months and 31 percent of the participants and 29 percent of the controls recidivating within six months (Homant & Osowski, 1981).

Concern has been expressed that Scared Straight programs may place undue psychological stress and pressure on many of the exposed youth, and the American Correctional Association recommends that extreme caution be exercised in implementing such an approach with juveniles (Travisono, 1979). Dean (1983) set out to determine whether Scared Straight–type programs adversely affect the attitudes and feelings of targeted youth. Twenty-eight male delinquents were randomly assigned to either a juvenile awareness program or a no-contact control condition and subjected to pre-post analysis. Paper-and-pencil tests revealed that participants acknowledged a shift in the direction of greater internal locus of control, but none of the negative side effects alluded to in the literature (for example, increased hostility, decreased self-esteem). Whereas these findings suggest that concerns about the dangers of youth awareness programs like Scared Straight may be overstated, this study suffers from several major design flaws, from an exceedingly small sample size to exclusive reliance on paper-and-pencil tests, to a pre-post comparison that fails to take into account the possibility of an interaction between the pretest and treatment.

Even when youth awareness programs are conducted without the scare tactics they are so famous for, they are found to produce little change in the behavior of adjudicated delinquents (Buckner & Chesney-Lind, 1983). Whether juvenile awareness programs like Scared Straight have a deleterious effect on a teenager's self-concept, there is little solid evidence that such programs are effective in forestalling future criminal involvement.

Shock Probation: This form of intermediate punishment consists of a brief period of confinement followed by a longer interval of community supervision. Research has determined that shock probation is most effective with youthful adult first-time offenders deriving from good educational or employment backgrounds (McCarthy, 1976; Vito & Allen, 1981). Vito (1978) adds that shock probationers incarcerated 30 or fewer days experienced better outcomes than shock probationers confined for periods in excess of 30 days. Inquiries pitting shock probation against regular probation, however, have produced few positive outcomes. The majority of studies have either identified no major differences in recidivism between shock probation and regular probation participants (Holmes, Sykes, & Revels, 1983; Parisi, 1981) or awarded a slight advantage to regular probation subjects (Vito & Allen, 1981; Vito, Holmes, & Wilson, 1985). Of the studies showing a positive outcome for shock probation (Boudouris & Turnbull, 1985), the effect has been known to fade with time. In short, there appears to be little affirmation of the deterrent value of shock probation.

Shock Incarceration: With its roots in challenge program philosophy, Scared Straight technology, and shock probation politics, shock incarceration (SI) appears to have the support of a large number of judges, law enforcement personnel, and members of the general public. By 1989 eight states and jurisdictions had

Table 7.3
Overview of Shock Incarceration Programs

Jurisdiction	Opening Date	Program¹ Capacity	Offender Age Limit	Current Offense	Program Length	Treatment² Options
Oklahoma	11/83	150(M) 40(F)	18-22	Non-violent	120 days	DA, RT, RX, IC, RC
Georgia	12/83	200(M)	17-25	No restrict.	90 days	
Mississippi	4/85	140(M) 60(F)	none	Non-violent	90 days	RT, RX, IC
Orleans Parish	1/87	60(M) 28(F)	none	Non-violent	120 days	DA, IC
Louisiana	3/87	120(M&F)	none	Parole Elig.	90-180 days	DA, RT, IC
South Carolina	7/87	96(M) 28(F)	17-24	Non-violent	90 days	DA, RC
New York	9/87	500(M)	16-24	Non-violent	180 days	DA, RT, IC, RC, TC
Florida	10/87	100(M)	none	No restrict.	90-120 days	DA, RT, RX

¹M = male; F = female.

²DA = drug and alcohol counseling; RT = reality therapy; RX = relaxation training; IC = individual counseling; RC = recreational therapy; TC = therapeutic community.

Source: Parent (1989).

installed shock incarceration programs and another eight were seriously contemplating the implementation of such programming in the near future (Parent, 1989). This publicly popular program has three main goals: developing self-discipline, promoting physical conditioning, and fostering a positive attitude toward authority (Sechrest, 1989). Dale Parent, who has conducted the most exhaustive review of the literature on shock incarceration to date, describes the program as such:

SI involves a short period of confinement, typically three to six months, during which young offenders convicted of less serious, non-violent crimes, who have not been imprisoned before, are exposed to a demanding regimen of strict discipline, military-style drill and ceremony, physical exercise and physical labor. Some, but not all, SI programs also offer vocational training, education, and rehabilitative services. (Parent, 1989, p. xi)

Characteristics of the eight programs active at the time of the Parent review are summarized in Table 7.3.

SI is being sold to the public as a less expensive alternative to incarceration. However, the cost per day of enrollment in SI programming is equal to, and in some cases exceeds, the cost per day of keeping an inmate in prison (Parent,

1989). Furthermore, the majority of offenders placed in SI would never have been incarcerated in the first place, but would likely have been granted probation, which, as we saw previously, is noticeably cheaper than both SI and confinement. Parent (1989) estimates that SI might reduce prison overcrowding by no more than 2 to 4 percent and so cannot be viewed as a realistic solution to the overcrowding problem facing the American correctional conglomerate.

Drawing comparisons between SI and military boot camps is inevitable; in fact, SI programs are often referred to as correctional "boot camps." However, the similarities between SI and military boot camps exist primarily on the surface. Military basic training is designed to prepare noncriminal youth for military service and war, while SI accepts the more difficult task of attempting to change the behavior and thinking of persons who have adopted a criminal way of life. Furthermore, military drill sergeants no longer rely on verbal confrontation and intimidation to control and train their troops, but place a great deal more emphasis on voice commands (Parent, 1989). To compare SI programs with military basic training is therefore misleading and ill advised.

Shock incarceration can probably be traced back to the work of penologist John Cray, who in 1821 attempted to relieve overcrowding at Auburn Prison in New York by instituting certain paramilitary practices. Similar efforts took place at New York's Elmira Reformatory just prior to the turn of the century, although this program was noted more for abusive punishment than for innovative penological practice (Morash & Rucker, 1990). The first organized attempt to implement a program of stress incarceration took place a decade or two ago in England, where it received mixed reviews. Thornton et al. (1984) performed a one-year follow-up of adolescents enrolled in several British boot camp programs and surmised that re-conviction rates varied little from outcomes obtained by youth released from traditional juvenile correctional centers.

In the United States, a 29-month follow-up of the Oklahoma program revealed that half the SI graduates had been returned to prison compared to 28 percent of a group of nonviolent controls (Parent, 1989). Return-to-prison rates in Florida demonstrated that 5.6 percent of the boot camp group and 7.8 percent of the controls, a difference which failed to achieve statistical significance, were returned to prison within one year (Florida Department of Corrections, 1989). Preliminary outcome data gathered in Georgia suggest that 39 percent of a group of SI-treated offenders returned to prison within three years, compared to a control comparison of 38 percent (cited in Sechrest, 1989). Re-arrest rates in Louisiana were 24.5 and 22.5 percent after nine months for graduates and regular parolees, respectively (MacKenzie, 1990), while in New York SI-versus-control re-arrest rates were on the order of 23 and 28 percent in one study (New York Division of Parole, 1989) and 19.8 and 18.5 percent in a second investigation (New York Department of Correctional Services, 1989).

The recidivism or re-arrest rate represents only a portion of the outcome we attempt to influence through implementation of secondary and tertiary preventive measures like shock incarceration. Inspecting preliminary data generated by the

New York SI program, Aziz (1988) discerned that SI graduates exhibited greater educational attainment in prison relative to that achieved by a group of nonparticipants. A comparison of shock incarceration and regular prison confinement in Louisiana highlighted superior adjustment and more prosocial attitudes on the part of subjects in the SI group 85 days into the program (MacKenzie & Shaw, 1990). It should be pointed out, however, that in addition to lacking a long-term follow-up, this study demonstrated a distinct pattern of differential mortality, in which SI enrollees withdrawing or being expelled from the program prior to the 85 day post-test (50%) displayed more negative pre-test attitudes than enrollees who completed the first 85 days of programming.

While it may not be quite time to close down the correctional boot camps, available research on these programs is far from encouraging. Controlled comparisons assessing the validity of SI should probably include groups of offenders on regular probation, since this is the population from whence many of the SI enrollees have been sampled. Still, research has been fairly consistent in showing that if there is a difference in the recidivism of probationers and incarcerates, then the advantage goes to the probationers (Wheeler & Hissong, 1988). Consequently, SI will probably fare no better when contrasted with a control group comprised of persons granted regular probation. There is also the possibility that the "dehumanizing" treatment youthful offenders may suffer at the hands of overzealous boot camp drill instructors does more harm than good with individuals already consumed by hostility and low self-esteem (Morash & Rucker, 1990).

Basing our intervention efforts on fear, regardless of whether the target behavior is venereal disease, smoking, or crime, has generally been found ineffective in changing behavior. This, in fact, may be one of the primary reasons why juvenile awareness and adult shock programs have yielded less than impressive results despite their popular and political appeal. Whereas available research insinuates that awareness programs may be modestly effective with first-time offenders (many of whom would probably never have offended again, even without benefit of treatment), these programs appear to be futile—and maybe even counterproductive—with persons who have had prior experience with the criminal justice system. Though of dubious merit even under the best of circumstances (with first-time offenders), awareness programs must be bolstered by regularly scheduled follow-up interventions to have any lasting impact on behavior, modest as this effect may be.

House Arrest and Electronic Monitoring. House arrest is another intermediate-level punishment, and electronic monitoring is one technique by which this sanction is commonly enforced. House arrest can be inserted at several different points in the criminal justice sequence: as a form of pretrial detention, as diversion from prison, or as a condition of release or parole (Morris & Tonry, 199). The first electronic monitoring program, in which the movements of targeted offenders were monitored electronically, was established in Palm Beach, Florida, in 1984. By 1988 electronic surveillance was being used in 33 states for the purposes of monitoring the activities of 2,300 offenders, with Florida and Michigan accounting for approximately half the electronically monitored cases in the United States (Schmidt, 1989). Organized according to the type of monitoring device utilized (continuously signaling devices and programmed contact devices), the information is fed into a computer at the monitoring agency and then analyzed by parole or probation staff. Major traffic offenses (for example, DWI), property crimes, and drug violations are the most common criminal acts for which electronic surveillance is currently being used (Schmidt, 1989), although there is no good data on the efficacy or cost-effectiveness of this approach to intermediate punishment.

Therapeutic Communities. With the advent of a more punitive correctional philosophy, therapeutic communities for lawbreaking adults and juveniles have generally fallen out of favor. We must examine the empirical literature, however, to determine whether the decision to move away from the therapeutic community approach to intervention was based on a rational reading of the data or simply a knee-jerk response to certain political exigencies. Cornish and Clarke (1975) were unable to detect differences in outcome for British youth randomly assigned to a modified therapeutic community or conventional school regime. A year earlier, McMichael (1974) had found much the same outcome, while Klein (1979) acknowledges that he was unable to identify significant variations in the level of recidivism experienced by subjects exposed to custodial and noncustodial forms of intervention. In a four-year follow-up of juveniles treated in an intensive community-based treatment program, it was determined that recidivism was appreciably lower than that witnessed in adolescents assigned to a custodial facility (Empey & Erickson, 1972). Though random assignment of subjects to conditions was not accomplished, experimental and control subjects had been carefully matched on several relevant dimensions.

The contradictory nature of these findings suggests that certain characteristics of the individual and treatment situation may interact in their effect on outcome. Palmer (1974), for instance, reports that "power-oriented" youth performed better in a traditional institution, while "neurotic" youth did better in a nontraditional therapeutic community. More research needs to be conducted on person × treatment interactions (see Chapter 6), although existing studies seem to suggest that the therapeutic community approach to intervention is often no more successful in reducing recidivism than is incarceration. However, therapeutic communities have the decided advantage of being less restrictive and possibly less detrimental to the psychological and emotional well-being of youthful rule breakers, many of whom will never go on to become serious adult offenders. Hence, while the therapeutic community approach to crime prevention has its limitations and is probably less effective than was once thought, it may prove useful in certain instances if issues of follow-up and criminal sophistication are taken into account.

CONCLUSION

The results of this review on crime prevention measures certify that there is no single method that is effective under all conditions. Consequently, we must consider several different measures in constructing a comprehensive crime-prevention package, incorporating procedures from each of the four functional categories introduced in this chapter: altering the incentives for criminal and noncriminal behavior; decreasing the opportunities for crime; increasing the opportunities for and benefits of prosocial behavior; increasing the cost of crime. The incentive-modifying leg of this model is anchored by parenting and school-based interventions, while target hardening, physical environmental modifications, community policing, and media-based surveillance (Crime Stoppers) serve to define the opportunity-reducing leg. Efforts to teach and reinforce prosocial forms of behavior have generated fewer positive findings, although challenge programs and certain categories of early release have produced moderately encouraging results. Procedures designed to raise the cost of crime (probation, intermediate sanctions, incarceration) round out our discussion of preventive strategies and serve as the fourth leg of our comprehensive system of crime prevention and control.

At a point early in this chapter we considered three categories of prevention—primary, secondary, and tertiary—which were then periodically referenced in the body of knowledge and discussions that followed. It may be helpful to examine how each of these three categories of intervention conform to the basic tenets of our comprehensive model of crime prevention.

The primary prevention goal might best be realized in early family and school interventions, as well as in environmental solutions like target hardening and defensible space. Secondary prevention could possibly be achieved through involvement in challenge programs, regular probation, and intermediate procedures, to include intensive probation supervision (IPS). Finally, tertiary prevention measures (for example, incarceration, parole, and Crime Stopper programs) must also be embraced if our model is to be truly comprehensive. It would be myopic of us to construe a system of crime control without taking into account the four primary functions (incentive-modification, opportunity-reduction, prosocial-augmentation, cost-elevation) and three general categories (primary, secondary, tertiary) of prevention.

A proper balance between formal and informal sources of social control must also be struck if our comprehensive system of crime prevention is to prove viable. By way of review, formal social control is expressed in written rules and laws and is enforced by the police, courts, and correctional system, while informal social control is lodged in custom and social mores and is enforced by the citizenry through surveillance, verbal reprimands, and other social pressures to conform to community standards. Police science research clearly denotes that law enforcement and community policing are interdependent to the extent that the efficacy of one demands the support of the other. Absent a clearly defined blueprint of formal-informal integration, our efforts will likely fall short of our goal of effectively managing the problem of crime. This rapprochement might be achieved by creating committees designed to facilitate communication and bring about the mutual cooperation of law enforcement, judicial, governmental, business, media, and community interests (possibly modeled along the lines established by Crime Stopper programs).

Implementing our comprehensive model of crime prevention, we will want to take advantage of important characteristics of both the victim and victimizer. Research investigations note that persons who engage in more risk-avoidance behaviors (those who refrain from carrying large sums of cash and who do not go out at night without an escort, dog, or weapon) are less prone to victimization than persons who engage in fewer risk-avoidance behaviors (Garofalo, 1977; Lavrakas, 1982). Lifestyle also plays a crucial role in one's vulnerability to crime, since persons involved with drugs, gambling, and gangs are at higher risk of victimization than persons eschewing such activities (Hindelang, Gottfredson, & Garofalo, 1978).

On the victimizer side of the equation, we have already seen the folly of ignoring the characteristics of potential offenders in research on defensible space theory (Mawby, 1977; Mayhew, 1979). Age and gender are two pivotal victimizer-relevant variables in the sense that crime is not proportionally distributed but is more highly concentrated in certain groups, such as adolescent males (Wilson & Herrnstein, 1985). Accordingly, studies show that public high schools elevate the crime rate of nearby neighborhoods (Roneck & Lobosco, 1983), while area crime rates tend to correlate inversely with their distance from a fast-food restaurant (Brantingham & Brantingham, 1982). Any approach to crime prevention would be incredulously incomplete if it were to overlook the potential characteristics of victims and victimizers.

In this chapter we have canvased the literature in an effort to form a comprehensive model of crime prevention. However, very little progress can be anticipated in the realization of this goal without a decided improvement in the methodological sophistication of studies addressing sundry preventive issues. Knowledge derived through anecdotal observation can be an invaluable source of intelligence in the preliminary stages of theory development, but the time has come for research on crime prevention to adopt a more rigorous test of its founding principles. Preliminary findings need to be probed with the aid of better designed studies. As part of this new methodology, we must begin paying closer attention to the individual components of prevention programs since it has been standard practice to roll several different interventions into a single treatment package. Hence, component analyses of crime prevention conglomerations, like subanalyses of person-oriented change programs, are required as we move forward toward a comprehensive system of crime prevention.

Reiterating a theme expressed throughout this chapter, prevention can be an incredibly powerful form of intervention, although to harness its full potential we must exercise greater conceptual control over the relationships hypothesized to exist between situational variables and crime, seek to reorganize our research methodologies, and then reevaluate initial conclusions on our way to developing a comprehensive system of crime control and prevention. Until this is accomplished, the vast wealth of crime prevention techniques will remain largely untapped and the dividends we might realistically anticipate unrealized. The exploration of social policy decisions and how they may affect criminal science outcomes is the organizing topic of the chapter that follows.

8

Situation-Oriented Intervention: Social Policy

Social policy, as a situation-oriented intervention, differs from the prevention techniques discussed in the previous chapter largely in terms of its scope. Whereas social policy decisions occur on a molar plane, prevention strategies call for a more molecular analysis of a particular problem or situation. In other words, social policy reflects how society contemplates, conceptualizes, and faces crime and crime-related issues, while prevention considers specific situation-oriented techniques designed to reduce crime through interventions affecting the relative costs and benefits of crime and noncrime. We might well refer to social policy and prevention as wide-band and narrow-band procedures, respectively.

There are many social policy issues that impact on criminal science investigations. In this chapter, however, we confine ourselves to three primary topics: capital punishment, legalization of drugs, and privatization. Nonetheless, as subsequent discussions will bear out, these three topics are more than adequate for the purposes of illustrating the kinds of issues, problems, and considerations that enter into any system of social-policy decision making. The reader should pay close attention to the manner in which each of these policy issues not only mirrors the attitudes of society but, in turn, perpetuates these same beliefs as part of a wider network of values and decisions.

THE DEATH PENALTY

The relative merits and drawbacks of capital punishment have become a core point of controversy since reinstitution of the death penalty in 1976. Opinions range wide and emotions run high when this issue is broached. Between 1930 and 1966 there were 3,859 death sentences carried out in the United States. In 1967 what would become a ten-year moratorium on the use of capital punishment began. Midway through this decade-long hiatus the Supreme Court ruled that pre-1967 death penalty statutes were discriminatory, although it did not find the

Figure 8.1
The Death Penalty in the United States as of July 1, 1990

notion of capital punishment to be unconstitutional (Furman v. Georgia, 1972). Four years later the Supreme Court approved a death penalty package compiled by authorities in Georgia (Gregg v. Georgia, 1976). Since the Gregg decision, 110 persons in 14 different states have been put to death. The 14 states that have carried out executions, along with the 23 states which have death penalty statutes but no post-Furman executions, are identified in Figure 8.1.

As of December 31, 1989, there were 2,250 prisoners under sentence of death in 34 states. Texas has the largest number of prisoners on death row (304), followed by Florida (289) and California (254). All except one of the inmates currently on death row in the United States have been convicted of murder and 69 percent have a record of at least one prior felony conviction. Interestingly, 41 percent of this group had been under the supervision of the criminal justice system (parole, probation, incarceration) at the time they committed the crime for which they eventually received a sentence of death. Of those on death row, 58 percent of are white, 99 percent male, and the average age at the time of the survey was 34 years (Bureau of Justice Statistics, 1990).

The form of execution has also become an issue in several jurisdictions owing to the fact that some techniques are viewed as more humane than others. At the end of 1988 lethal injection was the most popular method (authorized by 20 states), followed by electrocution (14 states) and the gas chamber (6 states). Seven states allow for more than one method, several out of concern that lethal injection may someday be found unconstitutional (Bureau of Justice Statistics, 1990). Since 1977 the average elapsed time between sentencing and execution has been six years, five months. This has been viewed as excessive by both supporters and opponents of the death penalty, although for very different reasons. Proponents of capital punishment contend that an average elapsed time of six years between sentencing and execution reflects bureaucratic inefficiency and financial waste, while opponents argue that this six-year gap constitutes a cruel and unusual form of punishment.

Attitudes Toward Capital Punishment

A recent Gallup poll shows that nearly eight out of every ten Americans support the death penalty for persons convicted of first-degree murder (Gallup & Gallup, 1988). This is the largest margin of support enjoyed by capital punishment since inception of the poll in 1936. Popular backing for the death penalty has always been strong in this country, and only once (1966 Gallup Poll) has opposition outweighed support. There is evidence, however, that many fewer people sanction execution of persons under the age of 18, even in states like Indiana and Ohio where a juvenile death penalty exists (Hamm [1989] and Skovron, Scott, & Cullen [1989], respectively). Bohm and Aveni (1985) assert further that Americans as a group are ignorant of the pertinent issues surrounding the capital punishment controversy, and while many persons are in favor of the death penalty in the abstract, most would be unwilling to personally administer this sentence, either through imposition of sentence of death in a courtroom situation or through participation in the execution itself.

What are some of the factors that might help explain the public's attitude toward the death penalty? One such explanatory concept is fear of crime. Surveys suggest that fear of crime has risen sharply in recent years (Bureau of Justice Statistics, 1984a). It stands to reason that fear or crime may help explain the popular endorsement of death penalty legislation. However, research on this issue has been divided, for while some studies show a positive association between fear of crime and death penalty approval (Bowers, 1984; van den Haag & Conrad, 1983), other studies have failed to generate support for the fear of crime explanation of death penalty countenance (Smith, 1975; Stinchcombe et al., 1980). Social demographic (being older, white, affluent, less educated, living in an urban area), occupational (being in a white-collar, agricultural, or manual labor occupation rather than holding a professional or business position), political (Republican), and religious (Catholic) variables were observed to correspond with support for capital punishment in a study directed by Vidmar and Ellsworth (1974). The results of a recent Gallup poll cast suspicion on several of these "correlates" of death penalty support, although race, gender, affluence, and political affiliation continued to evidence a strong correlation with attitudes toward capital punishment (Gallup, 1985).

Since legislators set social policy by formulating laws, it would seem especially important that we examine their posture on capital punishment. Cullen, Clark, Cullen, and Mathers (1985) surveyed the Illinois State Legislature and found that male legislators partial to a classical (free will) interpretation of offender behavior were more vocally supportive of capital punishment than legislators who conceptualized crime in positivist (social forces) terms. Using a design similar to Cullen et al.'s, McGarrell and Flanagan (1987) observed that conservative legislators were more likely than nonconservative policymakers to throw their support behind death penalty legislation. Likewise, Hamm (1989) notes that political affiliation is the most powerful discriminator of attitudes toward capital punishment, with Republicans more supportive of capital punishment legislation than Democrats. Though legislators often mirror the views and values of their respective constituencies, there is research to suggest that policymakers conceive of the public as being more supportive of punitive measures like the death penalty than is actually the case (Gottfredson & Taylor, 1984; Riley & Rose, 1980).

One might well wonder what factors could be used to help change attitudes toward social policy concerns like capital punishment. A factor that has received a great deal of attention from researchers investigating attitude change is education. We might suppose that education should influence public attitudes toward capital punishment, since research clearly indicates that the American public is grossly ill informed where the death penalty is concerned (Ellsworth & Ross, 1983). The use of educational programs, however, has typically failed to affect either death penalty opinions (Bohm & Aveni, 1985) or the reasons given for one's views on the death penalty (Bohm, Clark, & Aveni, 1990).

Retribution

Retribution has traditionally been the primary foundation upon which the death penalty in the United States has rested (Kohlberg & Elfenbein, 1975). Retributively based justification for capital punishment may be grounded in certain religious beliefs or moral credos adhered to by a major cross section of American society, or it may relate to a more individualized belief in revenge and retaliation. The Bible remains the most widely read religious document in this country, and supporters of the death penalty are quick to point out that it contains passages sympathetic to capital punishment. However, there are also biblical excerpts entirely discordant with the practice of putting to death society's lawbreakers (Bohm, 1987). It has also been stated that many of the aims of retribution could be achieved through implementation of less drastic measures (life imprisonment), while Wolfgang (1988) argues that capital punishment is inadequate even for retribution. Consequently, retribution by itself appears to provide a shaky foundation upon which to construct a social policy of capital punishment.

Discrimination

Opponents of the death penalty have long contended that this procedure has been applied arbitrarily in the past and that even today is used in a discriminatory manner. It is clear that the death penalty is not uniformly applied across all 50 states, or even across different jurisdictions within the same state. Approximately 60 percent of the nearly 4,000 executions taking place between 1930 and 1967 were in the South, and since the Furman decision Southern states have accounted for 93 percent of the executions in the United States (Baily & Peterson, 1989). This, in and of itself, is not sufficient grounds for claiming discrimination, although it has been noted that even within a single Southern state the probability of receiving the death penalty varies widely from one district to the next (Bowers, 1984).

It has been argued that the death penalty discriminates against blacks and other minorities, and research conducted prior to 1972 has tended to confirm this supposition, with a greater percentage of blacks than whites sentenced to death (Garfinkle, 1949; Mangum, 1940) and significantly fewer blacks with their death sentences commuted to life imprisonment (Koeninger, 1969; Wolfgang, Kelly, & Nolde, 1962). Kleck (1981) failed to identify a racial bias in studies probing use of the death penalty with persons convicted of murder, but did observe a racial disparity in persons sentenced for rape. Blacks found guilty of rape in Southern jurisdictions during a 20-year period (1945–1965) were discovered to have been executed at a rate 7 times that of whites convicted of the same offense, 17 times if the victim was white (Wolfgang & Riedel, 1973). A similar pattern was observed in a Northern jurisdiction (Philadelphia), although the discrepancy was much less dramatic: 88 percent of the blacks and 80 percent of the whites convicted under sentence of death actually were executed (Wolfgang et al., 1962). The apparent racial inequity of capital punishment practices prior to 1967 was, in fact, one of the factors contributing to the institution of a ten-year hiatus in application of the death penalty (1967–1976).

Studies conducted on death sentences carried out since 1977 also hint at potential racial inequalities. This has been observed in states as diverse as Florida (Radelet & Pierce, 1985); Texas (Henderson & Taylor, 1985); New Jersey (Bienin et al., 1988); South Carolina (Paternoster, 1983); and Illinois, Minnesota, North Carolina, Oklahoma, and Virginia (Gross & Mauro, 1984). Bowers and Pierce (1980) ascertained that blacks who murdered whites were substantially more likely to receive a post-Furman sentence of death than any other racial combination. However, it may be that this discrepancy reflects meaningful black-white offender differences in the frequency of past criminal behavior or in the severity of the current offense. Indeed, when the individual's past criminal record (Heilbrun, Foster, & Golden, 1989) or the circumstances surrounding the current offense (Arkin, 1980) are taken into account, racial discrepancies shrink considerably.

Barnett (1985) devised a measure of homicide severity that explained in toto the racial disparities of death sentences imposed by judges and juries in Georgia. While this measure was found useful in explaining a portion of the variance in Kentucky's use of capital punishment, prosecutors were still more inclined to seek the death penalty and juries more prone to sentence someone to death in cases involving a black defendant than when a white defendant was being tried (Vito & Keil, 1988). These same two investigators analyzed these data further and observed that blacks who killed whites were more likely to be charged with and receive the death sentence than blacks who killed blacks or whites who killed either blacks or whites, even after the severity of the offense, a defendant's criminal record, and the personal relationship between offender and victim were considered (Keil & Vito, 1990).

While it would appear that the death penalty may have been applied in a racially discriminatory manner in the past, taking a defendant's criminal history and the circumstances of the current offense into account reveals that modern versions of the death penalty are probably less discriminatory than were pre-Furman death penalty statutes. The Supreme Court's ruling in Coker v. Georgia (1977), which holds that the rape of an adult female is insufficient grounds for imposition of capital punishment, also helps limit the bias of moderate-day death penalty criteria. Bias may still exist on an individual level and it is likely that it operates on a wider scale in some jurisdictions than others, but there is no convincing evidence that present-day application of the death penalty discriminates system-wide on the basis of race.

If system-wide discrimination in how capital punishment is currently applied does, in fact, exist, then the culprit may well be positive bias in favor of affluent defendants rather than negative bias against black or minority defendants. Past speculation on the racially discriminatory nature of death-penalty legislation might therefore be explained by the fact very few blacks accused of murder have had the resources necessary to hire an experienced lawyer. It is rare indeed to find persons possessing the requisite funds necessary to retain superior legal counsel being sentenced to die in the gas chamber or electric chair, no matter how heinous the crime (Bedau, 1982). However, this does not appear to be sufficient grounds on which to find capital punishment unconstitutional, since it is a criticism which could be leveled against many aspects of the American system of jurisprudence.

Capital Punishment as a Deterrent

While retribution is thought to be the primary basis for people's support of the death penalty, most people point to deterrence as their rationale for endorsing capital punishment (Ellsworth & Ross, 1983). A recent Gallup poll established that 61 percent of a national sample of respondents concurred with the statement that capital punishment is a deterrent to murder (Gallup, 1986). The face validity of the deterrent argument is obvious. The empirical support generated by this argument, on the other hand, is less than impressive (Sellin, 1967). Contrasting pairs of adjacent states with and without capital punishment, Sellin observed that a state's death penalty status was uncorrelated with its homicide rate. Sellin was also unable to identify a deterrent effect when he compared the homicide rates of states before and after restoration or abolition of the death penalty. Likewise, there were no pre-post execution differences in homicide for cities in which executions took place.

Despite the importance of Sellin's (1967) findings, they have not gone unchallenged. Several of the more salient criticisms of the Sellin studies have been advanced by Wilson (1983) in his book *Thinking About Crime*. First, Wilson argues that it is difficult to match states with and without capital punishment since these states differ on more than just whether they ascribe to capital punishment. A second concern is that Sellin studied the overall homicide rate, but capital punishment may exert little impact on this figure since most murders are not potentially punishable by death. It would be more meaningful, though excruciatingly painstaking, to study just those homicides that are premeditated or sufficiently heinous to potentially warrant imposition of the death penalty. There are also problems with Sellin's definition of a state's death penalty status since several of his "capital punishment" states had not executed anyone in years even though they had a death penalty statute on the books (Wilson, 1983).

Recent investigations on the deterrent effect of capital punishment are of two kinds: cross-sectional studies, which compare two or more states at a particular point in time; and longitudinal studies, which examine homicide rates over time. Cross-sectional studies on the deterrent value of capital punishment have produced mixed outcomes. Controlling for selected variables, Ehrlich (1977) and Cloninger (1977) determined that the death penalty played a deterrent role in affecting homicide rates for 1940 and 1960, respectively. However, Passell (1975), inspecting outcomes for 1950 and 1960, and Forst (1977), canvasing results for 1960 and 1970, were unable to identify the proposed relationship between death penalty status and homicide after controlling for several possible intervening variables. The use of divergent methodologies, disparate data groups, and dissimilar control variables may help explain why a conclusion about the outcome of cross-sectional studies linking death penalty status with the homicide rate continues to elude us.

Ehrlich (1975) directed one of the first sophisticated longitudinal analyses of the proposed nexus between capital punishment and homicide. He examined yearly data on homicide and executions between 1933 and 1969, holding the unemployment rate, labor force participation, income, racial composition, and age distribution constant. The outcome of these analyses led Ehrlich to estimate an associated drop in the homicide rate of seven to eight murders for every execution accomplished. Wolpin (1978b) reviewed execution and murder rate data for England and Wales, and observed a pattern similar to that recorded in the Ehrlich study: each execution corresponded with a reduced number of murder victims, in this case the ratio was four murders to every execution carried out.

Though suggestive, the results obtained by Ehrlich (1975) and Wolpin (1978b) are subject to several criticisms. For one, an increased probability of execution may influence juries or judges to make less frequent use of the death penalty. This, in fact, was observed in England, where abolition of capital punishment was followed by a sharp decline in the number of defendants found insane and therefore spared the gallows (Wilson, 1983). It should also be noted that near the end of the time frames studied by Ehrlich and Wolpin there was a noticeable plunge not only in the use of capital punishment but also in the length of time served by nonexecuted murderers. In order to accept the conclusion that capital punishment is a deterrent to homicide we must be assured that the receding sentences of nonexecuted murderers do not account for the inverse correlation detected between homicide and executions. Finally, there is a statistical artifact in the Ehrlich (1975) study that finds executions falling to near zero and crime growing at an unprecedented rate at the end of the study period (1963–1969). Interestingly, if we drop these years from the investigation and restrict our analyses to the 1933–1962 period, the inverse execution-homicide relationship observed by Ehrlich becomes nonsignificant (Passell & Taylor, 1977).

The consensus of investigators addressing the relationship between capital punishment and homicide is that when the theoretical and methodological problems encountered in the earlier longitudinal studies are corrected, there is virtually no connection between death penalty status and homicide rate (Bedau, 1982; Bowers & Pierce, 1975). Avio (1979) correlated Canadian execution and homicide data but could not identify a significant association between the two, though he did note, in support of previous concerns directed at the Ehrlich and Wolpin studies, that the homicide rate demonstrated a significant inverse relationship with the amount of time nonexecuted murderers served in prison. A cross-national survey of capital punishment as a deterrent to crime also failed to support the presence of a connection between homicide and death penalty status (Archer & Gartner, 1984). There has been some speculation of late that capital punishment may actually exert a brutalizing effect by increasing rather than inhibiting future occurrences of homicide. Though speculative at this point, there have been several studies in which a brutalizing effect has been suggested (Amsterdam, 1982; Bedau, 1982; Bowers, 1984).

The general deterrent effect of capital punishment has also been explored in studies probing the influence of execution publicity on murders in a particular jurisdiction. Highly publicized executions in Philadelphia in 1927, 1929, 1930, 1931, 1932 (Dann, 1935), 1944, 1946, and 1947 (Savitz, 1958) correlated with increased, rather than decreased, levels of subsequent homicide. These findings were replicated in California for the years 1946 through 1955 (Graves, 1956) and in South Carolina for the years 1950 through 1963 (King, 1978). Phillips (1980), on the other hand, surmised that the 22 most highly publicized executions in England between 1858 and 1921 were followed by a 35 percent decline in the homicide rate during a two-week period subsequent to the execution, although he also witnessed a rebound effect in which homicides returned to their baseline level during the third through fifth weeks post-execution.

The methodology of research investigating the concordance between execution publicity and homicide has been questioned on several counts. Mindful of these issues, Stack (1987) inspected the relationship between level of execution publicity and monthly homicide rates in the United States between 1950 and 1980 in a study that introduced several methodological improvements over previous research in the area. The outcome of this inquiry revealed a significant decline in homicide following a high publicized execution, but no such change when the execution received only moderate or low amounts of publicity. Bailey and Peterson (1989) demonstrated even greater methodological finesse by providing better operationalization of terms, including an increased number of control variables, and extending the time frame of the study by 16 years (1940–1986). The resultant outcome was that they failed to identify an inverse relationship between the publicity surrounding an execution and the homicide rate one to six months later.

At present there are little data to support the argument that capital punishment is an effective deterrent to murder. Hence, while the complexity of the problem makes scientific resolution of the deterrence issue elusive, the preponderance of evidence suggests that capital punishment is not an effective general deterrent to crimes punishable by death. One of the more exhaustive reviews of this topic (Zimring & Hawkins, 1986) strongly supports this conclusion. As for the value of capital punishment as a specific deterrent to murder, research studies document that less than 1 percent of all murderers released from prison between 1900 and 1976 were returned to prison for homicide, regardless of whether or not they were residing in a death-penalty state (Bedau, 1982). More important, however, it is ludicrous to even consider the specific deterrent value of capital punishment, since the executed individual will never be given the opportunity to demonstrate whether the penalty had any impact on his or her future behavior.

Incapacitation

It is clear that the death penalty serves to incapacitate its recipients. Once executed, a murderer will never again harm another person. In the aftermath of a 1985 Gallup poll incapacitation was shown to be the fifth most popular argument in favor of the death penalty, though it may well be the single most defensible position upon which to construct a policy of capital punishment (Bohm, 1987). Defensible or not, if incapacitation is our primary justification for capital punishment, then it needs to be documented that less drastic or restrictive measures are incapable of achieving the same level of immobilization. It is uncertain whether capital punishment is any more incapacitating than, say, life imprisonment without the possibility of parole. Of course, there is always a chance that an individual serving a life sentence might escape from custody, although this possibility seems remote if the individual is housed in a maximum security penitentiary.

Affiliated with the incapacitation issue is the belief in the cost-effectiveness of capital punishment. Some contend that keeping a person confined for life in a maximum security prison is a drain on societal resources. While this is most decidedly true, the results of at least one study indicate that incarcerating an offender for a period of 50 years is actually less expensive (by approximately $500,000) than going through the many appeals and other legal safeguards required to execute someone under our current system of law (New York State Defenders' Association, 1982). Eliminating some of the steps and safeguards might reduce the expense of capital punishment but at the cost of certain personal freedoms. At this point I submit that incapacitation can be achieved in ways that are, in many ways, less harsh and less expensive than capital punishment.

Concerns about Executing an Innocent Defendant

One issue raised by opponents of the death sentence is that an innocent person might be executed before disconfirming evidence can be brought to bear on the case. Since the average wait on death row is six years, it seems improbable that this occurs very often. That it could occur at all, however, should give us cause to stop and evaluate our procedures and policies. Espy (1985) states that of the more than 14,000 persons executed in the United States between 1608 and 1985, approximately 700 (5%) were "innocent." Bedau and Radelet (1987) make note of 350 individuals convicted of murder, many of whom were condemned to die for the crime, who were eventually acquitted on appeal. In still another survey, Black (1981) reports that he identified 100 examples of innocent persons convicted of murder, 31 of whom were sentenced to die, and 8 of whom were eventually executed.

Supporters of the death penalty contend that present-day criteria provide sufficient protection and safeguards under nearly all circumstances. When pressed for an answer to the question of executing an innocent person these scholars reason that this is the price we must pay for administering a viable program of criminal jurisprudence (Berns, 1979). However, in light of questions about the credibility of capital punishment as a cost-effective deterrent to crime, we as a society may want to reconsider whether we are willing to risk the lives of a handful of innocent people in order to maintain a policy of executing persons who violate certain of society's rules.

Moral Issues

Ethical and moral issues have been raised by both supporters and opponents of capital punishment. Supporters comment that the death penalty provides society with the ability to express maximum condemnation for certain forms of behavior (see van den Haag's arguments in van den Haag & Conrad, 1983). They would contend that society has the right—nay, the obligation—to define the boundaries of acceptable conduct and assign the most severe penalties to those actions that are at the upper reaches of unacceptability. Without a death penalty, supporters asseverate, the line between acceptable and unacceptable behavior tends to blur and people experience a sense of uncertainty and anomie that is at once frightening and demoralizing.

Opponents of capital punishment argue that this most extreme form of sanctioning diminishes human potential and dignity, and that it is incompatible with the ideals of a democratic or humanistic society (Bohm, 1989; Bowers, 1984). Supporters counter that there is nothing about capital punishment inherently incompatible with a humanistic approach to life (Friedrichs, 1989). Conrad argues that capital punishment serves to perpetuate violence, adding that historically the more violent nations have been the ones that have relied more extensively on the death penalty (van den Haag & Conrad, 1983). When pondering the broader issue of societal sanctions and humanitarianism we might want to keep Winston Churchill's 1966 statement on this matter in mind: "The mood and temper of the public with regard to the treatment of crime and criminals is one of the most unfailing tests of the civilization of any country."

Kohlberg and colleagues have devised a system of moral development that seems potentially applicable to the moral issues discussed in this section. Kohlberg and Elfenbein (1975) hypothesize that as the moral development of a society proceeds, support for the death penalty should decline. The ascending level of endorsement afforded capital punishment by the American public in recent years leads us to one of two conclusions: either Kohlberg's reasoning is flawed or this country's moral development has regressed significantly since Kohlberg first made his predictions. Proponents of capital punishment argue the former, opponents the latter.

Discussion

In considering the proponent side of the capital punishment issue we can see that the moral argument of retribution is the strongest point in favor of the death penalty (see Table 8.1). Deterrence and cost-effectiveness, on the other hand, add little to the argument. While incapacitation certainly supports the position of death-penalty adherents, this goal can probably be accomplished through implementation of less drastic measures (life imprisonment). On the converse side of the issue, we can see that moral considerations involving the personal dignity of offenders and victims and efforts to model reasoned social control and restraint support the arguments of those opposing the death penalty. Arguments about reverse discrimination in favor of the affluent and concerns about the accidental execution of innocent defendants also weigh heavily on the opponent side of the capital punishment question.

As with most aspects of social policy, the ideas, attitudes, and values of the

Table 8.1
Arguments For and Against the Death Penalty

Pro Arguments	Support	Con Arguments	Support
Retribution	Strong	Discrimination	Moderate
Deterrence	Weak	Innocent Victims	Moderate
Incapacitation	Moderate	Moral Issues	Strong
Cost-efficiency	Weak		
Moral Issues	Moderate		

ruling elite will determine how we as a society approach the question of capital punishment. It is hoped that this policy reflects (at least indirectly) the will of the populace, and in the case of the U.S. death penalty this seems to be true. Of course, there is always the question of how well informed the American public is on the relevant issues surrounding the capital-punishment debate. This review is not intended to provide a definitive answer to the death-penalty question, but simply clarify the major positions and evaluate the available evidence. Nevertheless, to continue justifying capital punishment on the strength of its posture as a deterrent to homicide or cost-effective incapacitating alternative to other major sanctions (life incarceration) is inconsistent with the bulk of research data on this subject.

LEGALIZATION (DECRIMINALIZATION) OF DRUGS

On December 12, 1989, Federal District Judge Robert W. Sweet raised the eyebrows of those in the higher echelons of the political superstructure when, in a speech to a group at the Cosmopolitan Club in Manhattan, he advocated the legalization of drugs and the development of alternative measures to reduce addiction. His was not the first voice to be heard in what has become a growing volley of dissent directed at the present administration's handling of the drug situation, but this was the first time the call for legalization had come from someone so clearly entrenched in the legal system.

The legalization alternative has been championed by Professor Ethan Nadelmann of the Woodrow Wilson School of Public and International Affairs at Princeton University, and has received the endorsement of such luminaries as Nobel Prize–winning economist Milton Friedman, Mayor Kurt Schmoke of Baltimore, former Secretary of State George Schultz, and conservative columnist William F. Buckley. The principal thrust of persons calling for legalization is to question our traditional reliance on law enforcement as a solution to the problem of drugs and suggest alternative approaches to a very real problem (Nadelmann, 1989).

Figure 8.2
Percentage of Persons Responding "Yes" to a National Survey on the
Legalization of Marijuana (1973–1988)

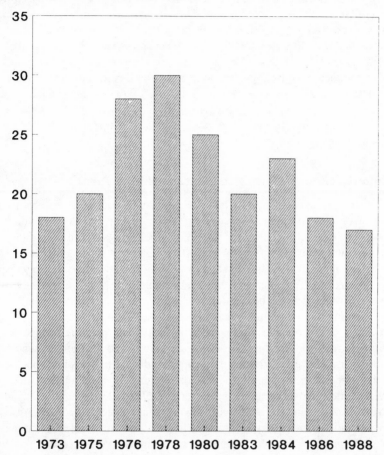

Source: Jamieson & Flanagan (1987).

Attitudes Toward Legalization

In an opinion poll taken by the National Opinion Research Center in April 1989, 1,537 adults were asked to state their opinions about the legalization or decriminalization of marijuana (Labaton, 1989). The results of this survey disclosed that opinions against legalization outnumbered the recommendations for legalization by a margin of 5 to 1. The recent decline in public support for the legalization of marijuana is graphically depicted in Figure 8.2. It seems that there is little popular support for legalization of drugs at this time, but just as we saw in reviewing the capital punishment literature, there are questions about how well informed the American public is on the pertinent issues surrounding the legalization controversy.

Interestingly, while 78 percent of those surveyed in an ABC News–*Washington Post* poll stated that they believed the U.S. government should spend as much money as necessary to stop the flow of drugs into this country, the majority of respondents in a CBS News–*New York Times* poll acknowledged that they regarded many of the proposals for increased spending on the "war on drugs" as motivated more by political goals than by a genuine desire to do something about the "drug problem" (Jamieson & Flanagan, 1987). We can only wonder whether the skepticism expressed by the respondents in the CBS poll represents the feelings of many Americans or accurately captures the true nature of the war on drugs as we enter the 1990s.

Current Policy: The Supply and Demand of Illicit Drugs

The strategy adopted by the last several administrations in combating the problem of drugs is aimed at reducing the supply of and demand for these substances. Efforts to control the supply of illicit drugs by limiting their flow into this country have traditionally met with only modest success (Reuter, 1988). Smugglers, in fact, have devised many creative and imaginative ways to transport their drugs over the border and through customs. The major effect of current drug-control policies has been to elevate the price of illicit substances, with a corresponding increase in the potential profit (as well as the incentive) for drug trafficking. The economics of drug dealing also bring pressure to bear on the consumer, who may then engage in illegal activities as a means of supporting his or her use of drugs. While current supply-reducing policies have been moderately effective in reducing the influx of foreign-grown marijuana which had previously flowed over the borders undetected, it has failed to significantly affect the volume of cocaine and heroin entering the United States from South America, Mexico, and Asia each day. Moreover, in order to compensate for diminished levels of imported cannabis, domestic marijuana harvesting operations have emerged in Western and Midwestern states, making the United States one of the world's largest producers of marijuana (Nadelmann, 1989).

Interventions designed to decrease the demand for drugs have centered on treatment and education. This would appear to be a potentially fruitful approach to the problem of drugs, although demand-reducing procedures have typically not received the level of governmental support law enforcement initiatives have. As we saw in Chapter 6 of this volume, when properly conceptualized, competently managed, and liberally stocked with motivated clients, drug-treatment programs can be effective. Unfortunately, motivated clients are often grouped with unmotivated ones, who then interfere with the treatment progress of the motivated subjects, depreciate the measured effect of the intervention, and add to the burgeoning waiting lists that make early response and immediate enrollment a luxury most low-budget programs cannot afford. Educational campaigns designed to reduce the demand for drugs await wide-scale empirical evaluation, although these procedures may very well be capable of effecting meaningful behavioral change in youngsters before they have had a chance to become enmeshed in a criminal or drug lifestyle.

The Cost of Current Policies

Nadelmann (1989) asserts that our present drug policies create many more problems than they alleviate. First, he points to the expense of enforcing drug laws. Between 1981 and 1987, federal expenditures for drug law enforcement more than tripled so that by 1987 state, federal, and local disbursements totaled more than $10 billion (National Drug Enforcement Policy Board, 1987). Furthermore, a substantial portion of the money spent on illegal drugs ends up in foreign banks, consequently draining essential assets from the national economy. Nadelmann (1989) states that if drugs were made legal, the government could go about the business of collecting billions of dollars in taxes instead of spending billions of dollars for law enforcement initiatives that have little apparent efficacy in stemming the tide of drug usage and drug-related criminal activity (Nadelmann, 1989). Studies conducted in Maine and California have established that decriminalization of marijuana was cost-effective primarily because it greatly reduced expenses incurred by the criminal justice system in the processing of marijuana law violators (Maloff, 1981).

The criminal justice system is a second area that has been adversely affected by our current policies on drugs. The U.S. Sentencing Commission (1987) estimates that by the year 2000 the federal prison population will number between 100,000 and 150,000 inmates, half of whom will be serving sentences for drug law violations. One-fourth of the 583,000 persons convicted of felonies in state courts during one 12-month period were there for drug possession or drug trafficking (Nadelmann, 1989). In Washington, D.C., the percentage of drug-law cases climbed from 13 percent in 1981 to 52 percent in 1986 (Greater Washington Research Center, 1988). It appears that the nation's court system is being encumbered and its correctional facilities inundated by an ever-growing number of drug cases, neither of which would occur if drugs were made legal.

A third misgiving scholars have about existing drug policies is that the lucrative drug trade has enticed and corrupted governmental officials at all levels and has helped create a new class of youthful and more violent criminals. Regarding the first point, there is evidence of corruption at the state, federal, and local levels that some say will decline with legalization (Shenon, 1988). Doubtlessly, legalizing drugs will no more eliminate black-market drug sales than legalized gambling has eradicated illicit games of chance (Perretti, 1989); it may, in fact, engender its own brand of bureaucratic corruption. Legalization may, however, do something about the youthful force of criminal offenders recruited by local drug lords. The stiffer penalties attached to drug dealing in recent years have led many traffickers to recruit juveniles, many of whom have grown up in the ghetto and view the drug dealer as a hero and a model of success, into their drug-running organizations. In the past the pattern has been for adolescents to start using drugs before they began selling them; today we see the reverse pattern—ghetto kids as young as seven or eight, with no previous history of drug usage, becoming involved in the drug trade (Mieczowski, 1986).

The Danger of Drug Legalization

There are those who argue that legalizing drugs will increase the threat or danger to both users and nonusers. In the United States, 320,000 people die each year from tobacco-related illnesses, 50,000 to 200,000 from causes linked directly to alcohol consumption, and 3,562 from all illicit drugs combined (Wicker, 1987). The question is whether decriminalization would substantially increase the rate of death from drugs presently illegal. There is no way to determine how many more new drug users legalization would create, but our experience in this country with repeal of Prohibition in 1933 and decriminalization of marijuana in several states during the mid-1970s seems to suggest that the increase might not be as great as opponents of legalization have led us to believe.

What is clear from our knowledge of drugs is that many of the negative physical effects of drug usage are more a function of the way these drugs are grown or processed than of the drugs themselves. Legalization would lessen the danger of impure, tainted, or poisoned substances being smoked, ingested, snorted, or injected by addicts through introduction of a system of quality control (Nadelmann, 1989). This same argument could be extended to the problem of acquired immunodeficiency syndrome (AIDS), of which intravenous drug use is one of the primary risk factors. It is estimated that approximately 25 percent of all cases of AIDS are transmitted by way of an infected hypodermic needle, and studies suggest that syringe exchange programs can dramatically reduce the incidence of AIDS without encouraging illicit drug usage (Des Jarlais & Hunt, 1988).

There are many myths and misconceptions that have sprung up around the issue of drugs in recent years. One is the concern about the danger and probability of addiction. A follow-up of 50 social-recreational users of cocaine revealed that after nine years half the group still used the substance socially and recreationally, while only 10 percent could be classified as compulsive users (Siegel, 1984). A survey of high school students revealed that 3.8 percent of the subjects who had tried cocaine reported that they tried to stop but couldn't compared to 7 percent of the people who had tried marijuana, and 18 percent of those who had tried tobacco (O'Malley, Johnston, & Bachman, 1985). All of this is not meant to overlook the truly serious nature of drug usage and addiction, but to keep the issues in perspective. History tells us that if we go beyond the data in instructing our children about the dangers of drugs we will eventually lose credibility with those we are trying to influence. We must also come to realize that the majority of people who experiment with drugs do not become addicted or even regular users of these substances, though there is a percentage of persons whose use of a substance, whether it be alcohol, marijuana, cocaine, tobacco, or any of the other drugs commonly misused, can only be described as abusive. Treatment appears to be a better option than jail in these particular cases.

Concerns about the possible dangers a user may pose to others have also been used to counter the argument that drugs can be effectively and safely legalized. This issue has become highly charged with emotion in light of the rising incidence of drug-related homicides in cities like Los Angeles and Washington, D.C. A study addressing the issue of dangerousness indicated that persons convicted of violent crimes in 1986 were, at the time of the offense, more likely to have been under the influence of alcohol or a combination of alcohol and illegal drugs than an illicit substance alone (Jamieson & Flanagan, 1987). The interpersonal danger presented by drug use remains a legitimate concern, however, particularly if it turns out that legalization leads to a significant increase in the use and abuse of such presently illegal substances as PCP, barbiturates, and high-grade stimulants.

Legal Sanctions as a Deterrent to Drug Use

The stated rationale for involving the criminal justice system in the war on drugs is that legal sanctions serve to deter the future use of these substances. Research, however, has failed to clearly corroborate the deterrent value of legal sanctions (Joint Committee on New York Drug Law Evaluation, 1977; Meier & Johnson, 1977; Meyers, 1980). Fish and Bruhnsen (1978/1979) pursued this issue in a survey of 85 drug dealers serving a college population. Those arrested were no more likely to terminate their involvement in drug trafficking or express the desire to stop dealing than those who had never before been apprehended. Moreover, of those subjects who were arrested, conviction apparently played no part in their decisions to remain involved in or exit from the drug trade. In fact, several dealers commented that they continued selling drugs in order to raise money for their legal defense.

Erickson (1976) studied 95 persons convicted for the first time of cannabis possession in Toronto, Canada, and found that most (84%) expressed intentions of continuing with the use of this drug. Neither the severity nor certainty of punishment had any authority over expressed intent to reuse marijuana. Contrary to what we might anticipate, more severe sanctions and a higher perceived certainty of punishment were actually associated with a greater percentage of subjects planning to continue their use of cannabis. The counter-deterrent effect of legal sanctions witnessed in this particular study may have been a consequence of subjects rebelling against what they perceived to be unjust treatment under the law. In New York State during the mid-1960s then-governor Nelson Rockefeller introduced legislation into law that increased the penalty for narcotics violations. An initial dampening effect on heroin involvement was noted, but this outcome was eventually shown to be transient and short-lived (Meyers, 1980).

There is some evidence that legal sanctions may exert a deterrent effect on drug usage in criminally involved addicts when these sanctions are reinforced by a parole or probation supervisor and coupled with urine surveillance. However, this deterrent effect normally disappears once supervision has been terminated (Speckart, Anglin, & Deschenes, 1989). It is possible, then, that drug-control laws do influence consumption under highly structured circumstances (supervision), although the costs and problems associated with this policy increase rapidly to the point where they soon outweigh any perceived benefits.

Perretti (1989), the attorney-general of New Jersey, has spoken out against legalization, in part because he believes removing criminal sanctions from drug usage would unleash a palpable increase in the number of drug users upon society. He goes on to state that surveys show that 89 percent of all high school students report having used alcohol, 49 percent relate having smoked marijuana, and 19 percent admit having tried cocaine. Perretti contends that the latter two figures will approach the level of current alcohol consumption (89%) if drugs like marijuana and cocaine are made legal. Nadelmann (1989), on the other hand, argues that there is little to suggest that legalization would lead to a burgeoning of nonalcohol drug usage and reminds us that alcohol is the primary intoxicant in most societies, even when other substances are legally available.

A way by which we might evaluate the prospect of a marked increase in drug usage with the removal of legal sanctions would be to inspect the rate of drug intake in jurisdictions that have either eliminated or relaxed drug laws. The Netherlands, for instance, has much less of a drug problem than the United States despite the fact that marijuana and several other drugs have been decriminalized. Before the decriminalization of marijuana in 1976, 3 percent of all 15- to 16-year-olds and 10 percent of all 17- to 18-year-olds in this nation of 14 million were using marijuana at least occasionally; nine years later the proportions had fallen to 2 and 6 percent, respectively, despite the fact marijuana use was now legal (Ministry of Welfare, Health, and Cultural Affairs, 1985). In our own country relaxation of marijuana laws in 11 states during the mid-1970s failed to usher in a noticeable wave of new cannabis use (Johnston, Bachman, & O'Malley, 1981). Maloff (1981) informs us that there was no increase in either drug trafficking or drug usage after marijuana was decriminalized in Maine, Nebraska, and Oregon.

Moral Issues

Perhaps the strongest argument against the legalization of drugs is that no matter how much care we exercise, decriminalization appears to constitute a tacit condonation of drug usage. It has been maintained that the use of drugs runs counter to everything we strive to teach our children and that it will result in a deterioration of the values upon which this nation was built. When such

Table 8.2
Arguments For and Against the Legalization of Drugs

Pro Arguments	Support	Con Arguments	Support
Economic	Strong	Dangerousness	Moderate
Criminal Justice System Relief	Moderate	Increased Drug Usage	Moderate
Decreased Corruption	Weak	Deterrence of Legal Sanctions	Weak
Moral Issues	Strong	Moral Issues	Strong

issues are raised the example of alcohol seems inevitable. The hypocrisy of airing anti-drug messages followed by commercials showing groups of ex-athletes extolling the virtues of a particular brand of beer is likely apparent to many youthful viewers who look up to these ex-athletes as heroes and role models.

We must seek a balance between concerns about the decay of traditional values through the demise of the American family on the one hand, and on the other hand, troubling assaults on informal derivations of social control that accompany policies that encourage people to inform on friends, neighbors, or family members suspected or using illicit drugs (Nadelmann, 1989). There are some who contend that citizens have a right to be free of state interference for behaviors that do not pose harm to others (Farr, 1990). According to this viewpoint, labeling a large segment of the population whose only violation is the use of presently illegal drugs as criminals will propagate anomie on the part of those so labeled. This argument appears to have some merit, particularly as a way of explaining how drug criminalization laws can dismantle the possibility of social cohesion in some quarters while igniting cynicism, disaffection, and mistrust in others.

Discussion

There are many benefits that this society could realize if drug usage were to be curtailed. These include decreased morbidity and mortality, increased productivity, lower medical costs, and fewer drug-related family and interpersonal problems (Kramer, 1978). The question is whether they can be accomplished through our present policy of imposing legal sanctions on those of our citizens who use drugs. Fact, reason, and informed debate, however, must replace the rhetoric and demagogy that too frequently characterize present-day dialogues on this subject. Contrasting the pros and cons of drug decriminalization, we see that both sides can point to cogent supporting arguments, with the slightest of advantages seemingly going to the proponent side of the drug-legalization debate (see Table 8.2). Proponents attest to the likelihood of reduced financial investment in drug-based law enforcement, relief for the criminal justice system, and increased social-moral cohesion within society with the passage of drug decriminalization laws, while the interpersonal dangerousness of drugs, fears of an increased incidence of drug usage, and moral concerns about a breakdown in traditional American values buttress the arguments of decriminalization opponents.

Legalization or decriminalization of drugs should in no way be viewed as a complete solution to the American drug problem, nor does it need be an all-or-nothing enterprise. I agree with opponents of legalization that instituting a policy of decriminalization at this point in time would invite nothing short of wide-scale disaster. Educational programs designed to teach young people that regular use of any drug (to include alcohol) will likely remove them further from their goals should precede any efforts to decriminalize drugs. Treatment programs must also be made more available to that portion of the citizenry who will abuse drugs regardless of their legal status. Once these initiatives have been accomplished we can then go about the business of seriously debating and investigating the feasibility of decriminalizing and/or legalizing drugs.

The drug problem can be conceptualized in one of several ways. In the past we have defined it as a medical problem, but the current emphasis in this country is on drugs as a legal issue. I submit that reframing drug abuse as a lifestyle or behavioral problem is infinitely more useful than either the legal or medical models currently in vogue. Once the groundwork has been paved with education and broad-based treatment, we must find the courage to honestly evaluate our options, several of which (for example, legalization) may not be politically popular. Decriminalization could be handled in a selective manner, whereby we begin by reducing and eliminating the legal sanctions for drugs situated at the lower end of the seriousness continuum (for example, marijuana) and then proceed gradually from here, always mindful that the process can be halted should it be determined that the policy's costs outweigh its benefits (Nadelmann, 1989). However, we will never know the possibilities if we do not at least consider the fact that there are options available to us that may transcend our current social policies on drugs.

PRIVATIZATION

Privatization of correctional institutions has a long and storied history, dating all the way back to the ancient Romans (Sellin, 1976). In our own nation, states and localities contracted for prison services with private companies for much of the nineteenth century and well into the mid-twentieth century. There were, in fact, several systems entirely owned and operated by private interests (DiIulio, 1988). The privatization of prison industries reached its zenith near the turn of the century but began to lose momentum with each passing decade, owing in large part to opposition from organized labor and rival manufacturers (Sexton, Farrow, & Auerbach, 1985). The interested reader is referred to an article by Durham (1989) for a more thorough accounting of the history of privatization in the United States. In this section we find ourselves scrutinizing the rebirth of privatization, a renaissance which owes its life to two primary considerations:

(1) the desire to relieve the problem of overcrowding without the delay and cost of new public prison construction; (2) the necessity of providing more specialized services to undeserved populations (chronically mentally ill, physically handicapped, and elderly inmates).

Attitudes Toward Privatization

Thirty-eight states and the federal prison system presently contract with various private organizations and companies for correctional services and products (Camp & Camp, 1984). What exactly is the public's attitude toward privatization? In two of the eight jurisdictions studied by Hackett and associates it was determined that controversy surrounded the construction of a private correctional facility (Hackett et al., 1987). However, much of the controversy centered on job-security issues, and in one of these instances the public outcry subsided once the contractor agreed to hire the majority of correctional facility staff from the local area. A great deal more needs to be accomplished in our efforts to understand public opinion on the value of private corrections.

Cost-Effectiveness of Privatization

One of the principal arguments in favor of privatization is that it is more cost-effective than public forms of correctional intervention. Proponents argue that privatization is capable of providing higher quality services at a reduced cost (Cikins, 1986; Mullen, 1985), lowering expenses by as much as 10 to 25 percent (DiIulio, 1988). Others fear, however, that entrepreneurial approaches to corrections may eventually compromise the integrity of institutional programs (Anderson, Davoli, & Moriarity, 1985). Marketplace monopolization, unnecessary retention of inmates, and inadequate monitoring of cases over time are additional factors some scholars believe will devour initial savings, thereby making private correctional institutions no more cost-effective than their public counterparts.

An evaluation of the Okeechobee (Florida) School for Boys by the American Correctional Association revealed a slight economic advantage for this private facility over that obtained by state-run institutions, although the study failed to demonstrate the dramatic cost savings anticipated (Levinson, 1985). There were no differences between a private juvenile facility in Kentucky and two state-run institutions, although a private juvenile facility in Pennsylvania (Weaversville) recorded an 11 percent savings over comparable state facilities (Hackett et al., 1987). Sellers (1989) visited three public and three private correctional facilities in New Jersey, Pennsylvania, and Tennessee that had been matched on size, location, structure, age, capacity, and staffing patterns. The average weighted per diem cost of the private facilities was $46.17, a 37 percent savings over the average weighted per diem registered by public institutions ($73.76).

There are several methodological problems with research contrasting the relative costs of private and public facilities. First, there is the problem of "comparing apples and oranges'' since private and public facilities often pursue different goals and frequently provide different categories of service to offender populations (Logan, 1990). Second, there are the hidden costs of corrections that do not find their way into the budget reports of administrators but are still charged to taxpayers (Logan, 1990). Third, private facilities may have a decided advantage in short-term comparisons, but this advantage may tend to dissipate with time.

Logan (1990) considered all three of these issues in exploring the annual savings of a prison farm in Hamilton County, Tennessee, that had made the transition from a public to a private facility. Enlisting a pre-post design, Logan discerned that programs and services provided during the post-privatization period increased rather than decreased and that privatization actually saved the county between 4 and 8 percent of its total annual correctional costs calculated over three years. Obviously, this study has shortcomings of its own, to include a single-case time series analysis that failed to control for the effects of political, social, and economic changes occurring in the county during and after the transition. Still, these results highlight the fascinating possibilities brought on by a system of privatization, at least where certain correctional services are involved.

Privatization of Prison Industries

Another argument for privatization is that it establishes a climate more receptive to the development of prison-based industrial operations. Sexton et al. (1985) discuss six models by which the private sector might become involved with prison industries: as employer, investor, customer, manager, joint venture, or controlling customer. In January 1985 there were 26 private-sector prison industries in operation, 15 of which followed the employer model. Sexton and his colleagues observed that communication and cooperation between prison and business officials were critical to the success of the operation, wage disparities between industry workers and nonindustry inmates were typically not a source of friction between prisoners, and prison-based business ventures benefited the private corporation but also created certain hidden costs (worker turnover, training expenses).

Problems with Privatization

Privatization is no panacea. There are potential problems, obstacles, and unanswered questions that need to be addressed if this field is to contribute significantly to the criminal science effort. Three of these issues—presented under the headings of legal, administrative, and moral—are discussed here.

Legal Issues. Questions concerning the legality of contracting for operation of a correctional facility have been raised. If there is no law prohibiting a state from granting private organizations the opportunity to provide correctional services, or run entire facilities for that matter, then there would not appear to be a problem with the legality of establishing privately owned and operated correctional facilities (Hackett et al., 1987). Personal liability, however, is quite another matter. It remains uncertain whether the state or private corporation would be liable in cases involving possible violations of prisoners' rights, although it is likely that both would be culpable under such circumstances (Robbins, 1988). Labor relations are a second legal issue facing the privatization movement in that, unlike public correctional officers, private employees would have the right to strike. Contractors state that they will attempt to avert such a possibility by furnishing staff with higher salaries and attractive fringe benefits, but it needs to be written into the contract that state officials will be alerted in the event of an ensuing strike so that corrective action might be taken (Hackett et al., 1987).

Administrative Issues. Use of force, inmate accountability, and prisoner discipline are issues that can be handled adequately by a private correctional corporation, although this will require publication of detailed guidelines and the establishment of a regulatory board tasked with assuring that these standards are followed. Some fear that the cost of regulation will negate any savings accrued through the more efficient operation of a private correctional facility (DiIulio, 1988). A further administrative issue is whether private contractors would be willing to tackle the responsibility of managing maximum security inmates. Institutions for higher security offenders are appreciably more arduous and expensive to operate than the minimum to medium security facilities that are the staple of privately owned correctional corporations. Researchers generally agree that this is less of an issue with the privatization of juvenile corrections (Sellers, 1989; Shichor & Bartollas, 1990).

Moral/Responsibility Issues. It has been argued that punishment is the responsibility of the government and that to pass this responsibility on to a private corporation is unacceptable (Elvin, 1985). The profit motive, they state, has no place in corrections for both ethical and practical reasons. There is evidence to suggest, for example, that the desire to realize a profit through corrections can lead to reduced numbers and quality of both staff and treatment programs (Shichor & Bartollas, 1990). More critical, though, is the fact that even if private contractors administered every correctional institution in this country free of charge, we would realize little overall savings because less than one cent of every dollar of government expenditure is earmarked for corrections (DiIulio, 1988). The United States was built on a foundation of free enterprise; however, corrections may be one area that does not conform well to the capitalistic ideal. To my way of thinking, there is something intrinsically and morally wrong with a system of correction that is geared more to profit than to rehabilitation, deterrence, or even incapacitation.

Discussion

Scanning the pros and cons of privatization (see Table 8.3), we can see that as a system-wide approach, privatization has many more problems than it has

Table 8.3
Arguments For and Against the Privatization of Corrections

Pro Arguments	Support	Con Arguments	Support
Increased Efficiency	Weak	Legal Issues	Moderate
Decreased Expense	Moderate	Decreased Programming	Weak
		Regulation Costs	Moderate
Long-Term Advantages	Weak	Moral/Ethical/ Responsibility Concerns	Strong
Expansion of Prison Industries	Moderate		

benefits. In concert with the moral or responsibility issue, legal and administrative concerns call into question the wisdom of system-wide application of the privatization paradigm. Proponents of privatization highlight the cost-effectiveness of this procedure, although it should be pointed out that these savings tend to be modest and there is great uncertainty as to their long-term stability. Besides, savings can be realized in ways more consistent with the ideals of public corrections, to include inmate-assisted prison construction (Carter & Humphries, 1987), leave-purchase financing (DeWitt, 1986), and prisons designed to facilitate direct supervision (Nelson, 1988). In sum, while contracting out medical, mental health, educational, or vocational training services to private interests may be advisable under select circumstances, large-scale privatization appears to create rather than allay problems for the American correctional establishment.

CONCLUSION

There are many features of social policy that were not included in this chapter, among them gun control legislation (Jung & Jason, 1988), sentencing reform (Hoffman & Handyman, 1986), and decisions concerning the distribution of resources among the member branches of the criminal justice system (Phillips & Votey, 1981). It is believed, however, that the present review adequately covers the general mechanisms involved in the social decision-making process and the types of policy considerations that come to the forefront when system-wide issues are raised. The three examples provided in this chapter (death penalty, legalization of drugs, privatization) illustrate many of the problems associated with efforts to balance divergent values and empirical outcomes. This can be accomplished, but not without taking into account the results of research studies reviewed in previous chapters, particularly Chapter 7. Obviously, wide-band (social policy) and narrow-band (prevention) situation-oriented interventions are complementary but must be skillfully coordinated and intelligently blended for maximum effectiveness.

As a way of concluding this chapter I would like to point out that criminal scientists can play a leading role in the social policy decision-making process. First, however, the research they publish must be made more relevant. Ruback and Innes argue that psychologists and other social scientists must create research questions that address issues utmost on the minds of societal policymakers. These include focusing on variables that lend themselves to change, that are viewed by policymakers as important, and that consider the role of values in policy-making research (Ruback & Innes, 1988). This last point demands further clarification. There is no way to avoid the fact that values often play a guiding role in social decision making. In fact, my intent in permitting some of my own values to surface in discussions on the death penalty and privatization was to demonstrate the necessity of including and identifying one's values in any meaningful discourse on social policy concerns.

Values are the substance of social policy; the populace embraces them, politicians enforce them, and criminal scientists study them. They are therefore important in the manner in which we go about living our lives. Without a doubt, we should clearly identify these values and, while exerting caution, not lose sight of the fact that these values must be wisely integrated with current knowledge if they are to contribute forcefully to our understanding of molar-level decision making. Otherwise, we are left with a system that, while ornate and showy, fails to assist us with the very real problem of devising a meaningful agenda for social policymaking.

9

Interaction-Oriented Intervention: The Person and the Criminal Justice System

On December 22, 1984, an electrical engineer by the name of Bernhard Goetz made headlines by shooting four black youth he surmised were about to rob him in a New York City subway. Goetz testified that after one youth asked him for $5 he looked up to find an individual with a smirk on his face and a "gleam in his eye." Believing he was about to be robbed, Goetz pulled out a revolver and gunned down each of his would-be aggressors. Though none of the youth died as a result of this attack, one was left permanently paralyzed from wounds inflicted by a man who many would come to call the "subway vigilante." Acquitted of assault by a jury of his peers, Bernhard Goetz stands as an example of the delicate and unsteady balance which exists between law, justice, and criminal procedure in this nation of 250 million people.

Many of us can probably identify with the fears that likely ran through Bernhard Goetz's mind as he was approached by what he perceived to be four menacing and potentially dangerous youths. Goetz's actions are even more understandable when we consider the fact that he had been accosted and mugged by a group of men just three years earlier. However, understanding does not always beget condonation. Goetz was carrying an unlicensed, and therefore illegal, handgun on December 22, 1984, and testimony suggests that he may have fired at several of his "attackers" as they were running away. The thorny task of deciding whether individuals like Goetz warrant the full brunt of societal sanctions remains before us. Of greater relevance to our purposes here is to point out that the Goetz case stands as an example of the complexity encompassing person × situation interactions occurring between an individual accused of violating the law and the justice system to which he or she is remanded.

Following the shootings, Bernhard Goetz and the city of New York became embroiled in a controversy that served as a kind of microcosm of the social interaction between individual offenders and the criminal justice system. Two general philosophies exist on the subject of criminal sanctioning, commonly referred to as *just deserts* and *utilitarianism*. The just deserts perspective emphasizes punishment in proportion to the amount of harm done and the rated culpability of the criminal actor. From the standpoint of the just deserts approach, jurors in the Goetz case were probably aware of the harm Goetz had created but judged him to be of low culpability because of his perception of threat from the juveniles he eventually attacked. The utilitarian decision maker, on the other hand, attempts to influence or predict the future occurrence of crime by deterring, incapacitating, or rehabilitating offenders. A utilitarian might argue that the criminal justice system was lenient with Goetz because there is no general or specific deterrent value to be found in the incarceration of a man judged to have been acting in self-defense. In this chapter we probe the interaction between the individual and criminal justice system according to five sentencing or sanctioning aims: retribution, deterrence, incapacitation, rehabilitation, and restitution.

RETRIBUTION

Retribution is based on a belief in the responsibility of the human organism. The philosophy of retribution can be traced back to Hammurabi ("an eye for an eye"), the Old Testament (*lex talionis*), and the ancient Romans. However, modern formulations of the retribution hypothesis have their philosophical roots in the writings of Immanuel Kant (1724–1804) and Friedrich Hegel (1770–1831). Kant believed that people had a moral obligation to obey the law and deserved to be punished if they did not fulfill their responsibilities in this regard. He reasoned further that if individuals were not punished for their transgressions that this released a collective guilt upon the whole of society. Hegel's contribution to the development of retribution as a meaningful goal of criminal justice procedure was his contention that punishment could only be legitimately applied to those persons able to rationally enter into a social contract with society. Modern proponents of the retributive approach to sanctioning (Plant, 1980; van den Haag, 1975; von Hirsch, 1976; Wilson & Herrnstein, 1985) have generally remained faithful to Kant and Hegel's original ideas.

Principle of Commensurate Deserts

The just desert model of sentencing is based on a philosophy of retribution. Founded on the Principle of Commensurate Deserts, the just desert model holds that punishment should be proportional to the seriousness of an offender's criminal conduct. This principle is defined by the harm done and the level of culpability attributed to the offender. We might estimate the harm of a particular criminal act by scaling public perceptions of the relative severity of various categories of criminal conduct. This was a procedure adopted by Sellin and Wolfgang (1964) in their research on public perceptions of crime severity. These two criminologists detected a high degree of reliability in public perceptions of relative seriousness but much lower estimates when absolute seriousness was scaled. These public perceptions may also contain moral judgments that are factually spurious or procedurally untenable (Monahan, 1982).

Culpability is even more troublesome to operationalize and evaluate than harm. Psychiatrists and psychologists have long realized the problem of assessing culpability in defendants with suspected mental health problems. Can we reasonably expect the average lay person to perform any better? Research conducted on public perceptions of culpability indicate that subjects often fail to consider factors the Principle of Commensurate Deserts suggests they should (Riedel, 1975) or focus on irrelevant factors and parameters (DeJong, Morris, & Hastorf, 1976). Of even greater concern is the effective operationalization of accountability (Gardner, 1976). Bedau (1977) acknowledges that commonsense guidelines for sentencing are necessary but maintains that the Principle of Commensurate Deserts demonstrates neither the objectivity nor reliability required to advance beyond these commonsense boundaries.

Criticisms of the Retribution Model

Besides the operationalization and reliability issues, there are additional problems associated with the practice of relying on a retributive ideal in sanctioning society's offenders. First, while the retribution hypothesis may be sound in theory, there are problems when we attempt to translate this theory into practice. The Kantian conceptualization of the retributive process assumes the presence of a just society. Given the uneven distribution of rewards and resources in all real-life societies, the question becomes how we might find justice in an unjust world (Cavender, 1984). There are also the related arguments that just desert philosophies are overly idealistic (Young, 1981) and have traditionally ignored the sociohistorical context of crime and justice (Jenkins, 1980). There are those who contend that the spirit of vengeance that characterizes retribution has no place in a civilized society (Menninger, 1968). The counterargument is that retribution is concerned more with resposibility and justice than with revenge and retaliation. Advocates also contend that retribution can prevent certain kinds of abuses from occurring, such as confining a minor offender with possible psychological problems to a mental hospital on the strength of a psychiatrist's finding of dangerousness.

A second criticism frequently leveled against the just desert approach to sentencing is that it may tend to discriminate on the basis of variables other than the harm caused by the act or the rated culpability of the defendant. Hence, a trio of sociologists from the University of Washington in Seattle (Bridges, Crutchfield, & Simpson, 1987) examined data on the race and ethnicity of all persons sentenced to prison in Washington between 1980 and 1982. They determined that minority status (black, Hispanic) predicted increased severity of sentences, based largely on the perception that such individuals were more criminally oriented, violent, and dangerous, even though a thorough review of individual case material failed to confirm many of the claims of increased dangerousness made by judges, prosecutors, and other officials. Additional studies on racial bias in sentencing have yielded equivocal findings (see Klein, Petersilia, & Turner, 1990; Zatz, 1987), although it has been suggested that bias may exist under specific historical (Pruitt & Wilson, 1983), geographic (Kleck, 1981), and attitudinal (Peterson & Hagan, 1984) conditions.

The spector of gender discrimination in sentencing has also been raised. Male-female differences in sentence severity have been noted in favor of both women (Bernstein, Cardascia, & Ross, 1979; Steffensmeier & Kramer, 1982) and men (Figueria-McDonough, 1985; Ghali & Chesney-Lind, 1986), while other studies have failed to identify any gender-based differences in sentence severity (Bishop & Frazier, 1984). Two investigators from the University of Amsterdam obtained results intimating that the relationship between gender and sanction severity may vary as a function of offense category: adolescent males were punished more severely for violent crimes—perhaps because they were viewed as more culpable than females—and female adolescents were punished more harshly for neutral status offenses—possibly based on the stereotypic belief that male crime is more acceptable than female crime (Willemsen & van Schie, 1989).

An interaction between race and gender was suggested in the results of a study by Unnever, Frazier, and Henretta (1980), in which white females received greater leniency than minority women (Unnever, Frazier, & Henretta, 1980). Peterson (1988) took up the question of sentencing variations in 16- to 18-year-old offenders in New York, and discovered that females were more likely to receive leniency during both the adjudication and sentencing stages, while blacks and Hispanics were more often adjudicated as adults and sentenced to incarceration than whites, but only in jurisdictions outside New York City. Similarly, Spohn and a group of colleagues found that prosecutors' decisions to reject or dismiss felony charges were biased in favor of females and against blacks and Hispanics (Spohn, Gruhl, & Welch, 1987).

The Role of Retribution in Criminal Justice Decision Making

Retribution is based on three founding principles: (1) respect for human dignity and the responsibility an individual has for his or her conduct; (2) an individual's obligation to atone for his or her criminal behavior; (3) reestablishing the social equilibrium that was lost when the offender transgressed against society (Cavender, 1984). The authority of retribution to foster a sense of responsibility in the general citizenry should be self-evident. However, retribution can also prevent the imposition of unduly severe punishment since it abides by the Principle of Commensurate Deserts, which states that punishment should be proportional to the amount of harm done. This does not mean, however, that retribution is a fully elaborated process or that variables like historical (Perry, 1980) or sociocultural (Berk et al., 1981) context do not affect the manner in which retribution is implemented, just that retribution need not be excessively punitive to be effective.

One attempt to refine the retribution hypothesis can be discerned in Monahan's modified just desert model of criminal justice sanctioning. As early as 1968 Packer realized that retribution and utilitarian concerns were not necessarily incompatible. Taking his cue from Packer, Monahan has argued for an integrated approach to criminal justice decision making, with the retributive process of commensurate deserts serving to mold the general boundaries and utilitarian concerns like deterrence, selective incapacitation, and rehabilitation fixing sanctions to specific points within these general guidelines. Monahan adds that the actual utilitarian procedure employed in criminal justice decision making should exhibit an acceptable level of demonstrated validity. Only time will tell whether a modified just desert approach to sentencing has any empirical merit, although it would appear to provide a pathway by which retribution and utilitarian concerns might be reconciled.

DETERRENCE

Deterrence is the process whereby a potential offender refrains from engaging in a particular criminal act because of the perceived adverse consequences of that act. Cesare Beccaria (1738–1794) introduced the classical version of deterrence theory in the late eighteenth century with his rational, hedonistic perspective on human nature. Another pioneer in the development of early deterrence theory was Jeremy Bentham (1748–1832), who argued that punishment was only justified if it produced positive outcomes sufficient to outweigh its negative side effects. The scholarly efforts of these two philosophers helped promote the formation of a deterrent approach to criminal sanctioning that finds its modern expression in sociological exchange theory and the utility model of economics.

Gibbs (1975, p. 15) succinctly summarizes the philosophy behind modern versions of deterrence theory: "The greater celerity, certainty, and severity of punishment for a type of crime, the more are individuals deterred from that type of crime." There are three mechanisms through which deterrence is said to exert control over human behavior. These include an internalization of norms, the threat of legal sanctions, and a fear of social disapproval (Grasmick & Green, 1980). In the sections that follow we examine how these three control mechanisms operate and interact to bring about social conformity along four dimensions: absolute deterrence, restrictive deterrence, general deterrence, and specific deterrence.

Absolute and Restrictive Deterrence

Absolute deterrence occurs when a potential offender refrains in toto from engaging in a particular criminal act for fear of the possible societally defined negative consequences of that action. Restrictive deterrence, by way of contrast, involves a reduction rather than elimination of subsequent offending based on a fear of the societal sanctions attached to such behavior. The significance of distinguishing between absolute and restrictive deterrence is that these two criminal justice goals often involve different cognitive mechanisms and therefore require divergent intervention strategies (Gibbs, 1986). Consequently, an offender may be differentially responsive to these two categories of deterrence.

Paternoster (1989a) examined the relative influence of absolute and restrictive deterrence on four offenses (marijuana use, drinking liquor under age, vandalism, petty theft) in a panel study of tenth graders tested on two separate occasions. Studying the absolute deterrent value of societal sanctions, Paternoster failed to identify a relationship between perceived severity of sanctions and self-reported offending, and in only one instance (marijuana) did perceived certainty of punishment correlate (inversely) with self-reported violations. The restrictive deterrence model also failed to reveal a connection between the perceived severity of punishment and a subject's propensity for crime, although it did signify an inverse association between the perceived certainty of punishment and self-reported marijuana use, under-age liquor consumption, and vandalism. Paternoster concludes that deterrence may operate along restrictive rather than absolute lines and that the perceived certainty of a sanction is more of a deterrent than its perceived severity.

General Deterrence

General deterrence involves dissuasion of potential offenders by exposing them to information about a lawbreaker who has been punished for a particular infraction. This form of deterrence has been studied using aggregate level data, cross-sectional studies, longitudinal investigations, and laboratory studies.

Aggregate Studies. Gibbs (1968) and Tittle (1969) have used aggregate-level data to compare Uniform Crime Report (UCR) and national prison statistics. The resulting correlations were found to be supportive of deterrence theory. Gibbs (1975), for instance, witnessed an inverse relationship between indices of certainty (number of prison admissions for homicide) and severity (median number of months served in prison for homicide) and the rate of homicide, with states serving as the subjects of investigation. Using aggregate-level data, Tittle and Rowe (1974) identified a "tipping effect" in which crime clearance rates (certainty) had to attain a certain level before the severity of punishment could exert an effect. This same outcome has been observed in perceptual studies addressing the deterrence hypothesis (Paternoster, 1987). In a study which failed to generate support for the deterrence doctrine, Bailey (1980) found that the celerity (swiftness) of death penalty imposition, as measured by the time interval between sentencing and execution, was unrelated to aggregate murder rates. However, a more adequate measure of celerity would have been the time interval between commission of the offense and execution.

There have been several criticisms lodged against aggregate investigations of the deterrence hypothesis. First, aggregate studies have been reproached for treating the certainty and severity of punishment as objective entities rather than as perceptual processes (Williams & Hawkins, 1986). Research clearly shows

Table 9.1

Zero-Order Correlations Between the Perceived Severity and the Perceived Certainty of Sanctions and Self-Reported Criminality: Cross-Sectional Studies

	Perceived Severity		Perceived Certainty	
	Crime Index	Specific Offenses	Crime Index	Specific Offenses
Waldo & Chiricos (1972)		-.14		-.58
Bailey & Lott (1976)		-.06		-.03
Kraut (1976)		-.19		-.24
Silberman (1976)	+.10	+.06	-.26	-.18
Teevan (1976)		-.15		-.24
Meier & Johnson (1977)		+.22		+.17
Tittle (1977)		-.22		-.16
Jensen et al. (1978)		-.14	-.39	-.38
Grasmick & Bryjak (1980)	-.10		-.34	
Grasmick & Green (1980)	-.40		-.40	

Note: Crime Index = use of a total crime composite; Specific Offenses = mean value obtained using individual offenses (e.g., marijuana use, larceny). Whenever possible, self-referenced risk, rather than risk to the "average person," was used.

a minimal level of concordance between actual and perceived expectancies of punishment (Erickson & Gibbs, 1978; Parker & Grasmick, 1979). Second, when crime and clearance rates are correlated a bias is introduced owing to the fact that both indicators contain a common element—that is, number of arrests (Chiricos & Waldo, 1970). The reader is referred to a recent article by Gibbs and Firebaugh (1990) for a more thorough review of this topic. Third, there are questions concerning the direction of the relationship between aggregate crime and clearance rates. When Greenberg, Kessler, and Logan (1979) correlated state-wide clearance and crime rate statistics for the same year they observed results consonant with the deterrence hypothesis, but when they temporally lagged these measures they discovered that crime rate was more likely to be the cause of clearance rate changes than vice versa. The next generation of deterrence studies, cross-sectional investigations, attempted to control for the first two methodological issues but did little to rectify the problem of determining the direction of the proposed relationships between perceived risk and criminal conduct.

Cross-Sectional Studies. The major cross-sectional studies investigating the deterrence hypothesis are profiled in Table 9.1. The principal contribution of this new generation of deterrence research was a shift away from objective indices of severity and certainty in favor of self-reported perceptions of punishment intensity and probability. Soon after, deterrence began to be viewed as a perceptual process. As previous reviews have shown (Paternoster, 1987), and as a cursory inspection of Table 9.1 reveals, cross-sectional studies provide a great deal more support for the deterrent value of sanction certainty than sanction severity in deterring crime. Grasmick and Bryjak (1980) took a somewhat different tact by asking respondents how much of a problem a particular sanction would create in their own lives and subsequently found confirmatory support for the deterrence hypothesis. It may very well be that sanction severity is capable of exerting a deterrent effect but has failed to receive corroborative empirical backing because of the manner in which it has been measured; specifically, risk is a more effective deterrent if conceptualized relative to oneself rather than relative to other people (Grasmick & Green, 1980; Jensen, Erickson, & Gibbs, 1978).

Though cross-sectional studies have assisted with the maturation of deterrence theory and methodology, they are plagued by their own set of encumbrances. As is the case with aggregate studies, cross-sectional investigations are incapable of distinguishing between deterrence and incapacitation effects (Anderson, 1979). Of even greater concern is the problem of determining causal order from the results of a cross-sectional study. Just as we saw with Greenberg et al.'s (1979) longitudinal analysis of aggregate-level data, criminal involvement may have more of an effect on perceptions of sanction severity and certainty than perceptions have on criminal involvement. Since cross-sectional studies probe perceptions and self-reported criminality measured contemporaneously (with the period covered by the self-report preceding the perceptions), it is difficult to tease out the individual contributions of cause and effect.

Proponents of the cross-sectional approach to deterrence research argue that perceptions of punishment are reasonably stable over time, although research conducted on this issue has failed to generate support for this claim (Minor & Harry, 1982; Paternoster, 1987; Saltzman et al., 1982). Experiential effects are therefore free to wield their effect on cross-sectional research results. Experience has taught the average criminal offender that he or she gets away with the majority of his or her criminal acts and once apprehended, they soon discover that society's sanctions are nowhere near as aversive as they had initially anticipated (Walters, 1990). Under such circumstances, criminal behavior may significantly alter perceptions of sanction severity and certainty, a possibility supported by the observation that experiential effects often outweigh deterrent effects when crime data are inspected longitudinally (Minor & Harry, 1982; Paternoster et al., 1983; Saltzman et al., 1982). So that we might investigate these issues further we now turn our attention to longitudinal studies of the deterrence hypothesis.

Longitudinal Studies. Longitudinal investigations were introduced in an attempt to ferret out the cause and effect of perceptions of legal punishment and criminal involvement. Except for a study administered by Bishop (1984), longitudinal deterrence studies have failed to confirm the founding tenets of deterrence theory (see Table 9.2). In contrast to the two-wave panel studies that are the staple of longitudinal deterrence research, Paternoster (1989b) has sought to bring the deterrence doctrine into theoretical focus by crossing it with principles

Table 9.2
Standardized Multivariate Coefficients for Perceived Severity, Perceived Certainty, and Extralegal Measures: Longitudinal Studies

Study	Sample	Dependent Measure	Perceived Severity	Perceived Certainty	Extralegal Measures		
					Peer Involve	Moral Beliefs	Informal Sanctions
Minor & Harry (1982)	488 college students	cocaine use		-.04			
Saltzman et al. (1982)	300 college students	petty theft		-.22			
Paternoster et al. (1983)	300 college students	composite criminality		+.06		-.11	-.17
Bishop (1984)	2147 high school students	composite criminality		-.16			-.12
Meier et al. (1984)	265 high school students	marijuana usage		-.16	+.49		
Paternoster & Iovanni (1986)	1173 high school students	composite criminality	+.02	-.01	+.30	-.17	
Pillavin et al. (1986)	3300 offenders, addicts, and youthful dropouts	composite criminality		-.06			
Paternoster (1989b)	1250 high school students	marijuana usage	-.18	-.14	+.33	-.40	-.10

derived from the social control and rational choice formulations and by collecting data at three points in time. Logistic regression analyses revealed that perceived severity had no effect on the decision to offend or desist from offending. Perceived certainty influenced subjects' decisions to commit an offense for two of the four crime categories (marijuana, vandalism), though these decisions were more strongly affiliated with moral values, opportunity, and informal social control. Perceptual changes in risk assessment revealed a deterrent effect at the third wave in the decisions of nonoffenders to refrain from marijuana usage and vandalism and of offenders to desist from under-age alcohol consumption.

Where longitudinal designs have contributed a great deal to the study of deterrence, they too suffer from certain methodological shortcomings. First, except for the Pillavin et al. (1986) study, longitudinal research addressing the deterrence doctrine has used conscripted samples of college and high school students. The problem with this procedure, as Williams and Hawkins (1986) point out, is that adolescents and young adults may harbor less stable perceptions of punishment than older adults. Furthermore, the juvenile justice system differs markedly from its adult analogue. A second failing of longitudinal studies is that most have centered on relatively minor offenses (marijuana usage, shoplifting, vandalism), which is understandable given that more serious offenses have such low base rates of occurrence that they preclude meaningful analysis. Of the two longitudinal studies examining felony-level offenses, one demonstrated a negative relationship between perceived certainty and criminal involvement (Bishop, 1984), while the other (Piliavin et al., 1986) failed to identify a deterrent effect.

A third issue with longitudinal research on the deterrence hypothesis concerns the time frame. Williams and Hawkins (1986) ask how far into the future perceptions measured at Time 1 should be expected to affect behavior at Time 2 and recommend that studies with follow-ups of differing lengths be conducted. As with all longitudinal studies, there is always the potential dilemma of attrition and differential mortality when data are inspected over time. Paternoster (1989b), however, tested this hypothesis in his three-wave panel investigation and found no evidence of a differential mortality effect. Finally, in keeping with one of the cardinal themes of this chapter, we must explore the effect of various person variables on deterrence as it is investigated over time. Bishop (1984), for instance, witnessed an interaction between race and the deterrent effect of sanctions in one of the first longitudinal investigations to address the deterrence hypothesis. Such an outcome reveals the necessity of considering characteristics of both the person and situation if our goal is the construction of a comprehensive theory of deterrence.

Laboratory Studies. The deterrence hypothesis has also been examined under the highly controlled conditions of the laboratory, although the generalizability of such studies is always open to question. Miranne and Gray (1987) randomly assigned 80 college students to conditions and experimentally manipulated several different variables as subjects participated in a computerized version of "chicken." Consistent with the results of cross-sectional studies, these investigators found an inverse relationship between the certainty of sanctions and cheating behavior but no association between sanction severity and cheating. In a second laboratory experiment on deterrence, Klepper and Nagin (1989) presented masters-level candidates in public management with vignettes depicting the prospects associated with tax law violations, and instructed subjects to estimate the probability of detection and criminal prosecution. The outcome of this particular study revealed support for both the severity and certainty of punishment. While caution needs to be exercised in interpreting the results of these two investigations, given the artificiality of the laboratory setting, these studies provide some encouragement that deterrence may still play a role in criminal science interventions.

Specific Deterrence

In contrast to general deterrence, specific deterrence asks whether an individual punished by the criminal justice system is him or herself deterred from further criminal action. An early investigation into the specific deterrent value of legal punishment by Caldwell (1944) discerned that 57 percent of the offenders who had been imprisoned and whipped at least twice in a county in Delaware re-offended, in comparison to 31 percent of a group of persons placed on probation. Despite the fact that such an outcome is inconsistent with the canons of deterrence theory, this was a grossly inadequate test of the deterrent hypothesis since it was common practice during this period in time, as it is today, to assign persons with more serious criminal records to prison rather than to probation. In an unrelated study, chronic juvenile offenders who had been involuntarily removed from the community had better outcomes than juveniles administered less severe sanctions, even after accounting for maturation and selectivity differences between the groups (Murray & Cox, 1979).

The severity of sanctions would appear to have received a vote of confidence from the results of a study by Sherman and Berk (1984), in which domestic assault suspects in Minneapolis were randomly assigned to one of three conditions: arrest, orders, and advice. Subjects who had been arrested were less likely to engage in later violence, as reported by both the victim and police, than suspects ordered to leave the premises for eight hours or given "advice" by the arresting officer. Unfortunately, there is no way to determine the perceived severity of arrest versus the other dispositions, although it would stand to reason that most persons conceive of the former as more severe. Anecdotal evidence provided in a study by Glassner et al. (1983) shows that some adolescents desist from criminal activities at age 16 because of the perceived severity of an adult conviction and the fear of going to jail.

The ambiguous nature of research findings on the issue of specific deterrence is no more clearly illustrated than in two studies addressing the effect of offense-disposition delay on subsequent offending. An Israeli investigation failed to find evidence of an association between recidivism and the amount of time separating traffic violations and sentencing (Shoham, 1974). However, a positive relationship was noted between the interval bridging initial contact and adjudication and later adult criminal convictions in a study by Brown et al. (1989). Additional factors like age or gender may also be critical in defining specific deterrence. Hence, Keane, Gillis, and Hagan (1989) surmised that contact with the police served to deter marijuana smoking in female adolescents but produced a converse effect in male juveniles. The celerity, certainty, and severity of legal sanctions in deterring an offender previously punished by the criminal justice system is uncertain, but it is likely that if a meaningful specific deterrent effect does exist it varies according to certain characteristics of the individual (age, gender, criminal background) and situation (family support).

The Role of Deterrence in Criminal Justice Decision Making

Taken as a whole, the evidence is not terribly supportive of the deterrence hypothesis. Research has shown that the severity of punishment is typically not an effective deterrent to criminal behavior, while celerity has received only scattered corroboration (Paternoster, 1987). The only branch of the deterrent formula receiving any measure of support has been the certainty of legal punishment, but even here our conclusions are equivocal in light of the generally discouraging results of longitudinal investigations. Paternoster (1987) notes that the deterrent effect of perceived certainty is strongest in studies that are weakest methodologically. As the results of a study by Grasmick and Bryjak (1980) imply, however, the manner in which severity has traditionally been measured may be at least partly responsible for the largely negative results obtained in research on deterrence. There are also problems with studies showing celerity and certainty to be unrelated to future criminal outcomes.

What can be done to rectify the confusing state of affairs surrounding research on the deterrence hypothesis? Further review is plainly required, but simply conducting more studies is not the answer if we wish to understand the impact of the perceived celerity, certainty, and severity of criminal justice sanctions on future criminal outcomes. Research in this area could benefit from procedures designed to blend longitudinal and cross-sectional concerns into a single package, capitalizing on the special strengths of each and minimizing their collective weaknesses. A related recommendation is that subjects participating in deterrence research be provided with more specific contextual cues so that they do not have to furnish their own context. This way the problem of increased random error that occurs when subjects must try to interpret the intentions of the investigator can be avoided (Klepper & Nagin, 1989).

Longitudinal designs have helped introduce deterrence researchers to multivariate statistics but have yet to alleviate a malady that has troubled this field of investigative endeavor since its inception: a lack of strong theoretical ties to the more general field of knowledge that is criminal science. We must also contemplate the effect of individual person and situation variables on the deterrent process. Miller and Anderson (1986) have found that white males are more strongly influenced by the perceived severity and certainty of legal sanctions than are black males, white females, or black females. Relying on a longitudinal methodology, Bishop (1984) discerned that experiential effects exceeded deterrent effects in white subjects, although the relationship was reversed in the case of black subjects. Additional research along these lines would be in order since deterrence, like retribution, incapacitation, rehabilitation, and restitution, is probably best conceptualized as an interaction between the individual offender and society as represented by the criminal justice system.

INCAPACITATION

Incapacitation involves prevention of crime through imposition of physical or psychological barriers (with the emphasis on physical restraint) designed to render an individual powerless to engage in criminal activity (Cohen, 1985). The rationale of incarceration as a vehicle for incapacitation is that if an offender is confined, he or she will be unable to prey on the community. Three assumptions subserve incapacitation as a philosophy of criminal justice intervention. First, it is presumed that all offenders are at risk for arrest, conviction, and incarceration. Second, it is supposed that crimes averted when an offender is incapacitated will not be superceded by the criminal acts of offenders remaining in the community. A third and final assumption held by advocates of incapacitation is that confinement will not extend an offender's criminal career (Visher, 1987).

The benefit of incapacitation is a function of the violation rate of the person being incapacitated. This figure, computed as an annual rate and referred to in the literature as lambda (λ), is a key parameter in the calculus upon which incapacitation policies are based. The value of lambda referenced by an investigator will have a profound effect on the final outcome of one's research and has been shown to vary from .5 (Greenwood, 1975) to 10 (Shinnar & Shinnar, 1975). Gottfredson and Hirschi (1986) take issue with the common practice of computing lambda from the records of active criminals and assert that all members of society should be included in this figure if it is to have any meaning. They go on to state that if lambda is calculated using the entire population the risk of arrest (λ) not only approaches zero but reveals itself to be of dubious value in formulating a social policy of incapacitation.

Collective Incapacitation

To follow a collective incapacitation line of reasoning would be to incarcerate all persons convicted of a specific offense for a set period of time. The trend that finds the United States incarcerating offenders in ever-increasing numbers (see Chapter 7 of this volume) is a prime example of collective incapacitation. This also illustrates the principal negative side effect of wide-scale collective

Table 9.3

**Collective Incapacitation Benefits and Costs Provided a Five-Year Sentence Were
Made Mandatory Following Conviction for Any Serious Offense**

Study	Location	Year	Target Offense[1]	Crime Reduction	Increase in Prison Pop.[2]
Shinnar & Shinnar (1975)	New York State	1970	"safety crimes"	80%	400%
Petersilia & Greenwood (1978)	Denver, Colorado	1970	violent crimes burglary	31% 42%	450%
Van Dine et al. (1979)	Franklin Co., Ohio	1973	violent crimes	17.8%	523%
Cohen (1982)	Washington, DC	1973	index crimes	13.7%	310%

[1]Increase in the prison population for the target offense.

[2]Homicide, rape, robbery, assault, burglary.

incapacitation: prison overcrowding. Cohen (1985) advises that between 1973 and 1982 the prison population more than doubled, but that this policy of collective incapacitation only prevented crimes like robbery and burglary at a rate of 6 to 9 percent. Other researchers estimate that current collective incapacitation policies reduce crime by 1 (Clarke, 1974) to 20 percent (Shinnar & Shinnar, 1975).

It has been proposed that establishing a minimum standard sentence for all serious felony offenses would produce an even greater collective incapacitation effect. While this is true, Blumstein et al. (1986) estimate that any reduction in the collective incapacitation effect beyond that currently achieved would require a 10 to 20 percent increase in the prison population for every 1 percent of crime reduction. Greenwood (1975) reports that a one-year mandatory prison term for all felony convictions would reduce the rate of serious crime by 3 to 4 percent at the cost of a twofold increase in the prison population. Studies that have calculated collective incapacitation and prison population effects were convicted felons to receive a minimum sentence of five years are profiled in Table 9.3. As is self-evident from even a brief examination of this table, the monumental increase in prison populations such a policy would bring about prohibits wide-scale implementation of collective incapacitation schemes.

Selective Incapacitation

Given the expense and severity of a program of exclusive collective incapacitation, some researchers have preferred to consider a policy of selective incapacitation. This procedure entails assigning individual sentences on the basis of predictions about who will and will not be high-rate offenders in the future. The target of selective incapacitation, the so-called career criminal, along with measurement or prediction issues and implementation of policy considerations is examined next.

Table 9.4
The Greenwood Scale

1. A prior conviction for the same offense.

2. Incarceration for more than half the preceding two years.

3. A conviction prior to age 16.

4. A commitment to a state juvenile authority.

5. Use of narcotic drugs, two years prior to present commitment.

6. Use of narcotic drugs as a juvenile.

7. State of unemployment for more than half the time in the
    preceding two years.

The Career Criminal. It has been observed time and again that a majority of the serious criminality committed in this and other countries is perpetrated by a minority of all offenders. These individuals have been variously referred to as habitual, high-rate, and recidivistic offenders, although career criminal is the label most often applied today. The perception that a relatively small portion of the total criminal population is responsible for a lion's share of all predatory criminal acts has not yet attained the status of a scientific law, although it has inspired an impressive amount of empirical corroboration. Studies relying on a wide assortment of different methodologies, to include the cohort technique (Wolfgang, Figlio, & Sellin, 1972), survey method (Viscusi, 1983), target sample procedure (Petersilia, Greenwood, & Lavin, 1978), and longitudinal criminal history approach (Blumstein & Cohen, 1979), have deduced the presence of a career criminal profile. These lawbreakers are said to commence their criminal careers sooner, desist from crime later, and engage in a much higher volume of serious violation than other offenders (Blumstein & Cohen, 1979). The question then becomes, how might we distinguish between the career criminal and other categories of offending?

Identifying the Career Criminal. There are several assumptions that underlie selective incapacitation, although of overriding significance is the presumption that high-rate offenders can be identified. Peter W. Greenwood (1982) of the Rand Corporation developed a seven-item rating scale designed to identify career criminality (see Table 9.4). Greenwood, in collaboration with Abrahamse (1982), validated this scale against the self-reports of prisoners in California, Michigan, and Texas and found it to be reasonably well correlated with retrospective accounts of past criminality. However, this scale has yet to be successfully cross-validated. Decker and Salert (1986), in one cross-validation study, reported that 14 percent of their national sample of 10,769 inmates earned scores of 4 to 7 (likely career criminal category). This represents a large segment of the inmate population and would place a substantial burden on any correctional system proposing use of the Greenwood scale to identify candidates for selective incapacitation. Decker and Salert add that the Greenwood scale predicted only 15

Table 9.5

Effects of Selective Incapacitation on Crime Rates and Prison Populations

Study	Target Population	Year	Incapacitation Policy	Offense	Crime Reduction	Prison Pop. Change
Greenwood (1982)	California inmates	1978	8 yrs for high rate robbers; 3.5 yrs for high rate burglars; 1 yr for all others.	Robbery Burglary	15-20% 11%	-1% nc
Cohen (1983)	Washington arrestees	1973	Additional 2-yr term upon re-conviction for all offenders.	Robbery Burglary	8% 6%	+17% +25%
Janus (1985)	Federal releasees	1978	Determined by SFS Risk Score.	HSO*	7%	nc
Spelman (1986)	California inmates	1978	4.5 yrs for high rate offenders; 1 yr for all others.	Robbery	.5%	-2%
Visher (1986)	California inmates	1978	8 yrs for high rate offenders; 1 yr for all others.	Robbery	13-14%	nc

*HSO = high severity offenses (e.g., burglary, sexual assault, kidnapping, willful homicide).

Note: For prison population change: − = decrease, + = increase, nc = no change.

percent of the variance in the past criminal records of subjects and was potentially biased against blacks, women, and persons originating from lower socioeconomic backgrounds. Two studies have included follow-up evaluations of the original California Rand sample and in both cases the Greenwood scale was able to predict outcome at a level only slightly better than chance (Greenwood & Turner, 1987; Klein & Caggiano, 1986).

The Greenwood scale has seemingly encountered problems at every turn. Of prime consideration here is the high rate of false positive predictions generated by this scale (Cohen, 1983; von Hirsch & Gottfredson, 1984). Several investigators have also expressed concern that this scale is too heavily dependent on self-report information (Chaiken & Chaiken, 1984; Cohen, 1983). A third criticism directed at the Greenwood scale is that it fails to consider the possibility of change (Blackmore & Welsh, 1983), and Greenwood's method of calculating the force of selective incapacitation on crime has been faulted for failing to account for the termination of a lawbreaker's career (Cohen, 1984). The generalizability of the Greenwood scale to groups of nonincarcerated offenders has also been questioned (Cohen, 1983). Generally, most scholars believe that Greenwood's original ideas had promise but that he went beyond the data in proposing certain social policy implications before his scale and procedure were more thoroughly researched (Chaiken & Chaiken, 1984).

Implementation of a Selective Incapacitation Strategy. With the problems inherent in identifying and predicting high-rate criminality, the entire selective incapacitation enterprise finds itself resting on the edge of a precipice. Studies directed at the question of selective incapacitation are outlined in Table 9.5, although the reader should take heed of the many criticisms lodged against this particular form of criminal science intervention. Besides the questions surrounding prediction, it is quite common to see selective incapacitation attacked on moral grounds. Hence, it has been argued that it is unjust to sentence offenders for crimes not yet committed (Cohen, 1983). Proponents of selective incapacitation counter that this is already done with a fair degree of regularity by judges and juries, and that they are simply attempting to make the process more systematic, equitable, and concise. Some have also doubted the validity of assumptions central to selective incapacitation theory—in particular that crime replacement and career extension are of no major consequence and have little impact on the validity of incapacitation policies (Janus, 1985). Finally, Gottfredson and Hirschi (1986) contend that, given the fact that crime declines with age, selective incapacitation would have to focus on 13- and 14-year-olds to be effective, a practice which runs counter to our current system of justice and belief in giving youngsters a "second chance."

The Role of Incapacitation in Criminal Justice Decision Making

Despite the rather negative review collective and selective incapacitation have received in this section, I believe incapacitation has a definite place in a rational system of criminal justice. There are certain individuals who, unless incarcerated or incapacitated in some fashion, will continue to victimize and prey upon the rest of society. The issue, then, becomes making more sensible use of collective incapacitation policies and marrying our selective incapacitation decisions to a coherent theory and well-validated clinical procedures that seek a more equitable balance between false positive and false negative determinations. Despite guarded support for the general goal of incapacitation, current studies do not appear to provide sweeping endorsement of broad-based incapacitation policies; nor should we allow the presence of scattered positive outcomes to blind us to the many fallacies contained in a system grounded primarily in incapacitation rhetoric (van den Haag, 1983).

REHABILITATION

Rehabilitation is aimed at changing the criminal behavior of offenders through interventions designed to promote a prosocial attitude, rational thinking, and responsible action. Rehabilitation rests on a mantle of four assumptions: change is possible; the criminal justice system is capable of fostering such change; we can recognize when such change has occurred; and people are willing to accept rehabilitated ex-offenders back into the fold of society (Lampe, 1985). The final assumption relates directly to people's attitudes toward rehabilitation, a topic of some interest to investigators and policymakers.

Attitudes Toward Rehabilitation

Public endorsement of rehabilitation has wavered some since Lou Harris conducted his public opinion poll on the subject a quarter of a century ago. Harris

Table 9.6
Percentage of General Public Respondents Supporting Rehabilitation as a Major Goal of the Criminal Justice System

Study	Location	Year	Percentage
Harris (1968)	National	1968	73%
Duffee & Ritti (1977)	Pennsylvania	1974	71%
Market Opinion Research Company (1978)	Michigan	1977	74%
Associated Press-NBC (1981)	National	1981	37%
Austin (1982)	California	1981	58%
Flanagan & Caufield (1984)	National	1982	44%
Warr & Stafford (1984)	Seattle, Washington	1981	59%
Cullen et al. (1985)	Texas	1982	79%
Thomson & Ragona (1987)	Illinois	1983	31%
Cullen et al. (1988)	Galesburg, Illinois	1982	55.5%
Cullen et al. (1990)	Cincinnati, Ohio	1986	54.7%
	Columbus, Ohio	1986	58.7%

(1968) recorded an approval rating of approximately 75 percent, a figure which has fallen, risen, and now appears to have leveled off at around 50 percent (see Table 9.6). Surveying the responses of 200 residents of a middle-size town in west-central Illinois, Cullen, Cullen, & Wozniak (1988) detected a punitive philosophy in the opinions of townspersons, although support for rehabilitation was far from dead. Employing a similar procedure in two Ohio cities, Cullen and another group of colleagues uncovered a ground swell of support for the global concept of rehabilitation, with educational and employment programs receiving the highest marks (Cullen et al., 1990). The percentages provided in Table 9.6 should be considered nothing more than a general index of public support for rehabilitation, since the wording of questions pertaining to rehabilitation has tended to vary across studies. We should also remain cognizant of Flanagan and Caulfield's (1984, p. 41) caveat that the public's attitude toward correctional reform is "diverse, multidimensional, and complex."

The opinions of correctional workers, prison administrators, and societal legislators on the rehabilitation issue are also more positive than one might anticipate, given the general atmosphere of fear and punishment which seems to permeate the modern American psyche. One hundred and fifty-five correctional officers working in a Southern correctional system were surveyed by Cullen et al. (1989), and while most expressed sentiments that indicated their primary affiliation was with the custody function of corrections and maintaining order within the institution, many communicated a favorable attitude toward rehabilitation and change. Interestingly, these same officers overestimated the degree to which their fellow officers supported a strictly custodial orientation, suggesting that correctional officers may exude uncharacteristically negative attitudes about inmates and the prospect of rehabilitation when in the company of fellow officers. One-hundred percent of the Illinois state correctional administrators surveyed by Cullen and Gilbert (1982) agreed that offenders should be provided the opportunity for rehabilitation, while 80 percent of the Indiana state legislators canvased by Hamm (1987) stated that they believed rehabilitation was as important as retribution or punishment in sentencing offenders.

The outcome of research addressing itself to public and professional attitudes toward rehabilitation suggests that the national climate is generally conducive to the implementation of rehabilitation programs provided these programs do not take precedence over the correctional philosophies of punishment and retribution. It should be kept in mind, however, that the manner in which a question is phrased can have a major bearing on the responses investigators obtain. Since the wording has tended to vary from survey to survey, it is difficult to compare responses across studies. Furthermore, a lawmaker who answers in the affirmative when questioned about his or her support for rehabilitation as a goal of the criminal justice system may turn around and respond very differently when asked to vote on a bill that will provide revenues for correctional rehabilitation programs. These issues should be kept in mind when reviewing the results outlined in Table 9.6.

Assessing the Validity of the Rehabilitation Ideal

During the golden age of rehabilitation in this country (1960–1972) a primary goal of the criminal justice system was promoting behavioral change in criminal offenders. Even before this era began, however, evidence had been accumulating to show that rehabilitation was no panacea (Cressey, 1958). It was not until Martinson published his "nothing works" article in 1974, however, that we see the pendulum taking a noticeable swing away from the rehabilitation ideal. This shift in ideology was based not so much on the scholarly merit of Martinson's arguments but on the fact that the time was ripe for anti-rehabilitation sentiment. Conservatives embraced Martinson's reading of the data because it reinforced their long-standing belief in the necessity of taking a more punitive approach in dealing with society's lawbreakers, while many liberals found solace in Martinson's conclusions because it tended to validate their lack of trust in state-run programming (Cullen & Gendreau, 1989). Martinson's paper simply fulfilled a preexisting interest in finding fault with the rehabilitation hypothesis.

The problem with the Martinson review is that it tells only part of the story. Martinson (1974) argued that there was no good evidence that rehabilitation works, however, he failed to mention that there was no solid evidence that rehabilitation doesn't work, either. In short, the research upon which the Martinson review is based was so flawed as to defy meaningful analysis and interpretation. Recent studies utilizing a more rigorous test of the rehabilitation hypothesis have shown Martinson's initial conclusions to have been overly pessimistic. The efficacy of treatment interventions with adult and juvenile offenders has been documented both qualitatively (Gendreau & Ross, 1979; 1987) and quantitatively (Andrews et al., 1990; Davidson et al., 1984; Garrett, 1985; Izzo & Ross, 1990). These outcomes lead me to the conclusion that rehabilitation programs do in fact work, although no program works for all offenders and some programs do not succeed with anyone. We must therefore identify the limits of these positive effects in an effort to answer the question posed in Chapter 6: Which procedures work best with which type offenders under which specific sets of circumstances?

The Role of Rehabilitation in Criminal Justice Decision Making

Though it is debatable whether all four of the assumptions underlying rehabilitation will ever be satisfied (for example, being able to determine when genuine change has occurred), rehabilitation would appear to have a place in a comprehensive system of criminal justice decision making. In order to avoid the mistakes of the past we would be well advised to consider why previous efforts at rehabilitation may have been less than fully successful. It should come as no surprise to anyone who has ever worked with an offender that there are some individuals who are unreceptive to and antagonistic toward rehabilitation programming. To include such persons in programs with motivated clients will not only interfere with the treatment progress of the latter group but also make it more difficult for the researcher to identify positive treatment effects (Glaser, 1975). Restricting ourselves to persons expressing an interest in change may narrow the range of individuals for whom rehabilitation is a reasonable correctional goal, but with a corollary gain in our ability to more adequately test the benefit of rehabilitation programs.

A review of past attempts at rehabilitation reveals that most were poorly conceptualized, myopically conceived, and improperly administered (Hamm & Schrink, 1989). We must therefore do a better job of integrating practice, research, and theory, to include identifying specific target behaviors we expect to change as a function of involvement in a particular rehabilitation program. To view rehabilitation programs as a cure-all is not only unrealistic but counterproductive, since the frustration of failing to find a "cure" for criminality when such a possibility does not even exist will likely divert our attention from the task of finding a workable solution that includes, but is not confined to, selected rehabilitation programs.

Unlike retribution or incapacitation, rehabilitation is not a goal that can be forced on the individual, although in the past this may very well have been the intent of some correctional administrators. It might be more realistic and productive to conceptualize rehabilitation as a goal that is the ultimate responsibility of the individual. The criminal justice system can assist in the realization of this goal by providing valid programs, but it should stop short of coercing inmates to participate in these programs and activities. We must emphasize to the offender that he or she chooses to enter a rehabilitation program, just as he or she decides whether to participate in crime—mindful, of course, that each option carries with it certain potential consequences (for example, a chance at a conventional lifestyle versus involvement in a continuing cycle of crime and incarceration).

RESTITUTION

Restitution, which concerns itself with reparations made to the victims of crime, was quite popular in ancient times. Under the Roman law of the Twelve Tribes, thieves who were apprehended paid double the value of the stolen object, triple the value if the thief escaped and was subsequently recaptured, and four times the value if the theft was accomplished by force (Peak, 1986). Reparation was almost exclusively monetary in the barbaric tribes of northern Europe before the fall of the Roman Empire. Even murder could be atoned for with a tribute in cattle or sheep (Gillin, 1945). The Ifugoa of North Lozon ruled that if a married man were to rape a married woman, then the victim's family, the victim's husband's family, and the offender's wife's family were entitled to collect damages from the rapist (Hoebel, 1954). After the Middle Ages, victim compensation began to lose momentum as governments began defining the state as the proper broker of punishments dispensed to lawbreaking citizens. It was not until the women's movement of the late 1960s and early 1970s that we see victims' rights resurfacing as an important social issue.

Attitudes Toward Restitution

Restitution would appear to enjoy a moderate to high degree of popularity with victims and victimizers alike. Schafer (1977) indicates that the majority of Florida inmates he interviewed expressed an interest in making reparations to their victims and the families of their victims. This sentiment was particularly strong in men who had been convicted of murder. Umbreit (1988) advises that burglary victims in Minnesota confided in him that they felt the youthful offenders who had burglarized their homes should be held accountable for their actions, but tempered this resolve with the hope that these young lawbreakers could receive counseling and the opportunity for reconciliation. Where rehabilitation programs have seen their funds cut and backers silenced, victim assistance and restitution programs have been steadily gaining allies. The victim-assistance movement reached new heights when President Ronald Reagan signed into law the Victims of Crime Act, which guaranteed funds to eligible state victim-compensation programs.

Figure 9.1
Funding Sources for State Victimization Programs

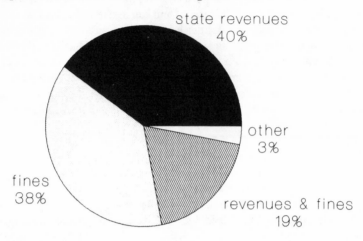

Victim Compensation

Peak (1986) reports that 43 states and the District of Columbia provide financial assistance to victims through various victim-compensation projects. Grants range from an average of $1,050 in New Mexico to $12,500 in Rhode Island, with a national mean of $3,113 and national median of $2,600 (McGillis & Smith, 1982). Several states have enacted ''Son of Sam'' statutes that mandate that a substantial portion of all proceeds realized as a result of one's criminal ventures (for example, book royalties, movie rights) be forfeited and redirected into a victim-compensation fund. Figure 9.1 provides an overview of how state victim-compensation programs are currently funded.

Restitution appears to be one of the more popular sanctioning options available for use with juvenile offenders. One group of investigators determined that 86 percent of the 133 juvenile courts surveyed reportedly utilized restitution in one form or another (Schneider et al., 1977). Researchers Zapf and Cole (1985) reviewed the results of a restitution program initiated in the Yukon Territory, Canada, and observed that 60.8 percent of the orders resulted in full payment, 3.8 percent in partial payment, and 35.4 percent in no payment. The enforcement of unpaid restitution was identified as a problem by Zapf and Cole, who report that in one out of every five cases the restitution orders had either been lost or forgotten. For this reason victims often prefer a system of state compensation whereby they are more likely to receive remuneration.

Victim-Offender Reconciliation Programs

Restitution is more commonly indemnified in money than in service (Zapf & Cole, 1985), but Victim-Offender Reconciliation Programs (VORP) show promise of recalibrating the balance of money and service. Financial payments are sometimes a part of the VORP agenda, although the primary goal of such programs is the interpersonal rapprochement of victims and offenders. Properly handled, VORPs can foster understanding on the part of offenders while promoting a sense of self-efficacy in victims (Green, 1984). In fact, mediation was viewed as helpful by 86 percent of the victims participating in a Victim-Offender Reconciliation Program in Minneapolis, Minnesota (Umbreit, 1989). Of course, personal contact between an offender and his or her victim is not always practical, possible, or even advisable, particularly when it comes to working with the victims of violent assault. Under such circumstances it might be best to fall back on a general model of victim-offender reconciliation, where unacquainted victims and offenders meet as a group.

Person-on-person reconciliation yields divergent outcomes as a function of the offender, victim, instant offense, and reparative model utilized. Blagg (1985), a lecturer in social policy at the University of Lancaster, identified two models of reparation for use with juvenile lawbreakers: the Institutional Reparative Model and the Personal Reparative Model. The Institutional Reparative Model demands that youth accused of an illegal act apologize to representatives of the organization or business they have victimized. Blagg finds this procedure to be largely unsatisfactory owing to the fact that it perpetuates the cycle of punishment experienced by adolescent lawbreakers and places the organizational representative in the role of punitive authority figure. Even if the encounter is handled properly by the representative, juveniles often come away from such interactions feeling persecuted, angry, and resentful (Blagg, 1985).

The Personal Reparative Model, on the other hand, affords the youthful offender the opportunity to apologize directly to the person he or she has victimized. According to Blagg (1985), this permits a more meaningful exchange of thoughts and feelings between victim and victimizer than can be realized through use of the Institutional Reparative Model. Blagg (1985) shares the positive experience of a youthful offender who agreed to meet with the owner of a home in England he had broken into and stole £25 and some sweets:

I was terrified when I went up to the house . . . but the guy shook my hand and said that I had been a man to have come. His two little daughters were sitting there, just out of the bath, he told me that the sweets were a birthday present from them to him. . . . They must have thought I was a criminal. I felt rotten. (p. 275)

Obviously, person-on-person reparation is not advisable under all conditions and is most problematic, and normally ill advised, in cases involving assault or physical violence.

The Role of Restitution in Criminal Justice Decision Making

The criminal justice goal of restitution appears to provide benefits to both the offender and victim. Restitution, especially in the form of victim-offender reconciliation, has been shown to empower victims who previously may have felt impotent and helpless after being exploited by the criminal actions of another (Symonds, 1980). Offenders benefit from the goal of restitution by gaining an augmented sense of self-worth and decreased feelings of guilt (Galaway & Hudson, 1980; Umbriet, 1989). These benefits do not accrue without a price, however, and many offenders remark that being confronted by victims (particularly their own victims) is more difficult than going to jail (Green, 1984). Restitution is said to fulfill the aims of rehabilitation (Eglash, 1975), punishment (McAnany, 1978), and deterrence (Tittle, 1978), but as Blagg (1985) warns, this particular goal of criminal justice intervention is a highly complex process that requires skillful and sensitive handling.

CONCLUSION

It should be obvious by now that none of the five goals of person × situation interaction explored in this chapter—retribution, deterrence, incapacitation, rehabilitation, restitution—are sufficiently robust to stand alone as the primary justification for criminal science intervention. Retribution comes closest to being a stand-alone procedure, but in a society that values scientific advancement and consideration of the individual condition, retribution in isolation is but a crude impersonation of what a comprehensive system of criminal justice ought to be. There is a seemingly natural conflict between fairness and equity in sentencing (retribution), the protection of society (incapacitation), and growth of the individual offender (rehabilitation). However, further analysis reveals that the five philosophies reviewed in this chapter are not necessarily incompatible (Moore et al., 1984). Wisely integrated, these philosophies appear to provide the framework for an effective system of checks and balances.

In offering a comprehensive intervention program of person × situation interaction we might want to follow the lead of Monahan (1982), who proposed that the retributive Principle of Commensurate Deserts be used to establish the upper and lower limits of a particular criminal sanction. The individual needs of the offender (rehabilitation), victim (restitution), general public (incapacitation), and system (deterrence) could then be a means of identifying a specific point within the range established by the Principle of Commensurate Deserts. As previously noted, these five goals, suitably arranged, could serve as the foundation for a comprehensive system of criminal justice decision making. Restricting people's rights under the law would increase the certainty of punishment and accomplish the goal of deterrence, just as executing all persons possessing two or more felony convictions would likely advance incapacitative aims. However, such seemingly oppressive practices could never exist in a system that pursues an equitable balance among the five primary goals of criminal science intervention.

There are, without question, problems with each of the five philosophies of criminal justice sanctioning explored in this chapter. However, to argue that deterrence is ineffectual, incapacitation unproductive, or rehabilitation a myth goes beyond the data that are currently available. Research suggests that under clearly defined circumstances each of these goals can be accomplished. If we have learned anything from the "nothing works" fiasco of the mid-1970s, it should be that to abandon a particular approach on the basis of inadequate research data is a strategy that will eventually backfire. None of the five goals surveyed in this chapter is sufficient in and of itself, but all are necessary as part of a comprehensive system of person × situation criminal justice intervention.

PART IV

CONCLUSION

10

Answering the Questions

The initial chapters of Volumes 1 and 2 contained several questions devised to guide our journey through the morass of data, ideas, and applications that are criminal science. Setting the stage for what would follow, these chapters examined several approaches to the study of crime and asked how crime might best be measured, formulated a definition of criminal behavior and explored ways this behavior could be more properly controlled, inquired into what was criminal science and wondered how we might proceed with the scientific study of criminal behavior, and delved into the question of application by considering the issues of assessment, prediction, and intervention. It seems fair to say that while these and several other questions were addressed in this two-volume text, few of these queries were answered in a manner sufficient to satisfy most criminal scientists, the present author included. Thus, despite the wealth of criminal science information currently available, we must continue to search for a system of knowledge upon which to base a congruent policy of criminal justice decision making.

The remaining pages of this chapter could be filled with a discussion of factors that hinder our ability to draw definitive conclusions to the questions posed in those initial chapters. Issues such as the need for augmented interdisciplinary cooperation, increased research sophistication, enhanced theoretical elaboration, and expanded integration come to mind when the problems facing criminal scientific investigation are broached. However, each of these issues has already been discussed with a reasonable degree of specificity. Our time might therefore be more wisely spent exploring matters not considered or else given only cursory treatment in the previous 19 chapters. I therefore invite the reader to join me on a brief excursion into what I call the foundations, functions, and overriding goals of criminal science.

FOUNDATIONS AND FUNCTIONS

The five foundations of criminal science should be thoroughly familiar to the reader by now. Adopting these five foundations we have come to realize that the criminal science movement is devoted to understanding crime in its socio-historical *context*, collecting pertinent *research* data; achieving a meaningful *theoretical integration* of these data; using these data and theory to *evaluate* and *predict* future criminal events; and applying these categories of understanding (context, research, theory, evaluation/prediction) to form a comprehensive system of *intervention*. However, in order that these objectives might be attained we must move from a general appreciation of these foundations to a discussion of the models that cut across criminal science inquiry. One such model is the condition-choice-cognition paradigm first enumerated in Walters' (1990b) research on the criminal lifestyle.

As conceptualized by Walters (1990b), conditions establish one's predisposition to criminality, either by increasing (risk factors) or decreasing (protection factors) one's chances of future criminal involvement. Conditions are of three types: (1) characteristics of the individual (person variables); (2) characteristics of the environmental situation (situation variables); or (3) characteristics of the interaction between person and situation variables (interactive variables). Among the person variables commonly cited for their ability to augment or mitigate the future risk of criminal conduct we find age, gender, intelligence, and cognitive style. Drugs and major agents of socialization (particularly the family, school, peers, and media) are of paramount significance as situational correlates of criminal behavior. However, a sentiment expressed many times in this text and reiterated here is that it is the person × situation interaction that is of prime consideration in investigating the behavior of criminal offenders.

Some scholars argue that we live in an ordered world, while others assert that this is nothing more than a fantasy born of our desire to find direction in a random universe. The truth may never be known, but in all probability it lies somewhere between these two extremes. In fact, the person × situation interaction helps bring this issue into focus. That person and situation variables interact in random fashion is evident in studies that show there is often no reasonable explanation for why certain events occur for one individual but not another. One of the horrors of serial murder is that the motive for homicide often has little to do with the behavior of the victim. Such randomness shatters our belief in a just world and leaves us feeling exposed, naked, and vulnerable. There is, nonetheless, some affirmation of an ordered universe in the three interactive domains discussed in Chapter 7 of Volume 1. Hence, the physical (stimulus modulation, internal-external orientation), social (attachment, social bonding or empathy), and psychological (self-image, role identity) domains of person × situation interaction may serve to bridge the gap between the randomness of human experience and the patterns into which this experience sometimes falls. One could argue, of course, that the three domains reviewed in this text are nothing more than a self-deceptive attempt by proponents of the ordered universe school to force order on a random series of events. However, the research reviewed in Chapter 7 of Volume 1 suggests that interactive experiences may, in fact, coalesce around a finite number of themes.

Moving to the second link in the condition-choice-cognition chain we can see that, despite the effect interactive influences may have on human behavior, these influences do not determine behavioral outcomes. The human being is an active decision maker who chooses to engage in a particular action based on a unique, albeit imperfect, view of the world. This world view grows into a cognitive style, the third link in the condition-choice-cognition continuum, a link which reflects the enduring human capacity for self-protection and self-preservation. Once a person decides to engage in a given criminal act, whether this act is an isolated event or part of a wider lifestyle, he or she must find ways to justify and rationalize this behavior through the development of a characteristic style of thought or cognition (Walters, 1990). The significance of the condition-choice-cognition sequence is that crime will not occur under circumstances in which it is not supported by the conditions, choices, and cognitions of one's life.

SCIENCE AND RESPONSIBILITY

There are several overriding considerations in addition to the condition-choice-cognition continuum that help direct and motivate the five foundations. The systematic pursuit of information on crime and criminals is one such consideration. The unremitting quest for new knowledge therefore characterizes the activities of the criminal scientist. Though indispensable to the criminal science effort, this search for understanding does not take place in a vacuum. Research investigations on the correlates of crime, for example, have identified certain groups (for example, youthful, male, urban blacks) as being at high risk for involvement in future criminal activity. To conclude from this, however, that blacks are innately more criminal than whites or that whites are inherently more law-abiding than blacks, given our current lack of understanding into the nature of this relationship, leaves one vulnerable to charges of racism, and rightfully so. On the other hand, to ignore the correlation between racial or ethnic status and crime would be scientifically irresponsible. Balancing the search for knowledge with restraint in interpreting one's findings is at the heart of the criminal science investigative effort.

The moral dilemmas facing the criminal scientist intent on probing "sensitive" issues highlight the necessity of tempering our quest for new knowledge with reasoned judgment, moral consternation, and ethical use of available data. Criminal scientists not only venture beyond the boundaries of current understanding but do what they can to guard against the possibility that this new knowledge will be misused or misinterpreted. A philosophical assertion of personal responsibility cannot ethically be used to justify a correctional policy that assigns inordinately long sentences to persons convicted of relatively minor offenses.

The criminal scientist is not only responsible for collecting, evaluating, and interpreting information on crime and criminals but does what he or she can to discourage inappropriate use of his or her findings, ideas, and conclusions. The ticklish ethical issues surrounding the use of scientific knowledge to develop and build nuclear weapons predate our present concerns but serve as a reminder of how difficult it is to strike a proper balance between the pursuit of knowledge and relevant ethical considerations. There are no simple answers to this perplexing state of affairs, although the reader should keep in mind that, above all else, criminal science is dedicated to preserving the dignity of the human organism and ascribes to the belief that those factors over which we have the greatest degree of control are the elements on which we should be judged.

One final matter requiring our attention relative to the scientific foundations of criminal investigation is the issue of objectivity. Criminal scientists strive to make the study of crime and criminal behavior as scientifically impartial as possible. Though we will probably never be able to completely eliminate subjectivity from our study of human behavior, it is this ability to function beyond the conditions of our lives that separates us from the lower organisms. Subjectivity deserves to be investigated in its own right, despite the fact that it injects uncertainty into the investigative process. It is well to keep in mind that subjectivity affects even the physical sciences, where renowned physicist Werner Heisenberg (1901–1976) demonstrated that efforts to measure a phenomenon often serve to modify the outcome of one's inquiry. Hence, whenever scientists insert themselves into a research situation they unwittingly influence the subject of their investigation. Criminal scientists are therefore obligated to expose the limitations of their scientific methods and make certain that the resulting knowledge is used wisely.

BALANCING THE DICHOTOMIES

Throughout this text we have seen evidence of multifarious dichotomies. Positivism-classicism, formal-informal social control, person-situation variables, and utilitarianism–just deserts are but a few that run through the criminal science literature. Criminal science seems a field of polarized ideas and concepts. The incompatibility of these concepts may be more apparent than real, however. A second overriding goal of the criminal science movement, therefore, is to blend, balance, and reconcile the concepts that have served to characterize this field of investigative endeavor. The key to resolving dichotomous thinking in the criminal sciences might be to reorganize the way we look at crime and criminals. Integrative attempts, such as the construction of a comprehensive system of crime prevention and criminal justice decision making, need to be developed further than was possible in this introductory research text.

Adopting a comprehensive approach to criminal science research was a point stressed throughout Volume 1. We learned in Chapter 7 of Volume 2 that primary, secondary, and tertiary prevention, as well as incentive-altering, opportunity-reducing, noncrime-benefit enhancing, and crime cost-augmenting intervention strategies, can be organized into a comprehensive system of crime prevention. We then entertained a comprehensive system of criminal justice intervention (Chapter 9, Volume 2) that achieved its integrating power by combining the five goals of criminal justice procedure: retribution, deterrence, incapacitation, rehabilitation, and restitution. In fact, this text is imbued with statements indicating that intervention and understanding must take place at all levels, from the individual offender to the neighborhood, to the upper reaches of social policy-making. It would seem, then, that a second fundamental aim of the criminal science movement is to dissolve the dichotomies that have too long plagued this field of investigative procedure.

THE AMERICAN CRIME PHENOMENON

A third overriding goal of criminal science endeavor is to find answers to questions that affect many people simultaneously. The problem of a spiraling rate of violent criminality would, for example, fit into this particular goal. Surveys show that the United States suffers a higher rate of per capita violent crime than the vast majority of other industrialized nations (Archer & Gartner, 1984). Of even greater significance, however, is explaining the nature of this phenomenon. Attempts were made to find answers to these questions in Chapters 2 and 3 of Volume 1. As the reader may recall, the crime curve in the United States began to deviate from those of other western nations shortly after the Civil War. Consequently, the war itself may have contributed to the American crime phenomenon by virtue of its violent nature, although we must consider additional factors in deriving a complete understanding of this phenomenon: formal versus informal sources of social control, the politicalization of crime, the mediazation of crime, and the adversarial nature of the U.S. system of law, in particular.

The necessity of designing a solid system of informal social support has been emphasized throughout this book. Data show that formal avenues of control (that is, law enforcement) are made substantially more efficacious when paired with informal reservoirs of social influence (Steenhuis, 1980). Likewise, informal sources of social control become appreciably more effective when coupled with and supervised by formal control agencies and organizations (Bennett, 1989). There is much less intercommunication and mutual support between formal and informal sources of social control in this country than in nations like Switzerland and Japan where, despite high industrialization, the rate of crime is much lower than in the United States. Perhaps we have stressed avenues of formal social control at the expense of informal methods of social influence. Hence, despite pledging support for the nuclear family, some politicians have implemented policies that, though they aid the formal social control network, inadvertently tear at the very fabric of such potent agents of informal social control as the family. Until the nation as a whole grasps the puissance of extralegal sources of social influence, it is likely that we will continue to be saddled with one of the highest crime rates in the industrialized world.

Many an election has been won on the strength of a candidate's stance on crime. Recalling once again the Willie Horton incident of several years ago, we can see the potential value of criminal science issues for those holding various political aspirations. Once the votes were counted, however, the Willie Horton case was all but forgotten, with no real impact on national policy. While this may be viewed by some as nothing more than a harmless case of political maneuvering, it is appreciably more serious because it shifts our attention away from the real issues. In addition, such a tactic often stimulates disillusionment and skepticism on the part of the public while increasing its fear of crime. This, in turn, may encourage less informed voters to support policies (such as increased police power) that, though they may have a mild suppressing effect on crime in the present, hold serious consequences for the survival of certain personal freedoms and liberties in the future.

The media also appear to have played a role in elevating the American public's sensitivity to and fear of crime. The radio, television, and print media have an obligation to inform the public. However, in order to attract as many listeners, viewers, and readers as possible they frequently spotlight the exceptional while ignoring the commonplace. As understandable as this may be, such a practice brings about several unintended and potentially destructive consequences, not the least of which is providing the public with a skewed or distorted picture of the world. Crimes of violence are among the more popular topics in newspapers or on television, although they account for only a small fraction of all crimes committed. When we review historical data we notice that the crime rate, as measured by victimization surveys, has exhibited a declining slope ever since the mid-1970s, although most people perceive that crime has risen dramatically in the last decade, based largely, I believe, on information disseminated by the media. Finally, both the news and entertainment media have seemingly fed our long-standing voyeuristic preoccupation with criminals as represented by news specials on alleged Mafia boss John Gotti and movies like *Scarface* and *The Godfather*.

As with many features of American life, legal procedure is often guided by an attitude of competition. It is the prosecution against the defense in a match-up that rivals the Super Bowl or World Series. Many lawyers and judges openly acknowledge that the American system of jurisprudence exists for the purpose of administering legal procedure rather than dispensing justice. The sad fact is that judicial equity and social harmony may be sacrificed in the process. Crime may even be encouraged in situations where courtroom victories take precedence over justice, in that such situations tend to augment opportunities for legal procedure. The oriental practice of employing attorneys as advisors rather than as adversaries may help reduce some of the unintended crime-promoting features of our current system of jurisprudence, although this issue requires a great deal more study before we can seriously consider its implementation.

In spite of what has been said in this section, it is the criminals—not the police, politicians, media, or lawyers—who are responsible for crime. The present discussion simply illuminates possible avenues by which we might deal more effectively with the problem of crime in the United States and was in no way intended to lay the blame for criminal behavior solely on the shoulders of America's social institutions. However, a principal objective of criminal science procedure is the accumulation of knowledge not only by scholars but by the general populace as well. Until people are educated on many of the issues discussed in this text, are able to separate the pertinent issues from the superfluous ones, and are willing to demand that certain societal changes take place, interventions aimed at the individual offender will remedy only a small fraction of the problem and the American crime phenomenon will likely continue at its present strength.

A FINAL COMMENT

There are, unfortunately, many more questions about crime than answers at this point. We can state with a reasonable degree of confidence, however, that this book has taken steps to delineate several of the more pertinent questions presently confronting the criminal science field. The purpose has been to reconstruct the relevant questions, provide several preliminary answers, and offer a framework by which we might answer an even greater number of inquiries in the future. The paradox is that with the accumulation of new knowledge this text will soon become outdated. In line with the first overriding goal of criminal science (knowledge development), this book has as a leading objective, its own obsolescence. Whether or not the book survives as new knowledge accumulates is immaterial, for if it promotes the scientific study of crime and criminal behavior, then it has fulfilled its author's intentions.

References

Aaland, R. L., & Schag, D. W. (1984). The assessment of continued threat to the community in mentally ill offender programs. *Journal of Criminal Justice, 22*, 81–86.

Abel, G. G., & Annon, J. S. (1982, April) *Reducing deviant sexual arousal through satiation.* Workshop presented at the 4th National Conference on Sexual Aggression, Denver, CO.

Abel, G. G., Blanchard, E. B., Barlow, D. H., & Flannagan, B. (1975, December). *A case report of the behavioral treatment of a sadistic rapist.* Paper presented at the annual meeting of the Association for the Advancement of Behavior Therapy, San Francisco, CA.

Abel, G. G., Blanchard, E. B., & Becker, J. V. (1978). An integrated program for rapists. In R. Rada (ed.), *Clinical aspects of the rapist* (pp. 161–214). New York: Grune & Stratton.

Abel, G. G., Rouleau, J. L., & Cunningham-Rathner, J. (1985). Sexually aggressive behavior. In W. J. Curren, A. L. McGarry, & S. A. Shah (eds.), *Forensic psychiatry and psychology* (pp. 289–313). Philadelphia: Davis.

Abramson, M. (1972). The criminalization of mentally disordered behavior. *Hospital and Community Psychiatry, 24*, 105–107.

Adams, K. (1983). Former mental patients in a prison and parole system: A study of socially disruptive behavior. *Criminal Justice and Behavior, 10*, 358–384.

——— (1986). The disciplinary experiences of mentally disordered inmates. *Criminal Justice and Behavior, 13*, 297–316.

Adams, S. (1961). *Effectiveness of interview therapy with older youth authority wards: An interim evaluation of the PICO project* (Research Report No. 20). Sacramento, CA: California Youth Authority.

Adams, T. C., & West, J. (1976). Another look at the use of the Minnesota Multiphasic Personality Inventory as an index to "escapism." *Journal of Clinical Psychology, 32*, 580–582.

Agee, V. L. (1986). Institutional treatment programs for the violent juvenile. In S. Apter & A. Goldstein (eds.), *Youth violence: Programs and prospects.* New York: Pergamon.

Aiken, T. W., Stumphauzer, J. S., & Veloz, E. V. (1977). Behavioral analysis of non-delinquent brothers in a high juvenile crime community. *Behavioral Disorders*, *2*, 212–222.

Alexander, F., & Staub, H. (1931). *The criminal, the judge, and the public*. New York: Macmillan.

Alexander, J. F., Barton, C., Schiavo, R. S., & Parsons, B. V. (1976). Systems-behavioral interventions with families of delinquents: Therapist characteristics, family behavior, and outcome. *Journal of Consulting and Clinical Psychology*, *44*, 656–664.

Alexander, J. F., & Parsons, B. V. (1973). Short-term behavioral intervention with delinquent families: Impact on family process and recidivism. *Journal of Abnormal Psychology*, *81*, 219–225.

———— (1982). *Functional family therapy*. Monterey, CA: Brooks/Cole.

Alexander, S. (1985). *Nut-cracker. Money, madness, murder: A family album*. New York: Dell.

Allen, R. P., Safer, D., & Covi, L. (1975). Effects of psychostimulants on aggression. *Journal of Nervous and Mental Diseases*, *160*, 138–145.

American Law Institute. (1955). *Model penal code, sec. 401(1)*.

American Medical Association. (1984). Insanity defense in criminal triads and limitations of psychiatric testimony: Report of Board of Trustees. *Journal of the American Medical Association*, *251*, 2967.

American Psychiatric Association. (1980). *Diagnostic and statistical manual of mental disorders: Third edition (DSH-III)*. Washington, DC: Author.

———— (1983). American Psychiatric Association statement on the insanity defense. *American Journal of Psychiatry*, *140*, 681–688.

Amsterdam, A. G. (1982). Capital punishment. In H. A. Bedau (ed.), *The death penalty in America* (3rd ed., pp. 346–358). New York: Oxford University Press.

Anderson, C. A. (1987). Temperature and aggression: Effects on quarterly, yearly, and city rates of violent and nonviolent crime. *Journal of Personality and Social Psychology*, *52*, 1161–1173.

Anderson, L. S. (1979). The deterrent effect of criminal sanctions: Reviewing the evidence. In P. J. Brantingham & J. M. Kess (eds.), *Structure, law, and power: Essays in the sociology of law* (pp. 120–134). Beverly Hills, CA: Sage.

Anderson, P., Davoli, C. R., & Moriarity, L. (1985). Private corrections: Feast or fiasco? *The Prison Journal*, *65*, 32–41.

Anderson, W. P., & Holcomb, W. R. (1983). Accused murderers: Five MMPI personality types. *Journal of Clinical Psychology*, *39*, 761–768.

Andrews, D. A. (1980). Some experimental investigations of the principle of differential association through deliberate manipulations of the structure of service systems. *American Sociological Review*, *45*, 448–462.

———— (1983). The assessment of outcome in correctional samples. In M. J. Lambert, E. R. Christensen, & S. S. DeJulio (eds.), *The assessment of psychotherapy outcome*. New York: John Wiley.

Andrews, D. A., Bonta, J., & Hoge, R. D. (1990). Classification for effective rehabilitation: Rediscovering psychology. *Criminal Justice and Behavior*, *17*, 19–52.

Andrews, D. A., Bonta, J., Motiuk, L. L., & Robinson, D. (1984, August). *Some psychometrics of practical risk/need assessment*. Unpublished paper presented at the meeting of the American Psychological Association, Toronto, Canada.

Andrews, D. A., & Friesen, W. (1987). Assessments of anticriminal plans and the prediction of criminal futures: A research note. *Criminal Justice and Behavior*, *14*, 33–37.

Andrews, D. A., Hoge, R. D., Robinson, D., & Hollett, J. (1986). *The family service assessment and evaluation project: Field report, phase I*. Ottawa: Family Service.

Andrews, D. A., & Kiessling, J. J. (1980). Program structure and effective correctional practices: A summary of CaVic research. In R. R. Ross & P. Gendreau (eds.), *Effective correctional treatment*. Toronto: Butterworths.

Andrews, D. A., Kiessling, J. J., Mickus, S. G., & Robinson, D. (1985). *The level of supervision inventory: Risk/needs assessment in community corrections*. Department of Psychology, Carleton University.

Andrews, D. A., & Wormith, J. S. (1984). *Criminal sentiments and criminal behavior*. Programs Branch User Report. Ottawa: Solicitor General of Canada.

Andrews, D. A., Zinger, I., Hoge, R. D., Bonta, J., Gendreau, P., & Cullen, F. T. (1990). Does correctional treatment work? A clinically-relevant and psychologically-informed meta-analysis. *Criminology*, *28*, 369–404.

Anglin, M. D. (1988). The efficacy of civil commitment in treating narcotic addiction. *National Institute on Drug Abuse: Research Monograph Series* (Monograph 86), 8–34.

Anglin, M. D., Brecht, M-L., & Maddahian, E. (1989). Pretreatment characteristics and treatment performance of legally coerced versus voluntary methadone maintenance admissions. *Criminology*, *27*, 537–557.

Annon, J. S. (1971). The extension of learning principles to the analysis and treatment of sexual problems. *Dissertation Abstracts International*, *32* (6–B), 3627.

———— (1975). *The behavioral treatment of sexual problems: Vol. 2. Intensive therapy*. Honolulu: Enabling Systems, Inc.

Apfeldorf, M., & Hunley, P. J. (1975). Application of MMPI alcoholism scales to older alcoholics and problem drinkers. *Journal of Studies on Alcohol*, *36*, 645–653.

Arbuthnot, J., & Gordon, D. A. (1986). Behavioral and cognitive effects of a moral reasoning development intervention for high-risk behavior-disordered adolescents. *Journal of Consulting and Clinical Psychology*, *54*, 208–216.

Archer, D., & Gartner, R. (1984). *Violence and crime in cross-national perspective*. New Haven, CT: Yale University Press.

Arkin, S. D. (1980). Discrimination and arbitrariness in capital punishment: An analysis of post-Furman murder cases in Dade County, Florida, 1973–1976. *Stanford Law Review*, *33*, 75–101.

Arvanites, T. M. (1988). The impact of state mental hospital deinstitutionalization on commitments for incompetency to stand trial. *Criminology*, *26*, 307–320.

Ashford, J. B. (1989). Offense comparisons between mentally disordered and non-mentally disordered inmates. *Canadian Journal of Criminology*, *31*, 35–48.

Ashford, J. B., & LeCroy, C. W. (1988). Predicting recidivism: An evaluation of the Wisconsin Juvenile Probation and Aftercare Risk Instrument. *Criminal Justice and Behavior*, *15*, 141–151.

Ashley, M. (1922). Outcome of 1000 cases paroled from the Middleton State Hospital. *State Hospital Quarterly*, *8*, 64–70.

Associated Press-NBC Poll. (1981, July). Reported in *St. Louis Globe-Democrat*, Prisons too soft, most in poll say, July 14, 1981, p. 1.

Austin, J. (1982). *The public mandate against the high cost of prisons.* Paper presented at the annual meeting of the Western Society of Criminology.

―――― (1983). Assessing the new generation of prison classification models. *Crime and Delinquency, 29,* 561–576.

―――― (1986). Using early release to relieve prison crowding—A dilemma in public policing. *Crime and Delinquency, 32,* 404–502.

Avio, K. L. (1979). Capital punishment in Canada. *Canadian Journal of Economics, 12,* 647–676.

Azcarate, C. L. (1975). Minor tranquilizers in the treatment of aggression. *Journal of Nervous and Mental Diseases, 160,* 100–107.

Aziz, D. (1988). *Shock incarceration evaluation: Preliminary data.* Albany, NY: Unpublished report to the New York Department of Correctional Services.

Baily, W. C. (1980). Deterrence and the celerity of the death penalty: A neglected question in deterrence research. *Social Forces, 58,* 1308–1333.

Baily, W. C., & Lott, R. P. (1976). Crime punishment and personality: An examination of the deterrence question. *Journal of Criminal Law and Criminology, 67,* 99–109.

Baily, W. C., & Peterson, R. D. (1989). Murder and capital punishment: A monthly time-series analysis of execution publicity. *American Sociological Review, 54,* 722–743.

Baird, S. C. (1981). Probation and parole classification: The Wisconsin model. *Corrections Today, 43,* 36–41.

―――― (1985). Classifying juveniles: Making the most out of an important management tool. *Corrections Today, 47,* 32–38.

Baldwin, J. D. (1984). Thrill and adventure seeking and the age distribution of crime: Comment on Hirschi and Gottfredson. *American Journal of Sociology, 90,* 1326–1330.

Ball, J. C., & Corty, E. (1988). Basic issues pertaining to the effectiveness of methadone maintenance treatment. *National Institute on Drug Abuse: Research Monograph Series* (Monograph 86), 178–191.

Bancroft, J. (1970). A comparative study of aversion and desensitization in the treatment of homosexuality. In L. E. Burns & J. L. Worley (eds.), *Behavior therapy in the 1970's* (pp. 1–22). Bristol: John Wright & Sons.

Bancroft, J., Jones, H. G., & Pullan, B. R. (1966). A simple transducer for measuring penile erection, with comments on its use in the treatment of sexual disorders. *Behaviour Research and Therapy, 4,* 239–241.

Bandura, A. (1969). *Principles of behavior modification.* New York: Holt, Rinehart, & Winston.

Barber, J. G., Bradshaw, R., & Walsh, C. (1989). Reducing alcohol consumption through television advertising. *Journal of Consulting and Clinical Psychology, 57,* 613–618.

Barlow, D. H., & Abel, G. G. (1981). Recent developments in assessment and treatment of paraphilias and gender-identity disorder. In W. E. Craighead, A. E. Kazdin, & M. J. Mahoney (eds.), *Behavior modification: Principles, issues and applications* (2nd ed.). Boston: Houghton-Mifflin.

Barnett, A. (1985). Some distribution patterns for the Georgia death sentence. *U. C. Davis Law Review, 18,* 1327–1374.

Barton, C., Alexander, J. F., Waldron, H., Turner, C. W., & Warbuton, J. (1985).

Generalizing treatment effects of functional family therapy: Three replications. *American Journal of Family Therapy, 13,* 16–26.

Baumrind, D. (1971). Current patterns of parental authority. *Developmental Psychology, 4* (Monograph I), 1–103.

Baxstrom v. Herold, 383 U.S. 107 (1966).

Beall, H. S., & Panton, J. H. (1956). Use of the MMPI as an index to escapism. *Journal of Clinical Psychology, 12,* 392–394.

Beck, A. J., & Shipley, B. E. (1987). Recidivism of young parolees. *Bureau of Justice Statistics Special Report.* Washington, DC: Bureau of Justice Statistics.

————. (1989). Recidivism of prisoners released in 1983. *Bureau of Justice Statistics Special Report.* Washington, DC: Bureau of Justice Statistics.

Beck, A. T. (1976). *Cognitive therapy and the emotional disorders.* New York: International Universities Press.

Beck, J. L. (1981). Employment, community treatment center placement, and recidivism: A study of released federal offenders. *Federal Probation, 45,* 3–8.

Bedau, H. A. (1977). Concessions to retribution in punishment. In J. Cederblom & W. Blizek (eds.), *Justice and punishment.* Cambridge, MA: Ballinger.

————. (ed.). (1982). *The death penalty in America* (3rd ed.). New York: Oxford University Press.

Bedau, H. A., & Radelet, M. L. (1987). Miscarriages of justice in potentially capital cases. *Stanford Law Review, 40,* 21–179.

Bell, R. Q., & Harper, L. V. (1977). *Child effects on adults.* Hillsdale, NJ: Erlbaum.

Bem, D. J., & Funder, D. C. (1978). Predicting more of the people more of the time: Assessing the personality of situation. *Psychological Review, 85,* 485–501.

Benjamin, A. (1981). *The helping interview* (2nd ed.). Boston: Houghton-Mifflin.

Bennett, L. A., & Ziegler, M. (1975). Early discharge: A suggested approach to increased efficiency in parole. *Federal Probation, 39,* 27–30.

Bennett, S. F., & Lavrakas, P. J. (1989). Community-based crime prevention: An assessment of the Eisenhower Foundation's neighborhood program. *Crime and Delinquency, 35,* 345–364.

Bennett, T. (1987). *An evaluation of two neighborhood watch schemes in London.* Executive summary of final report to the Home Office Research and Planning Unit. Cambridge, England: Cambridge University, Institute of Criminology.

Bennett, T. (1989). Factors related to participation in neighborhood watch schemes. *British Journal of Criminology, 29,* 207–218.

Bennett, T., & Wright, R. (1984). *Burglars on burglary: Prevention and the offender.* Aldershot, England: Gower.

Beran, N. J., & Hotz, A. M. (1984). The behavior of mentally disordered criminals in civil mental hospitals. *Hospital and Community Psychiatry, 35,* 585–589.

Berechochea, J. E., Himelson, A. N., & Miller, D. E. (1972). The risk of failure during the early parole period: A methodological note. *Journal of Criminal Law, Criminology, and Police Sciences, 63,* 93–97.

Berk, R. A., Rauma, D., Messinger, S. L., & Cooley, T. F. (1981). A test of the stability of punishment hypothesis: The case of California, 1851–1970. *American Sociological Review, 46,* 805–829.

Berkowitz, F. J., & Hazlewood, R. A. (1973). *Delinquency control through parent education. Evolution of crime control programs in California: A review.* Sacramento, CA: California Council on Criminal Justice.

Berns, W. (1979). *For capital punishment*. New York: Basic Books.

Bernstein, I. H., Cardascia, J., & Ross, C. (1979). Defendant's sex and criminal court decisions. In R. Alvarez & K. G. Lutterman (eds.), *Discrimination in organizations* (pp. 329–354). San Francisco: Jossey-Bass.

Bernstein, I. N. (1975). Evaluation research in corrections: Status and prospects revisited. *Federal Probation*, *39*, 56–57.

Berreuta-Clement, J. R., Schweinhart, L. J., Bennett, W. S., Epstein, A. S., & Weikart, D. P. (1984). *Changed lives: The effects of the Perry Preschool Program through age 19*. Ypsilanti: High/Scope Press.

Bienin, L., Weiner, N., Denno, D., Allison, P., & Mills, D. (1988). The reimposition of capital punishment in New Jersey: The role of prosecutorial discretion. *Rutgers Law Review*, *41*, 275–372.

Birk, L., Huddleston, W., Miller, E., & Cohler, B. (1971). Avoidance conditioning for homosexuality. *Archives of General Psychiatry*, *25*, 314–323.

Bishop, D. M. (1984). Deterrence: A panel analysis. *Justice Quarterly*, *1*, 311–328.

Bishop, D. M., & Frazier, C. E. (1984). The effects of gender on charge reduction. *Sociological Quarterly*, *25*, 385–396.

Bittner, E. (1967). Police discretion in emergency apprehension of mentally ill persons. *Social Problems*, *14*, 278–292.

Black, C. L. (1981). *Capital punishment: The inevitability of caprice and mistake* (2nd ed.). New York: Norton.

Black, G. S. (1991, January). *Partnership for a Drug-Free America attitude tracking study*. Paper presented at the NIDA National Conference on Drug Abuse Research and Practice, Washington, DC.

Blackmore, J., & Welsh, J. (1983). Selective incapacitation: Sentencing according to risk. *Crime and Delinquency*, *29*, 504–528.

Blagg, H. (1985). Reparation and justice for juveniles. *British Journal of Criminology*, *25*, 267–279.

Blair, C. D., & Lanyon, R. I. (1981). Exhibitionism: Etiology and treatment. *Psychological Bulletin*, *49*, 439–463.

Blakely, C. H., Davidson, W. S., Saylor, C. A., & Robinson, M. J. (1980). Kentfields rehabilitation program: Ten years later. In R. R. Ross & P. Gendreau (eds.), *Effective correctional treatment* (pp. 321–326). Toronto: Butterworths.

Blanchard, E. B., Bassett, J. E., & Koshland, E. (1977). Psychopathy and delay of gratification. *Criminal Justice and Behavior*, *4*, 265–271.

Bluglass, R. S. (1966). *A forensic psychiatry service at HM Prison, Perth*. Unpublished manuscript.

Blumstein, A., & Cohen, J. (1979). Estimation of individual crime rates from arrest records. *Journal of Criminal Law and Criminology*, *70*, 561–585.

Blumstein, A., Cohen, J., Roth, J., & Visher, C. (eds). (1986). *Criminal careers and "career criminals."* Washington, DC: National Academy Press.

Bohm, R. M. (1987). American death penalty attitudes: A critical examination of recent evidence. *Criminal Justice and Behavior*, *14*, 380–396.

Bohm, R. M. (1989). Humanism and the death penalty, with special emphasis on the post-Furman experience. *Justice Quarterly*, *6*, 173–195.

Bohm, R. M., & Aveni, A. F. (1985, November). *Knowledge and attitude about the death penalty: A test of the Marshall hypotheses*. Paper presented at the annual meeting of the American Society of Criminology, San Diego, CA.

Bohm, R. M., Clark, L. J., & Aveni, A. F. (1990). The influence of knowledge on reasons for death penalty opinions: An experimental test. *Justice Quarterly, 7*, 175–188.

Bohn, M. J. (1980). Inmate classification and the reduction of institution violence. *Corrections Today, 42*, 48–55.

Bolton v. Harris, 395 F.2d 642 D.C. Cir. (1968).

Bolton, A. (1976). *A study of the need for the availability of mental health services for mentally disordered jail inmates and juveniles in detention facilities*. Boston: Arthur Bolton Associates (mimeo).

Bonnie, R. J., & Slobogin, C. (1980). The role of mental health professionals in the criminal process: The case for informed speculation. *Virginia Law Review, 66*, 427–522.

Bonovitz, J. C., & Bonovitz, J. S. (1981). Diversion of the mentally ill into the criminal justice system: The police intervention perspective. *American Journal of Psychiatry, 138*, 973–976.

Bonovitz, J. C., & Guy, E. B. (1979). Impact of restrictive civil commitment procedures on a prison psychiatric service. *American Journal of Psychiatry, 136*, 1045–1048.

Bonta, J., & Motiuk, L. L. (1985). Utilization of an interview-based classification instrument: A study of correctional halfway houses. *Criminal Justice and Behavior, 22*, 333–352.

Bonta, J. L., & Nanckivell, G. (1980). Institutional misconducts and anxiety levels among jailed inmates. *Criminal Justice and Behavior, 7*, 203–214.

Booth, R., & Howell, R. (1980). Classification of prison inmates with the MMPI: An extension and validation of the Megargee typology. *Criminal Justice and Behavior, 7*, 407–422.

Borkovec, T. D. (1970). Autonomic reactivity to sensory stimulation in psychopathic, neurotic, and normal juvenile delinquents. *Journal of Consulting and Clinical Psychology, 35*, 217–22.

Borzecki, M. A., & Wormith, J. S. (1985). The criminalization of psychiatrically ill people: A review with a Canadian perspective. *Psychiatric Journal of the University of Ottawa, 10*, 241–247.

———. (1987). A survey of treatment programs for sex offenders in North America. *Canadian Psychology, 28*, 30–44.

Boudouris, J., & Turnbull, B. W. (1985). Shock probation in Iowa. *Journal of Offender Counseling, Services and Rehabilitation, 9*, 53–67.

Bowers, W. J. (1984). *Legal homicide: Death as punishment in America, 1864–1982*. Boston: Northeastern University Press.

Bowers, W. J., & Pierce, G. L. (1980). Arbitrariness and discrimination under post-Furman capital statutes. *Crime and Delinquency, 26*, 563–635.

Braithwaite, J. (1979). *Inequality, crime, and public policy*. London: Routledge & Kegan Paul.

Brantingham, P. J., & Brantingham, P. L. (1975). The spatial patterning of burglary. *Howard Journal of Penology and Crime Prevention, 14*, 11–24.

———. (1982). Mobility, notoriety, and crime: A study in crime patterns of urban nodal points. *Journal of Environmental Systems, 11*, 89–99.

Breslin, J. (1990). *America's most wanted: How television catches crooks*. New York: Harper & Row.

Bridges, G. S., Crutchfield, R. D., & Simpson, E. E. (1987). Crime, social structure and criminal punishment: White and nonwhite rates of imprisonment. *Social Problems, 23*, 345–361.

Bridges, G. S., & Weis, J. G. (1989). Measuring violent behavior: Effects of study design on reported correlates of violence. In N. A. Weiner & M. E. Wolfgang (eds.), *Violent crime, violent criminals* (pp. 14–34). Newbury Park, CA: Sage.

Brill, H., & Malzberg, B. (1962). Statistical report on the arrest record of male ex-patients released from New York State mental hospitals during the period 1946–48. In *Criminal acts of ex-mental hospital patients* (Supplement No. 153). Washington, DC: American Psychiatric Association Mental Hospital Service.

Brill, W. H. (1972, May). *Security in public housing: A synergistic approach.* Paper presented at the 4th National Symposium on Law Enforcement Science and Technology, University Park, MD.

Brown, B., & Spevacek, J. (1971). Disciplinary offenses and offenders at two differing correctional facilities. *Corrective Psychiatry and Journal of Social Therapy. 17*, 48–56.

Brown, B. B., & Altman, I. (1983). Territoriality, defensible space and residential burglary: An environmental analysis. *Journal of Environmental Psychology, 3*, 203–220.

Brown, C. R. (1978). The use of benzodiazepines in prison populations. *Journal of Clinical Psychiatry, 38*, 219–222.

Brown, W. K., Miller, T. P., Jenkins, R. L., & Rhodes, W. A. (1989). The effect of early juvenile court adjudication on adult outcome. *International Journal of Offender Therapy and Comparative Criminology, 23*, 177–183.

Bry, B. H. (1982). Reducing the incidence of adolescent problems through preventive intervention: One and five year follow up. *American Journal of Community Psychology, 10*, 265–275.

Buchanan, R. A., Whitlow, K. L., & Austin, J. (1986). National evaluation of objective prison classification systems: The current state of the art. *Crime and Delinquency, 32*, 272–290.

Buck, J. A., & Graham, J. R. (1978). The *4-3* MMPI profile type: A failure to replicate. *Journal of Consulting and Clinical Psychology, 46*, 344.

Buckner, J. C., & Chesney-Lind, M. (1983). Dramatic cures for juvenile crime: An evaluation of a prison-run delinquency prevention program. *Criminal Justice and Behavior, 10*, 227–247.

Bukatman, H. A., Foy, J. L., & DeGrazia, E. (1971). What is competency to stand trial? *American Journal of Psychiatry, 127*, 1225–1229.

Bureau of Justice Statistics. (1983a). *Prisoners and alcohol.* Washington, DC: Author.

———. (1983b). *Prisoners and drugs.* Washington, DC: Author.

———. (1984a). *Bulletin: The severity of crime.* Washington, DC: Author.

———. (1984b). *Probation and parole 1983.* Washington, DC: Author.

———. (1985). *Victimization risk supplement to the National Crime Survey.* Washington, DC: Author.

———. (1986). *State and federal prisoners, 1925–1985.* Washington, DC: Author.

———. (1989). *Correctional populations in the United States 1987.* Washington, DC: Author.

———. (1990). *Capital punishment 1989.* Washington, DC: Author.

Butcher, J. N., Dahlstrom, W. G., Graham, J. R., Tellegen, A., & Kaemmer, B. (1989). *Minnesota Multiphasic Personality Inventory–2 (MMPI–2): Manual for administration and scoring.* Minneapolis: University of Minnesota Press.

Butcher, J. N., & Tellegen, A. (1978). Common methodological problems in MMPI research. *Journal of Consulting and Clinical Psychology*, *46*, 620–628.

Byles, J. A., & Maurice, A. (1982). The juvenile services project. *Canadian Journal of Criminology*, *24*, 155–165.

Byrne, J. M., & Kelly, L. (1989). *Restructuring probation as an intermediate sanction: An evaluation of the Massachusetts intensive probation supervision program.* Final report to the National Institute of Justice, U.S. Department of Justice Research Program on the Punishment and Control of Offenders. Washington, DC: National Institute of Justice.

Cahalan, M. W. (1986). *Historical corrections statistics in the United States 1850–1984.* Washington, DC: Bureau of Justice Statistics.

Caldwell, R. G. (1944). The deterrent influence of corporal punishment upon prisoners who have been whipped. *American Sociological Review*, *9*, 171–177.

Callison, H. (1989). *Zephyr products: A story of an inmate-staffed business.* College Park, MD: American Correctional Association.

Camp, B. W. (1977). Verbal mediation in young aggressive boys. *Journal of Abnormal Psychology*, *86*, 145–153.

Camp, C. G., & Camp, G. M. (1984). *Private sector involvement in prison services and operations.* Washington, DC: National Institute of Corrections.

Camp, G. M., & Camp, C. G. (1988). *The corrections yearbook: 1988.* South Salem, NY: Criminal Justice Institute.

Campbell, D. T., & Stanley, J. C. (1966). *Experimental and quasi-experimental designs for research.* Chicago: Rand McNally.

Campbell, M., Small, A. M., Green, W. H., Jennings, S. J., Perry, R., Bennett, W. G., & Anderson, L. (1984). Behavioral efficacy of haloperidol and lithium carbonate. *Archives of General Psychiatry*, *41*, 650–656.

Carbonell, J. L., Megargee, E. I., & Moorhead, K. M. (1984). Predicting prison adjustment with structured personality inventories. *Journal of Consulting and Clinical Psychology*, *52*, 280–294.

Carey, R. J., Garske, J. P., & Ginsberg, J. (1986). The prediction of adjustment to prison by means of an MMPI-based classification system. *Criminal Justice and Behavior*, *13*, 347–365.

Carlson, K. A. (1982). *Manual for the Carlson Psychological Survey.* Port Huron, MI: Research Psychologists Press.

———. (1990). 1989 survey of psychological testing practices in prisons. *Correctional Psychologist*, *22*, 9–11.

Carr, T. W. (1980). *The effects of crowding on recidivism, cardiovascular deaths and infraction rates in a large prison system.* Unpublished doctoral dissertation, University of Michigan.

Carroll, J. (1980). Judgements of recidivism risk: The use of base-rate information in parole decisions. In P. Lipsitt & B. Sales (eds.), *New directions in psycholegal research* (pp. 68–86). New York: Van Nostrand.

Carson, R. C. (1969). Interpretive manual to the MMPI. In J. N. Butcher (ed.), *MMPI: Research developments and clinical applications* (pp. 279–296). New York: McGraw-Hill.

Carter, S. A., & Humphries, A. C. (1987). Inmates build prisons in South Carolina. *National Institute of Justice: Construction Bulletin.* Washington, DC: National Institute of Justice.

Cartwright, D. S. (1974). *Introduction to personality.* Chicago: Rand McNally.

Cassady, J. (1978). *The use of the MMPI for classification in a local county jail.* Unpublished manuscript.

Cautela, J. R. (1967). Covert sensitization. *Psychological Record, 20,* 459–468.

Cavender, G. (1984). Justice, sanctioning, and the justice model. *Criminology, 22,* 203–213.

Cedar Rapids (Iowa) Police Department. (1972). *Evaluation of the effects of a large-scale burglar alarm system.* Cedar Rapids: Prepared for Law Enforcement Assistance Administration, National Institute of Law Enforcement and Criminal Justice.

Chaiken, J., & Chaiken, M. (1982). *Varieties of criminal behavior.* Santa Monica, CA: Rand Corporation.

Chaiken, M. (1989). In-prison programs for drug involved offenders. *NIJ Issues and Practices Report.* Washington, DC: U.S. Government Printing Office.

Chaiken, M., & Chaiken, J. (1984). Offender types and public policy. *Crime and Delinquency, 30,* 195–226.

Chandler, C. L., Weissberg, R. P., Cowen, E. L., & Guare, J. (1984). Long-term effects of a school-based secondary prevention program for young maladapting children. *Journal of Consulting and Clinical Psychology, 52,* 165–170.

Chandler, M. J. (1973). Egocentrism and anti-social behavior: The assessment and training of social perspective-taking skills. *Developmental Psychology, 9,* 326–332.

Chapman, L. J., & Chapman, J. P. (1969). Illusory correlation as an obstacle to the use of valid psychodiagnostic signs. *Journal of Abnormal Psychology, 74,* 271–280.

Chellsen, J. A. (1986). Trial competency among mentally retarded offenders: Assessment techniques and related considerations. *Journal of Psychiatry and Law, 14,* 177–185.

Chiricos, T., & Waldo, G. (1970). Punishment and crime: An examination of some empirical evidence. *Social Problems, 18,* 200–217.

Churchill, W. (1966). *The struggle for survival, 1940–1945* (taken from the diaries of Lord Moran). Boston: Houghton-Mifflin.

Cikins, W. I. (1986). Privatization of the American prison system: An idea whose time has come? *Journal of Law, Ethics, and Public Policy, 2,* 445–464.

Cirel, P., Evans, P., McGillis, D., & Whitcomb, D. (1977). *Community crime prevention program: Seattle, Washington.* Washington, DC: National Institute of Justice.

Clanon, T. L., & Jew, C. (1985). Predictions from assessments of violent offenders under stress: A fifteen-year experience. *Criminal Justice and Behavior, 12,* 485–499.

Clark, J. H. (1948). Application of the MMPI in differentiating AWOL recidivists from non-recidivists. *Journal of Psychology, 26,* 229–234.

Clarke, R.V.G. (ed.). (1978). *Tackling vandalism.* Home Office Research Study No. 47. London: HMSO.

———. (1983). Situational crime prevention: Its theoretical basis and practical scope. In M. Tonry & N. Morris (eds.), *Crime and justice: An annual review of research* (Vol. 4, pp. 225–256). Chicago: University of Chicago Press.

Clarke, R.V.G., & Hough, J. M. (eds.) (1980). *The effectiveness of policing.* Farnborough: Gower.

Clarke, S. (1974). Getting 'em out of circulation: Does incarceration of juvenile offenders reduce crime? *Journal of Criminal Law and Enforcement, 65,* 528–535.

Clear, T. R., & Gallagher, K. W. (1983). Screening devices in probation and parole: Management problems. *Evaluation Review*, 7, 217–234.

Cleckley, H. (1976). *The mask of sanity* (5th ed.). St. Louis: Mosby.

Clements, C. B. (1980). Offender classification: Problems and prospects for correctional management. *Prison Law Monitor*, 2, 237–242.

Cloninger, C. R. (1987). Pharmacological approaches to the treatment of antisocial behavior. In S. A. Mednick, T. E., Moffitt, & S. A. Stack (eds.), *The causes of crime: New biological approaches* (pp. 329–349). New York: Cambridge University Press.

Cloninger, C. R., & Guze, S. B. (1970). Psychiatric illness and female criminality: The role of sociopathy and hysteria in the antisocial woman. *American Journal of Psychiatry*, 127, 303–311.

————. (1973). Psychiatric disorders and criminal recidivism: A follow-up study of female criminals. *Archives of General Psychiatry*, 29, 266–269.

Cloninger, D. O. (1977). Deterrence and the death penalty: A cross-sectional analysis. *Journal of Behavioral Economics*, 6, 87–106.

Clopton, J. R., & Neuringer, C. (1977). MMPI Cannot Say scores: Normative data and degree of profile distortion. *Journal of Personality Assessment*, 41, 511–513.

Cocozza, J. J. (1973). Dangerousness. *Psychiatric News* (August 15, 1973).

Cocozza, J. J., & Steadman, H. J. (1974). Some refinements in measurement and prediction of dangerous behavior. *American Journal of Psychiatry*, 131, 1012–1014.

Cocozza, J. J., & Steadman, H. J. (1978). Prediction in psychiatry: An example of misplaced confidence in experts. *Social Problems*, 25, 265–276.

Cohen, B-Z., & Sordo, I. (1984). Using reality therapy with adult offenders. *Journal of Offender Counseling, Services and Rehabilitation*, 8, 25–39.

Cohen, J. (1982). *Patterns of adult offending*. Umpublished doctoral dissertation, Carnegie-mellon University.

————. (1983). Incapacitation as a strategy for crime control: Possibilities and pitfalls. In M. Tonry & N. Morris (eds.), *Crime and justice: An annual review of research* (Vol. 5, pp. 1–84). Chicago: University of Chicago Press.

————. (1984, November). *Categorical incapacitation effects: Empirical issues*. Paper presented at the 1984 meeting of the American Society of Criminology, Cincinnati, OH.

————. (1985). *Empirical estimates of the incapacitative effect of imprisonment*. Paper presented at the annual meeting of the American Association for the Advancement of Science, Los Angeles, CA.

Cohen, L., & Freeman, H. (1945). How dangerous to the community are state hospital patients? *Connecticut State Medical Journal*, 9, 697–700.

Coker v. Georgia, 433 U.S. 584 (1977).

Coleman, R. P., & Neugarten, B. L. (1971). *Social status in the city*. San Francisco: Jossey-Bass.

Comstock, G. A. (1980). *Television in America*. Beverly Hills, CA: Sage.

Conrad, S. R., & Wincze, J. P. (1976). Orgasmic reconditioning: A controlled study of its effect upon the sexual arousal of adult male homosexuals. *Behavior Therapy*, 7, 155–166.

Cooke, G. (1969). The court study unit: Patient characteristics and differences between patients judged competent and incompetent. *Journal of Clinical Psychology*, 25, 140–143.

Cooke, G., Johnston, N., & Pogany, E. (1973). Factors affecting referral to determine competency to stand trial. *American Journal of Psychiatry*, *130*, 870–875.

Cooke, G., & Sikorski, C. R. (1975). Factors affecting length of hospitalization in person adjudicated not guilty by reason of insanity. *Bulletin of the American Academy of Psychiatry and the Law*, *11*, 251–261.

Cooper, R. P., & Werner, P. D. (1990). Predicting violence in newly admitted inmates: A lens model analysis of staff decision making. *Criminal Justice and Behavior*, *17*, 431–447.

Cooper, S. H., Perry, J. C., & Arnow, D. (1988). An empirical approach to the study of defense mechanisms: I. Reliability and preliminary validity of the Rorschach defense scales. *Journal of Personality Assessment*, *52*, 187–203.

Cordner, G. W. (1986). Fear of crime and the police: An evaluation of a fear-reducing strategy. *Journal of Police Science and Administration*, *14*, 223–233.

Cornish, D. B., & Clarke, R.V.G. (1975). *Residential treatment and its effect on delinquency*. Home Office Research Study No. 32. London: HMSO.

Costello, R. M., Fine, H. J., & Blau, B. I. (1973). Racial comparisons on the MMPI. *Journal of Clinical Psychology*, *29*, 63–65.

Cowden, J. E., Schroeder, C. R., & Peterson, W. M. (1971). The CPI vs. the 16PF at the reception center for delinquent boys. *Journal of Clinical Psychology*, *27*, 109–111.

Cressey, D. R. (1958). The nature and effectiveness of correctional techniques. *Law and Contemporary Problems*, *23*, 754–771.

Criminal Justice Newsletter. (1988, March). *Lower recidivism rate cited for youths sent to 'Vision Quest,'* pp. 5–6.

Criss, M. L., & Racine, D. R. (1981). Impact of change in legal standard for those adjudicated not guilty by reason of insanity, 1975–1979. *Bulletin of the American Academy of Psychiatry and the Law*, *8*, 261–271.

Cronbach, L. J. (1970). *Essentials of psychological testing* (3rd ed.). New York: Harper & Row.

Cross, D. T., Barclay, A., & Burger, G. K. (1968). Differential effects of ethnic membership, sex, and occupation on the California Psychological Inventory. *Journal of Personality Assessment*, *42*, 597–603.

Crouch, B. M., & Alpert, G. P. (1982). Sex and occupational socialization among prison guards: A longitudinal study. *Criminal Justice and Behavior*, *9*, 159–176.

Cubitt, G. H., & Gendreau, P. (1972). Assessing the diagnostic utility of the MMPI and 16PF indexes of homosexuality in a prison sample. *Journal of Consulting and Clinical Psychology*, *39*, 342.

Cullen, F. T., Clark, G. A., Cullen, J. B., & Mathers, R. A. (1985). Attribution, salience, and attitudes toward criminal sanctioning. *Criminal Justice and Behavior*, *12*, 305–331.

Cullen, F. T., Clark, G. A., & Wozniak, J. F. (1985). Explaining the get tough movement: Can the public be blamed? *Federal Probation*, *49*, 16–24.

Cullen, F. T., Cullen, J. B., & Wozniak, J. F. (1988). Is rehabilitation dead: The myth of the punitive public. *Journal of Criminal Justice*, *16*, 303–317.

Cullen, F. T., & Gendreau, P. (1989). The effectiveness of correctional rehabilitation: Reconsidering the "nothing works" debate. In L. Goodstein, & D. L. MacKenzie (eds.), *The American prison* (pp. 23–43). New York: Plenum.

Cullen, F. T., & Gilbert, K. E. (1982). *Reaffirming rehabilitation*. Cincinnati: Anderson.

Cullen, F. T., Lutze, F. E., Link, B. G., & Wolfe, N. T. (1989). The correctional orientation of prison guards: Do officers support rehabilitation? *Federal Probation*, *53*, 33–42.

Cullen, F. T., Skovron, S. E., Scott, J. E., & Burton, V. S. (1990). Public support for correctional treatment: The tenacity of rehabilitative ideology. *Criminal Justice and Behavior*, *17*, 6–18.

Cunningham, W. C., & Taylor, T. H. (1985). *The Hallcrest Report: Private security and police in America*. Portland, OR: Chancellor.

Curtis, L. A. (ed.). (1985). *American violence and public policy*. New Haven, CT: Yale University Press.

———. (1987). The retreat of folly: Some modest replications of inner-city success. *Annals*, *494*, 71–89.

Curtiss, G., Feczko, M. D., & Marohn, R. C. (1979). Rorschach differences in normal and delinquent white male adolescents: A discriminant function analysis. *Journal of Youth and Adolescence*, *8*, 379–392.

Cusson, M., & Pinsonneault, H. P. (1986). The decision to give up crime. In D. B. Cornish & R. V. Clarke (eds.), *The reasoning criminal: Rational choice perspectives on offending* (pp. 72–82). New York: Springer-Verlag.

Czudner, G. (1985). Changing the criminal. *Federal Probation*, *49*, 64–66.

Dahlstrom, W. G., Panton, J. H., Bain, K. P., & Dahlstrom, L. E. (1986). Utility of the Megargee-Bohn MMPI typological assignments: Study with a sample of death row inmates. *Criminal Justice and Behavior*, *13*, 5–17.

Dahlstrom, W. G., Welsh, G. S., & Dahlstrom, L. E. (1972). *An MMPI handbook, Volume I: Clinical interpretation* (rev. ed.). Minneapolis: University of Minnesota Press.

———. (1975). *An MMPI handbook, Volume II: Research applications*. Minneapolis: University of Minnesota Press.

Danesh, Y. (1989). Baton Rouge ex-offender's clearing house: A casualty of misguided savings. *International Journal of Offender Therapy and Comparative Criminology*, *33*, 207–214.

Dann, R. H. (1935). The deterrent effect of capital punishment. *Friends Social Services*, *29*, 1–20.

Davidson, P. R. (1984). *Behavioral treatment for incarcerated sex offenders: Post-release outcome*. Unpublished manuscript, Kingston Penitentiary, Kingston, Ontario.

Davidson, W. D., & Robinson, M. J. (1975). Community psychology and behavior modification: A community-based program for the prevention of delinquency. *Corrective and Social Psychiatry*, *21*, 11–12.

Davidson, W. S., Gottschalk, R., Gensheimer, L., & Mayer, J. (1984). *Interventions with juvenile delinquents: A meta-analysis of treatment efficacy*. Washington, DC: National Institute of Juvenile Justice and Delinquency Prevention.

Davis, K. R., & Sines, J. O. (1971). An antisocial behavior pattern associated with a specific MMPI profile. *Journal of Consulting and Clinical Psychology*, *36*, 229–234.

Davison, G. C. (1968). Elimination of a sadistic fantasy by a client-controlled counter conditioning technique. *Journal of Abnormal Psychology*, *73*, 84–90.

Dean, D. G. (1983). The impact of a juvenile awareness program on select personality traits of male clients. *Journal of Offender Counseling, Services and Rehabilitation*, *6*, 73–85.

Decker, S. H., & Salert, B. (1986). Predicting the career criminal: An empirical test of the Greenwood scale. *Journal of Criminal Law and Criminology*, 77, 215–236.

Deiker, T. E. (1974). A cross-validation of MMPI scales of aggression on male criminal criterion groups. *Journal of Consulting and Clinical Psychology*, 42, 196–202.

DeJong, W., Morris, W., & Hastorf, A. (1976). Effect of an escaped accomplice on the punishment assigned to a criminal defendant. *Journal of Personality and Social Psychology*, 33, 192–198.

Dell, S. (1980). Transfer of special hospital patients to the NHS. *British Journal of Psychiatry*, 136, 222–234.

DeLeon, G. (1984). *The therapeutic community: Study of effectiveness*. Treatment Research Monograph Series, National Institute on Drug Abuse, Washington, DC.

———. (1988). Legal pressure in therapeutic communities. *National Institute on Drug Abuse: Research Monograph Series* (Monograph 86), 160–177.

DeLeon, G., Wexler, H. K., & Jainchill, N. (1982). The therapeutic community: Success and improvement rates 5 years after treatment. *International Journal of the Addictions*, 17, 703–747.

DeLong, C. F. (1978). *Changes in prisoner perceptions of control over life decisions as a result of learning decision-making skills*. Unpublished doctoral dissertation, Temple University (Microfilm No. 7817295).

Dershowitz, A. M. (1973). Abolishing the insanity defense: The most significant feature of the administration's proposed criminal code—An essay. *Criminal Law Bulletin*, 9, 434–439.

Des Jarlais, D., & Hunt, D. E. (1988). AIDS and intravenous drug use. *National Institute of Justice: AIDS Bulletin*. Washington, DC: National Institute of Justice.

DeWitt, C. B. (1986). Ohio's new approach to prison and jail financing. *National Institute of Justice: Construction Bulletin*. Washington, DC: National Institute of Justice.

DiFrancesca, K. R., & Meloy, J. R. (1989). A comparative clinical investigation of the "How" and "Charlie" MMPI subtypes. *Journal of Personality Assessment*, 53, 396–403.

DiIulio, J. J. (1988). Private prisons. *National Institute of Justice: Crime File*. Washington, DC: National Institute of Justice.

Dixon, D. J. (1986). On the criminal mind: An imaginary lecture by Sigmund Freud. *International Journal of Offender Therapy and Comparative Criminology*, 30, 101–109.

Doctor, R. M., & Polakow, R. L. (1973, August). *A behavior modification program for adult probationers*. Paper presented at the annual meeting of the American Psychological Association.

Dole, V. P., & Joseph H. (1978). Long-term outcome of patients treated with methadone maintenance. *Annals of the New York Academy of Science*, 311, 181–189.

Donovan, E. J., & Walsh, W. F. (1986). *An evaluation of Starrett City Security Services*. Research project conducted by the Pennsylvania State University.

Doren, D. M., Megargee, E. I., & Schreiber, H. (1980). The MMPI criminal classification system's applicability to a juvenile population. *Differential View*, 10, 42–46.

Douds, A. F., Engelsjord, M., & Collingwood, T. R. (1977). Behavior contracting with youthful offenders and their parents. *Child Welfare*, 56, 409–417.

Dougher, M. J. (1988). Clinical assessment of sex offenders. In B. K. Schwartz (ed.), *A practitioner's guide to treating the incarcerated male sex offender* (pp. 77–84). Washington, DC: National Institute of Corrections.

Draguns, J., Haley, E., & Phillips, L. (1967). Studies of Rorschach content: A review of the research, Part I: Traditional content categories. *Journal of Projective Techniques and Personality Assessment, 13*, 247–284.

Driscoll, P. J. (1952). Factors related to the institutional adjustment of prison inmates. *Journal of Abnormal and Social Psychology, 47*, 593–596.

DuBow, F., & Podolefsky, A. (1982). Citizen participation in community crime prevention. *Human Organization, 414*, 307–314.

Duffee, D. E., & Ritti, R. R. (1977). Correctional policy and public values. *Criminology, 14*, 449–459.

Dunham, H. W., Phillips, P., & Srinivasan, B. (1966). A research note on diagnosed mental illness and social class. *American Sociological Review, 31*, 223–227.

Durbin, J. R., Pasewark, R. A., & Albers, D. (1977). Criminality and mental illness: A study of arrest rates in a rural state. *American Journal of Psychiatry, 134*, 80–83.

Durham v. United States, 214 F.2d 862, 876 (D.C. Cir. 1954).

Durham, A. M. (1989). Origins of interest in privatization of punishment: The nineteenth and twentieth century American experience. *Criminology, 27*, 107–139.

Dusky v. United States, 363 U.S. 402 (1960).

Dy, A. J. (1974). Correctional psychiatry and phase psychotherapy. *American Journal of Psychiatry, 131*, 1150–1152.

D'Zurilla, T. J., & Goldfried, M. R. (1971). Problem-solving and behavior modification. *Journal of Abnormal Psychology, 78*, 107–126.

Eck, J. E. (1982). *Solving crimes: The investigation of burglary and robbery.* Washington, DC: Police Executive Research Forum.

Eck, J. E., & Spelman, W. (1987). *Problem solving: Problem-oriented policing in Newport News.* Washington, DC: Police Executive Research Forum.

Edinger, J. D. (1979). Cross-validation of the Megargee MMPI typology for prisoners. *Journal of Consulting and Clinical Psychology, 47*, 234–242.

Edinger, J. D., Reuterfors, D., & Logue, P. E. (1982). Cross-validation of the Megargee MMPI typology: A study of specialized inmate populations. *Criminal Justice and Behavior, 9*, 184–203.

Edwards, A. L., & Diers, C. J. (1962). Social desirability and the factual interpretation of the MMPI. *Educational and Psychological Measurement, 22*, 501–509.

Eglash, A. (1975). Creative restitution: A broader meaning of an old term. *Journal of Criminal Law, Criminology, and Police Science, 48*, 284–290.

Ehrlich, I. (1975). The deterrent effect of capital punishment: A question of life or death. *American Economic Review, 65*, 397–417.

———. (1977). Capital punishment and deterrence: Some further thoughts and additional evidence. *Journal of Political Economy, 85*, 741–788.

Ekland-Olson, S., Barrick, D., & Cohen, L. E. (1983). Prison overcrowding and disciplinary problems: An analysis of the Texas prison system. *Journal of Applied Behavioral Science, 19*, 163–176.

Elion, V. H. (1974). The validity of the MMPI as a discriminator of social deviance among black males. *FCI Research Reports, 6*, 1–18.

Elizur, A. (1949). Content analysis of the Rorschach with regard to anxiety and hostility. *Rorschach Research Exchange and Journal of Projective Techniques, 13*, 247–284.

Elliott, D. S., & Voss, H. (1974). *Delinquency and dropout*. Lexington, MA: D. C. Heath.

Ellis, A. (1962). *Reason and emotion in psychotherapy*. New York: Lyle Stuart.

Ellis, D. (1984). Crowding and prison violence: Integration of research and theory. *Criminal Justice and Behavior, 11*, 277–308.

Ellsworth, P. C., & Ross, L. (1983). Public opinion and capital punishment: A close examination of the views of abolitionists and retentionists. *Crime and Delinquency, 29*, 116–169.

Elvin, J. (1985). A civil liberties view of private prisons. *The Prison Journal, 65*, 48–52.

Empey, L. T., & Erickson, M. L. (1972). *The Provo experiment: Evaluating community control of delinquency*. Washington, DC: D. C. Heath.

Emshoff, J. G., & Davidson, W. S. (1987). The effect of "good time" credit on inmate behavior: A quasi-experiment. *Criminal Justice and Behavior, 14*, 335–351.

Endicott, J., & Spitzer, R. (1978). A diagnostic interview: Schedule for Affective Disorders and Schizophrenia. *Archives of General Psychiatry, 35*, 837–844.

Englander-Golden, P. (1983). *Say it straight*. Norman, OK: Golden Communication Books.

Englander-Golden, P., Elconin, J., & Satir, V. (1986). Assertive/leveling communication and empathy in adolescent drug abuse prevention. *Journal of Primary Prevention, 6*, 219–230.

Englander-Golden, P., Jackson, J. C., Crane, K., Schwarzkopf, A. B., & Lyle, P. S. (1989). Communication skills and self-esteem in prevention of destructive behavior. *Adolescence, 24*, 481–502.

Engstad, P., & Evans, J. L. (1980). Responsibility, competence, and police effectiveness in crime control. In R.V.G. Clarke and J. M. Hough (eds.), *The effectiveness of policing* (pp. 139–162). Farnborough: Gower.

Enyon, T., Allen, H., & Reckless, W. (1971). Measuring the impact of a juvenile correctional institution by perceptions of inmates and staff. *Journal of Research in Crime and Delinquency, 8*, 93–107.

Erickson, M. L., & Gibbs, J. P. (1978). Objective and perceptual properties of legal punishment and the deterrence doctrine. *Social Problems, 25*, 253–263.

Erickson, P. G. (1976). Deterrence and deviance: The example of Canadian prohibition. *Journal of Criminal Law and Criminology, 67*, 222–232.

Erickson, W. D., Luxenberg, M. G., Walbek, N. H., & Seeley, R. K. (1987). Frequency of MMPI two-point code types among sex offenders. *Journal of Consulting and Clinical Psychology, 55*, 566–570.

Erikson, R. V., & Roberts, A. H. (1966). An MMPI comparison of two groups of institutionalized delinquents. *Journal of Projective Techniques and Personality Assessment, 30*, 163–166.

Erwin, B. S. (1986). Turning up the heat on probationers in Georgia. *Federal Probation, 50*, 17–24.

Erwin, B. S., & Bennett, L. A. (1987). New dimensions in probation: Georgia's experience with intensive probation supervision (IPS). *National Institute of Justice: Research in Brief*. Washington, DC: National Institute of Justice.

Espy, M. W. (1985). Personal communication (cited in Bohm, 1989).

Esses, V. M., & Webster, C. D. (1986). *Physical attractiveness, dangerousness, and the Canadian criminal code*. Unpublished manuscript, Clarke Institute of Psychiatry and the University of Toronto.

Evans, C., & McConnell, T. R. (1941). A new measure of introversion-extroversion. *Journal of Psychology*, *12*, 111–124.

Evans, D. R. (1967). An exploratory study into the treatment of exhibitionism by means of emotive imagery and aversive conditioning. *Canadian Psychologist*, *8*, 162.

Evans, R. M., & Picano, J. J. (1984). Relationship between irrational beliefs and self-reported indices of psychopathology. *Psychological Reports*, *55*, 545–546.

Exner, J. E. (1974). *The Rorschach: A comprehensive system, Volume 1*. New York: John Wiley.

Exner, J. E., & Weiner, I. B. (1982). *The Rorschach: A comprehensive system, Volume 3: Assessment of children and adolescents*. New York: John Wiley.

Fagan, J. (1990). Social and legal policy dimensions of violent juvenile crime. *Criminal Justice and Behavior*, *17*, 93–133.

Fallen, D. L., Apperson, C., Hall-Milligan, J., & Aos, S. (1981). *Intensive parole supervision*. Olympia, WA: Department of Social and Health Services.

Farr, K. A. (1990). Revitalizing the drug decriminalization debate. *Crime and Delinquency*, *36*, 223–237.

Farrington, D. P. (1979). Longitudinal research on crime and delinquency. In N. Morris & M. Tonry (eds.), *Crime and justice: An Annual review of research* (Vol. 1, pp. 289–348). Chicago: University of Chicago Press.

Fattah, D. (1987). The House of Umoja as a case study for social justice. *Annals*, *494*, 37–41.

Faulk, M. (1976). A psychiatric study of men serving a sentence in Winchester Prison. *Medicine, Science, and the Law*, *16*, 244–251.

Faupel, C. E. (1981). Drug treatment and criminality: Methodological and theoretical considerations. In J. A. Inciardi (ed.), *The drug-crime connection* (pp. 183–206). Beverly Hills, CA: Sage.

Feldman, M. P., & MacCulloch, M. J. (1971). *Homosexual behavior: Therapy and assessment*. New York: Pergamon.

Felson, R. B., Ribner, S. A., & Siegel, M. S. (1984). Age and the effect of third parties during criminal violence. *Sociology and Social Research*, *68*, 452–462.

Felson, R. B., & Steadman, H. J. (1983). Situational factors in disputes leading to criminal violence. *Criminology*, *21*, 59–74.

Felthous, A. R. (1981). Childhood cruelty to cats, dogs, and other animals. *Bulletin of the American Academy of Psychiatry and the Law*, *9*, 48–53.

Felthous, A. R., & Bernard, H. (1979). Enuresis, firesetting and cruelty to animals: The significance of two-thirds of this triad. *Journal of Forensic Science*, *24*, 240–246.

Felthous, A. R., & Kellert, S. R. (1986). Violence against animals and people: Is aggression against living creatures generalized? *Bulletin of the American Academy of Psychiatry and the Law*, *14*, 55–69.

Fenelon, J. R., & Megargee, E. I. (1971). Influence of race on the manifestation of leadership. *Journal of Applied Psychology*, *55*, 353–358.

Field, G. (1989). The effects of intensive treatment on reducing the criminal recidivism of addicted offenders. *Federal Probation*, *53*, 51–56.

Figgie Corporation. (1988). *The Figgie report, Part VI. The business of crime: The criminal perspective*. Richmond, VA: Author.

Figuera-McDonough, J. (1985). Gender differences in informal processing: A look at charge bargaining and sentence reduction in Washington, DC. *Journal of Research in Crime and Delinquency*, *22*, 101–133.

Finckenauer, J. (1982). *Scared Straight! and the panacea phenomenon*. Englewood Cliffs, NJ: Prentice-Hall.

Fischer, B. S. (1988). *Participating democracy in action: Crime prevention activities*. Unpublished doctoral dissertation, Northwestern University.

Fish, B., & Bruhnsen, K. (1978/1979). The impact of legal sanctions on illicit drug selling. *Drug Forum*, *7*, 239–258.

Flanagan, J. C., & Lewis, G. (1974). First prison admissions with juvenile histories and absolute first offenders: Frequencies and MMPI profiles. *Journal of Clinical Psychology*, *30*, 358–360.

Flanagan, T. J. (1982). Risk and the timing of recidivism in three cohorts of prison releasees. *Criminal Justice Review*, *7*, 34–45.

———. (1983). Correlates of institutional misconduct among state prisoners: A research note. *Criminology*, *21*, 29–39.

Flanagan, T. J., & Caulfield, S. L. (1984). Public opinion and prison policy: A review. *Prison Journal*, *64*, 31–46.

Florida Department of Corrections. (1989). *Research report, boot camp evaluation*. Tallahassee, FL: Bureau of Planning, Research, and Statistics.

Fo, W.S.O., & O'Donnell, C. R. (1975). The buddy system: Relationship and contingency conditions in a community intervention program for youth with nonprofessionals as behavior change agents. *Journal of Consulting and Clinical Psychology*, *42*, 163–169.

Ford v. Wainwright, 477 U.S. 399 (1986).

Forgac, G. E., & Michaels, E. J. (1982). Personality characteristics of two types of male exhibitionists. *Journal of Abnormal Psychology*, *9*, 287–293.

Forst, B. E. (1977). The deterrent effect of capital punishment: A cross-state analysis of the 1960s. *Minnesota Law Review*, *61*, 743–767.

Forst, B., Rhodes, W., Dimm, J., Gelman, A., & Mullin, B. (1983). Targeting federal resources on recidivists: An empirical view. *Federal Probation*, *46*, 10–20.

Forth, A. E., Hart, S. D., & Hare, R. D. (1990). Assessment of psychopathy in male young offenders. *Psychological Assessment: A Journal of Consulting and Clinical Psychology*, *2*, 342–344.

Frank, L. K. (1939). Projective methods for the study of personality. *Journal of Psychology*, *8*, 389–413.

Frazier, C., & Cochran, J. (1986). Official intervention, diversion from the juvenile justice system, and dynamics of human service work: Effects of a reform goal, based on labeling theory. *Crime and Delinquency*, *32*, 157–176.

Freedman, A. M., Warren, M. M., Cunningham, L. W., & Blackwell, S. J. (1988). Cosmetic surgery and criminal rehabilitation. *Southern Medical Journal*, *81*, 1113–1116.

Freeman, R. A., & Mason, H. M. (1952). Construction of a key to determine recidivists from non-recidivists using the MMPI. *Journal of Clinical Psychology*, *8*, 207–208.

Friburg, R. R. (1967). Measures of homosexuality: Cross-validation of two MMPI scales and implications for usage. *Journal of Consulting Psychology*, *31*, 88–91.

Friedrichs, D. O. (1989). Comment—Humanism and the death penalty: An alternative perspective. *Justice Quarterly*, *6*, 197–209.

Funkunaga, K. K., Pasewark, R. A., Hawkins, M., & Gudeman, H. (1981). Insanity plea: Interexaminer agreement and concordance of psychiatric opinion and court verdict. *Law and Human Behavior*, *5*, 325–328.

Furman v. Georgia, 408 U.S. 238 (1972).

Furstenberg, F. F., & Wellford, C. F. (1973). Calling the police: The evaluation of police service. *Law and Society Review, 7*, 393–406.

Gaes, G. G., & McGuire, W. J. (1985). Prison violence: The contribution of crowding versus other determinants of prison assault rates. *Journal of Research in Crime and Delinquency, 22*, 41–65.

Galaway, B., & Hudson, J. (1980). Restitution as a victim service. *Evaluation and Change*, 116–119.

Gallup, G., & Gallup, A. (1988). Public support for death penalty is highest in Gallup annals. *Los Angeles Times.*

Gallup Report. (1985). *The death penalty.* Princeton, NJ: Author.

Gallup Report. (1986). *The death penalty.* Princeton, NJ: Author.

Ganzer, V. J., & Sarason, I. G. (1973). Variables associated with recidivism among juvenile delinquents. *Journal of Consulting and Clinical Psychology, 41*, 1–5.

Gardner, M. (1976). The renaissance of retribution—An examination of "Doing Justice." *Wisconsin Law Review*, 781–815.

Garofalo, J. (1977). *Victimization and the fear of crime in major American cities.* Paper presented at the annual meeting of the American Association for Public Opinion Research, Buck Hills Falls, PA.

Garofalo, J., & McLeod, M. (1989). The structure and operations of neighborhood watch programs in the United States. *Crime and Delinquency, 35*, 326–344.

Garfinkle, H. (1949). Research note on inter- and intra-racial homicides. *Social Forces, 27*, 369–381.

Garrett, C. J. (1985). Effects of residual treatment on adjudicated delinquents: A meta-analysis. *Journal of Research in Crime and Delinquency, 22*, 287–308.

Garvin, L. M., & Goldstein, A. P. (1990, March). *Criminal thinking patterns: The relationship between errors in thinking and antisocial behavior.* Paper presented at the American-Psychology Law Society mid-year conference, Williamsburg, VA.

Gearhart, J. W., Keith, H. L., & Clemmons, G. (1967). *An analysis of the vocational training program in the Washington state adult correctional institution.* Research Review No. 23. State of Washington, Department of Institutions.

Gearing, M., Heckel, R., & Matthey, W. (1980). The screening and referral of mentally disordered inmates in a state correctional system. *Professional Psychology, 11*, 849–854.

Gendreau, P., Madden, P. G., & Leipciger, M. (1980). Predicting recidivism with social history information and a comparison of their predictive power with psychometric variables. *Canadian Journal of Criminology, 22*, 328–336.

Gendreau, P., & Ross, R. R. (1979). Effective correctional treatment: Bibliotherapy for cynics. *Crime and Delinquency, 25*, 463–489.

———. (1987). Revivification of rehabilitation: Evidence from the 1980s. *Justice Quarterly, 4*, 349–407.

Ghali, M., & Chesney-Lind, M. (1986). Gender bias and the criminal justice system: An empirical investigation. *Sociology and Social Research, 70*, 164–171.

Gibbons, D. C. (1970). Differential treatment of delinquents and interpersonal maturity level theory. *Social Sciences Review, 44*, 22–33.

———. (1975). Offender typologies—Two decades later. *British Journal of Criminology, 15*, 141–156.

————. (1988). Some critical observations on criminal types and criminal careers. *Criminal Justice and Behavior*, *15*, 8–23.

Gibbs, J. J. (1987). Symptoms of psychopathology among jail prisoners: The effects of exposure to the jail environment. *Criminal Justice and Behavior*, *14*, 288–310.

Gibbs, J. P. (1975). *Crime, punishment, and deterrence*. New York: Elsevier.

————. (1986). Deterrence theory and research. In S. L. Brodsky, G. B. Melton, & M. J. Saks (eds.), *Nebraska Symposium on Motivation 1985: The law as a behavioral instrument* (pp. 87–130). Lincoln, NE: University of Nebraska Press.

Gibbs, J. P., & Firebaugh, G. (1990). The artifact issue in deterrence research. *Criminology*, 347–367.

Gilberstadt, H., & Duker, J. (1965). *A handbook for clinical and actuarial MMPI interpretation*. Philadelphia: Saunders.

Gillin, J. L. (1945). *Criminology and penology*. New York.

Gillispie, R. W. (1980). Fines as an alternative to incarceration: The German experience. *Federal Probation*, *44*, 20–26.

Gills, A. R., & Hagan, J. (1982). *Bystander apathy and the territorial imperative*. Toronto: University of Toronto, Centre for Urban and Community Studies.

Giovannoni, J. M., & Gurel, L. (1967). Socially disruptive behavior of ex-mental patients. *Archives of General Psychiatry*, *17*, 146–153.

Glaser, D. (1975). Achieving better questions: A half century's progression in correctional research. *Federal Probation*, *39*, 3–9.

Glass, G. V., McGraw, B., & Smith, M. L. (1981). *Meta-analysis in social research*. Beverly Hills, CA: Sage.

Glasser, W. (1965). *Reality therapy*. New York: Harper & Row.

Glasser, W., & Zunin, L. M. (1979). Reality therapy. In R. J. Corsini (ed.), *Current psychotherapies* (2nd ed., pp. 302–339). Itasca, IL: F. E. Peacock.

Glassner, B., Ksander, M., Berg, B., & Johnson, B. D. (1983). A note on the deterrent effect of juvenile vs. adult jurisdiction. *Social problems*, *31*, 219–221.

Glazer, S. (1989). Can prisons rehabilitate criminals? *Editorial Research Reports*, pp. 430–442.

Glover, E. (1960). *The roots of crime: Selected papers on psychoanalysis. Vol. II*. London: Imago.

Glueck, B. (1918). A study of 608 admissions to Sing Sing Prison. *Mental Hygiene*, *2*, 85–151.

Glueck, S., & Glueck, E. (1968). *Delinquents and nondelinquents in perspective*. Cambridge, MA: Harvard University Press.

Golding, S. L., Roesch, R., & Schreiber, J. (1984). Assessment and conceptualization of competency to stand trial: Preliminary data on the Interdisciplinary Fitness Interview. *Law and Human Behavior*, *8*, 321–334.

Goldmeier, J., Sauer, R. H., & White, E. V. (1977). A halfway house for mentally ill offenders. *American Journal of Psychiatry*, *134*, 45–49.

Goldstein, A. P., & Stein, N. (1975). *Prescriptive psychotherapies*. Englewood Cliffs, NJ: Prentice-Hall.

Goldstein, G., & Hersen, M. (eds.). (1984). *Handbook of psychological assessment*. New York: Pergamon.

Good, M. I. (1978). Primary affective disorder, aggression, and criminality: A review and clinical study. *Archives of General Psychiatry*, *35*, 954–960.

Goodman, D. S., & Maultsby, M. C. (1974). *Emotional well-being through rational behavior training*. Springfield, Il: Charles C. Thomas.

Goodstein, L. I. (1980). The crime causes crime model: A critical review of the relationships between fear of crime, bystander surveillance, and changes in the crime rate. *Victimology, 5*, 133–151.

Gorelick, S. M. (1989). "Join our war": The construction of ideology in a newspaper crimefighting campaign. *Crime and Delinquency, 35*, 421–436.

Gorlow, L., Zimet, C., & Fine, H. (1952). The validity of anxiety and hostility Rorschach content scores among adolescents. *Journal of Consulting Psychology, 16*, 73–75.

Gottfredson, D. M. (1967). Assessment and prediction methods in crime and delinquency. In *Task Force Report: Juvenile delinquency and youth crime*. Washington, DC: U.S. Government Printing Office.

———. (1975, November). *Some positive changes in the parole process*. Paper presented at the annual meeting of the American Society of Criminology, Toronto, Canada.

Gottfredson, M. R., & Adams, K. (1982). Prison behavior and release performance. *Law and Policy Quarterly, 4*, 373–391.

Gottfredson, M. R., & Hirschi, T. (1986). The true value of lambda would appear to be zero: An essay on career criminals, criminal careers, selective incapacitation, cohort studies, and related topics. *Criminology, 24*, 213–234.

Gottfredson, M. R., Mitchell-Herzfeld, S. D., & Flanagan, T. J. (1982). Another look at the effectiveness of parole supervision. *Journal of Research in Crime and Delinquency, 19*, 277–298.

Gottfredson, S. D., & Gottfredson, D. M. (1980). Screening for risk: A comparison of methods. *Criminal Justice and Behavior, 7*, 315–330.

———. (1988). Violence prediction methods: Statistical and clinical strategies. *Violence and Victims, 3*, 303–324.

Gottfredson, S. D., & Taylor, R. B. (1984). Public policy and prison populations: Measuring opinions about reform. *Judicature, 68*, 190–201.

———. (1986). Person-environment interactions in the prediction of recidivism. In J. M. Byrne & R. J. Sampson (eds.), *The social ecology of crime* (pp. 133–155). New York: Springer-Verlag.

Gough, H. G. (1954). Some common misconceptions about neuroticism. *Journal of Consulting Psychology, 18*, 287–292.

———. (1957). *California Psychological Inventory manual*. Palo Alto, CA: Consulting Psychologists Press.

———. (1965). Cross-cultural validation of a measure of asocial behavior. *Psychological Reports, 17*, 379–387.

Gough, H. G., Wenk, E. A., & Rozynko, V. V. (1965). Parole outcome as predicted from the CPI, MMPI, and a base expectancy table. *Journal of Abnormal Psychology, 70*, 432–441.

Graham, J. R. (1987). *The MMPI: A practical guide* (2nd ed.). New York: Oxford University Press.

Grant, J. D. (1965). Delinquency treatment in an institutional setting. In H. C. Quay (ed.), *Juvenile delinquency: Research and theory* (pp. 263–297). Princeton, NJ: Van Nostrand.

Grasmick, H. G., & Bryjak, G. J. (1980). The deterrent effect of perceived severity of punishment. *Social Forces, 59*, 471–491.

Grasmick, H. G., & Green, D. E. (1980). Legal punishment, social disapproval and internalization as inhibitors of illegal behavior. *Journal of Criminal Law and Criminology, 71*, 325–335.

Graves, W. F. (1956). A doctor looks at capital punishment. *Journal of the Loma Linda University School of Medicine, 10*, 137–141.

Greater Washington Research Center. (1988). *Drug use and drug programs in the Washington metropolitan area: An assessment.* Washington, DC: Author.

Green, C. J. (1988). The Psychopathy Checklist. *Journal of Personality Disorders, 2*, 185–188.

Green, S. (1984). Victim-offender reconciliation programs: A review of the concept. *Social Action and the Law, 10*, 43–52.

Green, S. B., & Kelley, C. K. (1988). Racial bias in prediction with the MMPI for a juvenile delinquent population. *Journal of Personality Assessment, 52*, 263–275.

Greenberg, D. F. (1985). Age, crime, and social explanation. *American Journal of Sociology, 91*, 1–27.

Greenberg, D. F., Kesslor, R. C., & Logan, C. H. (1979). A panel model of crime rates and arrest rates. *American Sociological Review, 44*, 843–850.

Greenberg, S. W., & Rohe, W. M. (1984). Neighborhood design and crime: A test of two perspectives. *Journal of the American Planning Association, 49*, 48–61.

Greene, R. L. (1980). *The MMPI: An interpretive manual.* New York: Grune & Stratton.

Greenwood, D. (1975). The incapacitative effect of imprisonment: Some estimates. *Law and Society Review, 9*, 541–580.

Greenwood, D., Lipsett, L., & Norton, R. A. (1980). Increasing the job readiness of probationers. *Corrections Today, 42*, 78–79, 82–83.

Greenwood, P. W., with A. Abrahamse (1982). *Selective incapacitation.* Rand Report R–2815-NIJ. Santa Monica, CA: Rand Corporation.

Greenwood, P. W., & Turner, S. (1987). *Selective incapacitation revisited: Why the high-rate offenders are hard to predict.* Rand Report R–3397-NIJ. Santa Monica, CA: Rand Corporation.

Gregg v. Georgia, 428 U.S. 1543 (1976).

Griswold, B. D. (1978). A comparison of recidivism measures. *Journal of Criminal Justice, 6*, 247–252.

Gross, S. R., & Mauro, R. (1984). Patterns of death: An analysis of racial dispositions in capital sentencing and homicide victimization. *Stanford Law Review, 37*, 27–153.

Groth, A. N., & Hobson, W. F. (1983). The dynamics of sexual assault. In L. B. Schlesinger & E. Revitch (eds.), *Sexual dynamics of antisocial behavior* (pp. 159–172). Springfield, IL: Charles C. Thomas.

Grunfeld, B., & Noreik, K. (1986). Recidivism among sex offenders: A follow-up study of 541 Norwegian sex offenders. *International Journal of Law and Psychiatry, 9*, 95–102.

Grupp, S., Ramseyer, G., & Richardson, J. (1968). The effect of age on four scales of the California Psychological Inventory. *Journal of General Psychology, 78*, 183–187.

Guerra, N. G., & Slaby, R. G. (1990). Cognitive mediators of aggression in adolescent offenders: 2. Intervention. *Developmental Psychology, 26*, 269–277.

Gunn, J. (1973). *Violence in human society.* Newton Abbot, England: Davis & Charles.

Gunn, J., Robertson, G., Dell, S., & Way, G. (1978). *Psychiatric aspects of imprisonment*. London: Academic Press.

Guy, E., Platt, J. J., Zwerling, I., & Bullock, S. (1985). Mental health status of prisoners in an urban jail. *Criminal Justice and Behavior, 12*, 29–53.

Guze, S. B., Goodwin, D. W., & Crane, J. B. (1970). Criminal recidivism and psychiatric illness. *American Journal of Psychiatry, 127*, 832–840.

Guze, S. B., Tuason, V. B., Gatfield, P. D., & Stewart, M. A., & Picken, B. (1962). Psychiatric illness and crime with particular reference to alcoholism: A study of 223 criminals. *Journal of Nervous and Mental Disease, 134*, 512–521.

Guze, S. B., Woodruff, R. A., & Clayton, P. J. (1974). Psychiatric disorders and criminality. *Journal of the American Medical Association, 227*, 641–642.

Hackett, J. C., Hatry, H. P., Levinson, R. B., Allen, J., Chi, K. & Feigenbaum, E. D. (1987). Contracting for the operation of prisons and jails. *National Institute of Justice: Research in Brief*. Washington, DC: National Institute of Justice.

Hafner, H., & Boker, W. (1973). Mentally disordered violent offenders. *Social Psychiatry, 8*, 220–229.

Hakel, M. D. (1982). Employment interviewing. In K. M. Rowland & G. R. Ferris (eds.), *Personnel management*. Boston: Allyn & Bacon.

Hall, G.C.N. (1988). Criminal behavior as a function of clinical and actuarial variables in a sexual offender population. *Journal of Consulting and Clinical Psychology, 56*, 773–775.

Hall, G.C.N., Maiuro, R. D., Vitaliano, P. P., & Proctor, W. E. (1986). The utility of the MMPI with men who have sexually assaulted children. *Journal of Consulting and Clinical Psychology, 54*, 493–496.

Halpern, A. L. (1977). The insanity defense: A judicial anachronism. *Psychiatric Annals, 7*, 41–63.

Hamm, M. S. (1987). *Attitudes of Indiana legislators toward crime and criminal justice: A report of the state legislator survey—1986*. Terre Haute, IN: Indiana State University.

———. (1989). Legislator ideology and capital punishment: The special case for Indiana juveniles. *Justice Quarterly, 6*, 219–232.

Hamm, M. S., & Schrink, J. L. (1989). The conditions of effective implementation: A guide to accomplishing rehabilitative objectives in corrections. *Criminal Justice and Behavior, 16*, 166–182.

Hamparian, D. M., Schuster, R., Dinitz, S., & Conrad, J. P. (1978). *The violent few*. Lexington, MA: Lexington/D. C. Heath.

Hanson, R. W., Moss, C. S., Hosford, R. E., & Johnson, M. E. (1983). Predicting inmate penitentiary adjustment: An assessment of our classification methods. *Criminal Justice and Behavior, 10*, 293–309.

Hare, R. D. (1980). A research scale for the assessment of psychopathy in criminal populations. *Personality and Individual Differences, 1*, 111–119.

———. (1985). Comparison of procedures for the assessment of psychopathy. *Journal of Consulting and Clinical Psychology, 53*, 7–16.

Hare, R. D., & Cox, D. N. (1978). Clinical and empirical conceptions of psychopathy, and the selection of subjects for research. In R. D. Hare & D. Schalling (eds.), *Psychopathic behaviour: Approaches to research* (pp. 1–21). Chicester, England: John Wiley.

Harpur, T. J., Hakstian, A. R., & Hare, R. D. (1988). Factor structure of the Psychopathy Checklist. *Journal of Consulting and Clinical Psychology, 56*, 741–747.

Harpur, T. J., Hare, R. D., & Hakstian, A. R. (1989). Two-factor conceptualization of psychopathy: Construct validity and assessment implications. *Psychological Assessment: A Journal of Consulting and Clinical Psychology, 1*, 6–17.

Harris, J., & Parker, D. (1980). *The impact of increased population on disciplinary incidents.* Hartford, CT: Connecticut Department of Corrections.

Harris, L. (1968). *Corrections 1968: A climate for change.* Washington, DC: Joint Commission on Correctional Manpower and Training.

Harris, P. W. (1983). The interpersonal maturity of delinquents and nondelinquents. In W. S. Laufer & J. M. Day (eds.), *Personality, moral development and criminal behavior* (pp. 145–164). Lexington, MA: Lexington Books.

———. (1988). The interpersonal maturity level classification system: I-level. *Criminal Justice and Behavior, 15*, 58–77.

Hart, S. D., Kropp, P. R., & Hare, R. D. (1988). Performance of male psychopaths following conditional release from prison. *Journal of Consulting and Clinical Psychology, 56*, 227–232.

Hartman, A. A. (1940). Recidivism and intelligence. *Journal of Criminal Law and Criminology, 31*, 417–426.

Harwood, H. J., Napolitano, D. M., Kristiansen, P. L., & Collins, J. J. (1984). *Economic costs to society of alcohol and drug abuse and mental illness: 1980.* (RTI/2734/00–01FR). Research Triangle Park, NC: Research Triangle Institute.

Hathaway, S. R., & McKinley, J. C. (1940). A multiphasic personality schedule (Minnesota): I. Construction of the schedule. *Journal of Personality, 10*, 249–254.

Hathaway, S. R., & Monachesi, E. D. (1963). *Adolescent personality and behavior: MMPI patterns of normal, delinquent, dropout, and other outcomes.* Minneapolis: University of Minnesota Press.

Hawk, G. L., & Cornell, D. G. (1989). MMPI profiles of malingerers diagnosed in pretrial forensic evaluations. *Journal of Clinical Psychology, 45*, 673–678.

Hedlund, J. L., Sletten, I. W., Altman, H., & Evenson, R. C. (1973). Prediction of patients who are dangerous to others. *Journal of Clinical Psychology, 27*, 443–447.

Heilbrun, A. B. (1979). Psychopathology and violent crime. *Journal of Consulting and Clinical Psychology, 47*, 509–516.

———. (1990). The measurement of criminal dangerousness as a personality construct: Further validation of a research index. *Journal of Personality Assessment, 54*, 2–18.

Heilbrun, A. B., Foster, A., & Golden, J. (1989). The death sentence in Georgia, 1974–1987: Criminal justice or racial injustice? *Criminal Justice and Behavior, 16*, 139–154.

Heilbrun, A. B., Knopf, I. J., & Bruner, P. (1976). Criminal impulsivity and violence and subsequent parole outcome. *British Journal of Criminology 16*, 367–377.

Heller, M S., & Ehrlich, S. M. (1984). Actuarial variables in 19,600 violent and nonviolent offenders referred to a court psychiatric clinic. *American Journal of Social Psychiatry, 4*, 30–36.

Hellman, D. S., & Blackman, N. (1966). Enuresis, firesetting and cruelty to animals: A triad predictive of adult crime. *American Journal of Psychiatry, 122*, 1431–1435.

Helzer, J. E., Clayton, P. J., Pambakian, R., Reich, T., Woodruff, R. A., & Reveley, M. A. (1977). Reliability of psychiatric diagnosis. *Archives of General Psychiatry*, *34*, 136–141.

Henderson, J., & Taylor, J. (1985). Killers of blacks escape the death penalty. *Dallas Times Herald* (November 17, 1985).

Hess, J. H., & Thomas, T. E. (1963). Incompetency to stand trial: Procedures, results and problems. *American Journal of Psychiatry*, *119*, 713–720.

Hetherington, E. M., & Feldman, S. E. (1964). College cheating as a function of subject and situational variables. *Journal of Educational Psychology*, *55*, 212–218.

Hetherington, E. M., Stouwie, R., & Ridberg, E. H. (1971). Patterns of family interaction and child rearing attitudes related to three dimensions of juvenile delinquency. *Journal of Abnormal Psychology*, *77*, 160–176.

Hewitt, J. D., Poole, E. D., & Regoli, R. M. (1984). Self-reported and observed rule-breaking in prison: A look at disciplinary response. *American Journal of Sociology*, *90*, 437–447.

Hillsman, S. T., Mahoney, B., Cole, G. F., & Auchter, B. (1987). Fines as criminal sanctions. *National Institute of Justice: Research in Brief*. Washington, DC: National Institute of Justice.

Hindelang, M. J. (1973). Variations in personality attributes of social and solitary self-reported delinquents. *Journal of Consulting and Clinical Psychology*, *40*, 452–454.

Hindelang, M. J., Gottfredson, M. R., & Garofalo, J. (1978). *Victims of personal crime: An empirical foundation for a theory of personal victimization*. Cambridge, MA: Ballinger.

Hippchen, L. J. (1976). Biomedical approaches to offender rehabilitation. *Offender Rehabilitation*, *1*, 115–123.

Hirschi, T., & Hindelang, M J. (1977). Intelligence and delinquency: A revisionist review. *American Sociological Review*, *42*, 571–587.

Hobson, W. F., Boland, C., & Jamieson, B. (1985). Dangerous sexual offenders. *Medical Aspects of Sexuality*, *19*, 104–123.

Hoebel, E. A. (1954). *The law of primitive man*. Cambridge, MA.

Hofer, P. (1988). Prisonization and recidivism: A psychological perspective. *International Journal of Offender Therapy and Comparative Criminology*, *32*, 95–106.

Hoffman, P. B. (1982). Female recidivism, and the salient factor score: A research note. *Criminal Justice and Behavior*, *9*, 121–125.

———. (1983). Screening for risk: A revised salient factor score. *Journal of Criminal Justice*, *11*, 539–547.

Hoffman, P. B., & Beck, J. L. (1974). Parole decision-making: A salient factor score. *Journal of Criminal Justice*, *2*, 195–206.

———. (1980). Revalidating the salient factor score: A research note. *Journal of Criminal Justice*, *8*, 185–188.

———. (1984). Burnout—Age at release from prison and recidivism. *Journal of Criminal Justice*, *12*, 617–623.

———. (1985). Recidivism among released federal prisoners: Salient factor score and five year follow-up. *Criminal Justice and Behavior*, *12*, 501–507.

Hoffman, P. B., Gottfredson, D. M., Wilkins, L., & Pasela, G. (1974). The operational use of an experience table. *Criminology*, *12*, 214–228.

Hoffman, P. B., & Handyman, P. L. (1986). Crime seriousness scales: Public perception and feedback to criminal justice policy makers. *Journal of Criminal Justice, 14*, 413–431.

Hoffman, P. B., & Stone-Meierhoefer, B. (1979). Post release arrest experiences of federal prisoners. *Journal of Criminal Justice, 7*, 193–216.

———. (1980). Reporting recidivism rates: The criterion and follow-up issues. *Journal of Criminal Justice, 8*, 53–60.

Hoffman, P. B., Stone-Meierhoefer, B., & Beck, J. L. (1978). Salient factor score and release behavior: Three validation samples. *Law and Human Behavior, 2*, 47–63.

Hogan, R., Mankin, D., Conway, J., & Fox, S. (1970). Personality correlates of undergraduate marijuana use. *Journal of Consulting and Clinical Psychology, 35*, 58–63.

Holland, T. R., Beckett, G. E., & Levi, M. (1981). Intelligence, personality, and criminal violence: A multivariate analysis. *Journal of Consulting and Clinical Psychology, 49*, 106–111.

Holland, T. R., & Holt, N. (1980). Correctional classification and the prediction of institutional adjustment. *Criminal Justice and Behavior, 7*, 51–60.

Holland, T. R., Holt, N., Levi, M., & Beckett, G. E. (1983). Comparison and combination of clinical and statistical predictions of recidivism among adult offenders. *Journal of Applied Psychology, 68*, 203–211.

Hollingshead, A. B., & Redlich, F. C. (1958). *Social class and mental illness: A community study*. New York: John Wiley.

Holmes, R. M., Sykes, G. W., & Revels, J. (1983). Shocked and scared: Prison as a deterrent. *Perspectives, 7*, 1–3.

Homant, R. J. (1984). Employment of ex-offenders: The role of prisonization and self-esteem. *Journal of Offender Counseling, Services and Rehabilitation, 8*, 5–23.

Homant, R. J., & Osowski, G. (1981). Evaluation of the "scared straight" model: Some methodological and political considerations. *Corrective and Social Psychiatry and Journal of Behavioural Technology, Methods and Therapy, 27*, 130–134.

Hope, T. (1988). Support for neighborhood watch: A British crime survey analysis. In T. Hope & M. Shaw (eds.), *Communities and crime reduction* (pp. 146–163). London: HMSO.

Hoppe, C. M., & Singer, R. D. (1976). Overcontrolled hostility, empathy, and egocentric balance in violent and nonviolent psychiatric offenders. *Psychological Reports, 39*, 1303–1308.

Hough, J. M., Clarke, R.V.G., & Mayhew, P. (1980). Introduction. In R.V.G. Clarke & P. Mayhew (eds.), *Designing out crime*. London: HMSO.

Hovey, H. B. (1953). MMPI profiles and personality characteristics. *Journal of Consulting Psychology, 17*, 142–146.

Howell, R. J., & Geiselman, J. H. (1978). *Psycho-diagnostic study of restitution inmates*. Unpublished manuscript.

Hu, T., & Mitchell, M. E. (1981). *Cost effectiveness of the 1978 NIDA drug abuse prevention television campaign*. Draft final report prepared for the National Institute on Drug Abuse. Rockville, MD: National Institute on Drug Abuse.

Hubbard, R. L., Collins, J. J., Rachal, J. V., & Cavanaugh, E. R. (1988). The criminal justice client in drug abuse treatment. *National Institute on Drug Abuse: Research Monograph Series* (monograph 86), 57–79.

Humphreys, L., Forehand, R., McMahon, R., & Roberts, M. (1978). Parent behavioral training to modify child noncompliance: Effects on untreated siblings. *Journal of Behavior Therapy and Experimental Psychiatry, 9*, 235–238.

Hunt, R. C., & Wiley, E. D. (1968). Operation Baxstrom after one year. *American Journal of Psychiatry, 124*, 974–978.

Hunter, J. A., & Santos, D. R. (1990). The use of specialized cognitive-behavioral therapies in the treatment of adolescent sexual offenders. *International Journal of Offender Therapy and Comparative Criminology, 34*, 239–247.

Innes, C. A. (1986). Population density in state prisons. *Bureau of Justice Statistics Special Report*. Washington, DC: National Institute of Justice.

———. (1988). Profile of state prison inmates, 1986. *Bureau of Justice Statistics Special Report*. Washington, DC: National Institute of Justice.

Itil, T. M., & Wadud, A. (1975). Treatment of human aggression with minor tranquilizers, antidepressants, and newer psychotropic drugs. *Journal of Nervous and Mental Diseases, 160*, 83–99.

Izzo, R. L., & Ross, R. R. (1990). Meta-analysis of rehabilitation programs for juvenile delinquents: A brief report. *Criminal Justice and Behavior 17*, 134–142.

Jackson v. Indiana, 406 U.S. 715 (1972).

Jackson, M. W. (1986). Psychiatric decision-making for the courts: Lay people, judges, or psychiatrists. *International Journal of Law and Psychiatry, 9*, 507–520.

———. (1988). Lay and professional perceptions of dangerousness and other forensic issues. *Canadian Journal of Criminology, 30*, 215–229.

Jackson, P. C. (1983). Some effects of parole supervision on recidivism. *British Journal of Criminology, 23*, 17–34.

Jaman, D. R. (1969). *Behavior during the first year in prison, report 2—MMPI scales and behavior*. Sacramento, CA: California Department of Corrections.

James, J. F., Gregory, D., Jones, R. K., & Rundell, O. (1980). Psychiatric morbidity in prisons. *Hospital and Community Psychiatry, 31*, 675–677.

Jamieson, K. M., & Flanagan, T. J. (eds.). (1987). *Sourcebook of criminal justice statistics—1986*. Washington, DC: Bureau of Justice Statistics.

Jan, L. J. (1980). Overcrowding of inmate behavior. *Criminal Justice and Behavior, 7*, 293–301.

Janus, M. G. (1985). Selective incapacitation: Have we tried it? Does it work? *Journal of Criminal Justice, 13*, 117–129.

Jencks, C. S. (1985). How poor are the poor? A review of C. Murray (1984) "Losing ground: American social policy, 1950–1980." *New York Review of Books*, pp. 41–48.

Jenkins, I. (1980). *Social order and the limits of the law*. Princeton, NJ: Princeton University Press.

Jensen, G. (1977). Age and rule-breaking in prison: A test of sociocultural interpretations. *Criminology, 14*, 555–568.

Jensen, G. F., Erickson, M. L., & Gibbs, J. P. (1978). Perceived risk of punishment and self-reported delinquency. *Social Forces, 57*, 57–78.

Jesness, C. F. (1971). *The Jesness Behavior Checklist*. Palo Alto, CA: Consulting Psychologists Press.

———. (1974). *Sequential I-level manual*. Sacramento, CA: American Justice Institute.

———. (1986). Validity of Jesness Inventory classification with nondelinquents. *Educational and Psychological Measurement, 46*, 947–961.

Jesness, C. F., & Wedge, R. F. (1983). *Classifying offenders: The Jesness Inventory Classification System.* Sacramento, CA: California Youth Authority.

———. (1984). Validity of a revised Jesness Inventory I-level classification with delinquents. *Journal of Consulting and Clinical Psychology, 52,* 997–1010.

———. (1985). *Jessness Inventory Classification System supplementary manual.* Palo Alto, CA: Consulting Psychologists Press.

Johnson, D. L., & Breckenridge, J. N. (1982). The Houston parent-child development center and the primary prevention of behavior problems in young children. *American Journal of Community Psychology, 10,* 305–315.

Johnston, L. D., Bachman, J. G., & O'Malley, P. M. (1981). *Marijuana decriminalization: The impact on youth 1975–1980.* Monitoring the Future, Occasional Paper 13, University of Michigan Institute for Social Research.

Joint Committee on New York Drug Law Evaluation. (1977). *The nation's toughest drug law: Evaluating the New York experience.* New York: Association of the Bar of the City of New York.

Jones v. United States, 103 S.Ct. 3043 (1983).

Jones, D. A. (1976). *The health risks of imprisonment.* Lexington, MA: Lexington Books.

Jones, T., Beidleman, W. B., & Fowler, R. D. (1981). Differentiating violent and nonviolent prison inmates by use of selected MMPI scales. *Journal of Clinical Psychology, 37,* 673–678.

Joseph, H. (1988). The criminal justice system and opiate addiction: A historical perspective. *National Institute of Drug Abuse: Research Monograph Series* (Monograph 86), 106–125.

Jung, R. S., & Jason, L. A. (1988). Firearm violence and the effects of gun control legislation. *American Journal of Community Psychology, 16,* 515–524.

Kahneman, D., & Tversky, A. (1973). On the psychology of prediction. *Psychological Review, 80,* 237–251.

Kassebaum, G., Ward, D. A., & Wilner, D. M. (1971). *Prison treatment and parole survival: An empirical assessment.* New York: John Wiley.

Kazdin, A. E. (1987). Treatment of antisocial behavior in children: Current status and future directions. *Psychological Bulletin, 102,* 187–203.

Kazdin, A. E., Bass, D., Siegel, T., & Thomas, C. (1989). Cognitive-behavioral therapy and relationship therapy in the treatment of children referred for antisocial behavior. *Journal of Consulting and Clinical Psychology, 57,* 522–535.

Kazdin, A. E., & Bootzin, R. R. (1972). The token economy: An evaluative review. *Journal of Applied Behavioral Analysis, 5,* 343–372.

Keane, C., Gillis, A. R., & Hagan, J. (1989). Deterrence and amplification of juvenile delinquency by police contact. *British Journal of Criminology, 29,* 336–352.

Keil, T. J., & Vito, G. F. (1990). Race and the death penalty in Kentucky murder trials: An analysis of post-Gregg outcomes. *Justice Quarterly, 7,* 189–207.

Kellert, S. R., & Felthous, A. R. (1985). Childhood cruelty toward animals among criminals and noncriminals. *Human Relations, 38,* 1113–1129.

Kelling, G. L. (1988). Police and communities: The quiet revolution. *Perspectives on Policing, 1,* 1–8.

Kelling, G. L., Pate, T., Dieckman, D., & Brown, C. (1974). *The Kansas City prevention patrol experiment: A technical report.* Washington, DC: The Police Foundation.

Kelly, F. J. (1974, October). *Outward bound and delinquency: A ten year experience.* Paper presented at the conference on experimental education, Estes Park, CO.

Kelly, F. J., & Baer, D. J. (1971). Physical challenge as a treatment for delinquency. *Crime and Delinquency, 17*, 437–445.

Kelly, R. J. (1982). Behavioral reorientation of pedophiliacs: Can it be done? *Clinical Psychology Review, 2*, 387–408.

Kerlinger, F. N. (1973). *Foundations of behavioral research* (2nd ed.). New York: Holt, Rinehart, and Winston.

Kifer, R. E., Lewis, M. A., Green, D. R., & Phillips, E. L. (1974). Training predelinquent youths and their parents to negotiate conflict situations. *Journal of Applied Behavior Analysis, 7*, 357–364.

King, D. R. (1978). The brutalizing effect: Executive publicity and the incidence of homicide in South Carolina. *Social Forces, 57*, 683–687.

King, G. D., & Kelley, C. K. (1977). Behavioral correlates for spike-*4*, spike-*9*, and *4-9/9-4* MMPI profiles in students at a university mental health center. *Journal of Clinical Psychology, 33*, 718–724.

King, M. (1989). Crime prevention in France. *Canadian Journal of Criminology, 31*, 527–538.

Kipper, D. A. (1977). The Kahn Test of Symbol Arrangement and criminality. *Journal of Clinical Psychology, 33*, 777–781.

Kirchmer, R. E., Schnelle, J. F., Domash, M., Larson, L., Carr, A., & McNees, M. P. (1980). The applicability of a helicopter patrol procedure to diverse areas: A cost-benefit analysis. *Journal of Applied Behavior Analysis, 13*, 143–148.

Kitchener, J., Schmidt, A. K., & Glaser, D. (1977). How persistent is post-prison success? *Federal Probation, 4*, 9–15.

Klassen, D., & O'Connor, W. A. (1988). Crime, inpatient admissions, and violence among male mental patients. *International Journal of Law and Psychiatry, 1*, 305–312.

Kleck, G. (1981). Racial discrimination in criminal sentencing: A critical evaluation of the evidence with additional evidence on the death penalty. *American Sociological Review, 46*, 783–805.

Klein, M. W. (1979). Deinstitutionalization and diversion of juvenile offenders: A litany of impediments. In N. Morris & M. Tonry (eds.), *Crime and justice: An annual review of research* (Vol. I, pp. 145–201). Chicago: University of Chicago Press.

Klein, N. C., Alexander, J. F., & Parsons, B. V. (1977). Impact of family system intervention on recidivism and sibling delinquency: A model of primary prevention and program evaluation. *Journal of Consulting and Clinical Psychology, 45*, 469–474.

Klein, S., & Caggiano, M. (1986). *The prevalence, predictability, and policy implications of recidivism*. Rand Report R–3413-BJS. Santa Monica, CA: Rand Corporation.

Klein, S., Petersilia, J., & Turner, S. (1990). Race and imprisonment decisions in California. *Science, 247*, 812–816.

Klepper, S., & Nagin, D. (1989). The deterrent effect of perceived certainty and severity of punishment revisited. *Criminology, 27*, 721–746.

Knopp, F. H., Rosenberg, J., & Stevenson, W. (1986). *Directory of juvenile and adult sex offender treatment programs in the United States*. Syracuse, NY: Safer Society Press.

Koeninger, R. C. (1969). Capital punishment in Texas, 1924–1968. *Crime and Delinquency, 15*, 132–142.

Kohlberg, L., & Elfenbein, D. (1975). The development of moral judgments concerning capital punishment. *American Journal of Orthopsychiatry, 45*, 614–640.

Koppin, M. (1977). *Age, hospital stay and criminal history as predictors of post-release release danger*. Pueblo, CO: Colorado State Hospital.

Kozol, H. L., Boucher, R. J., & Garofalo, R. F. (1972). The diagnosis and treatment of dangerousness. *Crime and Delinquency, 18*, 371–392.

Kramer, J. C. (1978). Social benefits and social costs of drug control laws. *Journal of Drug Issues, 8*, 1–7.

Kraus, J. (1974). A comparison of corrective effects on probation and detention of male juvenile offenders. *British Journal of Criminology, 14*, 49–62.

Kraut, R. (1976). Deterrent and definitional influences on shoplifting. *Social Problems, 23*, 358–368.

Krupat, E., & Kubzansky, P. E. (1987). Designing to deter crime. *Psychology Today, 21*, 58–61.

Kurtzberg, R. L., Safer, H., & Mandell, W. (1969). Plastic surgery in corrections. *Federal Probation, 33*, 45.

Labaton, S. (1989). Federal judge urges legalization of crack, heroin, and other drugs. *New York Times* (December 12, 1989).

Lamb, H. R., & Grant, R. W. (1982). The mentally ill in an urban county jail. *Archives of General Psychiatry, 39*, 17–22.

Lampe, P. E. (1985). Assessing treatment of the offender: From probation to capital punishment. *Federal Probation, 49*, 25–31.

Lane, P. J., & Kling, J. S. (1979). Construct validation of the *O-H* scale of the MMPI. *Journal of Consulting and Clinical Psychology, 47*, 781–782.

Langevin, R., Paitich, D., Orchard, R., Handy, L., & Russon, A. (1983). Childhood and family backgrounds of killers seen for psychiatric assessment: A controlled study. *Bulletin of the American Academy of Psychiatry and the Law, 11*, 331–341.

Lanyon, R. I. (1986). Therapy and treatment in child molestation. *Journal of Consulting and Clinical Psychology, 54*, 176–182.

Lasky, G. L., Gordon, B. C., & Srebalus, D. J. (1986). Occupational stressors among federal correctional officers working in different security levels. *Criminal Justice and Behavior, 13*, 317–327.

Latessa, E. J., & Allen, H. F. (1980). Using citizens to prevent crime: An example of deterrence and community involvement. *Journal of Police Science and Administration, 8*, 69–74.

Latessa, E. J., & Vito, G. F. (1988). The effects of intensive supervision on shock probationers. *Journal of Criminal Justice, 16*, 319–330.

Lavrakas, P. J. (1982). Fear of crime and behavioral restrictions in urban and suburban neighborhoods. *Population and Environment, 5*, 242–264.

Lavrakas, P. J., & Bennett, S. (1988). *Cross-site impact evaluation report for the neighborhood anti-crime self-help program*. Draft final impact report to the Eisenhower Foundation. Evanston, IL: Northwestern University.

Lavrakas, P. J., & Herz, L. (1982). Citizen participation in neighborhood crime prevention. *Criminology, 20*, 479–498.

Lavrakas, P. J., & Kushmuk, J. W. (1986). Evaluating crime prevention through environmental design: The Portland Commercial demonstration project. In D. Rosenbaum (ed.), *Community crime prevention: Does it work?* (pp. 202–227). Beverly Hills, CA: Sage.

Laws, D. R., & Osborn, C. A. (1982). *A procedure to assess incest offenders.* Proposal submitted to the research committee, Atascadero State Hospital, Atascadero, CA.

———. (1983). Setting up shop: How to build and operate a behavioral laboratory to evaluate and treat sexual deviance. In J. G. Greer & I. R. Stuart (eds.), *The sexual aggressor: Current perspectives on treatment* (pp. 293–335). New York: Van Nostrand Reinhold.

Lee, R., & Haynes, N. (1980). Project CREST and the dual-treatment approach to delinquency: Methods and research summarized. In R. R. Ross & P. Gendreau (eds.), *Effective correctional treatment.* Toronto: Butterworths.

Lehman, J. A., & Conklin, J. E. (1973). Plastic surgery in prison: An apparently negative result. *Ohio State Medical Journal, 69,* 892–895.

Lerner, M. (1977). The effectiveness of a definite sentence parole program. *Criminology, 15,* 211–244.

Levine, R. L. (1969). The MMPI and Revised Beta as predictors of academic and vocational success in a correctional institution. *FCI Research Reports, 1,* 1–52.

Levinson, D., Darrow, C., Klein, E., Levinson, M., & McKee, B. (1978). *The seasons of a man's life.* New York: Knopf.

Levinson, R. B. (1980). Security designation systems: Preliminary results. *Federal Probation, 44,* 26–30.

———. (1985). *Private sector operation of a correctional institution.* Washington, DC: National Institute of Corrections.

———. (1988). Developments in the classification process: Quay's AIM approach. *Criminal Justice and Behavior, 15,* 24–38.

Levinson, R. B., & Gerard, R. E. (1986). Classifying institutions. *Crime and Delinquency, 32,* 291–301.

Levinson, R. B., & Ramsay, G. (1979). Dangerousness, stress, and mental health evaluations. *Journal of Health and Social Behavior, 20,* 178–187.

Lewis, A. J. (1985). The junk food made me do it: Is there a connection between diet and crime? *East West Journal,* pp. 66–71.

Lewis, D. A., Grant, J. A., & Rosenbaum, D. P. (1988). *The social construction of reform: Community organizations and crime prevention.* New Brunswick, NJ: Transaction Books.

Lewis, D. O., Lovely, R., Yeager, C., & Femina, D. D. (1989). Toward a theory of the genesis of violence: A follow-up study of delinquents. *Journal of the American Academy of Child and Adolescent Psychiatry, 28,* 431–436.

Lewis, D. O., Shanok, S. S., Grant, M., & Ripvo, E. (1983). Homicidally-aggressive young children: Neuropsychiatric and experimental correlates. *American Journal of Psychiatry, 140,* 148–153.

Lewis, D. O., Shanok, S. S., Pincus, J. H., & Glaser, G. H. (1979). Violent juvenile delinquents: Psychiatric, neurological, psychological and abuse factors. *Journal of the Academy of Child Psychiatry, 18,* 307–319.

Lewis, R. V. (1983). Scared straight—California style: Evaluation of the San Quentin squire program. *Criminal Justice and Behavior, 10,* 209–226.

Lewison, E. (1965). An experiment in facial reconstructive surgery in a prison population. *Canadian Medical Association Journal, 92,* 251–254.

Lightman, E. S. (1982). The private employer and the prison industry. *British Journal of Criminology, 22,* 36–48.

Lindzey, G. (1959). On the classification of projective techniques. *Psychological Bulletin, 56,* 158–168.

Lipsitt, P. D., Lelos, D., & McGarry, A. L. (1971). Competency for trial: A screening instrument. *American Journal of Psychiatry, 128,* 105–109.

Lipton, D., Martinson, R., & Wilks, J. (1975). *The effectiveness of correctional treatment: A survey of treatment evaluation studies.* New York: Praeger.

Liska, A. E., & Baccaglini, W. (1990). Feeling safe by comparison: Crime in the newspapers. *Social Problems, 37,* 360–374.

Loftin, C., & Parker, R. N. (1985). An error-in-variable model of the effect of poverty on urban homicide rates. *Criminology, 23,* 269–287.

Logan, C. H. (1990). *Private prisons: Cons and pros.* New York: Oxford University Press.

Logan, W. (1989). Description of challenge programs. In D. G. Parent (au.), *Shock incarceration: An overview of existing programs* (pp. 55–59). Washington, DC: National Institute of Justice.

Loper, R. G., Kammeier, M. L., & Hoffmann, H. (1973). MMPI characteristics of college freshmen males who later became alcoholic. *Journal of Abnormal Psychology, 82,* 159–162.

Lubin, B., Larsen, R. M., Matarazzo, J. D., & Seever, M. (1985). Psychological test usage patterns in five professional settings. *American Psychologist, 40,* 857–861.

Luedtke, G., & Associates. (1970). *Crime and the physical city: Neighborhood design techniques for crime reduction.* Springfield, VA: National Technical Information Council.

MacDonald, J. E., & Gifford, R. (1989). Territorial cues and defensible space theory: The burglar's point of view. *Journal of Environmental Psychology, 9,* 193–205.

MacDonald, J. M. (1963). The threat to kill. *American Journal of Psychiatry, 120,* 125–130.

MacKenzie, D. L. (1987). Age and adjustment to prison: Interactions with attitudes and anxiety. *Criminal Justice and Behavior, 14,* 427–447.

———. (1990). Boot camp prisons: Components, evaluations, and empirical issues. *Federal Probation, 54,* 44–52.

MacKenzie, D. L., Posey, C. D., & Rapaport, K. R. (1988). A theoretical revolution in corrections: Varied purposes for classification. *Criminal Justice and Behavior, 15,* 125–136.

MacKenzie, D. L., & Shaw, J. W. (1990). Inmate adjustment and change during shock incarceration: The impact of correctional boot camp programs. *Justice Quarterly, 7,* 125–150.

Maitra, A. K. (1985). Rorschach sign of aggression, sadism, and hostility. *Psychological Research Journal, 9,* 17–23.

Malak, P. A. (1984). *Early release.* Report prepared for the Colorado Division of Criminal Justice.

Maletzsky, B. M. (1974). "Assisted" covert sensitization in the treatment of exhibitionism. *Journal of Consulting and Clinical Psychology, 42,* 34–40.

Maller, C., & Thornton, C. (1978). Transitional aid for released prisoners: Evidence from the LIFE experiment. *Journal of Human Resources, 13,* 208–236.

Mallory, C. H., & Walker, C. E. (1972). MMPI *O-H* scale responses of assaultive and nonassaultive prisoners and associated life history variables. *Educational and Psychological Measurement, 32*, 1125–1128.

Maloff, D. (1981). A review of the effects of decriminalization of marijuana. *Contemporary Drug Problems, 10*, 307–322.

Maloney, M. P., & Ward, M. P. (1976). *Psychological assessment: A conceptual approach*. New York: Oxford University Press.

Mandall, W., Goldschmidt, P., & Grover, P. (1973). *Interdrug final report: An evaluation of treatment programs for drug abusers. Vol. 2: Summary*. Baltimore: Johns Hopkins University.

Mangum, C. S. (1940). *The legal status of the Negro*. Chapel Hill, NC: University of North Carolina Press.

Mannheim, M., & Wilkins, L. T. (1955). *Prediction methods in relation to Borstal training*. London: HMSO.

Marcus, A., & Conway, C. (1969). Dangerous sexual offender project. *Canadian Journal of Correction, 11*, 198.

Market Opinion Research Company. (1978). *Crime in Michigan: A report from residents and employers* (6th ed.). Detroit: Author.

Marks, P. A., Seeman, W., & Haller, D. L. (1974). *The actuarial use of the MMPI with adolescents and adults*. Baltimore: Williams & Wilkins.

Marlowe, H., Reid, J. B., Patterson, G. R., & Weinrott, M. (1986). *Treating adolescent multiple offenders: A comparison and follow-up of parent training for families of chronic delinquents*. Unpublished manuscript, Eugene, OR.

Martinson, R. (1974). What works?—Questions and answers about prison reform. *Public Interest, 10*, 22–54.

———. (1979). New findings, new views: A note of caution regarding sentencing reform. *Hofstra Law Review, 7*, 242–258.

Marx, G. T., & Archer, D. (1973). The urban vigilante. *Psychology Today, 7*, 45–50.

Maskin, M. B. (1976). The differential impact of work-oriented vs. communication-oriented juvenile correction programs upon recidivism rates in delinquent males. *Journal of Clinical Psychology, 32*, 432–433.

Matthews, A. (1970). Observations on police policy and procedure for emergency detention of the mentally ill. *Journal of Criminal Law, Criminology, and Police Science, 61*, 283–295.

Matthews, R. W., Paulus, P. B., & Baron, R. A. (1979). Physical aggression after being crowded. *Journal of Nonverbal Behavior, 4*, 5–17.

Mattick, H., Olander, C. K., Baker, D. G., & Schlegel, H. E. (1974). *An evaluation of operation identification as implemented in Illinois*. Chicago, IL: University of Illinois at Chicago, Center for Research in Criminal Justice.

Maultsby, M. C. (1975). *Help yourself to happiness through rational self-counseling*. New York: Institute for Rational Living.

Mawby, R. I. (1977). Defensible space: A theoretical and empirical appraisal. *Urban Studies, 14*, 169–179.

Mayhew, P. M. (1979). Defensible space: The current status of a crime prevention theory. *Howard Journal of Penology and Crime Prevention, 18*, 150–159.

Mayhew, P. M., Clarke, R. V., Sturman, A., & Hough, J. M. (1976). *Crime as opportunity*. London: HMSO.

McAnany, P. D. (1978). Restitution as idea and practice: The retributive process. In B.

Galaway & J. Hudson (eds.), *Offender restitution in theory and action* (pp. 15–31). Lexington, MA: D. C. Heath.

McAuliffe, W. E. (1990). A randomized controlled trial of recovery training and self-help for opioid addicts in New England and Hong Kong. *Journal of Psychoactive Drugs, 22*, 197–209.

McCarthy, A. J. (1976). *On shock probation*. Unpublished paper, University of Kentucky.

McCord, J. (1978). A thirty year follow-up of treatment effects. *American Psychologist, 33*, 284–289.

McCreary, C. P. (1975). Personality profiles of persons convicted of indecent exposure. *Journal of Clinical Psychology, 31*, 260–262.

McDonald, D. C. (1986). *Punishment without walls*. New Brunswick, NJ: Rutgers University Press.

McGahey, R. M. (1986). Economic conditions, neighborhood organization, and urban crime. In M. Tonry & N. Morris (eds.), *Crime and Justice: An annual review of the research* (Vol. 8, pp. 231–311). Chicago: University of Chicago Press.

McGarrell, E. F., & Flanagan, T. J. (1987). Measuring and explaining legislator crime control ideology. *Journal of Research in Crime and Delinquency, 24*, 102–118.

McGarry, A. L. (1965). Competency for trial and due process via the state hospital. *American Journal of Psychiatry, 122*, 623–631.

———. (1971). The fate of psychotic offenders returned for trial. *American Journal of Psychiatry, 127*, 1181–1184.

———. (1973). *Competency to stand trial and mental illness*. Washington, DC: U.S. Government Printing Office.

McGillis, D., & Smith, P. (1982). *Compensating victims of crime: An analysis of American programs*. Washington, DC: U.S. Government Printing Office.

McGuire, J. (1976). *Prediction of dangerous behavior in a federal correctional institution*. Unpublished dissertation, Florida State University.

McMichael, P. (1974). After-care, family relationship and re-conviction in Scottish approved school. *British Journal of Criminology, 14*, 236–247.

McShane, M. D., & Williams, F. P. (1989). The prison adjustment of juvenile offenders. *Crime and Delinquency, 35*, 254–269.

Meehl, P. E. (1954). *Clinical versus statistical prediction*. Minneapolis: University of Minnesota Press.

Meehl, P. E., & Rosen, A. (1955). Antecedent probability and the efficacy of psychometric signs, patterns, or cutting scores. *Psychological Bulletin, 52*, 194–216.

Megargee, E. I. (1970). The prediction of violence with psychological tests. In C. D. Spielberger (ed.), *Current topics in clinical and community psychology* (Vol. 2, pp. 97–156). New York: Academic Press.

———. (1972). *The California Psychological Inventory Handbook*. San Francisco: Jossey-Bass.

———. (1976). The prediction of dangerous behavior. *Criminal Justice and Behavior, 3*, 3–22.

———. (1977). The need for a new classification system. *Criminal Justice and Behavior, 4*, 107–114.

———. (1984). A new classification system for criminal offenders, VI: Differences among the types on the adjective checklist. *Criminal Justice and Behavior, 11*, 349–376.

Megargee, E. I., & Bohn, M. J. (1979). *Classifying criminal offenders*. Beverly Hills, CA: Sage.

Megargee, E. I., & Carbonell, J. L. (1985). Predicting prison adjustment with MMPI and correctional scales. *Journal of Consulting and Clinical Psychology, 53*, 874–883.

Megargee, E. I., Cook, P. E., & Mendelsohn, G. A. (1967). Development and validation of an MMPI scale of assaultiveness in overcontrolled individuals. *Journal of Abnormal Psychology, 72*, 519–528.

Megargee, E. I., & Dorhout, B. (1977). A new classification system for criminal offenders: Revision and refinement of the classification rules. *Criminal Justice and Behavior, 4*, 125–148.

Megargee, E. I., & Mendelsohn, G. A. (1962). A cross-validation of 12 MMPI indices of hostility and control. *Journal of Abnormal and Social Psychology, 65*, 431–438.

Megathlin, W. L., Magnus, R. E., & Christiansen, H. W. (1977). Classification in adult male correctional institutions. *Criminal Justice and Behavior, 2*, 107–112.

Meier, R. F., Burkett, S. R., & Hickman, C. A. (1984). Sanctions, peers and deviance: Preliminary models of a social control process. *Sociological Quarterly, 25*, 67–82.

Meier, R. F., & Johnson, W. T. (1977). Deterrence as social control: The legal and extralegal production of conformity. *American Sociological Review, 42*, 292–304.

Melton, G. B., Petrila, J., Poythress, N. G., & Slobogin, C. (1987). *Psychological evaluations for the courts: A handbook for mental health professionals and lawyers*. New York: Guilford.

Meichenbaum, D. (1977). *Cognitive behavior modification*. New York: Plenum.

Menninger, K. (1968). *The crime of punishment*. New York: Viking.

Menzies, R. J., Jackson, M. A., & Glasberg, R. E. (1982). The nature and consequences of psychiatric decision-making. *Canadian Journal of Psychiatry, 27*, 463–472.

Menzies, R. J., Webster, C. D., & Sepejak, D. S. (1985). The dimensions of dangerousness: Evaluating the accuracy of psychometric predictions of violence among forensic patients. *Law and Human Behavior, 9*, 49–70.

Merrill, M. A. (1947). *Problems of child delinquency*. Boston: Houghton-Mifflin.

Merry, S. E. (1981). *Urban danger: Life in a neighborhood of strangers*. Springfield, IL: Mombiosse.

Messner, S. F. (1982). Poverty, inequality, and the urban homicide rate: Some unexpected findings. *Criminology, 20*, 103–114.

Meyer, J., & Megargee, E. I. (1977). A new classification system for criminal offenders, II: Initial development of the system. *Criminal Justice and Behavior, 4*, 115–124.

Meyer, J. K., Hoopes, J. E., Jabaley, M. E., & Allen, R. (1973). Is plastic surgery effective in the rehabilitation of deformed delinquent adolescents? *Plastic and Reconstructive Surgery, 51*, 53–58.

Meyers, E. J. (1980). American heroin policy: Some alternatives. In Drug Abuse Council, *The facts about drug abuse* (pp. 190–247). New York: Free Press.

Mieczowski, T. (1986). Geeking up and throwing down: Heroin street life in Detroit. *Criminology, 24*, 645–666.

Miller, J. L., & Anderson, A. B. (1986). Updating the deterrence doctrine. *Journal of Criminal Law and Criminology, 77*, 418–438.

Miller, W. R., & Hester, R. K. (1986). The effectiveness of alcoholism treatment: What research reveals. In W. R. Miller & N. Heather (eds.), *Treating addictive behaviors: Processes of change*. New York: Plenum.

Ministry of Welfare, Health, and Cultural Affairs. (1985). *Policy on drug users*. Rijswijk, the Netherlands.

Minor, W. W., & Harry, J. (1982). Deterrent and experiential effects in perceptual deterrence research: A replication and extension. *Journal of Research in Crime and Delinquency, 19*, 190–203.

Miranne, A. C., & Gray, L. N. (1987). Deterrence: A laboratory experiment. *Deviant Behavior, 8*, 191–203.

Mischel, W. (1968). *Personality and assessment*. New York: John Wiley.

———. (1973). Toward a cognitive social learning reconceptualization of personality. *Psychological Review, 80*, 252–283.

M'Naghten Case, 10 Clark & Fin. 200, 8 English Report 718 (1843).

Monahan, J. (1973a). Abolish the insanity defense?—Not yet. *Rutgers Law Review, 26*, 719–739.

———. (1973b). The psychiatrization of criminal behavior. *Hospital and Community Psychiatry, 24*, 105–107.

———. (1978). The prediction of violent criminal behavior: A methodological critique and prospectus. In A. Blumstein, J. Cohen, & D. Nagin (eds.), *Deterrence and incapacitation: Estimating the effects of criminal sanctions on crime rates* (pp. 244–269). Washington, DC: National Academy of Science.

———. (1981). *The clinical prediction of violent behavior*. (Crime and Delinquency Issues Monograph, U.S. Department of Health and Human Services Publication No. ADM 81–921). Washington, DC: U.S. Government Printing Office.

———. (1982). The case for prediction in the modified desert model of criminal sentencing. *International Journal of Law and Psychiatry, 5*, 103–113.

———. (1984). The prediction of violent behavior: Toward a second generation of theory and policy. *American Journal of Psychiatry, 141*, 10–15.

Monahan, J., Caldeira, C., & Friedlander, H. D. (1979). Police and the mentally ill: A comparison of committed and arrested persons. *International Journal of Law and Psychiatry, 2*, 509–518.

Monahan, J., & Cummings, L. (1974). Prediction of dangerousness as a function of its perceived consequences. *Journal of Criminal Justice, 2*, 239–242.

Monahan, J., & Steadman, H. J. (1984). Crime and mental disorder. *National Institute of Justice: Research in Brief*. Washington, DC: National Institute of Justice.

Monahan, T. P. (1957). Family status and the delinquent child: A reappraisal and some new findings. *Social Forces, 35*, 250–258.

Moncrieff, M., & Pearson, D. (1979). Comparison of MMPI profiles of assaultive exhibitionists and voyeurs. *Corrective and Social Psychiatry and Journal of Behavioural Technology, Methods and Theory, 25*, 91–93.

Moore, D. R., Chamberlain, P., & Mukai, L. H. (1979). Children at risk for delinquency: A follow-up comparison of aggressive children and children who steal. *Journal of Abnormal Psychology, 7*, 345–355.

Moore, M., Estrich, S. R., McGillis, D., & Spelman, W. (1984). *Dangerous offenders: The elusive target of justice*. Cambridge, MA: Harvard University Press.

Moos, R. H. (1974). *Correctional Institutions Environment Scale manual*. Palo Alto, CA: Consulting Psychologists Press.

———. (1975). *Evaluating correctional and community settings*. New York: John Wiley.

Morash, M., & Rucker, L. (1990). A critical look at the idea of boot camp as a correctional reform. *Crime and Delinquency*, *36*, 204–222.

Moriarity, T. (1975). Crime, commitment, and the responsive bystander: Two field experiments. *Journal of Personality and Social Psychology*, *31*, 370–376.

Morris, N., & Miller, M. (1987). Predictions of dangerousness in the criminal law. *National Institute of Justice: Research in Brief*. Washington: DC: National Institute of Justice.

Morris, N. M., & Tonry, M. (1990). *Between prison and probation: Intermediate punishments in a rational sentencing system*. New York: Oxford University Press.

Morrow, W. R., & Peterson, D. B. (1966). Follow-up on discharged offenders—"not guilty by reason of insanity" and "criminal sexual psychopaths." *Journal of Criminal Law, Criminology, and Police Science*, *57*, 31–34.

Moss, C. S., & Hosford, R. E. (1982). Predicting violent behavior in a prison setting. *U.S. Department of Justice Progress Reports*, *1*, No. 2.

Moss, C. S., Johnson, M. E., & Hosford, R. E. (1984). An assessment of the Megargee typology in lifelong criminal violence. *Criminal Justice and Behavior*, *11*, 225–234.

Motiuk, L. L., Bonta, J., & Andrews, D. A. (1986). Classification in correctional halfway houses: The relative and incremental criterion validities of the Megargee-MMPI and LSI systems. *Criminal Justice and Behavior*, *13*, 33–46.

Mowbray, C. T. (1979). A study of patients treated as incompetent to stand trial. *Social Psychiatry*, *14*, 31–39.

Mrad, D. F. (1979). *Application of the Megargee criminal classification system to a community treatment program*. Unpublished doctoral dissertation, University of Missouri, St. Louis.

Mrad, D. F., Kabacoff, R., & Duckro, P. (1982). Validation of the Megargee typology in a halfway house setting. *Criminal Justice and Behavior*, *10*, 252–262.

Mullen, J. (1985). Corrections and the private sector. *The Privatization Review*, *1*, 10–19.

Mullen, P. E., (1984). Mental disorder and dangerousness. *Australian and New Zealand Journal of Psychiatry*, *18*, 8–17.

Mullen, P. E., & Reinehr, R. C. (1982). Predicting dangerousness of maximum security forensic patients. *Journal of Psychiatry and Law*, *10*, 223–231.

Munjack, D. J., Oziel, L. J., Kanno, P. H., & Leonard, M. D. (1981). Psychological characteristics of males with secondary erectile failure. *Archives of Sexual Behavior*, *10*, 123–131.

Murray, C. (1984). *Losing ground: American social policy, 1950–1980*. New York: Basic Books.

Murray, C. A., & Cox, L. A. (1979). *Beyond probation: Juvenile corrections and the chronic delinquent*. Beverly Hills, CA: Sage.

Musheno, M. C., Levine, J. P., & Palumbo, D. J. (1978). Television surveillance and crime prevention: Evaluating an attempt to create defensible space in public housing. *Social Science Quarterly*, *58*, 647–656.

Myers, L. B., & Levy, G. W. (1978). Description and prediction of the intractable inmate. *Journal of Research in Crime and Delinquency*, *15*, 214–228.

Myers, S. L. (1983). Estimating the economic model of crime: Employment versus punishment effects. *Quarterly Journal of Economics*, *98*, 157–166.

Nacci, P. L., Teitelbaum, H. E., & Prather, J. (1977). Population density and misconduct rates. *Federal Probation*, *41*, 26–31.

Nadelmann, E. A. (1989). Drug prohibition in the United States: Costs, consequences, and alternatives. *Science*, *245*, 939–947.

Narabayashi, H. (1979). Long-range results of medical amydalotomy on epileptic traits in adult patients. In T. Rasmussen & R. Marino (eds.), *Functional neurosurgery*. New York: Raven.

Nash, G. (1973). *The impact of drug abuse treatment upon criminality: A look at 19 programs*. Upper Montclair, NJ: Montclair State College.

National Advisory Commission on Criminal Justice Standards and Goals. (1973). *Report on corrections*. Washington, DC: U.S. Government Printing Office.

National Crime Prevention Council. (1987). *The success of community crime prevention*. Washington, DC: Author.

National Drug Enforcement Policy Board. (1987). *National and international drug law enforcement strategy*. Washington, DC: U.S. Department of Justice.

National Institute of Corrections. (1985). *Designs for contemporary correctional facilities*. Crofton, MD: Capitol.

Nelson, W. R. (1988). Cost savings in new generation jails: The direct supervision approach. *National Institute of Justice: Construction Bulletin*. Washington, DC: National Institute of Justice.

Newman, J. P., Patterson, C. M., & Kosson, D. S. (1987). Response prevention in psychopaths. *Journal of Abnormal Psychology*, *96*, 145–148.

Newman, O. (1972). *Defensible space: Crime prevention through urban design*. New York: Macmillan.

Newman, O., & Franck, K. A. (1980). *Factors influencing crime and instability in urban housing developments*. Washington, DC: U.S. Government Printing Office.

New York State Defender's Association, Inc. (1982). *Capital losses: The price of the death penalty for New York State*. Albany: Author.

New York State Department of Correctional Services. (1989). *Initial follow-up study of shock graduates*. Albany, NY: Unpublished report.

New York State Division of Parole. (1989). *Shock incarceration: One year out*. Albany, NY: Unpublished report.

Nichols, W. (1979). *The classification of law offenders with the MMPI: A methodological study*. Unpublished doctoral dissertation, University of Alabama (University Microfilms No. 80–15–583).

Nicholson, R. A. (1988). Validation of a brief form of the Competency Screening Test. *Journal of Clinical Psychology*, *44*, 87–90.

Nicholson, R. A., Briggs, S. R., & Robertson, H. C. (1988). Instruments for assessing competency to stand trial: How do they work? *Professional Psychology*, *19*, 383–394.

Nicholson, R. A., Robertson, H. C., Johnson, W. G., & Jensen, G. (1988). A comparison of instruments for assessing competency to stand trial. *Law and Human Behavior*, *12*, 313–321.

Noonan, S., & Latessa, E. J. (1987, March). *An evaluation of an intensive supervision program*. Paper presented at the annual meeting of the Academy of Criminal Justice Sciences, St. Louis, MO.

Nottingham, E. J., & Mattson, R. E. (1980). A validation study of the Competency Screening Test. *Law and Human Behavior*, *5*, 320–335.

Nuttall, C. P. (1989). Crime prevention in Canada. *Canadian Journal of Criminology*, *31*, 477–486.

O'Callaghan, M.A.J., & Carroll, D. (1987). The role of psychosurgical studies in the control of antisocial behavior. In S. A. Mednick, T. E. Moffitt, & S. A. Stack (eds.), *The causes of crime: New biological approaches* (pp. 312–328). New York: Cambridge University Press.

Ogloff, J. R., Wong, S., & Greenwood, A. (1990). Treating criminal psychopaths in a therapeutic community program. *Behavioral Sciences and the Law*, *8*, 181–190.

O'Keefe, J. (1980). *Massachusetts Department of Mental Health correctional study summary*. Boston: Massachusetts Department of Mental Health (mimeograph).

O'Malley, P. M., Johnston, L. D., & Bachman, J. G. (1985). Cocaine use among American adolescents and young adults. *National Institute of Drug Abuse Monograph Series* (monograph 61), 50–75.

Ono, N. (1980). The characteristic MMPI profile pattern of youthful Japanese delinquents. *Tohoku Psychologica Folia*, *39*, 105–112.

Ostrov, E., Offer, D., & Marohn, R. C. (1976). Hostility and impulsivity in normal and delinquent Rorschach responses. In S. Sanker (ed.), *Mental health in children* (Vol. II, pp. 479–492). Westbury, NY: PJD Publications.

Ostrov, E., Offer, D., Marohn, R. C., & Rosenwein, T. (1972). The impulsivity index: Its application to juvenile delinquency. *Journal of Youth and Adolescence*, *1*, 179–195.

Othmer, E., Penick, E. C., & Powell, B. J. (1981). *Psychiatric Diagnostic Interview (PDI) manual*. Los Angeles: Western Psychological Services.

Pablant, P., & Baxter, J. E. (1975). Environmental correlates of school vandalism. *American Institute of Planners Journal*, *241*, 270–279.

Packer, H. L. (1968). *The limits of the criminal sanction*. Stanford, CA: Stanford University Press.

Palmer, T. (1974). The Youth Authority's community treatment project. *Federal Probation*, *38*, 3–14.

———. (1975). Martinson revisited. *Journal of Research in Crime and Delinquency*, *12*, 133–152.

Palmer, T., & Wedge, R. F. (1989). California's juvenile probation camps: Findings and implications. *Crime and Delinquency*, *35*, 234–253.

Palmer, T., & Werner, E. (1972). *A review of I-level reliability and accuracy in the community treatment project*. Sacramento, CA: California Youth Authority.

Pantle, M. L., Pasewark, R. A., & Steadman, H. J. (1980). Comparing institutional periods and subsequent arrests of insanity acquittees and convicted felons. *Journal of Psychiatry and Law*, *8*, 305–316.

Panton, J. H. (1958a). MMPI profile configurations among crime classification groups. *Journal of Clinical Psychology*, *14*, 305–308.

———. (1958b). Predicting prison adjustment with the MMPI. *Journal of Clinical Psychology*, *14*, 308–312.

———. (1959). Inmate personality differences related to recidivism, age, and race as measured by the MMPI. *Journal of Correctional Psychology*, *4*, 28–35.

———. (1960). A new MMPI scale for the identification of homosexuality. *Journal of Clinical Psychology*, *16*, 17–21.

———. (1962a). The identification of habitual criminalism with the MMPI. *Journal of Clinical Psychology*, *18*, 63–67.

―――. (1962b). The identification of predispositional factors in self-mutilation in a state prison population. *Journal of Clinical Psychology*, *18*, 63–67.

―――. (1973). Personality characteristics of management problem prison inmates. *Journal of Community Psychology*, *1*, 185–191.

―――. (1978). Characteristics associated with male homosexuality within a state correctional population. *Quarterly Journal of Corrections*, *2*, 26–31.

Paramesh, C. R. (1987). The Competency Screening Test: Application to a state maximum security hospital population. *American Journal of Forensic Psychology*, *5*, 11–15.

Parent, D. (1989). *Shock incarceration: An overview of existing programs*. Washington, DC: National Institute of Justice.

Parisi, N. (1981). A taste of the bars. *Journal of Criminal Law and Criminology*, *72*, 1109–1123.

Parker, J., & Grasmick, H. G. (1979). Linking actual and perceived certainty of punishment: An exploratory study of an untested proposition in deterrence theory. *Criminology*, *17*, 366–379.

Parsons v. State, 81 Ala. 577, 596, 2 So. 854 (1886).

Pasewark, R. A., & Lanthorn, B. W. (1977). Disposition of persons utilizing the insanity plea in a rural state. *Journal of Humanics*, *5*, 87–98.

Pasewark, R. A., & Pantle, M. L. (1979). Insanity plea: Legislators' view. *American Journal of Psychiatry*, *136*, 222–223.

Pasewark, R. A., Pantle, M. L., & Steadman, H. J. (1979). Characteristics and disposition of persons found not guilty by reason of insanity in New York state, 1971–1976. *American Journal of Psychiatry*, *136*, 655–660.

―――. (1982). Detention and rearrest rates of persons found not guilty by reason of insanity and convicted felons. *American Journal of Psychiatry*, *139*, 892–897.

Pasewark, R. A., & Seidenzahl, D. (1980). Opinions concerning the insanity plea and criminality among mental patients. *Bulletin of the American Academy of Psychiatry and the Law*, *9*, 199–202.

Passell, P. (1975). The deterrent effect of the death penalty: A statistical test. *Stanford Law Review*, *61*, 61–80.

Passell, P., & Taylor, J. B. (1977). The deterrent effect of capital punishment: Another view. *American Economic Review*, *67*, 445–451.

Pate v. Robinson, 383 U.S. 375 (1966).

Pate, A. M. (1986). Experimenting with foot patrol: The Newark experience. In D. P. Rosenbaum (ed.), *Community crime prevention: Does it work?* (pp. 137–156). Beverly Hills, CA: Sage.

Pate, A. M., McPherson, M., & Silloway, G. (eds.). (1987). *The Minneapolis community crime prevention experiment*. Draft evaluation report. Washington, DC: Police Foundation.

Paternoster, R. (1983). Race of the victim and location of the crime: The decision to seek the death penalty in South Carolina. *Journal of Criminal Law and Criminology*, *74*, 754–785.

―――. (1987). The deterrent effect of the perceived certainty and severity of punishment: A review of the evidence and issues. *Justice Quarterly*, *4*, 173–217.

―――. (1989a). Absolute and restrictive deterrence in a panel of youth: Explaining the onset, persistence/desistence, and frequency of delinquent offending. *Social Problems*, *36*, 289–309.

————. (1989b). Decisions to participate in and desist from four types of common delinquency: Deterrence and the rational choice perspective. *Law and Society Review, 23,* 7–40.

Paternoster, R., & Iovanni, L. (1986). The deterrent effect of perceived severity: A reexamination. *Social Forces, 64,* 751–777.

Paternoster, R., Saltzman, L. E., Waldo, G. P., & Chiricos, T. G. (1983). Estimating perceptual stability and deterrent effects: The role of perceived legal punishment in the inhibition of criminal involvement. *Journal of Criminal Law and Criminology, 74,* 270–297.

Paterson, C. R., Dickson, A. L., Layne, C. C., & Anderson, H. N. (1984). California Psychological Inventory profiles of peer-nominated assertives, unassertives, and aggressives. *Journal of Clinical Psychology, 40,* 534–538.

Patterson, G. R. (1980). Treatment for children with conduct problems: A review of outcome studies. In S. Feshbach & A. Fraczek (eds.), *Aggression and behavior change: Biological and social processes* (pp. 83–132). New York: Praeger.

————. (1985). Beyond technology: The next stage in developing an empirical base for parent training. In L. L'Abate (ed.), *Handbook of family psychology and therapy* (Vol. 2, pp. 1344–1379). Homewood, IL: Dorsey Press.

Patterson, G. R., Chamberlain, P., & Reid, J. (1982). A comparative evaluation of a parent training program. *Behavior Therapy, 13,* 638–650.

Patterson, G. R., & Fleischman, M. J. (1979). Maintenance of treatment effects: Some considerations concerning family systems and follow-up data. *Behavior Therapy, 10,* 168–185.

Paulson, M. J., Afifi, A. A., Thomason, M. L., & Chaleff, A. (1974). The MMPI: A descriptive measure of psychopathology in abusive parents. *Journal of Clinical Psychology, 30,* 387–390.

Paulus, P., Cox, V., McCain, G., & Chandler, J. (1975). Some effects of crowding in a prison environment. *Journal of Applied Social Psychology, 5,* 86–91.

Peak, K. (1986). Crime victim reparation: Legislative revival of the offended ones. *Federal Probation, 50,* 36–41.

Pearson, F. S. (1988). Evaluation of New Jersey's intensive supervision program. *Crime and Delinquency, 34,* 437–448.

Pease, K. (1985). Community service orders. In M. Tonry & N. Morris (eds.), *Crime and justice: An annual review of research* (Vol. 6, pp. 51–94). Chicago: University of Chicago Press.

Pennell, S., Curtis, C., Henderson, J., & Tayman, J. (1989). Guardian Angels: A unique approach to crime prevention. *Crime and Delinquency, 35,* 378–400.

Penrose, L. (1939). Mental disease and crime: Outline of a comparative study of European statistics. *British Journal of Medical Psychology, 18,* 1–15.

Perretti, P. N. (1989). New Jersey's attorney general says legalizing drugs would be a devastating mistake. *Council for Alcohol/Drug Education of New Jersey News, 49,* 1.

Perry, J. B., & Pugh, M. D. (1989). Public support of the Guardian Angels: Vigilante protection against crime, Toledo, Ohio, 1984. *Sociology and Social Research, 73,* 129–131.

Perry, M. E. (1980). *Crime and society in early modern Seville.* Hanover: University Press of New England.

Persons, R. W. (1967). Relationship between psychotherapy with institutionalized boys and subsequent community adjustment. *Journal of Consulting Psychology, 31,* 137–141.

Persons, R. W., & Marks, P. A. (1971). The violent *4-3* MMPI personality type. *Journal of Consulting and Clinical Psychology, 36,* 189–196.

Petersilia, J., & Greenwood, P. W. (1978). Mandatory prison sentences: Their projected effects on crime and prison populations. *Journal of Criminal Law and Criminology, 69,* 604–615.

Petersilia, J., Greenwood, P. W., & Lavin, M. (1978). *Criminal careers of habitual felons.* Washington, DC: U.S. Government Printing Office.

Petersilia, J., & Honig, P. (1980). *The prison experience of career criminals.* Rand Report R–2511-DOJ. Santa Monica, CA: Rand Corporation.

Petersilia, J., & Turner, S. (1990). Comparing intensive and regular supervision for high-risk probationers: Early results from an experiment in California. *Crime and Delinquency, 36,* 87–111.

Petersilia, J., Turner, S., Kahan, J., & Peterson, J. (1985). Executive summary of Rand's study, "Granting felons probation: Public risks and alternatives." *Crime and Delinquency, 31,* 379–392.

Peterson, R. D. (1988). Youthful offender designations and sentencing in the New York criminal courts. *Social Problems, 35,* 111–130.

Peterson, R. D., & Hagan, J. (1984). Changing conceptions of race: Toward an account of anomalous findings of sentencing research. *American Sociological Review, 49,* 56–70.

Petrila, J. (1982). The insanity defense and other mental health dispositions in Missouri. *International Journal of Law and Psychiatry, 5,* 81–101.

Pfohl, S. J. (1979). Deciding on dangerousness: Predictions of violence as social control. *Crime and Social Justice, 11,* 28–40.

Philliber, S. (1987). Thy brother's keeper: A review of the literature on correctional officers. *Justice Quarterly, 4,* 9–37.

Phillips, B. L., & Pasewark, R. A. (1980). Insanity plea in Connecticut. *Bulletin of the American Academy of Psychiatry and the Law, 8,* 335–344.

Phillips, D. P. (1980). The deterrent effect of capital punishment: New evidence on an old controversy. *American Journal of Sociology, 86,* 139–148.

Phillips, E. L., Phillips, R. A., Fixsen, D. L., & Wolf, M. W. (1973). Behavior shaping works for delinquents. *Psychology Today, 6,* 75–79.

Phillips, L., & Votey, H. L. (1981). *The economics of crime control.* Beverly Hills, CA: Sage.

Pierce, D. M. (1971). The escapism scale of the MMPI as a predictive index. *Correctional Psychologist, 4,* 230–232.

———. (1972). Prison adjustment: Cross-validation of a MMPI scale. *Correctional Psychologist, 5,* 22–24.

———. (1973). Test and nontest correlates of active and situational homosexuality. *Psychology, 10,* 23–26.

Piercy, F., & Lee, R. M. (1976). Effects of a dual treatment approach on the rehabilitation of habitual juvenile delinquents. *Rehabilitation Counseling Bulletin, 19,* 482–492.

Piliavin, I., & Gartner, R. (1981). *The impact of supported work on ex-offenders.* New York: Manpower Demonstration Research Corporation.

Piliavin, I., Gartner, R., Thornton, C., & Matseuda, R. L. (1986). Crime, deterrence, and rational choice. *American Sociological Review, 51,* 101–119.

Plant, R. (1980). Justice, punishment and the state. In A. Bottoms & R. Preston (eds.), *The coming penal crisis: A criminological and theological explanation* (53–70). Edinburgh: Scottish Academic.

Platt, J. J., Labate, C., & Wicks, R. J. (1977). *Evaluative research in correctional drug abuse treatment.* Lexington, MA: D. C. Heath.

Platt, J. J., Perry, G. M., & Metzger, D. S. (1980). The evolution of a heroin addiction treatment program within a correctional environment. In R. R. Ross & P. Gendreau (eds.), *Effective correctional treatment.* Toronto: Butterworths.

Podolefsky, A. M., & DuBow, F. (1981). *Strategies for community crime prevention: Collective responses to crime in urban America.* Springfield, IL: Charles C. Thomas.

Pollock, H. H. (1938). Is the paroled patient a threat to the community? *Psychiatric Quarterly, 12,* 236–244.

Polonski, M. L. (1980). *Chronic young offenders.* Toronto: Ontario Ministry of Correctional Services.

Porporino, F. J., & Zamble, E. (1984). Coping with imprisonment. *Canadian Journal of Criminology, 26,* 403–422.

Powers, E., & Witmer, H. (1951). *An experiment in the prevention of delinquency: The Cambridge-Somerville youth study.* New York: Columbia University Press.

President's Commission on Law Enforcement and Administration of Justice. (1967). *The challenge of crime in a free society.* Washington, DC: U.S. Government Printing Office.

Pruitt, C. R., & Wilson, J. Q. (1983). A longitudinal study of the effect of race on sentencing. *Law and Society Review, 17,* 613–635.

Quay, H. C. (1965). Psychopathic personality as pathological stimulation-seeking. *American Journal of Psychiatry, 122,* 180–183.

————. (1973, November). *An empirical approach to the differential assessment of the adult offender.* Paper presented at the annual meeting of the American Society of Criminology, New York, NY.

————. (1977). The three faces of evaluation: What can be expected to work. *Criminal Justice and Behavior, 4,* 341–354.

————. (1984). *Managing adult inmates.* College Park, MD: American Correctional Association.

Quay, H. C., & Love, C. T. (1977). The effect of a juvenile diversion program on rearrests. *Criminal Justice and Behavior, 4,* 377–396.

Quay, H. C., & Peterson, D. R. (1975). *Manual for the Behavior Problem Checklist.* Unpublished manuscript.

Quinsey, V. L., & Ambtman, R. (1979). Variables affecting psychiatrists' and teachers' assessments of the dangerousness of mentally ill offenders. *Journal of Consulting and Clinical Psychology, 47,* 353–362.

Quinsey, V. L., Arnold, L. S., & Pruesse, M. G. (1980). MMPI profiles of men referred for a pretrial psychiatric assessment as a function of offense types. *Journal of Clinical Psychology, 36,* 410–417.

Quinsey, V. L., & Boyd, B. A. (1977). An assessment of the characteristics and dangerousness of patients held on warrants of the lieutenant governor. *Crime and Justice, 4,* 268–274.

Quinsey, V. L., & Maguire, A. (1983). Offenders remanded for a psychiatric examination: Perceived treatability and disposition. *International Journal of Law and Psychiatry, 6,* 193–205.

Quinsey, V. L., Maguire, A., & Varney, G. W. (1983). Assertion and overcontrolled hostility among mentally disordered murderers. *Journal of Consulting and Clinical Psychology, 51,* 550–556.

Quinsey, V. L., Pruesse, M., & Fernley, R. (1975). A follow-up of patients found unfit to stand trial or not guilty because of insanity. *Canadian Psychiatric Association Journal, 20,* 461–467.

Rabkin, J. G. (1979). Criminal behavior of discharged mental patients: A critical appraisal of the research. *Psychological Bulletin, 86,* 1–27.

Rachman, S., & Teasdale, J. (1969). *Aversion therapy and behavior disorders: An Analysis.* Coral Gables, FL: University of Miami Press.

Radelet, M. L., & Pierce, G. L. (1985). Race and prosecutorial discretion in homicide cases. *Law and Society Review, 19,* 587–621.

Rader, C. M. (1977). MMPI profile types of exposures, rapists, and assaulters in a court services population. *Journal of Consulting and Clinical Psychology, 45,* 61–69.

Raifman, L. (1979, October). *Interjudge reliability of psychiatrists' evaluations of criminal defendants' competency to stand trial and legal sanity.* Paper presented at the American Psychology-Law Society Convention, Baltimore, MD.

Randolph, J. J., Hicks, T., & Mason, D. (1981). The Competency Screening Test: A replication and extension. *Criminal Justice and Behavior, 8,* 471–481.

Rangaswami, R. (1982). Expression of hostility in criminal schizophrenics, schizophrenics and normals. *Indian Journal of Clinical Psychology, 9,* 131–135.

Rapaport, D., Gill, M. M., & Schafer, R. (1968). *Diagnostic psychological testing.* New York: International Universities Press.

Rappeport, J. R., & Lassen, G. (1965). Dangerousness—Arrest rate comparisons of discharged patients and the general population. *American Journal of Psychiatry, 121,* 776–783.

———. (1966). The dangerousness of female patients: A comparison of the arrest rate of discharged psychiatric patients and the general population. *American Journal of Psychiatry, 123,* 413–419.

Ray, J. B., Solomon, G. S., Doncaster, M. G., & Mellina, R. (1983). First offender adult shoplifters: A preliminary profile. *Journal of Clinical Psychology, 39,* 769–770.

Reitan, R. M., & Davison, L. A. (eds.), *Clinical neuropsychology: Current status and applications.* Washington, DC: Winston.

Reitsma-Street, M., & Leschied, A. W. (1988). The conceptual level matching model in corrections. *Criminal Justice and Behavior, 15,* 92–108.

Repetto, T. A. (1974). *Residential crime.* Cambridge, MA: Ballinger.

Reuter, P. (1988). Quantity illusions and paradoxes of drug interdiction: Federal intervention into vice policy. *Law and Contemporary Problems, 51,* 233–252.

Riedel, M. (1975). Perceived circumstances, influences of intent and judgments of offense severity. *Journal of Criminal Law and Criminology, 66,* 201–209.

Riley, D. (1980). An evaluation of a campaign to reduce car thefts. In R.V.G. Clarke & J. M. Hough (eds.), *The effectiveness of policing* (pp. 113–125). Farnborough: Gower.

Riley, P. J., & Rose, V. M. (1980). Public vs. elite opinion on correctional reform: Implications for social policy. *Journal of Criminal Justice, 8,* 345–356.

Robbins, I. R. (1988). *The legal dimensions of private incarceration*. Washington, DC: American Bar Association.

Robey, A. (1965). Criteria for competency to stand trial: A checklist for psychiatrists. *American Journal of Psychiatry, 122*, 616–630.

———. (1978). Guilty but mentally ill. *Bulletin of the American Association of Psychiatry and the Law, 6*, 374–381.

Robitscher, J., & Haynes, A. K. (1982). In defense of the insanity defense. *Emory Law Journal, 31*, 9–60.

Rodriguez Statement. (1982). Hearing before the Subcommittee on Criminal Justice, House Committee on the Judiciary (September 9, 1982).

Roesch, R., & Golding, S. L. (1980). *Competency to stand trial*. Chicago: University of Chicago Press.

Rofman, E. S., Askinazi, C., & Fant, E. (1980). The prediction of dangerous behavior in emergency civil commitment. *American Journal of Psychiatry, 137*, 1061–1064.

Rogers, J. L., Bloom, J. D., & Manson, S. M. (1984). Insanity defense: Contested or conceded? *American Journal of Psychiatry, 141*, 885–888.

Rogers, J. W. (1989). The greatest correctional myth: Winning the war on crime through incarceration. *Federal Probation, 53*, 21–28.

Rogers, R., & Cavanaugh, J. L. (1981a). A treatment program for potentially violent offender patients. *International Journal of Offender Therapy and Comparative Criminology, 25*, 53–59.

———. (1981b). Rogers criminal responsibility assessment scales. *Illinois Medical Journal, 160*, 164–169.

———. (1983). Usefulness of the Rorschach: A survey of forensic psychiatrists. *Journal of Psychiatry and Law, 11*, 55–67.

Rogers, R., Dolmetsch, R., & Cavanaugh, J. L. (1981). An empirical approach to insanity evaluations. *Journal of Clinical Psychology, 37*, 683–687.

Rogers, R., Thatcher, A., & Cavanaugh, J. L. (1984). Use of the SADS diagnostic interview in evaluating legal insanity. *Journal of Clinical Psychology, 40*, 1537–1541.

Rogers, R., Wasyliw, O. E., & Cavanaugh, J. L. (1984). Evaluating insanity: A study of construct validity. *Law and Human Behavior, 8*, 293–303.

Roman, D. D., Tuley, M. R., Villanueva, M .R., & Mitchell, W. E. (1990). Evaluating MMPI validity in a forensic psychiatric population: Distinguishing between malingering and genuine psychopathology. *Criminal Justice and Behavior, 17*, 186–198.

Romero, J. J., & Williams, L. M. (1985). Recidivism among convicted sex offenders: A 10-year follow-up study. *Federal Probation, 49*, 58–64.

Roneck, D. W., & Lobosco, A. (1983). The effect of high schools on crime in their neighborhoods. *Social Science Quarterly, 64*, 598–613.

Rooth, F. G., & Marks, I. M. (1974). Aversion, self-regulation and relaxation in the treatment of exhibitionism. *Archives of Sexual Behavior, 3*, 227–248.

Rose, G., & Marshall, T. F. (1974). *Counseling and school social work: An experimental study*. London: John Wiley.

Rosenbaum, D. P. (1988). Community crime prevention: A review and synthesis of the literature. *Justice Quarterly, 5*, 323–395.

Rosenbaum, D. P., Lewis, D. A., & Grant, J. A. (1986). Neighborhood-based crime prevention: Assessing the efficacy of community organizing in Chicago. In D. P. Rosenbaum (ed.), *Community crime prevention: Does it work?* (pp. 109–133). Beverly Hills, CA: Sage.

Rosenbaum, D. P., Lurigio, A. J., & Lavrakas, P. J. (1986). Crime stoppers—A national evaluation. *National Institute of Justice: Research in Brief.* Washington, DC: National Institute of Justice.

———. (1989). Enhancing citizen participation and solving serious crime: A national evaluation of crime stoppers programs. *Crime and Delinquency, 55,* 401–420.

Rosenblatt, A., & Pritchard, D. A. (1978). Moderators of racial differences on the MMPI. *Journal of Consulting and Clinical Psychology, 46,* 1572–1573.

Rosenberg, A. H., & McGarry, G. A. (1972). Competency on trial: The making of an expert. *American Journal of Psychiatry, 128,* 1092–1096.

Ross, H. L. (1981). *Deterring the drinking driver: Legal policy and social control.* Lexington, MA: Lexington Books/D. C. Heath.

Ross, R. R., & Fabiano, E. A. (1985). *Time to think: A cognitive model of delinquency prevention and offender rehabilitation.* Johnson City, TN: Institute of Social Sciences and Art.

Ross, R. R., Fabiano, E. A., & Ewles, C. D. (1988). Reasoning and rehabilitation. *International Journal of Offender Therapy and Comparative Criminology, 32,* 29–35.

Ross, R. R., & Lightfoot, L. V. (1985). *Treatment of the alcohol-abusing offender.* Springfield, IL: Charles C. Thomas.

Ross, R. R., & McKay, H. B. (1978). Behavioral approaches to treatment in corrections: Requiem for a panacea. *Canadian Journal of Criminology, 20,* 279–295.

Rossi, P. H., Berk, R. A., & Lenihan, K. J. (1980). *Money, work, and crime.* New York: Academic Press.

Rotton, J., & Frey, J. (1985). Air pollution, weather, and violent crimes: Concomitant time-series analysis of archival data. *Journal of Personality and Social Psychology, 49,* 1207–1220.

Roundtree, G. A., Edwards, D. W., & Parker, J. B. (1984). A study of the personal characteristics of probationers as related to recidivism. *Journal of Offender Counseling, Services and Rehabilitation, 8,* 53–61.

Ruback, R. B., & Innes, C. A. (1988). The relevance and irrelevance of psychological research: The example of prison crowding. *American Psychologist, 43,* 683–693.

Rubenfeld, S. (1965). *Family of outcasts.* New York: Free Press.

Rubenstein, H., Murray, C., Motoyama, T., & Rouse, W. V. (1980). *The link between crime and the built environment: The current state of knowledge. Vol. I.* Washington, DC: National Institute of Justice.

Rubin, B. (1972). Prediction of dangerousness in mentally ill criminals. *Archives of General Psychiatry, 27,* 397–407.

Russell, D. H. (1971). Diagnosing offender patients in Massachusetts court clinics. *International Journal of Offender Therapy* (Offender Therapy Series, Monograph 1).

Rutter, M., & Giller, H. (1984). *Juvenile delinquency: Trends and perspectives.* New York: Guilford.

Sacco, V. F., & Silverman, R. A. (1981). Selling crime prevention: The evaluation of a mass media campaign. *Canadian Journal of Criminology, 23,* 191–202.

Sacks, H., & Logan, C. (1979). *Does parole make a difference?* Storrs, CT: University of Connecticut School of Law Press.

Saltzman, L., Paternoster, R., Waldo, G. P., & Chiricos, T. G. (1982). Deterrent and experiential effects: The problem of causal order in perceptual deterrence research. *Journal of Research in Crime and Delinquency, 19,* 172–189.

Sarason, I. G. (1978). A cognitive social learning approach to juvenile delinquency. In R. D. Hare & D. Schalling (eds.), *Psychopathic behavior: Approaches to research* (pp. 299–317). New York: John Wiley.

Sarason, I. G., & Ganzer, V. J. (1973). Modeling and group discussion in the rehabilitation of juvenile delinquents. *Journal of Consulting Psychology, 20,* 442–449.

Savitz, L. (1958). A study of capital punishment. *Journal of Criminal Law, Criminology and Police Science, 49,* 338–341.

Sawyer, J. (1966). Measurement and prediction, clinical and statistical. *Psychological Bulletin, 66,* 178–200.

Sawyer, M. W. (1975). *The effects of community probation and services versus conventional probation services on recidivism by juvenile probationers.* Unpublished doctoral dissertation, Brigham Young University.

Schafer, S. (1977). *Victimology: The victim and his criminal.* Reston, PA: Reston Publishing Company.

Schaffer, C. E., Pettigrew, C. G., Blouin, D., & Edwards, D. W. (1983). Multivariate classification of female offender MMPI profiles. *Journal of Crime and Justice, 6,* 57–66.

Schimerman, S. R. (1974). *Project evaluation report: Operation identification.* St. Louis: Missouri Law Enforcement Assistance Council.

Schmidt, A. K. (1989). Electronic monitoring of offenders increases. *National Institute of Justice: Research in Action.* Washington, DC: National Institute of Justice.

Schmidt, D. E., & Keating, J. P. (1979). Human crowding and personal control: An integration of research. *Psychological Bulletin, 86,* 680–700.

Schmidt, P., & Witte, A. (1980). Evaluating correctional progress: Models of criminal recidivism and an illustration of their use. *Evaluation Review, 4,* 585–600.

Schneider, P. R., Schneider, A. L., Reiter, P. D., & Cleary, C. M. (1977). Restitution requirements for juvenile offenders: A survey of practices in American juvenile courts. *Juvenile Justice, 28,* 43–56.

Schoenthaler, S. J. (1983). Diet and delinquency: A multi-stage replication. *International Journal of Biosocial Research, 5,* 70–78.

Scholte, E. M., & Smit, M. (1988). Early social assistance for juveniles at risk. *International Journal of Offender Therapy and Comparative Criminology, 32,* 209–218.

Schretlen, D., & Arkowitz, H. (1990). A psychological test battery to detect prison inmates who fake insanity and mental retardation. *Behavioral Sciences and the Law, 8,* 75–84.

Schroeder, M. L., Schroeder, K. G., & Hare, R. D. (1983). Generalizability of a checklist for assessment of psychopathy. *Journal of Consulting and Clinical Psychology, 51,* 511–516.

Schuckit, M. A., Herrman, G., & Schuckit, J. J. (1977). The importance of psychiatric illness in newly arrested prisoners. *Journal of Nervous and Mental Diseases, 165,* 118–125.

Schuring, A. G., & Dodge, R. E. (1967). The role of cosmetic surgery in criminal rehabilitation. *Plastic and Reconstructive Surgery, 40*, 268–270.

Sechrest, D. K. (1989). Prison "boot camps" do not measure up. *Federal Probation, 53*, 15–20.

Seidman, E., Rappeport, J., & Davidson, W. S. (1980). Adolescents in legal jeopardy: Initial success and replication of an alternative to the criminal justice system. In R. R. Ross & P. Gendreau (eds.), *Effective correctional treatment*. Toronto: Butterworths.

Seiter, R. (1977). *Evaluating federal community treatment centers: A project overview*. Washington, DC: Office of Research, Federal Prison System.

Seitz, F., & Baridon, P. (1982). Release of NGI patients from St. Elizabeth's hospital. *American Journal of Forensic Psychiatry, 3*, 108–119.

Sellers, M. P. (1989). Private and public prisons: A comparison of costs, programs and facilities. *International Journal of Offender Therapy and Comparative Criminology, 33*, 241–256.

Sellin, T. (1967). *Capital punishment*. New York: Harper & Row.

———. (1976). *Slavery and the penal system*. New York: Elsevier.

Sellin, T., & Wolfgang, M. E. (1964). *The measurement of delinquency*. New York: John Wiley.

Sepejak, D., Menzies, R. J., Webster, C. D., & Jensen, F.A.S. (1983). Clinical predictions of dangerousness: Two-year follow-up of 408 pre-trial forensic cases. *Bulletin of the American Academy of Psychiatry and the Law, 11*, 171–181.

Serin, R. C., Peters, R. D-V., & Barbaree, H. E. (1990). Predictors of psychopathy and release outcome in a criminal population. *Psychological Assessment: A Journal of Consulting and Clinical Psychology, 2*, 419–422.

Sexton, G. E., Farrow, F. C., & Auerbach, B. J. (1985). The private sector and prison industries. *National Institute of Justice: Research in Brief*. Washington, DC: National Institute of Justice.

Shah, S. A. (1978). Dangerousness: A paradigm for exploring some issues in law and psychology. *American Psychologist, 33*, 224–238.

Shands, H. C. (1958). *A report on an investigation of psychiatric problems in felons in the North Carolina prison system*. Chapel Hill, NC: Department of Psychiatry, University of North Carolina.

Shapiro, A. (1977). The evaluation of clinical prediction: A method and initial application. *New England Journal of Medicine, 296*, 1509–1514.

Shatlin, L. (1979). Brief form of the Competency Screening Test for mental competence to stand trial. *Journal of Clinical Psychology, 35*, 464–467.

Shatlin, L., & Brodsky, S. H. (1979). Competency for trial: The Competency Screening Test in an urban hospital forensic unit. *Mount Sinai Journal of Medicine, 46*, 131–134.

Shavit, Y., & Rattner, A. (1988). Age, crime, and the early life course. *American Journal of Sociology, 93*, 1457–1470.

Shaw, C. R., & McKay, H. D. (1942). *Juvenile delinquency and urban areas*. Chicago: University of Chicago Press.

Shaw, S. H. (1973). The dangerousness of dangerousness. *Medicine, Science and the Law, 13*, 269–271.

Shenon, P. (1988). Enemy within: Drug money is corrupting the enforcers. *New York Times* (April 11, 1988). pp. A1, A12.

Sherman, L. W. (1983). Patrol strategies for police. In J. Q. Wilson (ed.), *Crime and public policy*. San Francisco: Institute for Contemporary Studies.

Sherman, L. W., & Berk, R. A. (1984). The specific deterrent effect of arrest for domestic assault. *American Sociological Review, 49*, 261–272.

Sherman, L. W., Gartin, P. R., & Buerger, M. E. (1989). Hot spots of predatory crime: Routine activities and the criminology of place. *Criminology, 27*, 27–55.

Shichor, D., & Bartollas, C. (1990). Private and public juvenile placements: Is there a difference? *Crime and Delinquency, 36*, 286–299.

Shinnar, S., & Shinnar, R. (1975). The effects of the criminal justice system on the control of crime: A quantitative approach. *Law and Society Review, 9*, 581–611.

Shoham, S. G. (1974). Punishment and traffic offenses. *Traffic Quarterly, 28*, 61–73.

Shore, A. (1977). *Outward bound: A reference volume*. New York: Topp Litho.

Shore, M. F., & Massimo, J. L. (1979). Fifteen years after treatment: A follow-up study of comprehensive vocationally-oriented psychotherapy. *American Journal of Orthopsychiatry, 49*, 240–245.

Shover, N. (1983). The later stages of ordinary property offender careers. *Social Problems, 31*, 208–218.

Shweder, R. A. (1977). Illusory correlation and the MMPI controversy. *Journal of Consulting and Clinical Psychology, 45*, 917–924.

Siassi, I. (1984). Psychiatric interview and mental status examination. In G. Goldstein & M. Hersen (eds.), *Handbook of psychological assessment* (pp. 259–275). New York: Pergamon.

Siegel, R. K. (1984). Changing patterns of cocaine use: Longitudinal observation, consequences, and treatment. *National Institute on Drug Abuse: Research Monograph Series* (Monograph 50), 92–110.

Silberman, M. (1976). Toward a theory of criminal deterrence. *American Sociological Review, 41*, 442–461.

Simmons, J. G., Johnson, D. L., Gouvier, W. D., & Muzyczka, M. J. (1981). The Meyer-Megargee inmate typology: Dynamic or unstable? *Criminal Justice and Behavior, 8*, 49–54.

Simon, R. J., & Baxter, S. (1989). Gender and violent crime. In N. A. Weiner & M. E. Wolfgang (eds.), *Violent crime, violent criminals* (pp. 171–197). Newbury Park, CA: Sage.

Simons, A. D., Lustman, P. J., Wetzel, R. D., & Murphy, G. E. (1985). Predicting response to cognitive therapy of depression: The role of learned resourcefulness. *Cognitive Therapy and Research, 9*, 79–89.

Simpson, D. D., & Sells, S. B. (1982). Effectiveness of treatment for drug abuse: An overview of the DARP research program, *Advances in Alcohol and Substance Abuse, 2*, 7–29.

Singer, A. (1978). Insanity acquittals in the seventies: Observations and empirical analysis of one jurisdiction. *Mental Disability Law Reporter, 2*, 407–417.

Skogan, W. G. (1987). *Disorder and community decline*. Final report to the National Institute of Justice. Evanston, IL: Northwestern University.

Skovron, S. E., Scott, J. E., & Cullen, F. T. (1989). The death penalty for juveniles: An assessment of public support. *Crime and Delinquency, 35*, 546–561.

Skrzypek, G. J. (1969). Effect of perceptual isolation and arousal on anxiety, complexity preference, and novelty preference in psychopathic and neurotic delinquents. *Journal of Abnormal Psychology, 74*, 321–329.

Slobogin, C., Melton, G. B., & Showalter, C. R. (1984). The feasibility of a brief evaluation on mental state at the time of the offense. *Law and Human Behavior*, *8*, 305–320.

Smith, C. S., Farrant, M. R., & Marchant, H. J. (1972). *The Wincroft youth project: A social work programme in a slum area*. London: Tavistock.

Smith, P. E., Burleigh, R. L., Sewell, W. R., & Krisak, J. (1984). Correlation between the Minnesota Multiphasic Personality Inventory profile of emotionally disturbed adolescents and their mothers. *Adolescence*, *19*, 31–38.

Smith, P. E., & Hawkins, R. O. (1973). Victimization, types of citizen-police contacts, and attitudes toward the police. *Law and Society Review*, *8*, 135–152.

Smith, R. L., & Graham, J. R. (1989). Clinicians' experience and the determination of criminal responsibility. *Criminal Justice and Behavior*, *16*, 473–485.

Smith, T. W. (1975). A trend analysis of attitudes toward capital punishment, 1936–1974. In J. E. Davis (ed.), *Studies of social change since 1948: Volume II* (pp. 257–318). Chicago: National Opinion Research Center.

Snortum, J. R., Hannum, T. E., & Mills, D. H. (1970). The relationship of self-concept and parent image to rule violations in women's prison. *Journal of Clinical Psychology*, *26*, 284–287.

Sommer, R. (1987). Crime and vandalism in university residence halls: A confirmation of defensible space theory. *Journal of Environmental Psychology*, *7*, 1–12.

Sosowsky, L. (1978). Crime and violence among mental patients reconsidered in view of the new legal relationships between the state and the mentally ill. *American Journal of Psychiatry*, *135*, 33–42.

————. (1980). Explaining the increased arrest rate among mental patients: A cautionary note. *American Journal of Psychiatry*, *137*, 1602–1605.

Speckart, G., Anglin, M. D., & Deschenes, E. P. (1989). Modeling the longitudinal impact of legal sanctions on narcotics use and property crime. *Journal of Quantitative Criminology*, *5*, 33–56.

Spelman, W. (1986). *The depth of a dangerous temptation: Another look at selective incapacitation*. Final report to the National Institute of Justice, Contract No. 80-NIJ–84. Washington, DC: Police Executive Research Forum.

Spelman, W., & Brown, D. K. (1984). *Calling the police: Citizen reporting of serious crime*. Washington, DC: U.S. Government Printing Office.

Spira, M., Chizen, J. H., Gerow, F. J., & Hardy, S. B. (1966). Plastic surgery in the Texas prison system. *British Journal of Plastic Surgery*, *19*, 364–371.

Spohn, C., Gruhl, J., & Welch, S. (1987). The impact of the ethnicity and gender of defendants on the decision to reject or dismiss felony charges. *Criminology*, *25*, 175–191.

St. Croix, S., Dry, R., & Webster, C. D. (1988). Patients on warrants of the lieutenant governor in Alberta: A statistical summary with comments on treatment and relapse procedures. *Canadian Journal of Psychiatry*, *33*, 14–20.

Stack, S. (1987). Publicized executions and homicide, 1950–1980. *American Sociological Review*, *52*, 532–540.

State of Illinois. (1982). *Report of the (Illinois) Department of Mental Health Committee on Criminal Justice and Mental Health Systems*. Springfield, IL: Author.

State of Maryland, Department of Public Safety and Correctional Services. (1973). *Maryland's defective delinquency statute—A process report*. Baltimore, MD: Author.

Steadman, H. J. (1973). Follow-up Baxstrom patients returned to hospitals for the criminally insane. *American Journal of Psychiatry*, *130*, 317–319.

———. (1977). A new look at recidivism among Patuxent inmates. *Bulletin of the American Academy of Psychiatry and the Law*, *5*, 200–209.

———. (1979). *Beating a rap: Defendants found incompetent to stand trial*. Chicago: University of Chicago Press.

Steadman, H. J., & Cocozza, J. J. (1974). *Careers of the criminally insane*. Lexington, MA: Lexington Books/D. C. Heath.

———. (1978). Selective reporting and the public misconceptions of the criminally insane. *Public Opinion Quarterly*, *4*, 523–533.

———. (1980). The prediction of dangerousness—Baxstrom: A case study. In G. Cooke (ed.), *The role of the forensic psychologist*, Springfield, IL: Charles C. Thomas.

Steadman, H. J., Cocozza, J. J., & Melick, M. E. (1978). Explaining the increased arrest rate among mental patients: The changing clientele of state hospitals. *American Journal of Psychiatry*, *135*, 816–820.

Steadman, H. J., & Felson, R. B. (1984). Self-reports of violence: Ex-mental patients, ex-offenders, and the general population. *Criminology*, *22*, 321–342.

Steadman, H. J., & Hartstone, E. (1983). Defendants incompetent to stand trial. In J. Monahan & H. J. Steadman (eds.), *Mentally disordered offenders: Perspectives from law and social science* (pp. 39–62). New York: Plenum.

Steadman, H. J., Keitner, L., Braff, J., & Arvantes, T. M. (1983). Factors associated with a successful insanity plea. *American Journal of Psychiatry*, *140*, 401–405.

Steadman, H. J., & Keveles, G. (1972). The community adjustment and criminal activity of the Baxstrom patients: 1966–1970. *American Journal of Psychiatry*, *129*, 304–310.

Steadman, H. J., Monahan, J., Duffee, B., Hartstone, E., & Robbins, P. C. (1984). The impact of state mental hospital deinstitutionalization on United States prison populations, 1968–1978. *Journal of Criminal Law and Criminology*, *75*, 474–490.

Steadman, H. J., Monahan, J., Hartstone, E., Davis, S. K., & Robbins, P. C. (1982). Mentally disordered offenders: A national survey of patients and facilities. *Law and Human Behavior*, *6*, 31–38.

Steadman, H. J., Pasewark, R. A., Hawkins, M., Kiser, M., & Bieber, S. (1983). Hospitalization length of insanity acquittees. *Journal of Clinical Psychology*, *39*, 611–614.

Steadman, H. J., Vanderwyst, D., & Ribner, S. (1978). Comparing arrest rates of mental patients and criminal offenders. *American Journal of Psychiatry*, *135*, 1218–1220.

Steenhuis, D. W. (1980). Experiments on police effectiveness: The Dutch experience. In R.V.G. Clarke & J. M. Hough (eds.), *The effectiveness of policing* (pp. 124–138). Farnborough: Gower.

Steffensmeier, D., & Kramer, J. H. (1982). Sex-based difference in the sentencing of adult criminal defendants: An empirical test and theoretical overview. *Sociology and Social Research*, *66*, 289–304.

Steuber, H. (1974). *Prediction of academic achievement with the Minnesota Multiphasic Personality Inventory (MMPI) and California Psychological Inventory (CPI) in a correctional institution*. Unpublished doctoral dissertation, Florida State University, Tallahassee.

Stewart, J. K. (1986). The urban strangler: How crime causes poverty in the inner city. *Police Review, 37*, 6–10.

Stinchcombe, A. L., Adams, R., Heimer, C. A., Scheppele, K. L., Smith, T. W., & Taylor, D. G. (1980). *Crime and punishment: Changing attitudes in America.* San Francisco: Jossey-Bass.

Stock, H., & Poythress, N. (1979, August). *Opinions on competency and sanity: How reliable?* Paper presented at the annual convention of the American Psychological Association, New York, NY.

Stone-Meierhoefer, B., & Hoffman, P. (1982). Presumptive parole dates: The federal approach. *Federal Probation, 46*, 41–57.

Stump, E. S., & Gilbert, W. W. (1972). Experimental MMPI scales and other predictors of institutional adjustment. *Correctional Psychologist, 5*, 141–154.

Sturz, E. L., & Taylor, M. (1987). Inventing and reinventing Argus: What makes one community organization work. *Annals, 494*, 19–26.

Sullivan, C. E., Grant, M. Q., & Grant, J. D. (1957). The development of interpersonal maturity: Applications to delinquency. *Psychiatry, 20*, 373–385.

Sutker, P. B., & Moan, C. E. (1977). Prediction of socially maladaptive behavior within a state prison system. *Journal of Community Psychology, 1*, 74–78.

Swank, G. E., & Winer, D. (1976). Occurrence of psychiatric disorder in a county jail population. *American Journal of Psychiatry, 133*, 1331–1333.

Sweetland, J. (1972). *"Illusory correlation" and the estimation of "dangerous" behavior.* Unpublished doctoral dissertation, Indiana University.

Symonds, M. (1980). The 'second injury' to victims. *Evaluation and Change*, pp. 36–38.

System Sciences Incorporated. (1973). *A comparative analysis of twenty-four therapeutic communities in New York City.* New York: Addiction Services Agency of the City of New York.

———. (1978). *Final report—Evaluation of TASC, phase II.* Bethesda, MD: Law Enforcement Assistance Administration.

Szasz, T. (1979). Insanity and irresponsibility: Psychiatric diversion in the criminal justice system. In H. Toch (ed.), *Psychology of crime and criminal justice* (pp. 133–144). New York: Holt, Rinehart, & Winston.

Taggart, W. A. (1989). Redefining the power of the federal judiciary: The impact of court-ordered prison reform on state expenditures for corrections. *Law and Society Review, 23*, 501–531.

Taub, R. P., Taylor, D. G., & Dunham, J. (1984). *Patterns of neighborhood change: Race and crime in urban America.* Chicago: University of Chicago Press.

Taylor, F. (1978). How the graffiti disappeared from the ladies' room. *Education, 27*, 286–290.

Taylor, R. B., Gottfredson, S., & Brower, S. (1981). *Informal control in the urban residential environment.* Final report to the National Institute of Justice. Baltimore: Johns Hopkins University.

Taylor, R. B., Gottfredson, S., & Schumaker, S. A. (1984). *Neighborhood responses to disorder.* Unpublished final report, Johns Hopkins University.

Teevan, J. J. (1976). Subjective perceptions of deterrence (continued). *Journal of Research in Crime and Delinquency, 13*, 155–164.

Teplin, L. A. (1983). The criminalization of the mentally ill: Speculation in search of data. *Psychological Bulletin, 94*, 54–67.

————. (1984). Criminalizing mental disorder: The comparative arrest rate of the mentally ill. *American Psychologist*, *39*, 794–803.

Tharp, R. G., & Wetzel, R. J. (1969). *Behavior modification in the natural environment.* New York: Academic Press.

Thompson, K. M. (1990). Refacing inmates: A critical appraisal of plastic surgery programs in prison. *Criminal Justice and Behavior*, *17*, 448–466.

Thomson, D., & Ragona, A. J. (1987). Popular moderation versus governmental authoritarianism: An interactional view of public sentiments toward criminal sanctions. *Crime and Delinquency*, *33*, 337–357.

Thornberry, T., & Jacoby, J. (1979). *The criminally insane: A community follow-up of mentally ill offenders.* Chicago: University of Chicago Press.

Thornton, D., Curran, L., Grayson, D., & Holloway, V. (1984). *Tougher regimes in detention centres: Report of an evaluation by the young offenders psychology unit.* London: Home Office.

Tien, J. M., O'Donnell, V. F., Barnett, A., & Mirchandani, P. B. (1979). *Street lighting projects.* National Evaluation Program Phase I Report. Washington, DC: U.S. Government Printing Office.

Tittle, C. R., (1969). Crime rates and legal sanctions. *Social Problems*, *16*, 408–423.

————. (1977). Sanction fear and the maintenance of social order. *Social Forces*, *55*, 579–596.

————. (1978). Restitution and deterrence: An evaluation of compatibility. In B. Galaway & J. Hudson (eds.), *Offender restitution in theory and action* (pp. 33–58). Lexington, MA: D. C. Heath.

Tittle, C. R., & Rowe, A. R. (1974). Certainty of arrest and crime rates: A further test of the deterrence hypothesis. *Social Forces*, *52*, 455–462.

Tittle, C. R., Villemez, W. J., & Smith, D. A. (1978). The myth of social class and criminality: An empirical assessment of the empirical evidence. *American Sociological Review*, *43*, 643–656.

Toch, H. (1977). *Living in prison.* New York: Free Press.

Toch, H., & Adams, K. (1986). Pathology and disruptiveness among prison inmates. *Journal of Research in Crime and Delinquency*, *23*, 7–21.

Toch, H., Adams, K., & Greene, R. (1987). Ethnicity, disruptiveness, and emotional disorder among prison inmates. *Criminal Justice and Behavior*, *14*, 93–109.

Tonry, M. (1990). Stated and latent functions of ISP. *Crime and Delinquency*, *36*, 174–191.

Travisono, A. (1979). Caution on Scared Straight. *On the Line*, *2*, 1.

Treffert, D. A. (1981). Legal "rites": Criminalizing the mentally ill. *Hillside Journal of Clinical Psychiatry*, *3*, 123–137.

Trojanowicz, R. C. (1986). Evaluating a neighborhood foot patrol program: The Flint, Michigan project. In D. P. Rosenbaum (ed.), *Community crime prevention: Does it work?* (pp. 157–178). Beverly Hills, CA: Sage.

Troyer, R. J. (1988). The urban anti-crime patrol phenomenon: A case study of a student effort. *Justice Quarterly*, *5*, 397–419.

Tupin, J. P., Smith, D. B., Clanon, T. L., Kim, L. I., Nugent, A., & Groupe, A. (1973). The long-term use of lithium in aggressive prisoners. *Comprehensive Psychiatry*, *14*, 311–317.

Turkington, C. (1987). New focus on preventing relapse. *APA Monitor*, *18*, 15–17.

Twaddle, A. C. (1976). Utilization of medical services by a captive population: An analysis of sick call in a state prison. *Journal of Health and Social Behavior, 17,* 236–248.

Twaddle, A. C., & Geile, S. (1976). *Getting shot: Predictors of disciplinary reports in a maximum security prison.* Unpublished manuscript, University of Missouri, Columbia, MO.

Twomey, J. F., & Hendry, C. H. (1969). MMPI characteristics of difficult-to-manage federal penitentiary offenders. *Psychological Reports, 24,* 546.

Umbreit, M. S. (1988). *Victim understanding of fairness: Burglary victims in victim offender mediation.* Minneapolis, MN: Minnesota Citizens Council on Crime and Justice.

———. (1989). Crime victims seeking fairness, not revenge: Toward restoration of justice. *Federal Probation, 53,* 52–57.

Unnever, J. D., Frazier, C. E., & Henretta, J. C. (1980). Race differences in criminal sentencing. *Sociological Quarterly, 21,* 197–205.

United States Sentencing Commission. (1987). *Supplementary report on the initial sentencing guidelines and policy statements.* Washington, DC: Author.

Valdiserri, E. V., Carroll, K. R., & Hartl, A. J. (1986). A study of offenses committed by psychotic inmates in a county jail. *Hospital and Community Psychiatry, 37,* 163–165.

Van Alstyne, D., & Gottfredson, M. R. (1978). A multidimensional contingency table analysis. *Journal of Research in Crime and Delinquency, 15,* 172–193.

van den Haag, E. (1975). *Punishing criminals: Concerning a very old and painful question.* New York: Basic Books.

———. (1983). Thinking about crime again. *Commentary,* pp. 73–77.

van den Haag, E., & Conrad, J. (1983). *The death penalty: A debate.* New York: Plenum.

Van Dine, S., Conrad, J. P., & Dinitz, S. (1979). *Restraining the wicked: The dangerous offender project.* Lexington, MA: Lexington Books.

Van Voorhis, P. (1986). *A cross-classification of five offender typologies: Results of the pilot study.* Unpublished manuscript, University of Cincinnati.

———. (1988). A cross classification of five offender typologies: Issues of construct and predictive validity. *Criminal Justice and Behavior, 15,* 109–124.

Veneziano, C., & Veneziano, L. (1986). Classification of adolescent offenders with the MMPI: An extension and cross-validation of the Megargee typology. *International Journal of Offender Therapy and Comparative Criminology, 30,* 11–23.

Vidmar, N., & Ellsworth, P. (1974). Public opinion and the death penalty. *Stanford Law Review, 26,* 1245–1270.

Visher, C. A. (1986). The Rand inmate survey: A reanalysis. In A. Blumstein, J. Cohen, J. Roth, & C. Visher (eds.), *Criminal careers and career criminals* (Vol. 2, pp. 161–211). Washington, DC: National Academy Press.

———. (1987). Incapacitation and crime control: Does a "lock 'em up" strategy reduce crime? *Justice Quarterly, 4,* 513–543.

Viscusi, W. K. (1983). *Market incentives for criminal behavior.* Unpublished paper, National Bureau of Economic Research.

Vitek v. Jones, 445 U.S. 480 (1980).

Vito, G. F. (1978). Shock probation in Ohio: A re-examination of the factors influencing the use of an early release program. *Offender Rehabilitation, 3,* 123–132.

Vito, G. F., & Allen, H. E. (1981). Shock probation in Ohio: A comparison of outcomes.

International Journal of Offender Therapy and Comparative Criminology, 25, 70–76.

Vito, G. F., & Keil, T. J. (1988). Capital sentencing in Kentucky: An analysis of the factors influencing decision making in the post-Gregg period. *Journal of Criminal Law and Criminology, 79,* 483–503.

Vito, G. F., Holmes, R. M., & Wilson, D. G. (1984). The effect of shock and regular probation upon recidivism: A comparative analysis. *American Journal of Criminal Justice, 8,* 152–162.

von Hirsch, A. (1976). *Doing justice: The choice of punishments.* New York: Hill & Wang.

von Hirsch, A., & Gottfredson, D. M. (1984). Selective incapacitation: Some queries on research design and equity. *New York University Review of Law and Social Change, 12,* 11–51.

von Hirsch, A., & Hanrahan, K. (1979). *The question of parole: Reform, retention, or abolition?* Cambridge, MA: Ballinger.

Vorrath, H., & Brendto, L. (1974). *Positive peer culture.* Chicago: Aldine.

Vuylsteek, K. (1979). *Health education: Smoking, alcoholism, drugs.* Copenhagen: World Health Organization.

Wade, T. C., Morton, T. L., Lind, J. E., & Ferris, N. R. (1977). A family crisis intervention approach to diversion from the juvenile justice system. *Juvenile Justice Journal, 28,* 43–51.

Wagner, M. W., & Almeida, L. (1987). Geophysical variables and behavior: XXXVII. Lunar phase, "no," weekend, "yes," month, "sometimes." *Perceptual and Motor Skills, 64,* 949–950.

Waldo, G. P., & Chiricos, T. G. (1972). Perceived penal sanctions and self-reported criminality: A neglected approach to deterrence research. *Social Problems, 19,* 522–540.

Walker, P. A., & Meyer, W. J. (1981). Medroxyprogesterone acetate treatment for paraphiliac sex offenders. In J. P. Hays, T. K. Roberts, & K. S. Salwax (eds.), *Violence and the violent offender* (pp. 353–373). New York: S. P. Medical and Scientific Books.

Waller, I. (1974). *Men released from prison.* Toronto: University of Toronto Press.

Walters, G. D. (1985). Scale *4 (Pd)* of the MMPI and the diagnosis antisocial personality. *Journal of Personality Assessment, 48,* 486–488.

———. (1986a). Correlates of the Megargee criminal classification system: A military correctional setting. *Criminal Justice and Behavior, 13,* 19–32.

———. (1986b). Screening for psychopathology in groups of black and white prison inmates by means of the MMPI. *Journal of Personality Assessment, 50,* 257–264.

———. (1988). Assessing dissimulation and denial on the MMPI in a sample of maximum security male inmates. *Journal of Personality Assessment, 52,* 465–474.

———. (1989). Comparability of the standard and interview versions of the Lifestyle Criminality Screening Form. *International Journal of Offender Therapy and Comparative Criminology, 33,* 49–58.

———. (1990). *The criminal lifestyle: Patterns of serious criminal conduct.* Newbury Park, CA: Sage.

———. (1991). Predicting the disciplinary adjustment of maximum and minimum security prison inmates using the Lifestyle Criminality Screening Form. *International Journal of Offender Therapy and Comparative Criminology, 35,* 63–71.

Walters, G. D., Chlumsky, M. L., & Hemphill, L. (1988). Reliability and stability of a structured diagnostic interview in a group of incarcerated criminal offenders. *International Journal of Offender Therapy and Comparative Criminology, 32,* 87–94.

Walters, G. D., Greene, R. L., & Solomon, G. S. (1982). Empirical correlates of the overcontrolled-hostility scale and the MMPI *4-3* high-point pair. *Journal of Consulting and Clinical Psychology, 50,* 213–218.

Walters, G. D., Mann, M. F., Miller, M. P., Hemphill, L. L., & Chlumsky, M. L. (1988). Serious emotional disorder in state, federal, and military offenders. *Criminal Justice and Behavior, 15,* 433–453.

Walters, G. D., Revella, L., & Baltrusaitis, W. J. (1990). Predicting parole/probation outcome with the aid of the Lifestyle Criminality Screening Form. *Psychological Assessment: A Journal of Consulting and Clinical Psychology, 2,* 313–316.

Walters, G. D., Scrapansky, T. A., & Marrlow, G. A. (1986). The emotionally disturbed military criminal offender: Identification, background and institutional adjustment. *Criminal Justice and Behavior, 13,* 261–285.

Walters, G. D., & White, T. W. (1988a). Crime, popular mythology, and personal responsibility. *Federal Probation, 52,* 18–26.

———. (1988b). Society and lifestyle criminality. *Federal Probation, 52,* 52–55.

Walters, G. D., White, T. W., & Denney, D. (in press). The Lifestyle Criminality Screening Form: Preliminary data. *Criminal Justice and Behavior.*

Walters, G. D., White, T. W., & Greene, R. L. (1988). Use of the MMPI to identify malingering and exaggeration of psychiatric symptomatology in male prison inmates. *Journal of Consulting and Clinical Psychology, 56,* 111–117.

Walters, R. H. (1953). A preliminary analysis of the Rorschach records of fifty prison inmates. *Journal of Projective Techniques, 17,* 437–446.

Warr, M., & Stafford, M. (1984). Public goals of punishment and support for the death penalty. *Journal of Research in Crime and Delinquency, 21,* 95–111.

Warren, M. Q. (1966). *Interpersonal maturity level classification: Juvenile diagnosis and treatment of low, middle, and high maturity delinquents.* Sacramento, CA: California Youth Authority.

———. (1971). Classification of offenders as an aid to efficient management and effective treatment. *Journal of Criminal Law, Criminology, and Police Science, 62,* 239–258.

———. (1978). Impossible child, the difficult child, and other assorted delinquents: Etiology, characteristics, and incidence. *Canadian Psychiatric Association Journal, 23,* 41–60.

Webster, C. D., & Menzies, R. J. (1987). The clinical prediction of dangerousness. In D. N. Weisstub (ed.), *Law and mental health: International perspectives.* New York: Pergamon.

Weiner, D. N. (1948). Subtle and obvious keys for the MMPI. *Journal of Consulting Psychology, 12,* 164–170.

Weisburd, D., & Chayet, E. S. (1989). Good time: An agenda for research. *Criminal Justice and Behavior, 16,* 183–195.

Wellman, H., & Chun, R. (1979). Homeward bound: An alternative to the institutionalization of adjudicated juvenile offenders. *Federal Probation, 74,* 52–58.

Wender, P. H., Reimherr, F. W., & Wood, D. R. (1981). Attention deficit disorder ("minimal brain dysfunction") in adults: A replication study of diagnosis and drug treatment. *Archives of General Psychiatry, 38*, 449–456.

Wenk, E., & Halatyn, T. (1973). *The assessment of correctional climates.* Davis, CA: National Council on Crime and Delinquency Research Center.

Wenk, E. A., Robinson, J. O., & Smith, G. W. (1972). Can violence be predicted? *Crime and Delinquency, 18*, 51–68.

Werner, E. (1975). Relationships among interpersonal maturity, personality configurations, intelligence, and ethnic status. *British Journal of Criminology, 15*, 51–68.

Werner, P. D., Rose, T. L., & Yesavage, J. A. (1983). Reliability, accuracy, and decision-making strategy in clinical predictions of imminent dangerousness. *Journal of Consulting and Clinical Psychology, 51*, 815–825.

West, D. J., & Farrington, D. P. (1973). *Who becomes delinquent?* London: Heinemann Educational.

Wexler, H. K., Kalkin, G. P., & Lipton, D. S. (1990). Outcome evaluation of a prison therapeutic community for substance abuse treatment. *Criminal Justice and Behavior, 17*, 71–92.

Wexler, H. K., Lipton, D. S., & Foster, K. (1985, November). *Prison drug treatment: Study of recidivism.* Paper presented at the annual meeting of the American Society of Criminology, San Diego, CA.

Wheeler, G. R., & Hissong, R. V. (1988). A survival time analysis of criminal sanctions for misdemeanor offenders: A case for alternatives to incarceration. *Evaluation Review*, 510–527.

Whitaker, C. J. (1986). Crime prevention measures. *Bureau of Justice Statistics Special Report.* Washington, DC: Bureau of Justice Statistics.

White, G. F. (1990). Neighborhood permeability and burglary rates. *Justice Quarterly, 7*, 57–67.

Whitehead, J. T., & Lab, S. P. (1989). A meta-analysis of juvenile correctional treatment. *Journal of Research in Crime and Delinquency, 26*, 276–295.

Whiteman, M., & Deutsch, M. (1968). Social disadvantage as related to intellective and language development. In M. Deutsch, I. Ketz, & A. R. Jensen (eds.), *Social class, race, and psychological development* (pp. 86–114). New York: Holt, Rinehart, and Winston.

Wicker, T. (1987). Drugs and alcohol. *New York Times* (May 13, 1987), p. A27.

Wildman, R. W., Batchelor, E. S., Thompson, L., Nelson, F. R., Moore, J. T., Patterson, M. E., & deLaosa, M. (1978). *The Georgia court competency test: An attempt to develop a rapid, quantitative measure of fitness for trial.* Unpublished manuscript, Forensic Services Division, Central State Hospital, Milledgeville, GA.

Willemsen, T. M., & van Schie, E.C.M. (1989). Sex stereotypes and responses to juvenile delinquency. *Sex Roles, 20*, 623–638.

Williams, K. R., & Hawkins, R. (1986). Perceptual research on general deterrence: A critical overview. *Law and Society Review, 20*, 545–572.

Williams, W., & Miller, K. S. (1977). The role of personal characteristics in perceptions of dangerousness. *Criminal Justice and Behavior, 4*, 241–251.

Williamson, S., Hare, R. D., & Wong, S. (1987). Violence: Criminal psychopaths and their victims. *Canadian Journal of Behavioral Science, 19*, 454–462.

Wilson, D. G., & Vito, G. F. (1988). Long-term inmates: Special needs and management considerations. *Federal Probation*, *52*, 21–26.

Wilson, L. A., & Schneider, A. L. (1978). *Investigating the efficacy and equity of public initiatives in the provision of private safety*. Paper presented at the annual meeting of the Western Political Science Association, Los Angeles, CA.

Wilson, J. Q. (1983). *Thinking about crime* (rev. ed.). New York: Basic Books.

Wilson, J. Q., & Boland, B. (1978). The effect of the police on crime. *Law and Society Review*, *12*, 367–390.

Wilson, J. Q., & Herrnstein, R. J. (1985). *Crime and human nature*. New York: Simon & Schuster.

Wilson, S. (1978). Vandalism and 'defensible space' on London housing estates. In R. V. Clarke (ed.), *Tackling vandalism*. London: HMSO.

Winchester, S., & Jackson, H. (1982). *Residential burglary: The limits of prevention*. London: HMSO.

Winkel, F. W. (1987). Response generalization in crime prevention campaigns. *British Journal of Criminology*, *27*, 155–173.

Winterdyk, J., & Roesch, R. (1981). A wilderness experimental program as an alternative for probationers: An evaluation. *Canadian Journal of Criminology*, *23*, 39–49.

Wish, E. D. (1988). *Drug use forecasting (DUF): April-June 1988 data*. Washington, DC: National Institute of Justice.

Wolf, S., Freinek, W. R., & Shaffer, J. W. (1966). Frequency and severity of rule infractions as criteria of prison maladjustment. *Journal of Clinical Psychology*, *22*, 244–247.

Wolfgang, M. E. (1961). Quantitative analysis of adjustment to the prison community. *Journal of Criminal Law, Criminology, and Police Science*, *51*, 608–618.

———. (1988). The medical model versus the just deserts model. *Bulletin of the American Academy of Psychiatry and the Law*, *16*, 111–121.

Wolfgang, M. E., Figlio, R. M., & Sellin, T. (1972). *Delinquency in a birth cohort*. Chicago: University of Chicago Press.

Wolfgang, M. E., Kelly, A., & Nolde, H. C. (1962). Comparison of the executed and commuted among admissions to death row. *Journal of Criminal Law, Criminology, and Police Science*, *53*, 301–311.

Wolfgang, M. E., & Riedel, M. (1973). Race, judicial discretion, and the death penalty. *Annals*, *407*, 119–133.

Wolpin, K. I. (1978a). An economic analysis of crime and punishment in England and Wales, 1894–1967. *Journal of Political Economy*, *86*, 815–840.

———. (1978b). Capital punishment and homicide in England: A summary of results. *American Economic Review*, *68*, 422–427.

Wormith, J. S., & Goldstone, C. S. (1984). The clinical and statistical prediction of recidivism. *Criminal Justice and Behavior*, *11*, 3–34.

Wright, K. N. (1988). The relationship of risk, needs, and personality classification systems and prison adjustment. *Criminal Justice and Behavior*, *15*, 454–471.

Wright, K. N., Clear, T. R., & Dickson, P. (1984). Universal applicability of probation risk-assessment instruments. *Criminology*, *22*, 113–134.

Wright, K. N., & Smith, P. (1985, November). *The violent and the victimized in prison*. Paper presented at the annual meeting of the American Society of Criminology, San Diego, CA.

Yin, R. K., Vogel, M. E., Chaiken, J. M., & Both, D. R. (1977). *Patrolling the neigh-*

borhood beat: Residents and residential security. Santa Monica, CA: Rand Corporation.

Yochelson, S., & Samenow, S. E. (1976). *The criminal personality, Vol. I: A profile for change*. New York: Jason Aronson.

York, P., & York, D. (1990). *Toughlove: A self-help manual for parents*. Doylestown, PA: Toughlove International.

Young, Arthur & Company. (1978). *Second year report for the Cabrini-Green High Impact Program*. Chicago: City Department of Development and Planning.

Young, I. (1981). Toward a critical theory of justice. *Social Theory and Practice, 7*, 279–302.

Zager, L. D. (1983). The MMPI-based classification system: A critical review of derivation procedures and recent investigations of its generalizability and dynamic features. *FCI Research Reports, 12*, 1–30.

———. (1988). The MMPI-based criminal classification system: A review, current status, and future directions. *Criminal Justice and Behavior, 15*, 39–57.

Zapf, M. K., & Cole, B. (1985). Yukon restitution study. *Canadian Journal of Criminology, 27*, 477–490.

Zatz, M. S. (1987). The changing forms of racial-ethnic bias in sentencing. *Journal of Research in Crime and Delinquency, 24*, 69–92.

Zigler, E., & Child, I. L. (1969). Socialization. In G. Lindzey & E. Aronson (eds.), *Handbook of social psychology: Vol. 3* (2nd ed., pp. 450–589). Reading, MA: Addison-Wesley.

Zimring, F. (1978). Background paper. In *Confronting youth crime: Report of the twentieth century fund task force on sentencing policy toward young offenders* (pp. 27–120). New York: Holmes and Meier.

Zimring, F. E., & Hawkins, G. (1986). *Capital punishment and the American agenda*. New York: Cambridge University Press.

Zitrin, A., Hardesty, A. S., Burdock, E. I., & Drossman, A. K. (1976). Crime and violence among mental patients. *American Journal of Psychiatry, 133*, 142–149.

Zivan, M. (1966). *Youth in trouble: A vocational approach*. Dobbs Ferry, NY: Children's Village.

Author Index

Subject Index

About the Author

GLENN D. WALTERS is coordinator of the comprehensive drug program at the Federal Correctional Institution in Fairton, New Jersey, and has served as a consultant for Mainstream Inc., Topeka, Kansas. He is the author of *The Criminal Lifestyle: Patterns of Serious Criminal Conduct*.